Finance 101:
The Whiz Kid's Perfect Credit Guide

Finance 101:
The Whiz Kid's Perfect Credit Guide

The Teen Who Refinanced His Mother's House and Car at 14

Danny Singh
All Profits Support the Children's National Medical Center
in Washington, DC for HIV Treatment Research

© 2012 Danny Singh. All rights reserved.

No part of this book may be reproduced, stored in a retrieval system, or transmitted by any means without the written permission of the author.

Cover was produced by YDG Studios.

This book is printed on acid-free paper.

Because of the dynamic nature of the Internet, any web addresses or links contained in this book may have changed since publication and may no longer be valid. The views expressed in this work are solely those of the author and do not necessarily reflect the views of the publisher, and the publisher hereby disclaims any responsibility for them.

About the Author

With an Indian background, **Danny Singh** was the first in his family to be born and raised in Orlando, Florida; by his mother and grandparents. Danny's mother, Rita, purchased her own house in 2001, moved in with Danny. She began working longer hours at two jobs, so she could manage all the expenses. Due to the limited availability of Rita, Danny could not be fully dependent upon her.

For this reason, in 2003, Rita added Danny, as an authorized user, on her account and gave Danny his first credit card, at the age of 11; thus beginning his financial journey. Danny knew very little about credit cards and only used his credit card; to purchase food, supplies for school, necessities he needed, and gifts for his mom; during his younger years. He would always make sure his credit card was with him in his pocket. Danny admits to purchasing items he always desired, such as, Yu-Gi-Oh Cards, movies, comic books, Slurpee's at the gas station, and items kids would want. He loved the spending power of the credit card.

Unexpectedly, Rita started becoming increasingly busy on her jobs. She began calling Danny; asking him to open the mail and make sure the credit card bill was getting paid. She expressed; if the credit card bill was paid late, it would ruin her credit. Danny did not know what credit was, but he did not want to see his mother stress. While handling his academic responsibilities; he maintained her credit card, by signing online and using her checking account. As he began reading all of his mother's mail, although he could not understand everything; interest started provoking him as he began getting involved with other financial aspects of the household. Danny began reading the terms and conditions of the credit cards and the fine print, on the bills. This led him into reading more about credit on the Internet. He started asking his mother, grandfather, or the customer service credit managers; questions or misconceptions he had about credit.

Danny began wanting to handle the utility bills, mortgage, insurance, other credit cards (he was not using), and any other bill that his mother was expected to pay. Danny wanted his mother to give him full authorization, to all the companies; so they would release any account information to him, if needed. With this type of authorization, he would be permitted to make account changes, if needed, when calling customer service. Danny's mother was skeptical, at first, but trusted Danny; given the fact that he was never late on paying the credit card he was using.

Rita added Danny to all her accounts. They were discrete; about Danny's financial life. Danny has had many financial successes including: getting the annual fees removed from several of his mother's credit cards, refinancing the mortgage and car, getting over $1300 in interest refunded from a credit card company, having interest rates reduced on all loans, increasing the credit limits on accounts so his mother's credit scores could increase, and ensuring that no deposit accounts were becoming negative; at just 14 years of age.

Danny managed to get her car and house insurance costs reduced; while maintaining the same coverage. He removed a delinquency from his grandmother's credit report; which caused his grandmother to be denied credit. Danny was able to get his grandmother's credit application approved. When Rita's bank account information was stolen and numerous fraudulent charges occurred; Danny was able to get all the charges refunded. He also reported the phony business, to the Better Business Bureau and Complaint Board; so other consumers

Danny Singh

would not be scammed. Seminole County commissioner, Bob Dallari; Florida House District 33 representative, Jason Brodeur; Texas governor, Rick Perry; First Lady Anita Perry, Senator Marco Rubio, and several news stations recognized Danny; referring to him as a "financial whiz kid." In 2011, Danny graduated with honors from the International Baccalaureate program of University High School.

To this day, Danny has developed about eight years of financial experience, with many different financial institutions managing all the financial aspects of his mother's house and has never been late, even by a day, on several credit cards or any bill. Proudly, Danny is part of the Art & Phyllis Grindle Honors Institute, at the Seminole State College in Florida. In September 2011, Danny officially started a non-profit and independent credit advising agency entitled "Students' Finance Success." The mission of his agency is to encourage consumers to build and maintain good credit. For this reason, Danny has been doing financial seminars trying to help students effectively repay their student loans and maintain excellent credit while saving the maximum amount of money for retirement and other financial goals. Besides students, he has been helping other consumers save their houses from foreclosures, cars from repossessions, getting fees refunded, and teaching them to avoid dangerous loans such as payday loans.

Danny is working towards earning a Bachelors of Science degree with Honors, in Business Administration, with a concentration in Finance, a second concentration on Management, and career certificates in Project Management, Entrepreneurship, Financial Operations, and Small Business Management. Danny is doing a minor in Law Enforcement. Later, he hopes to earn an MBA and Ph.D., in Finance, from an Ivy League school. By doing financial seminars, running a financial tips website (www.facebook.com/studentsfinance), and his independent and non-profit credit advising agency; Danny encourages others that bankruptcy, debt settlements, being late, or not paying the bills are never solutions and success can only be achieved, with a powerful credit history. Danny hopes to come back to Seminole State College as a professor and continue sharing his financial passion with students. Helping others is what makes Danny's passion grow; so please contact him, using the Face Book page, if you need financial help.

Endorsements

"Danny has demonstrated exceptional finance and accounting abilities and his accomplishments are impressive- especially considering his young age. His training has been invaluable. I am pleased to commend his excellence."
Rick Perry, Governor of Texas and First Lady Anita Perry

"I can say without reservation that Danny is a young man of impeccable character. Danny has taken a strong stand for his family as he began controlling the family finances. He is truly a unique individual who has had extremely different priorities."
Jason Brodeur, Florida State Representative, District 33

"Danny's extensive knowledge of credit and the banking industry that he shared with me greatly impressed me considering his young age. His financial talents are rare and he is with no doubt a very gifted individual with a bright future ahead."
Bob Dallari, Seminole County Commissioner, District 1

"Paying the bills and balancing a checkbook--all the task and responsibilities of being an adult. But one mom said she handed it all over to her son at just 11 years old."
Central Florida News 13

"Danny was a natural, a finance whiz kid. Soon, he was spending time reading the small print on each of his mom's credit card statements and every bill that came through. He started refinancing the ways banks work, how credit card companies calculate interest and what makes credit good."
East Orlando Sun

"Growing up Danny wanted to be a doctor. But that changed, the moment his mom gave him a new chore around the house. One that saved her thousands of dollars, and helped her son find a new path in life."
Dallas/Fort Worth WFAA-TV

"Danny accomplished the feat by negotiating with Bank of America was he was just 14 years old!"
Fox 35 News

"Feeling frustrated over finances? Need help managing a student loan? The Financial Whiz Kid may be able to help."
Seminole Chronicle

"You may have heard of Danny "Financial Whiz Kid" Singh. At the age of 11, the Orlando boy took over his mom's finances. By the age of 14, he had refinanced their home mortgage, persuaded banks to remove annual fees from his mom's credit cards and negotiated more than $1300 in refunds on interest and fees for her. His financial savvy attracted the attention of print and electronic media—and fellow high school students."
Seminole State College of Florida (Formerly, Seminole Community College)

"In reading Danny's book, Danny is truly a genius when it comes to finances because he is always giving advice, especially to college students. His information helped me make the financial decision, which was to put my savings into a more lucrative account so I would not

need to take out loans for college! I was not disappointed by his book and neither will you."
Lacey Kresen, Student at Valencia College, Orlando

"In Finance 101: The Whiz Kid's Perfect Credit Guide, Danny demonstrates he has an endless knowledge of finances. He himself has applied what he knows about money, loans, and other financial decisions and is now sharing this invaluable information with us. Danny truly cares about others and their finances and the purpose of his book is to help us remain debt free and happy."
Grace Love, Student at the Seminole State College of Florida, Sanford

"Danny's book proves he is incredibly knowledgeable when it comes to personal finance. The best part about his book is that he does not just want to help his fellow students begin their lives by making the best financial decisions possible but he also wants to make sure that they continue to use good spending habits into the future. I absolutely love how he does so in terms that anyone and everyone can understand."
Arisa Ramirez, Student at Rollins College, Winter Park

"Danny Singh is the man to go to for financial information. In his book, he breaks it down to a level that's understandable for anyone. He even goes above and beyond to provide financial assurance if you contact him directly."
Nicole Phillip, Student at the University of Central Florida, Orlando

"Danny has an extraordinary talent in finance. Through his book, he shares it with the world hopefully to help everyone. Not only did he help his mom with her credit, but he has freely helped in giving useful tips to friends on how to avoid debt and how to develop good credit; especially for us college students! Danny's book is vital for all consumers to have regardless of their financial conditions."
Nadia Williams, Student at the University of Central Florida, Orlando

"I have never read such a greatly detailed and yet, easy to understand book about credit and managing your finances. His book is as beneficial at the financial seminars he has performed at the college. I am an international student, and knew very little about the credit scoring system before reading Danny's book and now I have a perfect understanding of it. Despite being 19, I feel as though Danny clearly knows more about finance than a person with an MBA. I cannot stress the importance of reading this book because it saved me from making poor financial decisions and it is guaranteed to help others do the same."
Medge L. Parcily. Student at Seminole State College of Florida, Sanford

"Do not think the book will not help you succeed financially because Danny is extremely knowledgeable and has a gift for finance. His book has taught me the steps I always need to take before taking out a loan or applying for a new credit card! The book has been so helpful and serves as a guide to help me achieve the best credit possible and ultimately, save the most amount of money for retirement."
Kaitlyn Pennington, Student at Harmony High School, Orlando

"Danny is extremely brilliant when it comes to the finance world and the most important part of his book in the way he explains about credit cards and home financing: He knows what he is talking about and has many years of experience to support his knowledge. He also has the patience and ability to explain all these things well to people ignorant about the specific details when it comes to consumer finance."

Ratna Okhai, Student at the University of Central Florida, Orlando

"Danny is a professional in finance and he shows this in Finance 101: The Whiz Kid's Perfect Credit Guide. When I first opened up a checking account I had issues with overdraft fees and didn't understand how my account was handled. I also was a victim of credit card fraud. Danny's book has supported, explained, and given me tips as to how to survive the world of banking. He is not just a professional but a great friend to everyone who wants to achieve the dream of financial freedom."
Steven Silvernail, Student at the University of Central Florida, Orlando

"Danny's book is motivated to help consumers of all ages achieve unlimited financial success just as how he has achieved success with his mother's finances. He offers several tips on budgeting money so the maximum amount can be used towards paying loans and saving for retirement while taking care of everyday expenses. Doing so allows for me to improve my credit scores and save even more money on insurance. I was not aware about the significance of building credit early and how without credit, I could be denied for a job, house, or car. The book enlightened me on finance and I am so grateful for reading it. The book is the best investment I have ever made in my life."
Tyi Gardener, Student at Valencia College, Orlando

"Wow - what a knowledgeable book! Mr Singh covers everything from credit cards to student loans to retirement accounts. I would recommend using this book as more of a reference book since it is so full of information and will be something you will want to refer back to for many years."
Danny Kofke, author of "A Simple Book Of Financial Wisdom: Teach Yourself (and your kids) How To Live Wealthy With Little Money"

"Danny really is a "Financial Whiz Kid." His book helped dispel a lot of false information and put me on track to building better credit and finances. His book is a must-read for anybody in need of financial recovery after the recession."
John Morey, Consumer Advocate and Reader

"Danny is brimming with knowledge and experience in finances that are beyond his years. He has an almost giddy enthusiasm for various topics in finance, which paired with his support of others to avoid or recover from common financial pitfalls, is refreshing and inspiring. He holds much promise as a contributor to the marketplace."
-Dr. Marcia Roman, Vice President of Student Affairs at Seminole State College of Florida

Special Dedication

It has taken me about seven to eight months to complete this book while taking several courses in college. Originally, I thought it would take much more time. I surpassed my expectations and I feel as though what contributed to my motivation was the encouragement, of a very supporting friend, whom I cherish, everyday; for her grace and humor. She never fails to make me laugh. I met her freshmen year of high school, on a random day; I asked to sit with her on the school bus, when all the other seats were filled. I was nervous to start a conversation so I asked her a random question about what Math course she was taking but I did not notice the Algebra 2 textbook she was holding and think I unknowingly made a dumb impression. I now realize, that day was a blessing in disguise, because God bestowed upon me; a friend whose endless beauty comes, from her heart. I have been the recipient of her loyal support and friendship, for the past five years. She was especially, supportive, when my father passed away and it separates her from every other girl on the planet.

Like in all friendships, sometimes, we fight and drift apart but what pulls me back to her are the jokes, fun, and memories we have shared. This bond drives me to get a laugh out of her through whatever means necessary and save the friendship. Sometimes I fail to do so but she always admires my good intentions and sees how much I value her in my life.

I have asked her for suggestions to improve my financial seminars, my book, and her advice has helped me in more ways, than she will ever know. I attribute all my success to her. She has embedded a mark within my heart that will help me succeed, in all my academic challenges. For these reasons, I cannot thank her enough for being my inspiration.

Proudly, I dedicate this book to Michelle Windish and also acknowledge that I am so proud to know the most beautiful and gifted woman in the universe.

Special Dedication

The experience of writing and publishing a book was very stressful at times but I had the encouragement of a really supporting friend who kept motivating me to complete the book. He offered advice on creating the press release and it has been more than an honor attending University High School with him for the past 4 years.

This person tells the best jokes. Anyone around him will struggle not to laugh. He is doing the Pre-Med program at the University of Miami and I know he will surpass all his goals in life.

I cannot thank him enough for being the person he is and so with great pride, I dedicate this book to my good friend, Ashish Yamdagni.

Special Dedication

When an individual thinks of a friend then they think of someone who will always be there for them, support them, be honest, and show understanding whenever they feel frustrated. Luckily, God has blessed me with a friend who has these qualities and more and I will never be able to thank him enough for it. The encouragement of this friend allowed for me to further unlock my passion for business and share my knowledge with the world through this book. He is currently attending the University of Central Florida and hopes to become a vet. With his motivation and strong academic abilities, I have no doubt that he will become a world renowned vet. I am so proud I had the honor of attending University High School with him.

I show my deepest gratitude to Steven Silvernail.

Contents

Credit in Lamest Terms 1

Credit Checks 2
-What are Credit Checks? 2
-Hard Credit Checks Damage Credit 2
-Employers Perform Credit Checks 3
-Conditions of Employment 3
-Insurance and Other Companies That Use Soft Inquiry Credit Checks 4
-Myths about Credit Checks 4

Credit Scores 7
-What is a Credit Score? 7
-Different Credit Scoring Models- Vantage Score and FICO Score 7
-Will a Business use the FICO or Vantage Score Model? 8
-Scores for Different Business Purposes 10
-Credit Reports are Free but Not Credit Scores 11
-Weaknesses of Credit Scores 11
-Inauthentic Credit Scores (FAKO Scores) 14

Check Credit with all Agencies 15

The Credit CARD Act of 2009 16
-Credit Card Act Changes 17
-The Four Types of Balances 21

Credit, Debit, Prepaid, and ATM Cards 29
-Automated Teller Machine Cards (ATM Card) 29
-Prepaid Cards 29
-Credit Cards 29
-Credit Cards are Safest Form of Payment and Build Credit 30
-Dangers of Debit, Prepaid, and ATM Cards 30
-Prepaid Cards = Fees, Fees, and More Fees 31
-Save Money on Withdrawing Money through Allpoint Network 31
-What is ChexSystems? 32
-Relationship of ChexSystems Report with Credit Profile 33
-Use a Credit Card for Maximum Security 34

Handling Credit Cards Wisely 35
-Interest Rate Reductions and Removal of Annual Fees 35
-Improvement that should be made with Credit Reports 35
-Bank Credit Cards verses Department Store Credit Cards 36
-Credit Card Debt Elimination Strategy 36

Credit Cards 40
-Credit Card Arbitration 40
-Business Credit Cards 40
-Card Numbers Cannot Appear on Receipts 40
-Raising Credit Card Minimum Payments 40
-Credit Card Terms and Conditions—Loan Contract with the Disclosures 42
-Avoid Overdraft Fees by wisely using Credit Card 44
-Keep Credit Cards Open for Long Time 44
-Do Not Just Make Minimum Payments 45
-Credit Card is Not Source of Income or Alternative to Not Having Money 46
-Legitimate Purpose of Credit Card 46
-The History of the Credit Card 46

Deposit Accounts and FDIC or NCUA 48
-Insured Deposit Accounts are Imperative 48
-Credit Unions offer NCUA Insured Accounts 48
-Detect Fraudulent Financial Institutions 49
-Community Banks are Beneficial 49
-Be Cautious of International Financial Institutions 50
-FDIC and NCUA Does Not Affect Loans 50
-Types of Deposit Accounts 50
-Deposit All Money into Deposit Accounts for Maximum Protection 51
-Average Daily Balances and Fees 52
-Online Bill Pay Feature 53
-Online Bill Pay Protection 54

Deposit Account Basics 63
-Rewards Checking Accounts 63
-Use Debit Card as Credit 63
-ATM Cards Do Not Save Money 63
-Free Overdraft Protection can Save Hundreds in Fees 63
-Benefits of Overdraft Protection 65
-Get Accounts that Offer Bonuses 66
-Free Online Bill Pay Saves Time and Money 67
-No Minimum Balance Requirements 67
-Insured Deposit Accounts Only 67
-No Fee-Based Accounts Ever 68
-Get Competitive Interest Rate Accounts 68
-Denial for Deposit Account- Serious Issue 68

Loans 70
-Recourse and Non-Recourse Loans 70
-Common Types of Recourse Loans 70
-Common Types of Non-Recourse Loans 71
-Signature Loans can be Expensive 71

-Tax Anticipation Refund Loans..71
-Microloans...72
-Mortgage Tip..72
-Loan-To-Value Ratio Suggests Likelihood of Defaulting...............................73
-Financial Institutions Asked for Little or No Down Payment......................73
-Federal Funds Rate 74
-Prime Lending is Best..74
-Subprime Lending is failing in Economy 75
-Think 6 Times before Cosigning 75
-Credit Reports do not Show Interest Rates of Loans 76
-Interest Rates Appearing on Credit Reports would Protect Businesses........77
-Have All Types of Credit 77
-Life Insurance Loan 78

Criteria for Loan Approvals..79
-Income Score..79
-Household Review 79
-Delinquency Ratio 81
-Debt-to-Credit Ratio..83
-Closure of Credit Cards = Not Wise 84
-Length of Credit History 87
-Debt-to-Income Ratio 88
-Carrying Balances is a BAD Habit and Hurts Credit......................................90

Credit Denials 91
-Do Not Just Accept Denial..91
-Look for Letter of Reason for Denial 91
-No-Income Verification Loans 113
-Business Risks of Subprime Lending...114

Credit Rights..115
-Through the Fair Credit Reporting Act..115
-Active Duty Alert Prevents Fraud 115
-Fair Debt Collections Practices Act..115
-Information that Shows on the Credit Reports.. 116
-Innovis Background Information (The 4th Credit Bureau)........................117
-Pay Attention when Reading Credit Reports...117
-Credit Agencies and Trade Lines 118
-Purpose of Needing Credit 118
-Free Copy of Credit Report is a Right upon Denial of Credit or Service 118
-Just Being Rich is Not Enough.. 119
-Companies view Consumers with Bad Credit as Low in Character............. 119
-Abuse of Credit in Relationships 119
-Creditworthiness is Trustworthiness 120
-Annual Fee is Profit Strategy 120

-Business Management of Credit 121
-Behavior Score suggests Profit 123
-USA Patriot Act 123
-Utility Bills are Important... 124
-Paying Bills in a Timely Manner is Not Enough 125
-Income has No Relationship with Credit.. 125

Bad Credit means Many Problems 126
-Bad Credit causes some Financial Institutions to "Blacklist" Consumers 129
-Do Not Pay Thousands to Credit Repair Agencies.. 129
-Freezing Credit Reports will Not Hide Information from Companies 130

Good Credit means a Good Life, Good Future, and No Cons 131
-Denied for Credit? Do Not Give Up!... 132
-Look for Denial Letter with Reasons 133
-Reconsideration helps Credit 133
-Account Approval helps Credit... 133
-Do Not Give Up on Getting Approval... 133
-Use Certified Mail to Send Reconsideration Letters 134

Loan Modification 137
-Loan Modification Warnings and Tips.. 139

All Things Auto 145
-Cash is Great but a Car Loan Is Better 145
-Get the Longest Loan Term Possible.. 145
-Good Credit means Cheap Insurance 146
-Family Member as Cosigner..146
-"Bad Credit Car Dealerships" = Death of Thousands of Dollars! 147
-Bad Quality Cars 148
-Alternatives to Buying an Automobile from a "Bad Credit Dealership" 148
-Finance with Credit Unions and Not Dealerships 150
-0% Promotion—Does It Really Save Money? 150
-Repossessed and Used Cars = Risky Purchases 151
-Negotiate for Cheaper Costs Always! 152
-Multiple Cars.. 153
-Returning a Car.. 153
-Caution about Gap Insurance 154
-Repossession of a Vehicle... 154
-Use Retirement Account to Save Automobile.. 156
-Attorneys to Help with Repossession Case 156
-Umbrella Insurance is Ideal for Risky Drivers 157
-Vehicles can Develop Negative Equity like Houses 157
-Car Refinancing 158
-Other ways in which Consumers can save Money with their Auto Loan 158

Insurance Brokers and Agents 160

Insurance 164
-Health and Dental Insurance 164
-Employment Discounts on Insurance 164
-CIGNA is an Ideal Insurance Company 164
-Medicaid 164
-Medicare 164
-4 Insurance Policies to Avoid 165
-Snapshot Auto Insurance Discount 165

Health Savings Account 166

Real Estate 167
-Apartment and Condo Hunting 167
-Real Estate Agents can find Great Deals 167
-Roth IRA can help Save Money Faster 167
-Mortgage Prepayment Scams 168
-Pay down Student Loans before getting Apartment 168
-Housing Crisis of 2000s: Mistakes of Congress and the Federal Reserve 168
-The Credit Crisis in Relation to the 2000s Housing Crisis 170
-Loan-to-Value Ratio in Relation to the 2000s Housing Crisis 173
-Be Careful of No Closing Costs Mortgages! 174
-Property Taxes 174
-Credit Disclosure Notice 174
-Private Mortgage Insurance is a Money Killer 174
-Consumers must Request for Removal of Private Mortgage Insurance 175
-Mortgages and Grace Period = Warning! 176
-Mortgage Lenders are More Consumer Friendly than Brokers 176
-Mortgage Types 176
-Mortgages for Consumers with Financial Struggles 178

Caution About Mortgages 181
-Buying a house 181
-Vital factors to Consider before buying a house 181
-Steal of a Deal 183
-Cash-out Refinance 183
-Closing Costs Tips 183
-Alternative to Refinancing with No Fees 184
-Mortgage Classifications 184
-Adjustable-rate mortgage (ARMs) 185
-Mortgage Tip in Paying Down Balance 187
-Save House from Foreclosure 187

Home Equity Loans 188
-How the Amount of Equity is Determined...188
-House Appraisers help Determine Equity 189
-The Thinking of House Appraisers..189
-Financial Institutions Spy on Consumers' Assets...189
-Credit Profile determines Amount of Loan Money 191
-Be Careful of Recourse Loans... 191
-Finalizing of Loans... 191
-Handle Payments Wisely..192
-Tax Benefits of Home Equity Loans and Home Equity Line of Credit Products............192
-Benefits of Home Equity Loans 193
-Tax Deduction Limitations 193
-Be Careful when Closing Home Equity Line of Credit Products.......................194
-Distribution of Home Equity Line of Credit Product Money 195
-Dangers of Home Equity Line of Credit Product- Very Expensive 196
-Variable Interest Rate of Home Equity Line of Credit = Problems....................196
-The Abuse of Home Equity Loans and Equity Line of Credit Products............197
-Warnings about Home Equity Loans and Home Equity Lines of Credit 197
-Negative Equity is Bad 198

Short Sales..199
-Short Sale is Better than a Foreclosure..199
-Short Sales during the 2000s Housing Crisis..199

Mortgage Score 200
-CoreLogic... 200

Fraud..207
-Phishing 207
-Review ChexSystems Report to Prevent Fraud and Financial Crisis 211

Bankruptcy and Debt Settlement.. 212
-Bankruptcy Codes 212
-Two Types of Debts.. 212
-Response of Financial Institutions to Bankruptcy... 213
-Impact on Credit Reports 213
-Bad Credit saved in Records 213
-Bad Credit damages Economy.. 214
-Bad Credit raises Needs to make Profit 214

Bankruptcy and Debt Settlement Alternatives 215
-Credit Counseling 215
-Be Careful when Trusting Credit Counseling Agencies 215
-Credit Counseling Fees: Pay HIGH Attention 215
-Credit Counseling Limitations.. 216
-Credit Counseling is a Last Resort 216

-Seek Government Approved Credit Counseling Agencies 216
-Risks of Credit Counseling and Its Impact on Credit 217
-Get a New Loan with a Low and Fixed Interest Rate 218
-Credit Unions save Money 218
-National Credit Union Association 219
-Interest Rates are Never Guaranteed 219
-Credit Report Disputes can Improve Scores 220
-Balance Transfers Can Save Money 221
-Methods to Request Balance Transfer 222
-Transferring Secured Loans to Unsecured Loans 223
-Scenario in which Balance Transfer is Beneficial 224
-Limitations of Balance Transfers 224
-Denial of Credit Card and No Balance Transfer 225

Pawnshop Loans 228
-No Credit Checks 228
-Collateral 228
-Excessive Interest 228
-No Credit Data Reporting 228

Cell Phones 229
-Save Money on Cell Phones 229
-Consumers Should Not Pay for Phones 229
-Qualities Sought in a Phone Plan 229
-SIM Cards save Money 230
-Cell Phone Insurance 230

Minors and Credit 232
-Minors Should Not Ignore Bills 232
-Be Honest about Financial Mistakes with Children 232
-Parents Abusing the Credit Profiles of their Children 236
-Credit Card offers sent to Minors = Sign of Danger 237
-Opt-out of Receiving Offers 237

High School and College Students Finances 239
-College Degree is never a Hole of Debt 241
-Job Difficulties 248
-FAFSA 252
-FAFSA Weaknesses and Criticisms 254
-College Cost Reduction Act of 2007 260
-Specific Government Student Loans 260
-Warning about ALL Stafford loans 261
-The Evil Private and Uncertified Student Loans 262
-Crucial Tips for ALL Private Student Loans (and other Loans too) 264
-Student Loan Relief Fraud 275
-Student Loan Relief Options 276

-Obama Student Loan Reform 280
-Quest Bridge 281

"School-as-Lender" Program 282

Weddings and Finance 283
-Weddings do not mean Debt 283
-Home Equity Loan is Sometimes a Safe Method to Finance Wedding 283
-Roth IRA can be Safe Financing Method for Wedding 283
-Ways to Keep Low Expenses for Wedding 284

Pregnancy and Finance 285

Financial Protection and Safety Strategies 287
-Safety Precautions 287
-Scam College Aid 287
-Credit Card Abuse 287
-Personal Line of Credit 287
-Timeshare 289
-Auto lease 289
-Saving for Children's Education 290
-529 College Savings 290
-Education IRA (Coverdell Education Savings Account) 291
-Third Party Manages Store Branded Credit Cards 291
-Revocable Living Trust 297
-Statue of Limitations 298

Building and Rebuilding Good Credit 299

Incarceration 305
-Notice of Deficiency 305
-Tax Audits are Serious 305
-Tax Evasion 306
-Incarceration Damages Credit 306
-Incarceration suggests No Integrity to Repay Bills 306

Certified Checks and Starter Checks 308

Retirement 309
-Seek Cheap Utilities 309
-Self-employed Consumers have Unique Retirement Accounts 309
-Retirement Accounts of Government Employees 310

Saving Money 311
-Save Money on Gift Cards 311
-Self-Publishing is a Great Source of Extra Money 311

- Name Brands can be Wallet Killers 311
- Premium Gas 312
- Fees for Checking in Bags at Airports 312
- Newspapers 312
- Surge Protector Power Strips = Inexpensive Electricity Bill 312
- Avoid Expensive Gyms and Health Care Clubs 312
- Avoid "Gas Saving" Devices 312
- Dollar Store Deals 313
- Saving Money on Sending Mail 313
- Avoid Hotel Fees 313
- Safe Deposit Boxes are Not Insured 313
- Extended Warranties on Items 314
- Fake Charities 314
- Vacation Finance 314
- Rent-to-Own is Expensive 314
- Companies that Buy Gold 315

Safe Online Shopping 316

Emergency Fund 317

Credit Report Dispute Forms 320

Experience with Financial Institutions 323

Credit Department Contact Numbers 324

Acknowledgements 326
- University High School International Baccalaureate Class of 2011 326
- 2011-2012 The Art and Phyllis Grindle Honors Institute at
    Seminole State College of Florida 333

My Recognition of Excellence 335
- Riverdale Elementary School in Orlando, Florida 335
- Odyssey Middle School in Orlando, Florida 336
- University High School in Orlando, Florida 337
- Seminole State College of Florida in Oviedo, Florida 338
- Family Acknowledgements 340

Index 343

Credit in Lamest Terms

Credit is any type of loan or service a consumer must apply for, such as an auto loan, mortgage (home loan), student loan, or credit card. The consumer may be denied or approved depending upon the financial information showing on their credit reports. Credit reports may be called "credit profiles." Services can include electricity, water, cell phone, insurance, and if the consumer has bad or limited credit history then the service issuers may want security deposits so they feel protected from a financial loss happening. A security deposit is when a consumer gives money up front to the company and in the event that the consumer does not pay the bill, and then as a consequence the company gets to keep the security deposit but may cancel the service.

If a consumer is approved for a service or loan, credit has been extended to the consumer by the financial institution and this is a financial achievement. Credit can be thought of as a pay-later system because the consumer gets to take immediate possession of the item such as a house or car, but must pay for it over time to the creditor, often with interest.

When consumers use a service or loan then they are in debt until they fully pay it back. Debt is any owed money to someone or a company. The financial institution, bank, or company that has extended the credit is considered to be the "creditor" of the consumer. Some consumers refer to the creditor as the "issuer of the loan."

Interest is usually not charged on services such as electricity, water, utilities, or insurance. Interest can be avoided depending upon how fast the entire amount of the loan is paid back and no fees are charged on the loans. Fees can be considered to be interest, become part of the balance, and the fees can accumulate more interest if the balances are not paid off immediately. Interest also accumulates more interest.

Credit Checks

What are Credit Checks?

When companies/employers, check the credit reports and scores of consumers, this is known as a "credit check." When a credit check happens with one or more of the three major credit bureaus, a "credit inquiry" is created; and shows on the credit report. The inquiry is evidence, to a consumer, that their credit was checked. Consumers must know who checks their credit; so they know that their personal information is not being compromised. A credit inquiry can be either "soft" or "hard." Consumers need to avoid having too many hard credit inquiries done on them, because they will lower the credit scores. The hard credit inquiries can be viewed by the consumer, any company, or employer that checks the credit in the future. For example, if Ashish applies for a Citibank credit card on February 21st, because he needs credit to buy his girlfriend an engagement ring; Citibank would check his credit that very same day. A hard inquiry credit check, from Citibank, would show on the Equifax credit report of Ashish. In April, Ashish decides to buy a house and applies for a mortgage with Bank of America. Bank of America would check his Equifax credit report and see that in February, Ashish had applied for a Citibank credit card. If in May, Ashish were to apply for an auto loan with Suntrust Bank, then Suntrust would check his credit and see Ashish had applied for a Citibank credit card, in February, and a mortgage with Bank of America in April.

Hard Credit Checks Damage Credit

The hard credit inquiry stays on credit reports for two years and they suggest that the consumer is seeking to obtain credit; which usually means they are trying to get into debt. This sends a negative message to financial institutions. Too many hard credit inquiries cause financial institutions to look at consumers, with risk. This financial behavior may give the impression that the consumer is financially unstable; because it makes no sense to them, why a consumer would need so much credit. For example, it would be considered very abnormal, to Bank of America, if Ashish had applied for five credit cards, in February. In the eyes of the financial institutions, consumers applying for credit aggressively have no intention of paying back the financial institutions; or are planning on getting into high levels of debt, that they will never be able to pay back. As a result, the financial institutions will have a loss. For such reasons, Ashish needs to make sure companies were not checking his credit without his authorization. It is possible for the same financial institution to make multiple hard inquiry credit checks, on the consumer, as a result of a system glitch. Consumers need to be aware of what is showing up on their credit reports and contact the financial institutions immediately, if they performed multiple credit inquiries for one credit product. Most financial institutions are comfortable with two to three credit checks, with each credit report, of the consumer. Soft credit inquiries are different from hard credit inquiries, because they do not lower credit scores. When consumers check their own credit then it is considered a soft inquiry.

Employers Perform Credit Checks

Any company or employer can perform a soft credit inquiry, without needing the authorization of a consumer. Usually, when a company performs a hard inquiry credit check; they must get permission from the consumer, before doing so. If a consumer is denied for a job, due to having bad credit; the employer will inform them.

On the Human Resources webpage of Seminole State College of Florida; it indicates the requirements for the available jobs and what types of checks will be done. There are many jobs, on the market, that require a soft inquiry credit check on candidates, which want a job. For this reason, do not ever stop paying on bills or declare a bankruptcy or commit to debt settlement.
Source: http://www.seminolestate.edu/hr/jobs/?id=101390

Conditions of Employment

"The College will conduct various types of background checks which may include, but are not limited to: criminal background, **credit check**, driver's license check, previous employment and references."

Financial institutions use **soft credit checks** for Account Reviews; they do **soft inquiries**, for the purpose of specializing and marketing; credit offers to consumers based on their individual credit histories. Additionally, financial institutions that are already doing business with a consumer periodically perform soft credit check inquiries on the credit reports. They want to make sure a consumer is not being delinquent on any loans, applying for credit aggressively, closing too many credit cards, or building high levels of debt. Such actions suggest, the financial conditions of a consumer are unusual or weak. For this reason, when a credit account is established with a company, their computer system monitors the credit profile, of the consumer, to detect any major changes. If major changes occur, then the financial institution will review the credit account that the consumer has with them; they may close it down, reduce the credit limit, or increase the interest rate.

For example, if Michelle is a credit card customer of Capital One; their computer system will monitor her credit profile, for the time she has the credit card open. If Michelle becomes delinquent with the credit card she has with Wells Fargo then Capital One will detect a negative change with her credit profile. They will perform a soft inquiry on her credit reports, and a credit analyst will do an **"account review"** with the credit card account Michelle has with Capital One. The fact that, Michelle was delinquent on a credit card; suggests she has become financially weak. Capital One will now look at Michelle, with risk, because if Michelle was delinquent with Wells Fargo it is feasible that she will become delinquent with Capital One or stop paying at all. For this reason, Capital One may take an adverse action against Michelle, such as increasing her interest rate. They want to make as much profit as possible for the time Michelle is making her payments in a timely manner. When a financial institution decides to increase the interest rate, on a loan or credit card to the penalty default rate; even when the consumer has never been late with them but with another financial institution, the financial institution is doing what is called **universal default**. In the case of Michelle, Capital One is doing universal default with her. However, Capital One may even close the account and this will damage the credit profile of Michelle. Departments within the financial institution that usually make such decisions on high risk consumers are called the **"portfolio risk department,"** **"account review department,"** or the **"credit department."** These departments are safeguards for the financial institution, in the event that the consumer makes poor financial decisions after establishing a credit account. Consumers are expected to always maintain excellent credit in order to keep their accounts open and receive incentives, such as interest rate reductions, credit limit increases, and fee refunds.

Insurance and Other Companies That Use Soft Inquiry Credit Checks

Insurance and other service related companies usually do soft credit inquiries, because they do not want to provide services to high risk consumers that are unlikely to pay their bill. They not perform hard credit inquiries, because getting a service such as electricity, water, insurance, or a phone is different than getting credit. With credit, a consumer has the ability to purchase anything and so financial institutions must do hard credit inquiries when consumers apply for credit for the purpose of protecting themselves. Hard credit inquiries cost more money, for the service providers, to obtain than soft inquiries and they do not make as much profit as financial institutions do. Upon doing the soft inquiry credit check, the service company will decide whether or not the consumer needs to provide a security deposit, due to their poor or limited credit history.

Myths about Credit Checks

Myth: Opening a loan or credit card hurts credit.

Fact: Opening a loan or credit card **initially** lowers the credit scores due to the credit check, most consumers unfortunately build a balance, and because the account is new it has no payment history. Ten percent, of the FICO credit scoring models, look at the credit checks, thirty percent look at the balances on accounts, and fifteen percent look at the length of history established on accounts. After three to four months, the credit scores increase again because the payment history starts building on the new credit account and the debt-to-credit limit ratio becomes less. In addition, the consumer has access to more available credit than they did before the account was established. The consumer should be using less than thirty percent of all the available credit for the purpose of maintaining a low utilization rate, which leads to higher credit scores. This shows the consumer is not financially weak. Financial institutions can often determine if consumers are financially weak; when they are using a large portion of all the credit that is available to them. This will cause financial institutions to close accounts, reduce credit limits, increase interest rates, and other adverse actions because they fear that the consumer will default.

After two years, the hard inquiry credit check that was done, when the consumer applied for the new account, will drop off the credit report. This is how the credit agencies have set up their systems, when managing the credit reports of consumers. Hard inquiry credit checks dropping causes the credit scores to become higher. Opening a new credit account is not negative information because it does not send the message that the consumer is going to cheat the financial institution. However, if a consumer were to open multiple credit accounts, within a short time period then this action could hurt credit. This is because it sends a negative message to financial institutions. Financial institutions assume most consumers that open several credit accounts, in a short time, do not pay them. For example, if Charlotte opened six credit cards within a week then a financial institution would think they are at high risk, of her defaulting. They would not understand why Charlotte opened so many accounts or her intentions. They might also be led to think that Charlotte is damaging her own credit, because six credit accounts mean six or more hard credit check inquiries. Inquiries lower credit scores and the financial institutions may think Charlotte does not care about having damaged credit. It considered unusual to apply for many credit accounts at once, because there is no need for so much credit. Finally, the financial institutions may think that Charlotte's personal information has been compromised and a criminal is applying for credit, with the intention of making numerous purchases. For such reasons, the financial institutions may take negative actions against Charlotte; such as closing her credit accounts, raising her interest rates, or reducing her credit limits. These actions can damage Charlotte's credit profile.

When credit accounts are established, they are immediately reported to the credit agencies, with the date they were opened, and future creditors can see this information. For example, if Charlotte opens up too many credit accounts, during two months, such as December and January, ten or less years pass, and Charlotte applies for credit again; although her credit scores may not reflect it, the financial institutions will notice the excessive number of accounts that Charlotte opened during December and January upon reviewing her credit reports. This will cause them to look at her with risk and they may take unfavorable actions against her; including denying her credit. They will think Charlotte is "credit needy", due to the fact; she opened so many credit accounts at one point in time. The high number of newly opened accounts may cause financial institutions to do a background check on Charlotte; to see if she is a victim of fraud or if she has been convicted of stealing. Such may explain why Charlotte has such unusual credit behavior. Financial institutions may also see how many credit applications have been submitted; under the social security number belonging to Charlotte. Consumers cannot see all the credit applications submitted under their name, on the credit reports. In order to see the credit applications, consumers would need to contact the credit agencies or the Fair Isaac Corporation and sign up for one of their credit monitoring services, which will cost money. Some states have special benefits for consumers that are victimized by fraud and they may receive free credit monitoring, up to a certain timeframe. The credit agencies usually store the credit applications electronically within their computer databases for up to two years. In fraud cases, authorities have the authority to request for the applications. An example of such a case would be if credit applications are being submitted under the social security number of an individual who is deceased.

In contrast, if Charlotte only opened one or two credit cards within a month then the financial institution will not think she is likely to default. They will likely think Charlotte is trying to make her credit stronger, made a large purchase and received a discount for opening an account, or cosigned for another person to help make their credit stronger. Such intentions are considered normal for consumers and financial institutions feel comfortable. They are less likely to take unfavorable actions against her.

Advice: Be conscious of how many credit accounts are established within a short time frame. There is no need to open many credit accounts within a month or year. This results in too many credit checks happening, which damages credit. Consumers should not let financial institutions do multiple credit checks on them especially when they are only applying for one credit account. If this happens then consumers should immediately contact the financial institutions and request for them to remove the extra credit check inquiries. Other financial institutions cannot tell if the credit check inquiries are legitimate or if the financial institution made a mistake. They will think an excessive number of credit check inquiries means the consumer is applying for credit aggressively and they may take negative actions against the consumer. For this reason, having the least number of inquiries should be the goal of every consumer. Consumers should be periodically monitoring their credit profiles for the purpose of preventing fraud. Criminals tend to apply for credit aggressively the minute they compromise personal information and if they are successful in opening accounts. The consumers are liable for all the fraudulent charges unless they report it immediately to the financial institutions. Unfortunately, many consumers are not aware of the fraudulent activity taking place until their credit has been ruined and as a result, their credit cards start getting closed and decline at the stores.

Myth: Consumers will hurt their credit by checking their own reports.

Fact: When consumers check their credit, their scores are not affected in any manner. This is because consumers are not trying to grant themselves credit or services. Credit scores can become low when companies that are trying to extend credit or a type of service check the credit profile of the consumer. This generates a hard inquiry credit check. Every consumer has four credit reports. One report is maintained by each credit agency. The agencies are Equifax, Experian, TransUnion, and Innovis. A company may check credit reports with all the agencies, maybe two agencies, or just one agency. It depends on the individual lending policies of the financial institution. Consumers are encouraged to check their credit often so they can avoid fraud and can detect any mistakes when the financial institutions report credit data to the credit agencies. Consumers can check their credit as many times as they feel necessary. Credit usually changes every month.

Advice: Consumers should check their credit monthly, anytime that fraud happens, and before they apply for credit so they can make sure all the information is correct. Consumers are in danger of being denied credit or being a victim of fraud if they are not continuing to check their credit.

Credit Scores

What is a Credit Score?

A credit score is a ranking given to a consumer based on the positive and negative information showing on their consumer agency reports. It is the "risk score" to the business; which suggests the likelihood of a consumer in paying back the loan without defaulting, becoming late or not paying at all. The credit scoring models are trying to help the businesses avoid losses. The models score the consumers lower, when they see consumers are doing financial actions that suggest they are likely to default. Statistically, other consumers in the past, that have done the same financial actions, such as; building high balances, applying for credit aggressively, or being late have stopped paying the loans and usually, they have declared a bankruptcy or debt settlement. The credit scoring models and the financial institutions assume that consumers, who are doing the same financial actions, as previous consumers that have financially failed are going to one day stop paying. Similarly, the credit scoring models score consumers higher when they are doing financial actions that previous consumers have done and financially succeeded. Such positive financial actions include paying down and keeping little or no balances, not applying for credit aggressively, and having different types of loans and credit. These actions suggest a consumer is unlikely to one day stop paying and the financial institutions will be more prone to treat them positively.

Different Credit Scoring Models- Vantage Score and FICO Score

There are different brands of credit scoring models, which the consumer reporting agencies use to calculate a credit score. The scoring models have their own algorithms set up by the businesses, which means they have their own ways of analyzing and treating sets of data. An algorithm can be thought of as being a mathematical calculation. One of the most popular credit scoring brands is the FICO score created by the Fair Isaac Corporation and it has a scale of 300 - 850. In order for consumers to receive an authentic copy of their Equifax and TransUnion FICO scores, they must order them from MyFico.com. In order to receive an authentic copy of their Experian FICO score, they must obtain it from the creditor to whom they submit a credit application or contact Experian directly but it may not be called an Experian FICO score but just an Experian credit score. Experian no longer allows consumers to access their Experian FICO score through any website including MyFico.com. Experian was not making enough money in their business relationship, with the Fair Isaac Corporation. If consumers attempt to order their Equifax, TransUnion, and Experian FICO scores from other websites besides MyFico.com then the scores are known as "FAKO scores." This is because other websites including the websites of the credit bureaus try to replicate the scoring model of FICO and a replication is not the same as the calculation done by the actual model. The scores given by websites other than MyFico.com are simply estimates as to what the authentic FICO scores are of the consumers. The second brand is the Vantage Score that was created by Vantage Score Solutions LLC and it has a scale of 501 - 990 along with a letter score of A - F. A is the highest letter score possible whereas F is the lowest score possible. Vantage Score Solutions LLC; was a company started by Equifax, TransUnion, and Experian in an attempt to beat the FICO scoring model of the Fair Isaac Corporation. Vantage Score Solutions LLC; was hoping more businesses would use the Vantage Score model than the FICO score model. The Vantage Score model and the FICO score model can be thought of as competitors.

Will a Business use the FICO or Vantage Score Model?

Businesses will usually select the credit score brand that is; the cheapest for them to use, best helps them achieve their particular business goals, or the credit score issuing company with whom they have the best relationship. Additionally, some businesses may use the information on the credit report, of the consumer, to calculate their own score using their programs.

For example, auto loan issuers usually calculate an "auto-enhanced score." The greatest portion of an auto-enhanced score focuses on the payment histories of a consumer; on their previous and current installment credit loans. However, if the business wants; it can order an auto-enhanced score from the Fair Isaac Corporation, Vantage Score Solutions LLC, Equifax, Experian, TransUnion, Innovis, or another company, depending upon which score issuing company with whom the business has the best relationship and if the score issuing company even offers the particular type of score that they want. Similarly, all types of insurance companies can order an "insurance risk score" from the Fair Isaac Corporation, Vantage Score Solutions LLC, or one or all of the consumer reporting agencies. Insurance risk scores focus on all the factors that a FICO credit score or Vantage Score would focus on such as payment history, balances on accounts, number of credit checks, and the length of history established on credit accounts. It is likely, if a consumer has good credit, then their insurance risk score will be good whereas if their have bad credit then their insurance risk score will be bad. Insurance companies assume that if consumers are responsible enough to handle their credit accounts properly then they are likely able to handle their items properly; for which they want insurance such as a boat, automobile, or house. Vantage Scores can be ordered through Experian on http://www.experian.com/consumer-products/vantage-score.html or by calling 1-888-322-5583.

Vantage Score Calculation Scale

Source of image: http://www.experian.com/consumer-products/vantage-score.html

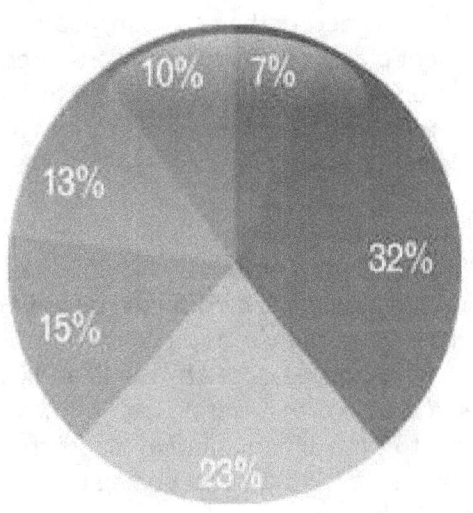

Recent credit (10%): This portion is influenced by the number of credit checks the consumer has had within the last two years and how many new credit accounts they opened within the last year. Too many credit checks or too many, newly opened credit accounts; send a bad message to the financial institutions about the consumer. They think the consumer has a bad intention of getting into large amounts of debt and not repaying that debt. Consumers should not keep applying for credit even if they are denied, regardless of the reasons because employers are also going to speculate as to why a consumer would damage their own credit profile by letting so many companies check their credit. This makes the employer think that the consumer is irresponsible. When consumers are approved for credit then they should stop applying for more credit and build at least two years worth of history on the account for which they were just approved before applying for credit again.

Available credit (7%): Consumers should not use more than 30% of the credit limit on a credit card and they should never carry balances on multiple credit cards because such lowers the amount of available credit to which they have access. Having too many balances or a high balance on loans increases the debt-to-credit limit ratio and it looks like the consumer is using credit excessively and will one day get into so much debt that they will have no choice but to stop paying because they will not be able to afford all the payments. For this reason, financial institutions do not like consumers who are using almost the entire credit limit on a credit card or loan.

Payment history (32%): This is the meat of any credit score or credit report. Consumers cannot be late ever on making payments or stop paying all together no matter how much income they make, what hardships they are facing, or what interest rates they are paying. Debt does not magically disappear. The unpaid debt will increase the hardships of the consumers because in most cases, financial institutions take drastic actions against consumers who stop paying their bills and other bills will increase in their amounts. The consumers will be in such a bad financial state that they will not be able to do anything for their children such as when their children need a cosigner for their car loan, apartment, or student loan. The financial institutions have payment plans for unemployed consumers in which the payments can possibly be deferred or the interest rates can be cut likely at the cost of the account getting closed, but the consumers need to inform the financial institutions before the due dates of their bills arrive. Employers dislike late payments because such suggests that the consumer is irresponsible and thus, does not deserve a job.

Utilization (23%): Consumers should not use more than 30% of the credit limit on their credit card. Only one credit card should be used for everyday purchases. However, consumers should ultimately use all their credit cards at least once every 6 months for the purpose of protecting them from getting closed by the financial institution for inactivity. If the credit cards get closed then it causes the utilization level of the consumer to be higher because the consumer has access to a lower amount of available credit. A low amount of available credit in relation to the overall level of debt belonging to the consumer can suggest the consumer is using credit excessively.

Balances (15%): The balances on credit cards and other revolving credit loans that have a credit limit should not be higher than 30% of the credit limits; if they are higher then the consumer needs to pay them down immediately; This is because in the eyes of the financial institutions and credit scoring models, the balances over 30% of the credit limit are considered high. The consumer is likely to let their accounts become delinquent because they will spend so much to the point that they will not be able to afford the payments. Even if consumers are always prompt in making their payments, if they have high levels of debt then their credit scores will be low.

Depth of credit: (13%): The depth of credit is the length of time that has been established on the credit accounts. The longer that the number of years pass and the consumer maintains a positive payment history on the credit account then the more their credit scores will increase. Consumers do not have to carry balances on the credit cards in order for them to remain open. Consumers simply need to make sure they are not used fraudulently. If consumers close their credit accounts, then they hurt their credit scores because in seven to ten years, the accounts with their payment histories fall off the credit reports and their average length of history shortens. Such defeats the purpose of having ever made all the payments in a timely manner. Additionally, the depth of credit focuses on the types of credit and variety of loans that are being handled by the consumer. Financial institutions want to see installment loans such as car loans, mortgages (home loans), student loans and revolving loans such as credit cards, home equity lines of credit, line of credit, line of credit or any loan that has a spending limit. Revolving and installment loans can be either secured, meaning there is an item or money that can be repossessed by the financial institution; or unsecured, mean there is nothing that can be repossessed by the financial institution in the event that the consumer stops paying on the loans.

Scores for Different Business Purposes

For "auto insurance scores" only, which mean scores that automobile insurance providers would obtain, they are not always influenced by the driving records of consumers depending upon the company that is calculating the auto insurance score. They are only based off of credit information.

For example, according to www.Creditkarma.com "the auto insurance score provided by TransUnion does not take into account the driving record or any other information outside the credit report." If businesses ordered an auto insurance score from another score issuing company other than TransUnion then the auto insurance score calculation may take into consideration the driving records of the consumer. Auto-enhanced, auto insurance, insurance risk scores, and all scores for different purposes have their own scales and how they weight factors, depending upon from which score issuing company the business orders the score from. In most cases, if a consumer damages their credit then they will damage any type of credit scores that can be pulled on them by different types of companies. The score issuing companies are all competing with each other to become the most popular in the business industry.

Credit Reports are Free but Not Credit Scores

Thanks to the Fair and Accurate Credit Transactions Act of 2003, which is abbreviated as the FACTA or FACT Act, credit reports are free for consumers to access once every year or in circumstances in which they have been victimized by fraud or identity theft on www.annualcreditreport.com with Equifax, Experian, and TransUnion. Currently, credit scores are still not free. This is because credit scores are not part of a credit report. Credit scores are simply extra information that may suggest creditworthiness. Each of the three agencies ranks the consumer using a score and individual report. Therefore, a consumer will have three different credit scores and three different credit reports. This is because not all companies report the account histories to all the credit agencies. Some companies may report to only one or two of the credit bureaus and some companies may not report data at all, which does not benefit the consumer. A consumer should want their positive payment history to reflect on their report. It is similar to the situation if a student was to take a class and it would not appear on the transcript.

Weaknesses of Credit Scores

Credit scores do not always indicate the most accurate picture of the financial conditions of a consumer. A high credit score does not always guarantee a consumer will be approved for credit or will receive the lowest interest rates. Similarly, a low credit score does not always guarantee a consumer will be denied for credit or will receive the highest interest rates. For this reason, the credit scoring models are considered by some consumers and businesses to have flaws and be weak. Financial institutions focus on content, which is the payment histories on accounts, when they reviewing the credit reports of consumers.

Credit scores can become high or low for minor reasons, which is why credit scores do not always indicate if a consumer has good or bad credit. For this reason, consumers should not waste money always buying credit scores. It is possible for a consumer to have no delinquencies but a low credit score due to a credit check, short history established on credit accounts, excessive debt, not enough loans, and the opening or closing of a credit account. These reasons are minor because they do not send the message that the consumer has cheated the creditor. In relation to personal experience, my credit scores are low because I have never had a secured installment credit loan, which is a common type of credit consumers would get if they wanted to purchase a car, house, or boat. If a financial institution looked at my scores alone then they would think that Danny does not pay his bills or is often late on making payments. This is not true because I simply have had no need to buy a car, house, or boat right now. When the financial institutions look at my credit reports then they will realize I do not cheat my bill issuers. My scores are low because I do not have enough credit types reflecting on my credit reports. This is out of my control and for this reason, credit score calculations are sometimes considered weak. When I do get an installment credit loan to buy a car, house, or boat and establish a positive payment history then my scores will increase.

As another example, it is possible for Brandon to graduate college and have a low credit score because Brandon has $60,000 student loan debt. If a business did not look at the credit reports and just the scores then they would think Brandon has been defaulting on their loans, which is not the case. It is also possible for a consumer to have delinquencies but a high credit score. The financial institution will be upset about the delinquencies and will not give value to the high credit score. This is similar to the situation in which a student receives poor grades in their freshmen year of high school. The student has a low grade point average. However, the students manages to get perfect grades their sophomore year of high school and this causes the grade point average to become high. When the high school student applies to college, the college applications review department will not be pleased with the poor performance during freshmen year. They will not value how much the grade point average increased. Similar to creditors, they will focus on the content of the transcript, which is the grade received in each course. For this reason, consumers need to focus on paying off balances quickly so they can avoid the risk of being late and not ruin their credit.

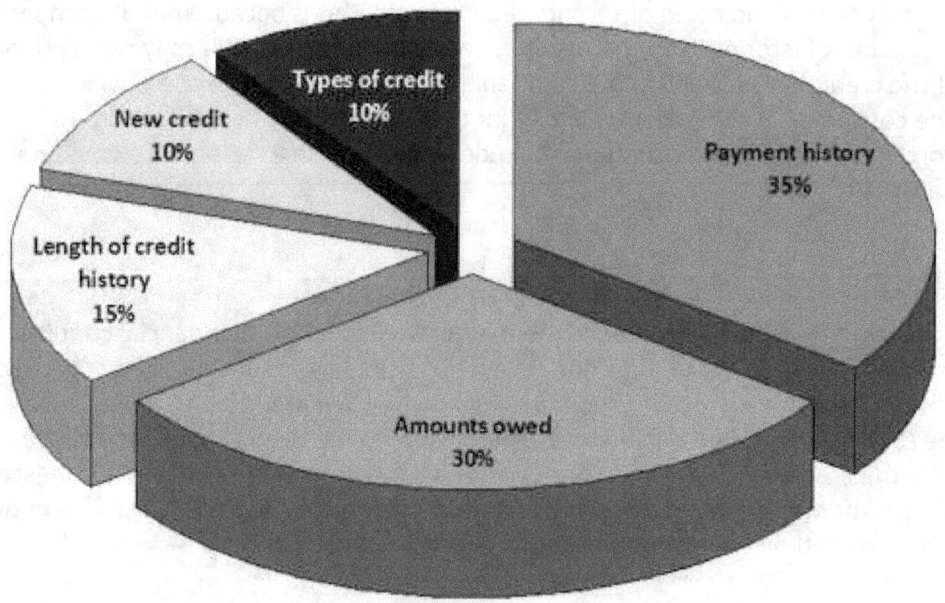

The **FICO** scoring model focuses on credit criteria areas that are similar to the credit criteria areas that are focused on by the Vantage Score model.

Payment history (35%): This is the meat of any credit score and credit report, because it is the key element that is focused on by financial institutions and employers when they are trying to financially judge the consumer. It tells them whether or not the consumer is trustworthy.

If consumers have delinquencies then it means the consumer is not trustworthy, in being able to do anything such as their job duties and repaying their loans. No delinquencies (past due accounts) or collection accounts mean the consumer is trustworthy.

Amounts owed (30%): Consumers should not use all their credit cards or use any credit card very heavily because doing so causes their credit scores to drop. This is because the consumer is building excessive debt and in this sense, they are utilizing too much loan money. Balances on credit cards should never exceed more than 30% of their credit limits. When consumers are excessively using credit cards and other loans then it sends the message that the consumer is very likely to build up so much debt that they will need to declare a bankruptcy or debt settlement because they will not be able to repay it. This will result in the loss for the financial institutions. For this reason, they will be reluctant to grant credit to consumers that have large volumes of debt or they will grant credit but the loan will have a higher than average interest rate and/or fees because they want to make as much profit as possible for the time that the consumer is able to successfully make payments.

Length of credit history (15%): Consumers should build many years of payment histories on all their credit cards and any loan that has a credit limit such as a home equity line of credit because doing so causes their credit scores to increase. However, consumers should use all their revolving loans with a credit limit only once every six months to make a small purchase and not use all the loans everyday. Using all the loans periodically prevents them from being shut down by the financial institutions and this will hurt the credit scores. Only one credit card should be used for everyday purchases.

New credit accounts (10%): This portion of the credit score is influenced by the recent hard inquiry credit checks done on the consumer by financial institutions and newly opened credit accounts. When a credit check occurs and/or a new credit account is opened then by default, the credit scores of the consumer drop by a certain number of points. The reason for this is because newly opened accounts and credit checks imply to companies that the consumer may be trying to get into debt. If the consumer only opens one to two new credit accounts within one to two years and/or has one to two hard credit check inquiries per credit report within two years then they do not think the consumer is likely to get into a large amount of debt, which they will not be able to repay. If the consumer has opened four to five or more new credit accounts within one to two years and/or has about four to seven or more hard inquiry credit checks then the financial institutions will think the consumer is financially weak due to the fact they want so much loan money. In most cases, when consumers are aggressively applying for credit then they have the bad intention of using all the loan money and not repaying any of the companies. The financial institution may also think that a criminal has compromised the information of the consumer and is using it to try and obtain loan money. Regardless of what they think is happening, financial institutions will shut down the credit accounts of consumers because their business risk management software will detect many new credit checks and/or credit accounts are being established under the social security number of the consumer. New financial institutions will notice the dates as to when the new accounts were opened and will see all the credit checks and for such reasons, will deny the consumer for new credit.

Types of credit used (10%): Financial institutions want to see consumers that have a variety of revolving and installment, secured and unsecured, loans on their credit reports for the purpose of better accessing their financial abilities.

Inauthentic Credit Scores (FAKO Scores)

Credit scores are not free, because they are not part of a credit report. They are only rankings given to consumers, by scoring models, and are used by businesses; to measure how consumers with certain scores handle their accounts. Credit scores do not always depict the accurate financial status of consumers and, for this reason, financial institutions focus more on the content showing on the credit reports. There are many credit scoring programs with several names such as; "Experian ScoreX Plus," "Equifax Plus score," "TransUnion Empirica score," "Equifax Beacon," "NextGen FICO score," "CE score," and the "TransUnion TransRisk score." All these programs are trying to replicate the FICO scoring model of the Fair Isaac Corporation. Replications are not considered authentic FICO scores and for this reason, they are considered "FAKO scores." If a consumer were to order all these scores then the consumer would notice that they are all different from each other.

It costs money for businesses and credit agencies to develop their software, which is used to calculate the credit scores of their customers, and they pass on some of these costs to consumers. It is likely that businesses and credit bureaus will develop more credit risk scoring programs in the future and discontinue their previous ones. Their goal is to create the ideal scoring program that will help them achieve the best lending standards possible so they can avoid lending to high risk consumers that will result in them having losses.

Advice: Consumers should only check their credit scores on www.myfico.com. In doing so, consumers are getting the most authentic information regarding their scores. www.myFico.com is run by the Fair Isaac Corporation and there are no score replications. The FICO scoring model is what most businesses use to calculate their scores. Consumers are wasting money by ordering credit scores from other websites because they are not authentic FICO scores. Such scores will likely be inaccurate. If consumers want to view their credit reports or scores multiples times during the year then it might be a good idea to sign up for credit monitoring with MyFico.com rather than pay for a credit report every time they want to view it. Some credit card issuers may offer free credit reports and scores to their consumers as a benefit for being a customer. Consumers that are denied credit have the right to request a free credit score from the financial institution that denied them and a free credit report from the credit agency that the financial institution used to pull a credit report.

Unfortunately, Experian terminated their relationship with the Fair Isaac Corporation and consumers can only order their authentic Experian credit report and score on www.experian.com. An Innovis credit report can only be ordered on www.innovis.com. Innovis currently has no business relationship with any of the credit agencies or the Fair Isaac Corporation.

Check Credit with all Agencies

Equifax, Experian, TransUnion, and Innovis all have different information regarding consumers that reflect on their credit reports. They may have similar information, but there is no guarantee that they have the same information. It may be possible that each report shows a different date of birth, social security number, address, or any other type of information which potentially could be incorrect. It is also possible that a financial institution may report the payment history regarding the credit account of a consumer to one or two of the credit agencies but not all of them. For example, Paul has a Commerce Bank credit card with nine years of positive history that is showing on his Equifax and Experian credit reports but the account is not showing on his TransUnion credit report. For this reason, the credit scores of Paul are high with Equifax and Experian but they are low with TransUnion due to the lack of history established on credit accounts. Paul needs to contact Commerce Bank and TransUnion and let them both know about the credit card account not showing on the TransUnion credit report.

If Paul ignores this issue and applies for credit. The financial institution may not check the credit reports with Equifax and Experian but only with TransUnion and it is likely they may deny Paul or approve him with a high interest rate and/or annual fee. There is no way to tell which credit agency the financial institution uses and the customer service agents are usually not trained to know such information. Thus, Paul will not get told such information by the customer service agent. The credit reports may all have different credit accounts showing because not all financial institutions report to all the agencies for the likely reason that it may cost them too much money to do so or they have data reporting glitches that they do not notice.

If consumers put incorrect information about themselves on applications or the financial institution misreads the application then incorrect information about the consumer may be reported to the credit agencies. When financial institutions are trying to verify the identity of the consumer, then they match the information on the application with the information on the credit profile. When they are doing such matching, they are also reporting the personal information on the application to the credit agencies and the credit agencies are collecting and storing this information within their databases, which may appear on the credit reports of the consumer. For example, if Danny spelled his name as "Danni" on the credit application or the associate at the lending department misread the spelling of his name as "Danni," then it is very likely that the credit report of Danny will show an incorrect spelling of his name as "Danni." When Danny applies for credit again and he puts his name as "Danny" on the credit application, then he may get denied by the financial institution but they will think he is using the social security number of "Danni" to fraudulently obtain credit. In their eyes, they think "Danny" and "Danni" are two different people.

The Credit CARD Act of 2009

To help improve the overall financial conditions of consumers and ensure more financial industries were doing ethical lending. On May 22, 2009, the 44th president of the United States, Barack Obama signed the Credit CARD Act into law.

Overall, the CARD Act was a reform act that would restrict financial institutions from charging too much interest and fees to consumers of all credit types; in this sense, financial institutions would be more consumer-friendly. These new credit card laws were expected to help lower the number of consumers that default on their credit cards. As a result, a lower number of financial institutions would have loan losses. Most of the changes presented by the CARD Act took effect on February 22, 2010.

However before this date, some angry consumers had expressed that their credit card issuers increased their interest rates, fees, and imposed new annual fees; despite being faithful in paying their bills. The Federal Reserve had predicted the credit card issuers would do such, because they wanted to make the highest amount of profit possible before the effects of the CARD Act took place. Some consumers and financial experts thought financial institutions did this because they were trying to make up for the losses they had off of consumers that did not pay their credit cards and other loans. Some financial institutions that increased the fees and interest rates, on all consumers, were not being fair to consumers, who always paid their credit cards. Other financial institutions were increasing rates and fees only on consumers; with bad or limited credit histories. For this reason, they were being fairer to consumers that always paid their credit cards and bills.

The CARD Act did have some cons; due to the fact credit card issuers could not make as much profit off of consumers as they used to; they had to lay off some of their employees and close some of their offices. It has become so difficult for consumers with bad or limited credit to get approved for new credit cards because in the eyes of financial institutions, such consumers are likely to default and due to making little profit. Financial institutions cannot afford losses. This is hurting business owners, because it is common for businesses to need access to credit; in order to purchase needed merchandises and services. Without access to credit, it is less likely entrepreneurs will proceed with their plans to start businesses and by not doing so, new jobs cannot be created. The level of overall spending, which is called aggregate demand, goes down and this potentially can hurt an economy.

Financial institutions are reviewing the credit accounts of some consumers. The consumers with bad or limited credit histories, with whom they currently do business and are taking adverse actions against them such as lowering the credit limits or closing down the accounts. Financial institutions are doing everything possible to lower business risks.

Credit Card Act Changes

Some financial institutions possibly shut down, because they did not follow these changes with their credit card lending practices. They are required by law to follow the CARD Act changes. Other loans, other than credit cards, may be exempt from following the CARD Act changes such as student loans, auto loans, and mortgages (home loans) and so consumers need to be more careful ensuring; financial institutions that grant them these products do not charge high interest or fees. Consumers have raised concerns though, as to why the changes imposed by the CARD Act, were not imposed earlier in America; such as when credit cards were first created. The changes may have helped avoid some of the severe effects of the recession and the credit crisis.

a) Credit card companies are not allowed to grant credit to consumers, under the age of 21 that do not have a strong source of income, such as a job. If they do not have a job; then the consumer will need a cosigner with a good credit history and strong source of income. The financial institution must verify the income in any case. For this reason, the consumer may be required to show an authentic pay stub or W-2. A W-2 is a tax document that shows how much income the consumer reported to the Internal Revenue Services and how much income tax they paid during the year that the W-2 shows. Consumers can get a copy of their W-2 or pay stub from their employer. A possible supporting reason why the government imposed the change of credit card companies not being able to grant credit to consumers under the age of 21 without verifying their incomes is because statistically, teenagers, college, and high school students were the groups that most often defaulted on their credit cards. It is likely these groups did not understand the dangers of paying late or not paying at all and were building large amounts of debt.

b) A credit card statement is simply the credit card bill. It shows the balance that the consumer owes to the financial institution; the interest rate that the consumer is paying; the charges and payments that took place on the account during the course of the month; and the required amount that the consumer must pay on or before the due date. Credit card companies are now required to include a "Late Payment Warning," "Minimum Payment Warning," and a number for a credit counseling agency when they print credit card statements, which will usually show underneath the "Payment Information" section of the statement.

Consumers need to understand; paying the minimum payment only does them no good because the interest charged by the financial institution eventually causes the balance to double. Consumers should pay the highest amount possible that they can towards the credit card without letting other bills become late. If consumers cannot pay the entire balance then they should at least to try and pay more than the suggested amount showing underneath the "minimum payment warning." For example, on the statement image, the suggested amount to pay above the minimum payment requirements is only $54.00. Consumers should pay more than just $54.00, so they can save money on interest; because they are reducing their "average daily balance" faster and their credit scores will increase due to having less debt. It is likely the credit card companies will put a suggested amount to pay that will still cause them to make a great deal of profit off of a consumer. Not all financial institutions are putting a suggested above the minimum payment requirements amount consumers should pay due to the likely reason of greed.

Consumers should immediately contact the credit card issuer and the credit counseling agency if they cannot afford to make the minimum payment by the due date so they can protect their credit and work out some type of extended payment plan without penalties even if they are currently unemployed. The consumer can possibly have the minimum payment deferred. Not contacting a credit counseling agency or the credit card issuer and just letting the account become delinquent will <u>always</u> damage credit. Consumers should only work with non-profit credit counseling agencies and before getting into business with them, consumers should do an interest search using the company name of the credit counseling agency to see if there are any major complaints against them.

   c) Credit card companies can only increase an interest rate, to the penalty default interest rate; when a consumer is more than sixty days late in making the minimum payment. However, when the consumer is late by thirty days alone, then the credit card issuer will report the credit account as one month delinquent to the consumer reporting agencies, ruin the credit profile of the consumer, and charge a late fee. When the consumer is late, by another thirty days, then the credit card issuer will report the credit account as two months delinquent and charge another late fee. The late fees become part of the balance and they start accumulating interest. In many cases, default interest rates and late fees will cause credit card balances to triple and the extra debt will mean lower credit scores. The CARD Act does not put restrictions on how high credit card issuers can make their default interest rates. For such reasons, consumers should not take the risk and miss any payment.

   d) Credit card issuers can only increase an interest rate when a promotional period ends. For example; Devi signs up for a Sear's credit card that indicates she will receive a 0% interest rate for twelve months, for purchasing a $2,000 television. After twelve months, Citibank, who is the issuer of the Sears credit card, will increase her interest rate from 0% to 13.43%. 13.43% is the standard purchase interest rate on all purchases excluding cash advances and it is the rate Devi must pay, on any remaining balance on the Sears credit card from the purchase of the $2,000 television. When credit card issuers offer promotional interest rates, such as the one Devi received, then they sometimes also indicate payments are not required within the twelve months period without any negative credit impact; unless the consumer chooses to make payments anyway. Consumers should always make payments despite the offer because the goal of the credit card issuer is to make as much profit as possible off of the consumer. They will charge the full standard purchase interest rate to the consumer on the credit card balance when the promotional interest rate period ends. In the case of Devi, if she did not make payments for the twelve months then Citibank would be able to make a great deal of profit off of her because they could charge the full 13.43% interest rate on the $2,000 television.

   e) Credit card companies can increase interest rates on credit cards that have variable interest rates. Besides promotional and variable rate credit cards, any other situation in which a credit card company would increase an interest rate or fees such as an annual fee, instead of two weeks, they must give the consumers a 45 days notice; with a new "terms and conditions" or "card member agreement", of the credit account, as required by the **Truth in Lending Act** of 1968. Consumers have the right to "opt-out" and reject the changes. If consumers do this, then it is likely the credit card account will be shut down; by the financial institution, but in a way that it would not hurt the credit profile of the consumer. The account will indicate a status that says "closed by consumer." The consumer will get to continue paying the original interest rate on any remaining balance that they agreed to when they signed up for the credit card. A forty-five day notice is hoped to give the consumer more time to find a new credit card provider or making arrangements for paying the balance. If a consumer wants to keep their current credit account open, then it is likely they will have to accept the new terms and conditions of the credit account.

f) Instead of 14 days, credit card issuers must send consumers their credit card bills twenty-one days before the due date, using mail or email. Consumers still have the obligation to pay the credit cards even if they do not receive the bill. They cannot use credit card and simply forget to pay it or their credit will suffer. If consumers do not receive the bill then they should <u>always</u> contact the credit card issuer <u>immediately</u>.

g) Credit cards companies can no longer increase interest rates, on consumers due to universal default. Universal default is when a financial institution increases the interest rate on a credit card; to the penalty interest rate during a periodic account review. An account review is when the financial institution does a soft credit check, on the consumer through one or more of the credit agencies and ensures the consumer is maintaining the same or better credit profile; that they had when the financial institution approved them for the credit account. The credit report that was used to approve the credit account is saved within their database. If during the account review, the financial institution pulls credit and sees that a consumer has defaulted on any loan such as a credit card, mortgage, student loan, or car loan and for this reason, the credit profile has become damaged then the financial institution may do universal default with the consumer and increase the interest rate on the credit card that the consumer has with them even though it has never been late. This is because the consumer is at high risk of defaulting. Defaulting on one or more loans sends the message that the consumer is capable defaulting on any loan including a credit card. The CARD Act has eliminated universal default and if a consumer defaulted on one loan with a company and another company noticed this default; then they cannot increase the interest rate on the credit card that the consumer has with them.

For example, Beth has three credit cards.
Capital One Bank MasterCard
Interest rate: 0%
Balance: $0

HSBC Bank Visa
Interest rate: 10.24%
Balance: $895.35

Nationwide Bank Visa
Interest rate: 14.24%
Balance: $1502.49

Beth defaults on her Nationwide Bank credit card, by being 30 days late in making the payment. Her credit scores drop, the delinquency reflects on her credit reports, and when Beth reaches the 60 days delinquency mark then Nationwide Bank increases her interest rate to the penalty rate, which is 31.99%. The systems of Capital One Bank and HSBC Bank alert them; that the credit profile of Beth has been damaged. This initiates a credit analyst at both banks to do an account review on the credit cards; that Beth has with them. They both do universal default with her upon reviewing her credit reports and finding out she defaulted with Nationwide.

Now, this is the financial scenario of Beth due to universal default.
Capital One Bank MasterCard
Interest rate: 29.99%
Balance: $0

HSBC Bank Visa
Interest rate: 30.99%
Balance: $895.35

Nationwide Bank Visa
Interest rate: 31.99%
Balance: $1502.49

This financial scenario with Beth cannot happen now because universal default no longer exists. Only Nationwide Bank will be able to increase her interest rate, because she was late with them.

The CARD Act eliminating universal default may have a negative consequence. This is because it is possible some consumers will be more likely to become irresponsible in handling their loans, due to the fact, there are less consequences. Some consumers may get a new credit card and not worry about their old credit cards and loans letting them become delinquent. The banks will have losses and this can mean increased loan costs on all consumers and decreased interest paid on their deposit accounts such as checking, savings, certificate of deposit, IRA, and money market.

h) The CARD Act has eliminated double-cycle billing, sometimes called double-interest billing, which means the credit card companies cannot charge consumers interest based on the balance that the consumer carried on their credit card for 2 months. For example, if Jyoti has a balance of $2,000 on her Nordstrom Bank credit card, for the month of December, and makes a payment of $1,800 then in January, she will have a balance of $200 on the credit card. Under double-cycle billing, Nordstrom Bank will charge Jyoti the interest based on the $2,000 balance that she carried for two billing cycles, which are usually two months. Due to the fact that Jyoti did not pay off the entire $2,000 balance, in December, in their eyes, she carried a balance on the credit card for two months and so she should be charged two months worth of interest. Thanks to the CARD Act, no financial institution can charge interest to a consumer, in such a manner, using double-cycle billing. Nordstrom Bank would charge Jyoti interest; based on a one month balance of $200. As a result, Jyoti is able to save money.

i) The total balance of a bank credit card such as a Visa, MasterCard, American Express, and Discover branded credit card is broken into four portions. Each portion is considered to be a type of balance. Each balance type is usually charged a different interest rate, but there are situations when multiple balance types are charged the same interest rate. The CARD Act now requires, for credit card issuers, to apply the amount of money paid above the minimum payment; towards the balance type that is being charged the highest interest rate.

The Four Types of Balances

Purchases: Accumulated from the everyday spending of the consumer using the credit card.

Cash advances: When consumers pull physical cash out of their credit cards, by using an automated teller machine, or going to the financial institution; that issued the credit card.

Overdraft protection: This prevents the deposit account, usually the checking account, from going into the state of overdraft; which means it is negative, because it has been overdrawn. If consumers used their debit card or wrote a check and in either case; the checking account did not have enough money to pay for the purchases. The checking account can use the credit limit of their credit card to pay for the purchases but consumers have to set up their checking account to do so with the financial institution before the situation actually occurs. When the credit limit of a credit card is used cover the purchases then a fee is accessed to the consumer by the financial institution for the service. Although consumers should not spend to the point that they need overdraft protection, paying a fee for the overdraft protection is better than paying multiple overdraft fees. Each charge, which requires an amount higher than the current balance, in the checking account, and prevents the financial institution from reporting negative information about the consumer to Chex Systems indicating several charges were bounced. However, consumers must immediately pay off the amount; that was pulled from the credit card for the overdraft protection; otherwise the interest will cause it to compound. The balance on the credit card will potentially become higher; than the total amount that the consumer would have paid in overdraft fees if they had no overdraft protection.

Balance transfers: When consumers transfer the balances, from their high interest loan debts, such as credit cards, student loans, car loan, collection accounts, and just any kind of debt to their credit card; in the hopes of being able to pay a lower interest rate. Balance transfers help consolidate, which means combine, the debts so consumers only have to make a single monthly payment.

Store branded credit cards such as Kohl's and Macys do not have these balance types because store branded credit cards can only be used for in-store purchases.

Bank credit card statement example

Balance Type	Annual Percentage Rate (APR)	Balance
PURCHASES	15.24% (v)	$2,193.39
CASH ADVANCES	19.24% (v)	$0
BALANCE TRANSFERS	15.24 %	$477.12
OVERDRAFT PROTECTION	19.24% (v)	$0

If the minimum payment requirement were $45.00 and the consumer paid $55.00 then without the CARD Act, the full $55.00 would be applied to the balance transfers balance type, because it is being the charged the lowest interest rate. The financial institutions wanted to make the maximum amount of profit, off of the consumer, and so they would ensure the balance type being charged the highest interest rate. In this scenario, the purchases would take the longest time for the consumer to pay off; since all their payments were being applied to the lowest interest rate balance type first. With the CARD Act, if $55.00 was paid by the consumer then $10.00 would be applied to the purchases balance type and the $45.00 would be applied to the balance transfers balance type. For this reason, consumers always need to pay above the minimum payment but if possible; they should pay the balance in full.

As a personal analysis, the government should instruct the financial institutions to apply all payments and not just the amounts paid above the minimum payment requirements towards the highest interest rate balance type, in all situations. This is because the consumer will be more likely to pay off the entire loan balance and they will be less likely to declare a bankruptcy, debt settlement, or stop paying all together. As a result, the financial institution will not have a loss.

Note: the **"v" stands for *variable interest rate*, which means the interest rate can increase or decrease at any time. For this reason, consumers should not carry balances. If the interest rate is fixed, meaning it will not change unless the consumer defaults or the promotional interest rate period ends, then a "v" will not appear next to the interest rate. Variable interest rates on any consumer loans such as adjustable rate mortgages, home equity lines of credit, private student loans, and credit cards are determined by the financial institution using a ***prime rate***.

A *prime rate* is the rate at which the Federal Open Market Committee of the Federal Reserve Boards determines; the financial institutions should be charging consumers on their loans. It is a rate that is expected to be affordable by most consumers and for this reason; they will likely be successful in paying their loans. As a result, the economy will likely prosper; because the profits that the financial institutions make off of the interest will enable them to grant more loans to consumers. The consumers will be able to expand upon their businesses more easily and create jobs, and the financial institutions can pay more interest, on the deposit funds of consumers such as in their retirement, money market, checking, and savings accounts. Consumers will likely deposit more of their funds, within deposit accounts, so they can make more interest. This will cause the assets of the financial institutions to increase and they can continue lending, in the highest amounts and make profits. The goal of the prime rate is to ensure that the economy does not decline and consumers are not being charged an interest rate; which will cause the majority of them to default because this hurts the productivity function level, of the financial institutions. Financial institutions will become more likely to become bankrupt, without a decent prime rate and this will hurt the economy because it is almost impossible to expand upon a business without loans. The Federal Open Market Committee, which can be abbreviated as FOMC, publishes the prime rate in the Wall Street Journal and they usually meet every six weeks to discuss the rate and current economic conditions. FOMC can decide, at any time, to increase or decrease the prime rate. The financial institutions are always reviewing the Wall Street Journal for changes with the prime rate. If the prime rate increases; then the loans of consumers will become more expensive whereas if the prime rate decreases then the loans of consumers will become cheaper. Financial institutions add their own interest rate for each balance type with the prime rate to determine the total annual, which means yearly, interest rate that the consumer will be paying on their loan. The interest rates for the balance types will be revealed on the terms and conditions document, which the consumer is supposed to read before applying for the loan.

Finance 101: The Whiz Kid's Perfect Credit Guide

Bank credit card statement example

Balance Type	Annual Percentage Rate (ARP)	Balance
PURCHASES	15.24% (v)	$2,193.39
CASH ADVANCES	19.24% (v)	$0
BALANCE TRANSFERS	15.24 %	$477.12
OVERDRAFT PROTECTION	19.24% (v)	$0

Credit card terms and conditions example

Prime Rate: Variable annual percentage rates (APRs) are based on the 3.25% Prime Rate as of February 22nd, 2010.

11.99% margin interest is added, to the prime rate, to determine the Purchase/Balance Transfer APR. In connection to the bank credit card statement example, 11.99% + 3.25% = 15.24%, which is the purchase and balance transfers interest rate.

15.99% margin interest is added to the prime rate to determine the Cash/Overdraft Advance APR. 15.99% + 3.25% = 19.24%, which is the cash advance and overdraft protection interest rate.

26.99% margin interest is added to the prime rate to determine the Penalty APR. This means 26.99% + 3.25% = 30.24%. Maximum penalty APR cap is 29.99%, which is the highest interest rate that the consumer could end up paying on *all their balance types,* if they are late on making their credit card payment by more than 60 days. It makes no sense to stop paying the bills, because it only causes the bills to increase in amounts due to penalty interest rates and late fees.

Bank credit card statement example of a consumer who has been late by more than 60 days

Balance Type	Annual Percentage Rate (APR)	Balance
PURCHASES	29.99% (v)	$2,193.39
CASH ADVANCES	29.99% (v)	$0
BALANCE TRANSFERS	29.99 % (v)	$477.12
OVERDRAFT PROTECTION	29.99% (v)	$0

j) The CARD Act prohibits financial institutions, from changing their credit card due dates every month; because this has caused some consumers to default on making their payments. The credit card payment will be due the same day, every month. For example, if the Discover credit card payment of Shannon is due on the 21st of November then this means her next monthly payments will be due on the 21st of December, January, February, and so on; unless she requests for the financial institution to change her due date. Changing the due date will not affect the current credit card bill; but only future bills. Consumers need to be careful when changing due dates; it is possible some financial institutions may review the credit account and think that a consumer who has changed their due date several times is likely to default and they will take adverse actions against the consumer such as closing the credit account or reducing the credit limit and these actions will lower the credit scores of the consumer. Financial institutions may also add more days to their billing cycle, without notifying the consumer. A billing cycle is the number of days that a consumer has to pay off their credit card balance and the number of days in which a balance is carried, on the credit card. Consumers do not want more days getting added to the billing cycle unless they are having financial difficulties in making the minimum payment, because an increased number of days in a billing cycle mean that the consumer will get charged more interest because they have had more time to pay their credit card balance. They get charged interest based on the average daily balance formula, which is Average Daily Balance x Annual Percentage Rate (APR) x Number of Days in Billing Cycle ÷ 365 days in a year. This is the formula all financial institutions use to determine how much interest the consumer will be charged on their credit card. This formula is programmed into their computer systems that generate the credit card statements.

For example, Paola has a balance of $2,000 on her American Express Blue credit card and she wants to know how much interest she will have to pay on it if she does not pay off the balance in full.

Average daily balance: $2,000
Annual percentage rate: 11.24%
Number of days in billing cycle: 31
**Note: 28-31 days is the average number of days within a billing cycle depending upon the number of days within the month and such is the number of days consumers should want to see on their credit card statement in order to avoid having to pay excessive interest. The credit card statement generates after the last day of the billing cycle.
$2,000 x .1124 x 31 days = 6,968.80
6,968.80 ÷ 365 days = $19.09, which is the amount of interest that Paola will pay on the $2,000 balance. The $2,000 balance will now become a $2,019.09 balance.

The employer of Paola indicates she will receive her paycheck late due to computer difficulties in doing the direct deposit into her checking account. For this reason, Paola calls American Express and asks for a different due date. American Express grants her request. Paola receives her American Express credit card bill with the new due date. However, she notices that the interest she has been charged is higher than normal considering her balance. She also notices her American Express bill indicates 39 days in the billing cycle.

Average Daily Balance x Annual Percentage Rate (APR) x Number of Days in Billing Cycle ÷ 365 days in a year
Average daily balance: $2,000
Annual percentage rate: 11.24%
Number of days in billing cycle: 39
$2,000 x .1124 x 39 days = 8,767.20
8,767.20 ÷ 365 days = $24.02.

The American Express bill that had 31 days in the billing cycle charged Paola $19.09 in interest, but due to the additional eight days in the billing cycle, she now has to pay $4.93 more on the $2,000 balance. Although the extra $4.93 may not seem to be a large amount, it will compound itself with interest. If the number of days in the billing cycle were more than 39 days; then she would have been charged more interest. The goal of all consumers needs to be to save every penny so they can put those funds into investments and savings and ultimately, pay off their credit card and other debts as soon as possible. Paola would need to call American Express and notify them that they did not inform her about adding more days to her billing cycle. She would need to request for them to refund all or a portion of the interest because it is not fair to her to have to pay extra interest.

k) If a consumer is delinquent on their credit card account; meaning they have not made a payment in a long time and as a result, their interest rate is increased by the financial institution to the 30% penalty interest rate. After six months of successfully making the minimum payment amount requirements or more in a timely manner, the credit card provider must reduce the interest rate on the credit card of the consumer back to the normal purchase interest rate.

l) If the credit card company increases the interest rate or imposes an annual fee on the credit card, due to economic conditions, then the consumer can opt-out of this by having the credit card account closed. Although the closure of the credit card will have a negative impact on the credit profile of the consumer, they will be allowed to pay off their credit card balance at their existing interest rate and save money. In this situation, closing the credit card is needed best; otherwise the consumer will struggle to pay off the credit card if they accept the interest rate increase change. However, if consumers are carrying no balance on their credit card then it should not matter whether or not the credit card company is increasing the interest rate. Consumers should negotiate with the financial institution to prevent them from imposing an annual fee and should periodically use and pay off the credit card so they are making profit. Making profit is needed for any business and a healthy economy.

m) Consumers must make their payments on or before 5 PM, on the due date, in order to prevent their credit card from becoming delinquent. Consumers can ask their credit card company for the time zone. For example, Capital One credit card customers must submit their payment online, before 5 PM Eastern Time or Capital One should have already received the payment before this time, even if it has not yet posted on the account. Consumers can call the credit card provider to check if the payment has been received. If the credit card company indicates they have not received their payment, then consumers should be safe and simply pay an over the phone payment. This is better than paying a late fee, which is usually $30 or more and compounds with interest itself. Consumers should not cancel the previous payment they had sent; especially if it is a low amount because the credit card company may receive that payment, try to cash it, and as a result of the consumer canceling the payment, the credit card company will charge them a returned payment fee. Ideally, consumers should always pay a couple days early so financial institutions know they are financially strong and are more willing to offer interest rate reductions.

n) Credit card companies are not allowed to charge late fees, if the consumer shows them proof that they electronically submitted or mailed in a payment no less than seven days before the due date. Consumers could fax in the proof, to the credit card company or possibly call the branch, and ask if they can come in to show the proof. Proof can include a copy of the check or a bank statement that shows the withdrawal of the payment, from the account.

o) When consumers are pre-approved for a credit card and they do not want it then they can reject the offer, without their credit scores being lowered because a pre-approved offer does not mean a hard inquiry credit check was done or that an account was ever established. Pre-approved credit cards only do soft inquiry credit checks and such checks do not ever affect credit scores. Consumers should not activate the credit card if they do not want it, because if they activate it then a hard inquiry credit check will be done on them by the financial institution, an account will be established on the credit reports, and this will lower the credit scores, especially if they close the account after activating it. The credit check will go to waste and will stay on the credit report for two years. For this reason, it is never recommended to close a credit card if a consumer has been approved for one, unless it has an expensive annual fee. If consumers have been denied for a secured credit card due to their bad credit profiles then they have no choice but to pay the annual fee because they need a credit card to fix their credit profile. The bad credit profiles are suggesting to financial institutions; that the consumer is very likely to one day stop paying on the credit card. For this reason, they must charge the annual fee so they can compensate for the loss when it happens. However, after two to three years, consumers with bad credit profiles should look into applying for a secured or unsecured credit card again, that has no annual fee. If consumers cannot afford to pay the annual fee then they should not get the credit card, otherwise they will cause more damage to their credit profile than good because it is likely they will become delinquent on the credit card.

p) Credit card companies must produce statements and terms and conditions contracts with legible font styles and sizes; so consumers can read them with ease. Some consumers have claimed they could not read the credit card contracts or statements. As a result, they defaulted on their credit cards due to ignorance. They did not know about the fees, interest rates, or due dates.

q) Despite the credit limit, consumers have the option to set spending limits caps on their credit card so they do not get tempted to overspend and as a result, endure over-the-credit limit fees. For example, if Fiorella was approved for a Barclays Bank credit card with a limit of $5,000. She can call them and request for a spending limit cap of $500 to be placed on the credit card. This means the credit card will decline, if she attempts spending more than $500. If Fiorella adds joint or authorized users to her credit card account, then she can set a limit on their cards too. If Fiorella had no spending limit cap, on her credit card and she spent money over $5,000 then she would be a charged an over-the-credit limit fee of $30 or more and the fee would compound with interest itself. Consumers should always ask to be refunded the fee as a one time courtesy even if the financial institution has refunded them a fee before. There is no guarantee if the financial institution keeps a record of the refunds that they issued to the consumer. However, consumers really need financial help if they have a habit of continuously spending over the credit limit, and as a result, damaging their credit profile. Such consumers have the option of requesting that the financial institution can let any transactions go through if they are going over the credit limit. A spending limit cap is different than a credit limit reduction. A **credit limit reduction** is when the consumer requests for the financial institution to reduce their credit limit and this can negatively affect the credit scores because it will cause the debt-to-credit ratio of the consumer to become higher. In lamest terms, it will look like the consumer is using a higher amount of all their available credit (loan money) that is coming from all their loans with spending limits. If consumers are using a high amount of all their loan money then it suggests they are more likely to default. A credit limit reduction will show on the credit reports and will raise the question to financial institutions as to why a consumer or credit card provider would reduce their credit limit. It will make them think that the consumer is financially weak. In the case of Fiorella, she can ask Barclays Bank to reduce her credit limit from $5,000 to $500 and other banks with whom she applies for credit; such as Bank of America, Wells Fargo, PNC Bank may wonder why the credit limit was reduced. Additionally, the banks have no way of knowing if it was Fiorella who requested for the credit limit reduction; or if it was Barclays Bank, because they felt as though she could not successfully repay them. The credit reports will not reflect how the credit limit reduction was initiated. In contrast, a spending limit cap is safe and does not affect the credit scores in anyway.

r) If the credit card balance goes over the credit limit, due to an annual fee, interest charges, and credit protection plan charges (plan that cancels the credit card payments until the consumer is financially stable but causes the balance to continue growing), then the financial institution is not allowed to charge an over-the-credit limit fee.

Example
Natalie has a balance of $1,481.49 on her First National Bank of Omaha (FNBO) credit card and her credit limit is $1,500. She is charged a $30 annual fee by FNBO because she has an airline rewards program. Her card balance is now $1,511.49 and it is considered to be over the credit limit. FNBO will not charge her an over-the-credit limit fee because Natalie had no control over when she would be charged the annual fee. Without the CARD Act, it may have been possible that FNBO may have charged her an over-the-credit limit fee along with the annual fee.

If the consumer is late in making their payment and they are charged a late fee which causes the credit card balance to go over the credit limit; then the financial institution is allowed to charge an over-the-credit limit fee because it is the fault of the consumer. However, financial institutions cannot charge more than three over-the-credit limit fees on the credit card balance.

Example
Victoria has an Iberia Bank Visa credit card. It has a balance of $1,991.23 and the credit limit is $2,000.00. Her credit card bill due date is April 4th but the bank never receives her payment. As a result, they charge her a late fee of $35.00. This causes the credit card balance to become $2,062.23 and the balance is now considered over the credit limit. Iberia Bank will charge Victoria a $30.00 over-the-credit limit fee; because she is at fault for being late. Her balance is now $2,092.23. It will continue growing with interest and fees until she pays down the balance. Iberia Bank can only charge Victoria two more over-the-credit limits but there are no restrictions on how many late fees they can charge her. For this reason, consumers should never carry balances on credit cards.

s) Consumers with bad credit profiles are targeted by subprime financial institutions; meaning they grant credit to consumers with bad credit profiles, that cannot get approved for credit by other financial institutions. The business strategy of subprime financial institutions is to charge consumers with bad credit profiles **many** and high fees, on their credit cards. They think the consumers are very likely to accept their credit card products, which are greatly advertised on the internet, because they are desperate.

For example, there is a subprime financial institution that offers credit cards with fixed interest rates of 39%, 59%, and 79% along with a $75 annual fee and other monthly fees. To an extent, they are draining the money out of consumers. For this reason, it is recommended consumers with bad credit profiles should always aim at getting approved for secured credit cards with credit unions or community banks because they are much cheaper than subprime financial institutions and if they cannot get approved then they should try to dispute the negative information off of their credit reports or wait for some of the information to fall. To control the fees that the subprime financial institutions charge, the CARD Act requires that they charge no more than 25% of the credit limit in fees. If there are fees more expensive than 25% of the credit limit then the financial institution must ask money from the consumer for those fees before approving the credit card application.

Example
Nicky is getting a credit card from a subprime financial institution because she has a bad credit profile. The credit card has a total of $110 in fees. It has a credit limit of $300. 25% of $300 is $75.00 and this can explain why the annul fee of the credit is only $75.00. The financial institution cannot charge Nicky more than 25% of the credit limit in fees. For this reason, they are going to ask Nicky to pay a $35.00 application fee before they approve her for the credit card. The $35.00 will not be charged on the $300 credit limit and so the financial institution will be safe from getting into trouble with the government.

t) Credit card companies must send their data to Congress every year regarding their profits made, interest rates on credit cards, and fees on credit cards. The purpose of doing this is for the government to ensure the credit card companies are not draining consumers, of their money, by charging high fees and interest.

u) Financial institutions are not allowed to promote their credit cards at the campuses of the colleges and/or universities; by offering free gifts and items, for the purpose of trying to get students to sign up for them. It is okay for consumers to sign up for credit cards and take advantage of the promotions, but it is not okay for them to build high balances and default on them.

v) Credit card companies must periodically send their terms and conditions credit card contracts that contain the interest rates and annual fees, if any, that consumers are paying on their credit cards, to the Federal Reserve Board. These credit card contracts should also be made available on their websites for consumers to access them. At any time, consumers should be able to request a copy of their credit card contract from the financial institution.

w) The CARD Act made an impact on the retail industry regarding how they manage their gift cards. Retailers are no longer allowed to set expiration dates less than five years after the consumer purchases the gift card. It is not fair, to the consumer, for the gift card to expire and as a result, they lose their money because they get nothing for it. Additionally, retail stores are not allowed to charge inactivity or service fees unless 12 months have passed since the gift card was purchased.

Credit, Debit, Prepaid, and ATM Cards

Automated Teller Machine Cards (ATM Card)

A credit card, debit card, prepaid, and an ATM card are all issued by financial institutions to consumers, but they are different. ATM cards are known as "automated teller machine" cards. They usually do not have rewards programs, because they are not part of the MasterCard, American Express, Visa, or Discover Card programs. These programs can be thought of, as card brands. For this reason, ATM cards do not have the MasterCard, American Express, Visa, or Discover Card logos. Similar to debit cards and some prepaid cards, ATM cards require a pin number when used in the store and can be used to withdraw money from ATM systems, which are often found at gas stations, bank branches and gas stations. Some of the machines charge fees when making withdrawals. For this reason, some consumers do not make withdrawals using the machines because it makes no sense to pay fees. ATM cards pull money from the savings, checking, or money market accounts; depending upon how the consumer has set up their particular account. Not all stores accept ATM cards when consumers purchase items.

Prepaid Cards

A prepaid card can be used as a debit card, but it does not withdraw money from a checking or savings account. Consumers must load prepaid cards with money before using them. They can do so at some stores and financial institutions. Consumers may advise their employers to deposit their paychecks directly into the prepaid card account; when they set up their "direct deposit." Consumers that usually have damaged ChexSystems profiles or damaged credit, tend to get prepaid cards because financial institutions will not approve them for a traditional savings or checking account. Consumers that have stopped paying on their loans or have declared a bankruptcy or debt settlement will get prepaid cards because they are worried that the financial institutions will levy their bank accounts and seize all the money. Debit and credit cards are accepted almost everywhere by merchants and they do save money due to their rewards programs. Prepaid cards have fees they charge to the consumers and they do not save money.

Credit Cards

Unlike ATM cards; debit, prepaid, and credit cards are part of the MasterCard, American Express, Visa, or Discover Card programs. The financial institutions determine what program their debit, prepaid, and credit card products will be assigned. The financial institutions will usually choose the program that will be the cheapest for them and bring the most profit, because the financial institutions have to pay for the programs. For this reason, they charge merchants whenever consumers use their debit, prepaid, or credit cards. Not all merchants accept the MasterCard, American Express, Visa, or Discover Card programs, because they may lose too much profit from the fees they must pay. There are other card programs out there such as Revolution Card, Diner's Club International, and JCB but these programs are not considered as large. The programs help determine the dispute rights of the consumer such as when they purchase items that are defective. When consumers dispute a charge, then they can get their money back. Dispute rights are also maintained by the **Fair Credit Billing Act**. However, consumers should not abuse their dispute rights by trying to dispute legitimate charges because then the credit card provider may get the impression that the consumer is trying to escape paying their bill. As a result, the credit card provider will close the credit card and this will lower the credit scores, of the consumer. On the credit reports, the credit card account will indicate "closed by credit grantor" and this sends a negative message to financial institutions about the ability of the consumer, to repay their loans.

Credit Cards are Safest Form of Payment and Build Credit

Each card program has their benefits. Unlike ATM, debit, or prepaid cards; credit cards pull money from credit limits, which can also be called "credit lines." A credit limit is the amount of money a consumer can spend, but must pay back. For this reason, a credit card is considered a loan and can positively or negatively affect the credit reports and scores of a consumer, based upon the payment history and how much the credit card is utilized. Credit cards are usually more secure than ATM, debit, and prepaid cards because most credit card issuers have twenty-four customer service centers that are open every day of the week including holidays.

If fraudulent charges were to happen on a credit card, the credit card issuer would immediately credit the charges back to the consumer. The consumer is not liable for those charges, as maintained by the Fair Credit Billing Act. The credit card number is changed immediately and often, credit card issuers can ship a new credit card to the consumer using overnight mail. Credit card issuers may have certain locations where consumers can go and have a new credit card created. Credit card companies have special security monitoring software that monitors credit card accounts and they will immediately block accounts, if charges are taking place; that are not part of the normal spending trend of the consumer, too many purchases are taking place online, or if the locations of the charges are far from the home address. For example, the special software would raise a red flag for the fraud department if a consumer has charges coming in from Mumbai; and the consumer lives in Orlando. The software would indicate a consumer has a high "fraud score." The computer and business software of financial institutions have own fraud score scales and such information is likely unavailable to consumers. In general, when a fraud score is high then that means the transaction is likely to be a fraudulent transaction. In contrast, if the fraud score is low, then that means the transaction is unlikely to be fraudulent. For this reason, consumers must inform credit card companies before doing long distance travel and using their credit card. Fraud scores are also used to evaluate credit applications. If financial institutions notice there are many applications for credit under the social security number of the consumer or if the address and telephone information provided by the consumer on the credit application, does not match public records then it is likely the risk management computer software will indicate the consumer has a high fraud score. The financial institution will think they are granting credit to a criminal and there is a high likelihood of a credit account going into default.

Dangers of Debit, Prepaid, and ATM Cards

In contrast, debit, ATM, and prepaid cards have less security. According to www.Kiplinger.com, if fraud were to happen on a debit card and the consumer did not inform the financial institution within two days or less; then the liability of the consumer can "jump to $500," which means they will be responsible for the first $500 worth of fraudulent charges that happen. Additionally, the Fair Credit Billing Act does not help consumers if fraudulent charges were to happen, with their debit cards or they needed to dispute charges. Financial institutions promise zero liability on credit cards but they do not always promise zero liability on debit cards. The consumer has a loss until the financial institution can conduct an investigation and recover the funds. Institutions may require a police report to be submitted. If criminals get a hold of debit, ATM, and prepaid card account numbers or the personal identification numbers, abbreviated as PIN, then they can clean out the accounts. The MasterCard and Visa programs offer protection "only to non-PIN transactions" likely because debit card payment processing transactions cost them more money. As a result, the consumer will have no funds.

Criminals cannot max out credit cards because financial institutions will likely require authorization from the consumer before allowing the transactions. Due to the fact that financial institutions do not make as much profit on debit, prepaid, and ATM cards as much as they do on credit cards, they usually do not have twenty-four hour customer service centers consumers can call whenever issues arise, on debit cards. Another advantage credit cards have over debit, ATM, and prepaid cards is that if a merchant were to swipe a credit card multiple times, such as when they think their credit card payment processor is not working. It is possible the processor will charge the consumer multiple times and the consumer will not notice this until looking at the bank statement. Multiple charges on debt, ATM, or prepaid cards could result in "overdraft fees" because there may be attempts to pull more money than the balances in the accounts. Credit cards do not have such fees and often, the credit card issuers can immediately credit the extra charges back to the consumer. Finally, due to the fact most credit cards have more money to spend than debit, ATM, or prepaid cards, it is only natural they would have more security.

Prepaid Cards = Fees, Fees, and More Fees

Prepaid cards of any type, (credit or debit), for consumers that cannot get approved for traditional checking and/or savings accounts are expensive, due to the fact they have many fees. Consumers have to get some type of bank account, because almost all bills and financial-related activities are online now. For example, making a purchase online requires a bank account or credit card. For this reason, to save the most money possible, consumers should only get a prepaid card through a credit union or community bank if they offer it. However, consumers should also check the Approved Card, which in my research, is the cheapest and best prepaid credit card in America. It was created by world renowned financial expert, Suze Orman. The US News and World Reports named the Approved Card as one of the best prepaid cards available. Consumers can apply for the Approved Card on http://www.theapprovedcard.com/. Currently, the card has a $3.00 monthly maintenance fee because as a business, the financial institution is taking on risk by granting a bank account to consumers who cannot be approved for traditional checking or savings accounts from banks. In their eyes, such consumers are likely to one day make the bank account negative and this raises the need to make maximum profit off of them so that the financial institution will not have as great a loss when and if the consumer makes the prepaid card account negative. However, the Approved Card has no other fees unless the consumer uses the card to spend more money than what they have available in their account or if the consumer uses an ATM system to withdraw money from their prepaid card that is not part of the Allpoint free ATM system usage network.

Save Money on Withdrawing Money through Allpoint Network

Financial institutions and credit unions have a business relationship with the Allpoint network not to charge fees to their customers for using the Allpoint ATM systems. There are Allpoint ATM systems in all 50 states within America. The ATM systems will usually indicate if they are with the Allpoint network on their computer screens. Consumers can find the nearest Allpoint

ATM system near their location by calling 1 (800) 809-0308 or by going on the Allpoint network website, which is http://www.allpointnetwork.com/. Regardless of what financial institution consumers do their banking with, they should not use ATM machines that are not part of the Allpoint network and waste their money on fees. Besides the Allpoint network, consumers can avoid fees if they use the ATM systems located at the branch offices of their financial institutions. Consumers will be charged fees if they withdraw money from the ATM system at a branch office of a financial institution that is not the financial institution, with which they do their banking. For example, if Sean does his banking with Suntrust Bank and uses his Suntrust Bank debit card to withdraw money at an ATM system; located at a Bank of America branch office, unless the ATM machine at Bank of America is part of the Allpoint network, then he will get charged fees. Sean is better off withdrawing money using an Allpoint network ATM machine located closest to him or going to a Suntrust Bank branch office, to withdraw money. Despite getting a prepaid card or debit card, consumers still must one day get a credit card to rebuild or build their credit history. It is natural that consumers are going to be responsible, with their own money that is within the debit and prepaid card accounts and for this reason; the financial institutions neither do the credit agencies consider how consumers handle their prepaid and debit card accounts to be very important when deciding whether or not to grant credit. They want to see how consumers handle credit cards and loans, because the consumer is handling the money belonging to a financial institution and it is not their own money. The trustworthiness level of consumers is being accessed when financial institutions and employers review how they are handling their loans and credit cards.

Note: Making a debit, ATM, or prepaid card account negative by spending more money than what is available in the account and getting charged numerous fees can be reported as negative information to the credit agencies and ChexSystems, which means high insurance costs and little or no chances of being able to get a good job.

Myth: Debit, ATM (Automated Teller Machine), and prepaid cards help build credit.

Fact: Debit, sometimes called check cards, and ATM cards issued by financial institutions and the prepaid cards such as the ones advertised on television or the internet do not build credit. If consumers are told otherwise then the business only hopes that they open up accounts so they can make profit off of them. Debit, ATM, and prepaid cards do not involve borrowing money from a company and paying it back. For this reason, debit cards and prepaid cards do not report any data or history to the credit bureaus. Consumers are using their own money to spend. However, if consumers were to make their checking accounts or prepaid cards negative by excessively using them and not having enough money in the accounts. This can negatively affect credit. This is because if consumers do not make their accounts positive in a timely manner, then the financial institutions may report them as unpaid and past due debts to the credit agencies. If the debts go unpaid for a long time frame then the financial institutions will assume the consumer has cheated them and may sell the unpaid debts to a collection agency. This will make the debts into collection accounts. Collection accounts ruin credit. Negative checking, savings, and prepaid card accounts are also reported to ChexSystems.

What is ChexSystems?

Although ChexSystems is not a credit agency, it is still considered a consumer reporting agency; but one that only collects information regarding deposit accounts such as checking, savings, certificate of deposit, and money market. The Chex Systems Incorporation makes money, because when consumers or financial institutions order ChexSystems reports then they pay fees. If the financial institutions report negative deposit accounts to the ChexSystems profile of a consumer; then their report will be ruined. These consumers will be denied for new deposit accounts or will be approved for deposit accounts with fees. This is because when consumers try and open new deposit accounts, financial institutions always check the ChexSystems report of the consumer to look for negative deposit accounts. Negative deposit accounts send the message that the consumer is very likely to make any new deposit account negative by excessively using it and this will cause the financial institution to have a loss. Financial institutions may report consumers that are continuously bouncing checks by writing check amounts greater than the amounts in their deposit accounts. Excessively bounced checks will show as negative information on a ChexSystems report. When checks are bounced, the financial institution charges a "non-sufficient funds fee," which can be abbreviated as an "NSF fee," to the consumer for each returned check. NSF fees are sometimes called returned check fees or overdraft fees or vice versa. Financial institutions must charge these fees in order to maintain a strong business reputation and performance. It costs financial institutions money when they process checks, process debit card payments, and order checks or debit cards for consumers. They cannot afford to pull money from deposit accounts that do not have enough funds.

Relationship of ChexSystems Report with Credit Profile
In addition to checking credit reports, creditors may also check a ChexSystems report and upon finding the negative information, they may deny credit to a consumer. This is because negative checking accounts suggest a consumer is financially unstable. This raises the chance that the consumer will default.

Example of a consumer with a negative ChexSystems profile

1. Citibank Checking Account
Status: Overdrawn since 01/05
Balance: $-48.39

2. Regions Bank Savings Account
Status: Overdrawn since 11/09
Balance: $-193.92

3. Trust co Bank Money Market Account
Status: Overdrawn since 04/06
Balance: $-9.21

Example of a consumer that overdraws accounts

Fifth Third Bank Checking Account

Balance: $103.04

1. Check written to Orange County Utilities for $42.49

$103.04 - $42.49 = $60.55

Current balance: $60.55

2. Debit card used at Publix for $62.69

$60.55 - $62.69 = $-2.14

Overdraft fee of $35.00 occurs for overdrawing the checking account. Fifth Third Bank allows for the $62.69 transaction.

$-35.00 + $-2.14 = $-37.14

Current negative balance: $-37.14

The consumer must deposit the $37.14 into the checking account immediately otherwise Fifth Third Bank will close down the checking account and report it as an overdrawn account to ChexSystems. Depending upon their policies, Fifth Third Bank may also report the unpaid debt to the credit agencies.

Use a Credit Card for Maximum Security

Good credit can only be established when consumers are borrowing money and paying it back in a timely manner. For this reason, consumers are better off using a credit card to pay for all purchases and paying off the credit card immediately. Unlike debit cards and prepaid cards, credit cards have no overdraft fees. They offer more protection against damaged or defective merchandise or services and more protection against fraud. For example, if a criminal took a debit card number and cleaned out the checking account of all its money then the consumer has no money until the financial institution can conduct an investigation, notify the police, and recover the funds. In contrast, financial institutions have twenty-four fraud detection departments that will block the card immediately if they notice suspicious activity. Any fraudulent charges found are credited to the consumer immediately and the consumer is not liable for them. The consumer has access to the entire credit limit and the fraudulent charges do not reduce it. Consumers should use a credit card as carefully as they would a debit card. They earn reward points, which help save money but only if huge balances, are not carried on credit cards. Such balances are charged interest by the financial institutions unless they are paid off immediately in a timely manner.

Handling Credit Cards Wisely

Interest Rate Reductions and Removal of Annual Fees

Consumers should always ask for interest rate reductions; even if the balances are being paid off in full or the credit cards are rarely being used. This is because the consumer is preparing themselves for any unexpected emergency purchases such as medical expenses, automobile maintenance, or house maintenance. Such situations can hurt the financial situation of a consumer but they will not be as damaging if a consumer has a low interest rate. They can pay off the balances quickly but should still pay above the minimum payment requirements. This is because the minimum payment is usually only three to four percent of the balance and paying only the minimum allows for the financial institutions to make large profits in charging interest. Low interest rates mean lower minimum payments and this can be beneficial in the event that the consumer is laid off from their job. They can at least make the minimum payments using their savings until they are employed again so their credit is not damaged.

Improvement that should be made with Credit Reports

Currently, the interest rates of credit accounts and loans do not reflect on credit reports because the credit agencies do not collect this information from the financial institutions with which consumers have credit. It may be a business weakness of financial institutions not to be able to see the interest rates consumers are paying when they review credit reports. This is because it is likely consumers that have high balances on credit accounts with high interest rates are at high risk of giving up on paying the debts. They will default, which results in a loss for the financial institution and increased costs on all consumers such as on loans and less interest paid on their deposit accounts. There have been cases in which interest rates on credit accounts were increased to the penalty rates due to too many returned payments. Credit reports do not reflect any information regarding the returned payments on credit accounts but if financial institutions can see the interest rates on credit accounts being 29% or more, which usually means the credit account is being charged a penalty interest rate, and then they may be able to determine that the consumer did not handle the credit account responsibly. The financial institution will be reluctant, as they should be, in extending credit to the consumer. Seeing the interest rates that consumers are paying on credit accounts may help financial institutions better market their credit products with lower interest rates than what the consumers are currently paying. Consumers will be more likely to sign up for the new credit products so they can save money on interest. If financial institution can see the interest rates consumers are paying on their accounts then they can better tell how successfully consumers are paying down their balances every month. It stands to reason that it is going to be more difficult for consumers to pay down the balances of credit accounts that have high interest rates. It is not a case in which a consumer is merely using their accounts aggressively until they are maxed out and that is when the consumer will stop paying. However, credit accounts that have low interest rates should be easier for consumers to pay down. It should send a red flag to the financial institution that a balance on a low interest rate credit card is not dropping as fast as it should in relation to the income level of the consumer because low interest rates accounts such as 13% or below have lower minimum payments than high interest rate accounts such as 14% or above. The consumer may have the bad intention of not paying off the credit account. Finally, if the financial institutions can see the interest rates of accounts on which the consumer made late payments then they should deny the consumer a credit product that will have the same or similar interest rate because it is likely the consumer will default on it.

Bank Credit Cards verses Department Store Credit Cards

In most cases, consumers only have the option of getting their interest rates reduced on bank credit cards. Bank credit cards have brands on them such as MasterCard, Visa, American Express, Discover, or some other credit card brand or program. Consumers cannot get their interest rates reduced on department store cards such as Macys, Kohl's, and Wal-Mart because usually, all consumers that have the same store card, regardless of their individual credit profiles, have the same interest rates. Most department store credit cards have regular purchase interest rates above 20% because unlike bank credit cards, the issuers of the department store credit cards send coupons to the consumers and give them a discount just for opening the account. The coupons will likely cause the consumers to make large purchases at the stores and the goal of the financial institutions is to make up for the savings they gave the consumers through the discount and coupons by charging high interest on the balances of the department store credit cards. Another reason why department store credit card issuers charge high interest is because they want to be able to approve many consumers with good, bad, or no credit. Charging high interest helps the financial institutions offset the potential of risk because they can make a great deal of profit for the time that the consumer is successfully making payments on the department store credit accounts. Finally, the department store credit card issuers charge high interest because department store cards can only be used within the certain store or affiliated stores. Unlike bank cards, they cannot be used by consumers to make purchases at other stores nor do cash advances and this can mean less profit for the financial institution because the consumer is less likely of building up a high balance. For this reason, the financial institution wants to charge as much interest as they can off of the balance that the consumer did build by making the purchases at the certain store. Consumers should save the coupons that department store card issuers send them, make purchases, and immediately pay them off so they can avoid paying interest. In doing so, consumers are saving money and maintaining excellent credit.

Credit Card Debt Elimination Strategy

Credit card debt is dangerous because unlike car loans, home loans, student loans, and other types of loans and bills, the interest rates can jump to 30% along with expensive late fees if the consumer is significantly late on making payments. This will cause the overall level of debt belonging to the consumer to increase because credit cards with high interest rates and fees make it more difficult to pay other bills and save money for retirement and children. Paying off credit card balances is not fun, takes patience, and a consumer must remain motivated to pay it off and stop spending beyond their means. Building debt is never the purpose of a credit card and using bankruptcy or debt settlement as a solution is abuse in the eyes of businesses and employers.

Here is my personal credit card pay off plan that should work for most consumers

1. Make payments above the minimum payment requirements on credit cards with the highest balances without letting the checking account become negative and only pay the minimum payments on the credit cards with the lowest balances. This is because the highest balances tend to accumulate the most interest whereas the lowest balances tend to accumulate the least amount of interest regardless of the interest rates. If possible, consumers should make payments, even small ones, everyday on the highest balance credit cards so they are getting paid down significantly and the financial institutions are more likely to be impressed of the strong payment history and offer cheaper interest rates. Additionally, if for whatever reason,

the consumer is late on making a payment then it is better to have a 30% interest rate on a credit card balance for example, $500 verses a balance of $5,000. However, please do not aggressively use the credit cards with the lowest balances otherwise the debt will not be getting paid down but will continue growing. Any balance above $1,500 is considered high. The goal is to get all credit card balances below $1,000. Reducing the largest balances causes the credit scores to increase faster.

2. Consumers should ask for the annual fee to be waived or permanently removed from the credit card account without having it closed otherwise the credit scores will drop. Annual fees accumulate interest themselves and make it harder to get out of debt.

3. For consumers that rarely get into accidents and/or get tickets, they should increase their car insurance deductible so the monthly payment drops. Consumers should also reduce the number of minutes on their phone plans or get a cheaper plan as well as investigate if they can get a cheaper television provider or plan. It makes no sense to have numerous minutes or numerous channels if the consumer does not use it all. The savings from the cheaper insurance and utilities should be applied towards the credit cards with the highest balances. If possible, use a credit card with no balance to pay the insurance and utilities and pay off the balance immediately because the rewards save money and mailing check payments can be dangerous because there is a possibility it could get lost in the mail.

4. Apply a portion of tax refunds received towards credit card payments. If the consumer has a 10 months emergency fund saved up then they should apply all of their tax refunds and extra money towards credit card payments. If a consumer has been using their credit cards to support their children then they should also use their child support money to make extra payments.

5. Keep calling the credit card providers every 3-4 months and ask for a cheaper purchase interest rate.

6. If for some reason, a consumer has no money to make payments then should immediately contact the credit card provider, defer the payment, work out a payment plan, and if the credit card provider does not cooperate then they should contact a non-profit credit counseling agency.

7. If received, consumers should always consider balance transfer offers because in certain situations, regardless of the one time balance transfer fee, they save money and help pay down balances much faster especially balance transfer offers from credit unions. For example, if Andy has a balance of $3,000 with an interest rate of 13.24% on a Chase credit card and he receives a balance transfer offer from McCoy Federal Credit Union in which he will receive an interest of 0% for 12 months and afterwards, an interest rate of 11% then in this situation, he will save money. Andy should transfer the $3,000 balance with Chase to the credit card with McCoy Federal Credit Union. He should keep the Chase credit card open but not use it until his $3,000 debt is paid off. If the offer from McCoy Federal Credit Union indicates the interest rate will be 15% and/or there will be an annual fee after the 12 months promotion then the offer will not save Andy money unless he has little or no debts with other companies because then it is likely he will be able to significantly or fully pay off the $3,000 balance within the 12 months.

8. If possible, explain the situation to a family member, and borrow money from them because consumers do not have to pay interest to their family members but be faithful in repaying them because money can ruin relationships.

9. If the consumer has an average to excellent credit profile and the closing costs, which are fees for getting the loan, are not expensive then they can consider getting a personal loan with a low interest rate from a credit union and paying off all the credit cards using the personal loan money. The interest rates of personal loans are not always cheaper than the interest rates of credit cards.

10. Do not take a cash advance, which is taking physical cash, from credit cards because in most cases, consumers that are taking cash advances will never be able to get them out of debt. Cash advances have a fee just for getting the cash and the interest rates are usually above 20%. The only situation in which it may be a good idea to take a cash advance is if the consumer is trying to save their checking account from being charged numerous overdraft fees.

Myth: It is okay to use the entire credit limit of a credit card as long as it is paid on time.

Fact: It is not okay to use the entire credit limit of a credit card and this is known as "maxing out" the card. Maxing out credit cards hurt the credit profile of the consumer despite their perfect payment histories. This is because it makes a bad impression to the financial institution that the consumer used a large amount of credit so quickly even if they pay it off immediately. It suggests that the consumer is more likely to get into a large amount of debt, which they will not be able to pay back. For example, it is not normal to use the entire five thousand dollars credit limit of a credit card in one day. In the thinking of the financial institution, it raises the question why a consumer is spending so much. Consumers are only supposed to use thirty percent or less of their credit limit on their credit card. This is because the credit bureaus record the highest balance accumulated on a credit card as the "high balance." The high balance is not the same as the current balance. Consumers should not want the high balance to be more than thirty percent because it shows on the credit reports forever. Spending over the credit limit causes the high balance to become higher than the credit limit. Future creditors will think consumers with credit cards of which their high balances were very close to the credit limits are prone to get into high levels of debt and overextend themselves. Such consumers are considered to have some risk in defaulting. Despite the high balances, if the consumers have no delinquencies or high debts then it is possible they may get approved for new credit but with low credit limits and higher than average interest rates.

Example of a consumer with unusually high balances

Wells Fargo credit card
Credit limit: $600
Current balance: $24.04
High balance: $581

Discover credit card
Credit limit: $2100
Current balance: $0
High balance: $1800

Bank of America credit card
Credit limit: $5000
Current balance: $293.50
High balance: $5049

A bank would question why the consumer utilized their credit cards so greatly even if they had managed to pay them off in a timely manner.

Wells Fargo credit card
High balance/credit limit = Highest proportion credit card was utilized
$581/$600 = 97% (rounded) utilized

Discover credit card
High balance/credit limit = Highest proportion credit card was utilized
$1800/$2100 = 86% (rounded) utilized

Bank of America credit card
High balance/credit limit = Highest proportion credit card was utilized
$5,049/$5,000 = 101% (rounded) utilized.
Note: This credit card went over the credit limit and thus, is considered to have been overly utilized.

Advice: As a change imposed by the President Obama in 2009 through the "Credit CARD Act," most financial institutions conduct an account review every six months to ensure the credit account is being actively used and the financial institution is not having a loss by keeping it open. For this reason, use all the credit cards at least once every six months so they do not get closed for inactivity but do not make large purchases. Use the credit card that has the highest credit limit and most rewards for everyday purchases but make sure no more than thirty percent of the credit limit is used.

For example, if a credit card has a credit limit of one thousand dollars, which is the amount of available credit a consumer can spend. A consumer should not spend more than three hundred dollars because that is thirty percent of the credit limit. Utilizing a credit card too much can cause a financial institution to close the account or reduce the credit limit fearing that the consumer will not be able to pay back the debts. The credit scores are guaranteed to drop due to the excessive utilization of credit cards. It may become difficult for a consumer to obtain new loans with decent interest rates. If situations approach in which a consumer must use the entire credit limit of their credit card such as college tuition then they should pay in advance towards the credit card and then use the credit card to pay for the expense. This way the credit bureaus will not receive information from the financial institutions indicating the entire credit limit of the credit card was used and the credit scores will not drop

Credit Cards

Credit Card Arbitration

Some consumers sue their credit card companies in court, which is arbitration. They feel as though the credit card companies were unfairly charging fees and interest. Usually, there are fees such as court fees to sue the credit card company and it is not easy to win against them; because the question will arise in court if the consumer felt as though they will being billed unfairly then why were they continuing to use the credit card. When multiple consumers sue a credit card company for the same reason, this is known as a class action lawsuit and all the customers of the credit card company will receive a notice regarding the lawsuit.

Business Credit Cards

The CARD Act does not affect business credit cards, which are credit cards used by consumers to make purchases for their business. The credit card company can charge big over-the-credit limit fees, they do not give 21 days to send in the payment, and the payments above the minimum payment are applied to the lowest interest rate balance first on the credit card. For this reason, avoid business credit cards because they are expensive unless the consumer can pay off the balance at the end of the month.

Card Numbers Cannot Appear on Receipts

When consumers make purchases, merchants are not allowed to print the full credit or debit card numbers on receipts or proof of purchases. This is considered "truncating," which means shortening the account number. No more than five digits of the card number used to make the purchase can be printed; otherwise the merchants can potentially be fined. The likely reason why the government enforced this law is because there were cases in which consumers would carelessly discard their receipts and criminals would get a hold of them. They would copy the card numbers listed on the receipts and make purchases for which the consumer was liable.

Raising Credit Card Minimum Payments

Due to the credit crisis, an increasing number of credit card companies are sending notices to their consumers that they are increasing the minimum payment amount that is due every month. A higher percentage of the balance will be getting paid down through a higher minimum payment and as a result, the credit card company will make more profit through the consumer and be less likely to fail as a business. The reason why credit card companies are taking this action against some consumers is because it is possible for a consumer to make small minimum payments on their credit card for the purpose of ensuring it does not decline when they attempt to use it to purchase items but when the entire credit limit is used then they will not bother to pay it or will likely declare a bankruptcy. As a result, the financial institution will have a loss.

     Example of consumer credit card abuse
Adrian has a credit card with Capital One Bank with a credit limit of $1,500.
It has a balance of $1,200 with a minimum payment due every month of $35.00.

First bill
Balance: $1,200.00
Minimum payment: $35.00.
Balance after payment is received: $1,165.00
Adrian spends $100 at Radio Shack, the card does not decline because he paid the minimum payment, and the credit card balance becomes $1,265.00. Notice that the balance has grown higher instead of decreasing with the payment.

Second bill
Balance: $1,265.00
Minimum payment: $35.00
Balance after payment is received: $1,230.00
Adrian spends $200 at Wal-Mart, the card does not decline because he paid the minimum payment, and the credit card balance becomes $1,430.00. Notice that the balance has grown even higher than the first bill. It is still not decreasing with the payments.

Third bill
Balance: $1,430.00
Minimum payment: $35.00
Balance after payment is received: $1,395.00
Adrian spends $150 at a game store, the card does not decline because he paid the minimum payment, and the credit card balance becomes $1,545.00. Notice that the balance has gone over the credit limit and Adrian will now be charged a $35.00 over-the-credit limit fee which makes the balance $1,580.00.

Months pass by and Capital One receives no payments from Adrian. Capital One ruins Adrian's credit profile, he gets to keep all the merchandise he purchased for free, and they sell the debt to a collection agency. Capital One selling the debt allows for them to partially make up for the loan loss.

Unfortunately, a growing number of consumers like Adrian are still abusing their credit cards. For this reason, financial institutions purposefully raise the minimum payment amounts for all consumers so they can avoid having major losses.

In the case of Adrian, if Capital One had required a minimum payment from him of $60.00, instead of $35.00, then they would not have had as great a loan loss. Adrian would have saved money too on interest with a higher minimum payment. When consumers receive the notice usually called "a change in terms and conditions" indicating that the minimum payment due every month is increasing then they can opt-out which means they will agree to have their credit card account closed so the minimum payment amount does not change and they can pay off the credit card balance more successfully with low chances of becoming delinquent. Consumers need to be aware that if the credit card is closed then it will lower their credit scores but if they authentically cannot afford to make the higher minimum payments then it is the best financial decision to opt-out because consumers want to avoid becoming delinquent on the credit card. Compared to a closed credit card, a delinquent credit card will do the most damage to their credit scores and chances of being able to earn a good job. The reason why credit card companies close the credit card account if a consumer opts out of the minimum payment amount being increased is because it stands to reason that if consumers are opting out then they likely cannot afford to make the higher minimum payments. For this reason, the financial institution considers them to be financially weak and very likely to one day default on the credit card. As a business, the financial institution cannot afford to take this risk.

If consumers can afford to make the higher minimum payments or better yet, pay off the entire balance, without becoming delinquent on another bill then they should not opt-out because then the financial institution will not close the credit card and with the increased payments, the credit scores of the consumers will increase faster. This means cheaper insurance premiums and being able to save more money to apply payments towards mortgages and student loans, the silent financial killers.

Credit Card Terms and Conditions—Loan Contract with the Disclosures
When consumers are deciding whether or not they should apply for a credit card, they need to look for these elements on the credit card contract.

Annual Percentage Rate (APR) for Purchases
This is the interest rate that the consumer will pay on the credit card if they carry a balance. Consumers can divide the interest rate by 12 months to determine the interest they will pay every month. For example, a 19.8% would be 0.198. 0.198 divided by 12 months would be an interest rate of 1.65% charged every month on the credit card balance. Consumers should call the credit card issuer every two to three months and ask for an interest rate reduction as a reward for always being timely in making the payments.

APR for Transfers
When consumers transfer, which means move, a balance from one loan or credit card to the credit card for which they are applying then this is the interest rate that they will pay on the balance.

APR for Cash Advances
This is the high interest rate consumers would pay if they used their credit card at an ATM machine and withdrew physical cash. Consumers should never do cash advances. They are expensive and have no protection against fraud or scam merchants.

Penalty APR and When It Applies
With an exception to credit cards issued by credit unions, most penalty APRs on credit cards are about 30%. This means if the consumer is significantly late on making their payment then their interest rate will be increased to 30%. After six months of timely payment history then the financial institution will lower the interest rate back to the normal annual percentage rate.

Annual Fee
This should always say none. An annual fee is a flat fee that the consumer will pay to the financial institution every year even if they never use the open credit card. Consumers want to avoid credit cards with annual fees because the fees will compound with interest themselves

if the consumer does not immediately pay them or is late on making the credit card payment, which will result in a late fee being charged.

Transaction Fees

Transfer: This is the fee, which is usually 3% to 4% of the balance amount, to do the balance transfer. The fee itself compounds with interest because it becomes part of the new balance on the credit card. Credit unions usually do not have balance transfer fees on their credit cards. Ideally, consumers should not get themselves into so much debt that they need to do a balance transfer.

Cash Advance: This is a fee that consumers must pay in order to withdraw physical cash using their credit card. The fee compounds with interest itself because it becomes part of the balance on the credit card. Most cash advance fees are $10 or 3% to 4% of the cash advance amount. Consumers should never do cash advances. It makes no sense to do so and pay fees along with the high cash advance interest rate. Consumers should not do cash advances to pay another loan or credit card. Such is a very bad habit that will lead to financial failure.

Penalty Fees: *All* fees become part of the credit card balance and compound with interest themselves.

Late Payment: This is the fee that the consumer will pay if they are late in making their credit card payment.

Over-The-Credit-Limit: This is the fee that the consumer will pay if they spend over their credit limit, which is the amount of loan money they are allowed to spend using a credit card. If a consumer is charged an over-the-credit limit fee then they need to get serious help with budgeting because they are getting into high levels of debt.

Returned Payment: If the consumer makes a payment, on a credit card or any loan, using a checking or savings account; which does not have enough money, then the payment will get denied by the issuer of the bank account; The payment will get returned to the credit card and as a result, the credit card balance will increase instead of decrease. Part of the minimum payment is interest so if the minimum payment made is returned to the credit card then in a sense, interest will be charged on interest.

Example: If Vikram makes a minimum payment, on his National City Bank credit card of $20.00 and 50% of the minimum payment amount is interest then this means the $10.00 within the $20.00 is interest. If the payment is returned by Wells Fargo, who is the issuer of his checking account, then the $20.00 will go back into the balance of the National City Bank credit card. The $10.00 interest within that $20.00 minimum payment will now compound with interest itself. This is considered capitalization because interest is being billed on interest.

Grace Period: Before getting a loan of any type or credit card, Consumers should always ask the financial institution if there is a grace period; meaning if the financial institution does not receive their payment on the due date, then the consumer has a certain number of days after the due date to still send in the payment, without being charged a late fee.

For example, my mother has a credit card with Commerce Bank. The due date on the credit card is the 7th of every month. The credit card has a one day grace period meaning; if

Commerce Bank receives a payment, by the 8th of the month, then they will not charge her a late fee or extra interest. Grace periods are very beneficial, in saving money. However, consumers should not make it a habit of always sending in the payment on the last day of the grace period; because it may send the message to the financial institution that the consumer is financially struggling and is very likely to one day default on the loan. As a result, the financial institution may reduce the credit limit, close the credit account, or increase the interest rate. In the case of my mother, if she makes it a habit of always sending in the payment on the 8th of every month then Commerce Bank may think she is financially unstable and they may reduce her credit limit, close her account, or take another adverse action against her as a means of protecting their business from enduring a loss. For this reason, my mother and I make sure that the credit card balance is paid off immediately after the day it is used.

Avoid Overdraft Fees by wisely using Credit Card

Good credit can only be established; when consumers borrow money and pay it back in a timely manner. For this reason, consumers are better off using a credit card to pay for all purchases, and then paying off the credit card immediately. Unlike debit cards and prepaid cards, credit cards have no overdraft fees. They offer more protection, against damaged or defective merchandise or services, and more protection against fraud.

For example, if a criminal took a debit card number and cleaned out the checking account of all its money; then the consumer has no money until the financial institution can conduct an investigation, notify the police, and recover the funds. In contrast, financial institutions have twenty-four fraud detection departments that will block the card immediately if they notice suspicious activity. Any fraudulent charges found are credited to the consumer immediately, and the consumer is not liable for them. The consumer has access to the entire credit limit, and the fraudulent charges do not reduce it. Consumers should use a credit card as carefully as they would a debit card. They earn reward points, which help save money but only if huge balances, are not carried on credit cards. Such balances are charged interest by the financial institutions unless they are paid off immediately in a timely manner.

Keep Credit Cards Open for Long Time

Financial institutions look at the length of history established on credit accounts. If a consumer only has an average, of six to seven months, of history built on their credit cards then the financial institution may be reluctant to extend new credit until the consumer has established more history. Credit scores tend to be higher when consumers have long history established on credit accounts, such as for ten years or longer. For this reason, consumers should not close credit accounts; even if they are not using them unless there are expensive annual fees that cannot be removed. Additionally, it is never too early to start building credit. Consumers should start trying to get their first credit card when they reach the legal age as permitted in their state and get a job. Financial institutions look at the number of hard inquiry credit checks, that the consumer has had within the past two years. Too many credit checks suggest the consumer is desperate for credit and this usually means the consumer is not financially strong. Financial institutions can deny credit to consumers with too many credit checks. Finally, financial institutions want to see consumers have a variety of loans such as student loans, auto loans, house loan (mortgage), and credit cards. When consumers have a variety of loans then this means they are taking on a high momentum level. If all the loans are being paid on time and in full then it will send the message to the financial institution that the consumer is financially stable and is capable of handling more credit.

Advice: Consumers need to make sure their credit is strong in all areas as measured by the FICO scoring model in order to have the best credit possible. These areas include the payment history, amounts owed on accounts, types of credit, length of history established on accounts, and a low number of credit checks as well as new accounts established within a short time period. One of these areas being weak could lead to a low credit score. Some of these areas consumers cannot improve immediately and simply must allow for time to pass and let their credit grow. An example of such an area is the length of history established on accounts. Consumers that get their first credit card will be weak in this area and they have to allow for years to pass in order for the area to improve. However, despite the weakness, their credit is not considered bad, but simply underdeveloped. Their credit scores may be low due to the low history but for this reason, financial institutions will focus on the content showing on their credit report such as if they have any delinquencies, too many credit checks, or high balances.

In order to ensure a consumer has a variety of loans and credit, a suggested idea would be even if a consumer has cash and does not need a certain loan, such as an auto loan. The consumer should still get the loan and use the cash to pay it off immediately. The auto loan will show as paid, on credit reports and the scores will increase. By paying off the loan immediately, the consumer will pay little or no interest. In order for consumers to maintain a low number of hard credit checks, they should not keep applying for credit even if they are getting denied. Instead, consumers should try and correct the reasons for which they are being denied by submitting credit report disputes to the credit agencies. Consumers can also contact the financial institutions and ask for a reconsideration of the credit application. Consumers must be confident over the phone or in the letter they submit for the purpose of making the financial institution feel confident they are at low risk of the consumer defaulting. Finally, even if consumers are not a victim of fraud or are not applying for credit, they can consider freezing their credit reports so they do not get tempted to apply for credit aggressively. They can remove the credit freeze whenever they are fully confident they need a certain loan.

Do Not Just Make Minimum Payments

Consumers should try their best to pay above the minimum payment, not just because it saves them money on interest; but because the financial institutions are less likely to take adverse actions against the consumer, such as; closing the credit account. They sometimes think consumers that are only paying the minimum payments have the intention of one day stopping to pay when the credit card is maxed out and has little or no available credit. This is because it raises the question to the financial institutions as to why the consumers are not making more payments towards their credit cards and if they plan on ever going out of debt. Unemployed consumers should only make minimum payments on the credit cards because they need extra money to spend on the everyday necessities of life. Unemployed consumers should not live off of their credit cards and other loans because it will only make life more expensive and harder to save money. Truthfully, despite becoming unemployed, consumers should never have plunged into such a high debt level. The amount of debt belonging to a consumer should never be higher than half the total amount of their assets. If the debt amount is exceeding the amount of assets belonging to the consumer then technically, they are considered bankrupt, sometimes called insolvent, even though they have not declared bankruptcy in the legal sense. Consumers should never become bankrupt by spending beyond their means even if they are running a business.

Credit Card is Not Source of Income or Alternative to Not Having Money

This is the biggest myth that has ruined the economy. Credit cards are not meant to be used when consumers do not have the funds to make a purchase and consumers should never have the attitude that they will later have enough funds to pay the credit card company. This is because any negative event can happen with the consumer such as losing their job, ending up having to pay medical bills, or becoming parents and financially supporting their children. Any of these events may cause the consumer to be late in making the payment on the credit card, being charged a late fee, the financial institution will increase the interest rate usually to 30% or more on the credit card, and the credit profile of the consumer will reflect a delinquency that happened with the credit card. This will cause the consumer to end up paying thousands on high interest mortgages and car loans and they may struggle to get approved for a decent paying job or low insurance premium. Such will increase the chances of the consumer getting into large debts because it stands to reason if a consumer cannot get a decent paying job due to bad credit, then they may not be able to make enough money to pay all the bills as well as the everyday expenses of living.

Legitimate Purpose of Credit Card

The purpose of a credit card is to build an excellent credit history so consumers have a high chance at getting approved for a low mortgage interest rate, low insurance premium, and being granted a decent paying job. Consumers are supposed to use a credit card so they can save money through the rewards programs and be protected against fraudulent merchants and scammers who have the intention of stealing all the money within the bank accounts of the consumers. Additionally, there is no way for a business to know whether or not a consumer will repay them for the services or loan money without checking their credit reports. If businesses assumed consumers with limited or bad credit profiles will repay them then the economy would be a disaster. On the credit reports, the businesses want to see that consumers have successfully managed their credit cards meaning the consumers have always repaid them in full and have never been late on making the payments.

For such reasons, when consumers have enough money to make a purchase then they should use a credit card and pay it off immediately. This way, the consumers do not plunge themselves into large debts. As a personal analysis, the only loan that is justified to be taken when a consumer cannot afford an expense, specifically college, is a student loan.

The History of the Credit Card

Sioux Falls, South Dakota is the source of where most mail credit card offers come from and where consumers send in their payments, to multiple credit card companies. This explains why most of the return addresses and payment mailing addresses of the credit card companies indicate South Dakota. This is because the credit card industry mostly emerged, in Sioux Falls. During the mid-1900's, South Dakota had a major recession in which financial institutions issued very few mortgages and loans. For this reason, South Dakota had strict laws imposed by their government on the interest rates that financial institutions could charge consumers on loans. The cap set by the government on loan interest rates was considered a "usury law." Usury is the practice of granting loans with excessively high interest rates and/or fees to consumers. For the purpose of trying to cause a boom within the economy and the banking industry, South Dakota eliminated its usury law in 1979.

As support, Bill Jacklow, the governor of South Dakota back then, said in an interview with PBS; that the usury law's elimination would allow for them "to lift the ceilings on usury so [they] could free up and get capital in South Dakota." During this time, the credit card division of Citibank in New York was having major loan losses because inflation and bad economic conditions caused interest rates to go up to 20 percent but Citibank could only charge consumers no more than 12 percent interest on their credit card accounts. This is because New York had strict usury laws similar to the ones in South Dakota originally, preventing financial institutions from charging excessive interest to consumers on their loans. Citibank was paying 20 percent interest on their money which they were lending to consumers; but getting paid 12 percent was causing their business to fail, especially considering that some consumers did not repay their credit cards.

In a sense, Citibank was spending more than what they were gaining in profit. In 1981, Citibank fixed this problem by moving their credit card division from New York into South Dakota because they could use the fact that South Dakota eliminated its usury law to its business advantage. They could charge consumers high interest rates on the credit cards because they had little or no limits on the interest rates imposed on them by the government. Not just Citibank but many other financial institutions such as Bank of America, First Chicago of Illinois, Chase Manhattan Bank, Manufacturers Hanover Bank, Chemical Bank, and Bank of New York started or moved their credit card divisions within South Dakota, and all this activity was adding growth to the credit card industry. These banks were creating jobs, so it was helping the economy of South Dakota recover from their recession. A major boom occurred with the credit card industry when the United States Supreme Court passed the Marquette Bank decision. This decision allowed for the financial institutions to charge the interest rates that it was charging to consumers on loans and credit cards within its own state to consumers in other states despite if the other states had strict usury laws. As an example of this practice, Bill Jacklow said during his interview "if South Dakota had a 25 percent ceiling, then [banks] could charge 25 percent, even to a loan in Florida." Such a loan can include a credit card.

All the financial institutions were taking advantage of the Marquette Bank decision and were expanding their credit card businesses. The Marquette Bank decision likely is what allowed for the financial institutions to structure their credit card products in the way that if the consumer was significantly late on making the monthly payment then they could increase the interest rate up to about 30 percent. All the economic success South Dakota was having caused Delaware to put fewer restrictions on their usury laws like South Dakota had done so. This caused financial institutions to move or originate credit card divisions also within Delaware because had the freedom to charge consumers high interest rates on credit cards. As a result, the credit card industry has become the "most profitable sector of banking" and they make more than "$30 billion" in profits considering about 144 million Americans and growing use credit cards as supported by PBS' "Secret History of the Credit Card" segment. The bottom line is that consumers should never carry balances on credit cards, so they can avoid paying high interest fees, and also avoid getting themselves into high debts. Consumers should pay off their balances immediately. If they cannot pay off their credit card immediately, then they should never use it to make a purchase.

Deposit Accounts and FDIC or NCUA

Insured Deposit Accounts are Imperative

When getting any deposit account such as; a savings, checking, or retirement account, it should always be insured by the **Federal Deposit Insurance Corporation**, which is abbreviated as **FDIC**. The financial institution will indicate if the deposit account is FDIC insured or not.

The Federal Deposit Insurance Corporation is a chartered agency financially supported by the government, of the United States, in which all the funds that consumers deposit into their accounts at any financial institution, only within the United States, are ensured up to a certain amount; in the event that the financial institution fails. The amount of protection that FDIC provides for each type of deposit account will be disclosed by the financial institution to the consumer. In most cases, the amount of which the consumer is insured is up to $250,000 for each FDIC insured financial institution with which they have deposit accounts. $250,000 is the coverage amount for all the deposits within each financial institution. Consumers would need check with the financial institutions regarding their policies as to what a consumer must do for more insurance if they are going to deposit more than $250,000 into their deposit accounts. With FDIC insurance, the funds of the consumer are not lost and they will be compensated for them. FDIC ensures that the financial institutions do not attempt deceptive practices with the funds of consumer.

For example, a financial institution that offers FDIC insured deposit accounts cannot take money from those accounts and use them with the bad intention of stealing from the consumer. FDIC could shut down a financial institution for such fraudulent practices. FDIC also protects the funds in an **individual retirement account**, which is abbreviated as an **IRA**. An IRA can be considered a deposit and investment account with tax benefits that the consumer can contribute (deposit) money, at any time they wish to do so. A consumer can think of any FDIC insured deposit account as having insurance for the funds so that they can never be lost. For this reason, a consumer should **never** get an account that is not FDIC insured because they are putting their money at risk of being lost, which could lead to them becoming homeless. Not all financial institutions offer FDIC insured deposit accounts because it costs them money for the program and they have to pass certain government regulations and inspections.

Credit Unions offer NCUA Insured Accounts

Credit unions do not offer FDIC insured deposit accounts, because the government has the credit union consumer accounts protected by; the insurance of **National Credit Union Association** or **NCUA** It is a different program but similar to the FDIC insurance and provides the same amount of coverage, which is $250,000. FDIC and NCUA insurance are free for consumers. Consumers should deposit all their money into an FDIC or NCUA insured deposit account, because they are taking a huge risk keeping the money, due to the fact they have no insurance if their house or apartment burns down or they are robbed. Homeowner's insurance or law officials are not able to compensate the consumer of all the money that was kept in the house or car. No matter how severe the economic conditions, money within FDIC and NCUA insured deposit accounts can never be lost. Some consumers make the mistake of withdrawing all their funds from their deposit accounts when the economic conditions become bad; such as when the 2000 *housing crisis* took place, in America and these consumers paid a heavy price, because they lost their money through some kind of unexpected cause such as a robbery.

Detect Fraudulent Financial Institutions

Credit unions that do not offer the NCUA insurance on their deposit accounts may be a sign that they are fraudulent. Similarly, in some cases, financial institutions that do not offer FDIC insured deposit accounts or any credit union or bank that wants extra fees from the consumer for providing any insurance; may be a sign that they are fraudulent because it is possible for any individual or company with sufficient funds to start a bank. As evidence, some individuals or private businesses start community banks.

A community bank is not as large as a traditional bank such as Bank of America or Chase Bank, because it usually has fewer assets. This is due to the fact its customers mostly come from the geographical area near the locations of the community bank. In fact, many of the workers of the community bank reside within the communities that it serves and are customers themselves. "Family owned banks" are usually considered community banks. A financial institution that has the word, "community" within their title does not always mean that it is an actual community bank, because some traditional banks and credit unions have the word, "community" within their titles. A community bank focuses on financially assisting the families and businesses living within the area and may be less strict than traditional banks when evaluating credit profiles for the purpose of approving credit applications and charging fees. They are not so focused on making high profits because unlike traditional banks, community banks do not have overly paid directors or executives and they do not have many branches, which saves them money and they can pass the savings onto the consumers. Consumers will tend to get more interest paid on their deposits and cheaper interest rates. For this reason, consumers are encouraged to check the loan rates of community banks and compare them to the loan rates of credit unions. A community bank or credit union, in the majority of cases, will be cheaper than traditional banks.

Community Banks are Beneficial

Some consumers may be reluctant to join a community bank, because the low number of branches will make it difficult for them to do transactions; such as deposits and withdrawals, especially when they are traveling out of the state or country. Community banks are more likely to fail than traditional banks if they have too many loan losses. Due to the recession, many community banks failed and a fewer number of businesses and individuals want to start a community bank. Part of the reason why some community banks failed is because they were offering deposit accounts; that were not FDIC insured but only privately insured, by the community bank themselves. They did not want to pay for the FDIC program and wanted to pass on the savings to consumers. They lost the deposits of consumers by granting them as loans to other consumers that did not pay them back. As a result, there are now lawsuits against some community banks. Currently, most states within the United States now require that all financial institutions and credit unions must be FDIC insured but there are a few states that may not depending upon their legislatures. Financial institutions with few assets may not be required to be FDIC insured. It is likely the most fraud, such as money laundering, is going to occur with financial institutions that are not FDIC insured. It is also likely that the majority of phony financial institutions will reside within the states that do not require for the financial institutions to be FDIC insured. It is possible that some privately insured financial institutions may be more expensive with their loans and have deposit accounts with higher fees, if any, compared to the loans and deposit accounts of FDIC insured banks. For this reason, consumers should read the terms, conditions, and disclosures of the loan and deposit account products of multiple financial institutions and compare them to see which products are the most consumer friendly because they offer the most savings. Consumers should also do an internet search with the name of the community bank and next to the name, type in "complaints" for the purpose of checking their reputation. Two recommended websites that store the complaints regarding companies are www.ripoffreport.com and www.complaintsboard.com. Consumers also need to be aware that is possible for any criminal to start a website, on the internet, indicating they are any random bank, credit union, or just any kind of company because they want to steal the personal information of consumers.

Be Cautious of International Financial Institutions

Financial institutions outside countries outside of the United States, especially the countries that have low level economies, may have financial institutions that have no insurance for the funds of consumers. Consumers should try their best to avoid such financial institutions and go to institutions that offer some type of insurance. Depending upon the amount of money that the consumer is depositing, it may be a smart decision to pay a fee to the financial institution, if possible, for the insurance of the funds.

FDIC and NCUA Does Not Affect Loans

FDIC does not provide any insurance protection for investments or loans. Investments can always lose or gain value and the government cannot compensate the consumers for the losses. FDIC does not control the interest rates on loans and they cannot compensate the consumers for the interest that consumers pay on their credit accounts. For this reason, consumers need to be careful when using loans, especially loans that have variable interest rates.

Types of Deposit Accounts

The funds within the deposit accounts are considered the liquid assets of the consumer. With an exception to a **certificate of deposit** (**CD**), the deposit accounts that accumulate interest have variable interest rates that can potentially change depending, upon the conditions of the economy and the **Federal Reserve**.

The Federal Reserve is different from the **Wall Street Journal**. The Wall Street Journal is the financial market office, of the United States, located in Manhattan, New York; where stock brokers, investors, and analysts conduct stock exchanges and other financial related businesses. Publicly traded companies such as Bank of America, Wells Fargo, and Suntrust also conduct stock exchanges at Wall Street Journal. The Wall Street Journal influences the interest rates on credit cards, student loans, home equity loans, car loans, and other loans with an exception to mortgages. The interest rate set by the Wall Street Journal is called the **prime rate**. In addition to deposit accounts, the interest rates on mortgages are influenced by the Federal Reserve, which is considered the central bank of the United States. The interest rate set by the Federal Reserve is called the feds fund rate. The loan contract will usually say if its interest rate is influenced by the Federal Reserve or the Wall Street Journal but if the interest rate is fixed then it will not change despite the changes that occur with the Federal Reserve or the Wall Street Journal. Car title loans, payday loans, tax refund loans, pawn shop loans, and

Finance 101: The Whiz Kid's Perfect Credit Guide

loans with exorbitant interest rates at 60% and above are usually not influenced by the Federal Reserve or the Wall Street Journal but only by their loan issuers.

Deposit All Money into Deposit Accounts for Maximum Protection

Consumers should always have all their money within some type of deposit account or multiple deposit accounts, because their money is protected by the government. If the financial institutions were to fail then the consumers would still never lose their money. Money is very dangerous to keep within a house, car, or just anywhere besides a financial institution; because if the consumer is robbed or the location where the money is being kept burns down then the consumer has a major financial loss. The interest made within deposit accounts is taxable, usually if the accounts begin making about $1,500 or more in interest.

Checking Account: A bank account, sometimes called a "demand account," that allows for a consumer to make unlimited deposits and withdrawals. In order to pay merchants, a consumer can write checks or use their debit card. Consumers should try to avoid writing too many checks because they have the account number on them next to the routing number. A criminal can potentially get a check, use the account number to clear the checking account of all its funds, and a consumer will not realize this until it is too late. Consumers need to be careful not to lose their checkbooks and if they do then they must change their checking account numbers immediately.

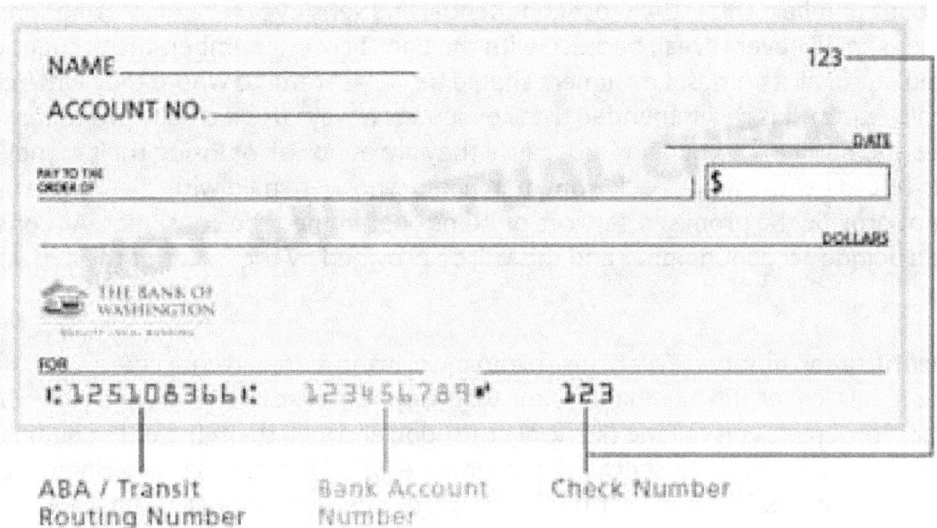

Source of image: http://www.the-bank.com/help-center.html

Routing transit number (RTN): The routing number verifies the financial institution that is the issuer of the checking account. This helps prevent criminals from creating fraudulent checks because it is possible a criminal can produce a check with the image of any bank logo. A routing number that begins with 00 usually means it is a check that will retrieve the funds from a United States government account. In contrast, routing numbers that begin with 21 through 32 usually mean that the check will retrieve its funds from a financial institution such as a credit union, community bank, or traditional bank. The routing number is sometimes called the "**ABA number**," which means the **American Bankers Association number**.

The American Bankers Association is simply a group in the United States that maintains a healthy relationship between its member financial institutions and the government. The American Bankers Association may bring up any issues that the majority of the financial institutions are experiencing to the government with the purpose of wanting to work out a solution. Usually, financial institutions that are part of the American Bankers Association will call the first nine digits of the check an ABA number because the American Bankers Association assigns a unique routing number to each financial institution. According to www.ehow.com, about 95% of financial institutions are part of the American Bankers Association; making it the largest banking group in the United States. These financial institutions have their assets maintained in accounts, with the Federal Reserve. Financial institutions that are not part of the American Bankers Association may have their checks, for consumers, structured in a different manner. For example, they may not have a routing number. Without a checkbook, consumers can still obtain the routing number by calling the financial institution. Some financial institutions post their routing numbers on their websites such as Wells Fargo. The routing numbers of financial institutions can also be found on www.routingnumbers.org. It is personally always recommended that consumers confirm the routing number with one of the representatives of the financial institution. This is because incorrect routing numbers can mean returned check fees and other fees from the billing company that was trying to cash the check. For the same reason, consumers should immediately contact financial institutions that merge or are bought out by another financial institution because it is possible the routing number may change.

Bank account number: This is the most confidential and sensitive piece of information; that a consumer should never reveal, because with the bank account number, the account can be cleaned out of all its funds. Consumers should be very careful to whom they write checks and for this reason, it is recommended that consumers always use a credit card to make the purchases and pay it off immediately, because they are at no risk of losing their money. It is often difficult to get the funds back from merchants who were paid with checks or a debit card and did not provide the promised services or items or scammed the consumer. All consumers will have a unique account number and this will be provided by the issuer of their checking account.

Check identification number: This helps the financial institution and consumer; track the check, in the event, it is lost or the merchant claims that they never received the check payment, in the mail. Consumers can call the financial institution and give them the check number. Consumers need to record the check number and the name of the merchant whom will be paid using the check before mailing off the check. The check number also helps the consumer dispute the check, in the event, that the consumer does not receive the promised service or merchandise from the merchant; or if they feel as though a merchant has withdrawn more money than the amount that was written on the check. Fraud merchants sometimes write in numbers in the box where the consumer writes the amount of how much money that the merchant should be paid. In fact, this is one of the reasons why consumers are discouraged from using checks to pay merchants; because such fraud cannot happen when consumers use a credit card.

Average Daily Balances and Fees

Some checking account products offered by financial institutions; make interest and they are usually called an **"interest checking account"** or a **"money market checking account."**

However, to make interest, consumers are usually required to maintain a minimum average daily balance and if they do not then some financial institutions may impose fees. There are no limits for making deposits. Consumers that plan on doing many withdrawals should not get interest bearing or money market checking accounts; unless there are no minimum balance requirements. Consumers need to make sure the financial institution does not limit the number of withdrawals that can be done with interest or money market checking accounts. This is because if consumers exceed the limits; then they may be charged "excess activity fees."

Regular checking and savings accounts, that do not make interest, do not have withdrawal limits; but in some rare scenarios, depending upon the policies of the financial institutions, some regular deposit accounts may have withdrawal limits and average daily balance requirements. It may be likely; that the financial institution is trying to make more profits by getting the consumers to use their credit cards more often for purchases. The reason why financial institutions may require minimum average daily balances and may limit the number of withdrawals on any type of interest or money market deposit account is because the funds within those accounts are considered assets of the financial institution. They use the assets as money to lend to other consumers in the form of loans. When consumers pay interest and fees on the loans then the financial institution will make a profit and share some of that profit by paying interest on the deposit accounts. The financial institution cannot lend money easily using the assets if consumers do not have sufficient funds or are always withdrawing money. The financial institutions charge the fees to lower the likelihood of excessive withdrawals happening, give the consumer more motivation to maintain the proper average daily balance because they are not going to want to be charged fees, financial intuitions will not be wasting their money hiring customer service agents and purchasing computer database software to manage deposit accounts that have little or no funds. As a result, the financial institution can grant loans more easily. This will allow for the financial institution to increase its cash flow and its overall aggregate of assets, which means amount of money. Consumers can close their checking account, any type, but the financial institution may require that it remain open for a certain number of days before a consumer can close it without being imposed any fees.

Online Bill Pay Feature

Most checking accounts, in the United States, come with a service called the "online bill pay," which is usually free, as a benefit to the consumer and is maintained by the **Check Free Corporation**, who is a division of the company called *Fiserv*. The financial institutions have a business relationship with Fiserv and pay them for the online bill pay service. Online bill pay is a program that allows for consumers to enter the information of all their bills; such as student loans, credit cards, rent payments, utility bills, and literally every bill possible. The program then saves all the information regarding the bills and a consumer simply has to enter the amount due for each bill and clicks send to submit the payments. The money is then immediately withdrawn from the checking account and sent to each bill issuer electronically or by mail through a check. Due to the fact it may cost the bill issuer more money, in payment processing, to accept the payment electronically, not all bill issuers except electronic payments and for this reason; the financial institution would mail them a check. The beauty of the online bill pay service is that it already has all the information saved about the bill issuers in its database; such as the payment mailing address and if they want an electronic or check payment because almost all consumers have the same types of bills with the same companies. When they enter the information about the bill issuer then the bill pay service will save the information and share it with another consumer who has a service with the same bill issuer.

Example:
Parth enters the information regarding his Chase credit card into the online bill pay system, which are the Chase credit card payment mailing address and his account number. The online bill pay will save this information.

Ashley enters her Chase credit card account number and based on the information Parth had entered, the online bill pay service recognizes Ashley has a Chase credit card and it immediately displays the payment mailing address without Ashley having to type it. All other consumers, like Ashley, that have a Chase credit card bill will not have to worry about entering all the information for their bill. As a result, they will be able to save time.

It is personally recommended to use online bill pay because it is a major tool that has allowed for me to never be late on any of the bills, belonging to my mother. Fiserv ensures all the payments sent through the online bill pay are received by the bill issuers and tracks all the electronic and check payments in case they were to get lost. If the online bill pay program indicates that a bill issuer will receive a payment by a certain date and they do not receive it then the customer service department managing the online bill pay will contact the bill issuer on the behalf of the consumer and get all late fees refunded. The consumer will face no penalties because they are not at fault. The online bill pay service makes it easy to keep the checking account balanced and prevents it from becoming negative, because it shows the consumer how much money will be left over after the bill payments are sent. Consumers are able to save money because they do not have to pay fees for postage or stamps as they would if they mailed out a check themselves. Consumers do not have to buy checkbooks anymore. Consumers can be more organized with their bills.

Online Bill Pay Protection

The online bill pay service is able to electronically retrieve most bills, not all, indicating how much money the consumer must pay to the issuer and the due date. The consumers will not receive paper bills, which at times, can be dangerous in the event a criminal were to get a hold of the bills and compromise the information about the consumer. Credit card paper bills are the major concern because some of them have account numbers on the bill. For this reason, financial institutions benefit as a business from the online bill pay program because they are less vulnerable at fraud occurring with the accounts of their consumers. Fraud results in a loss for the financial institution such as when the criminal uses the credit account numbers to purchase items. The financial institution does not know it is a criminal using the account fraudulently until the consumer reports it but until then, the financial institution assumes it is the correct consumer and lets the purchase transactions go through and the financial institutions pays the credit payment processing fees. When the consumer does report that fraudulent activity occurred then the financial institution dismisses the fraudulent charges but they do have a partial loss because until the investigation is completed, they pay for the fraudulent charges. Another reason why financial institutions favor online bill pay is because it costs them less money and time to process payments compared to the payment processing fees they would have to pay if consumers used their debit cards or checkbooks. They do not have to pay fees to order debit cards or checkbooks. They are able to make more money because they get paid by the bill issuer who receives the payment for the safe delivery. They pass on these savings to the consumers, which is why most financial institutions offer the bill pay service free. Consumers should not do business with financial institutions that charge

Finance 101: The Whiz Kid's Perfect Credit Guide

fees for their online bill pay service because it is a waste of money to pay for the service when consumers can simply move their checking account to a financial institution that offers the exact same service for free. When consumers login into their online banking then they should be a tap or link that says "bill pay." Some financial institutions may require for the consumer to request for the online bill pay service by contacting them directly. The financial institution will then release the program to the consumer whenever they log into online banking to view their transactions and balances. Consumers also have the option of going to the website of the Check Free Corporation, signing up for the free bill payment service, and living a stress free life. The website is www.mycheckfree.com. If a consumer does not like the service then they can stop using it. There is no commitment or contract required. There are other companies that offer bill pay services similar to that of Fiserv but they are not free and for this reason, they are not recommended.

Savings Account: A bank account that in most cases pays interest to the consumer and allows for the savings account balance to grow. The account may require for the consumer to maintain an average daily balance such $500 or fees may be imposed and the account may also be shut down. Consumers do receive checks for a savings account and an **automated teller machine** (**ATM**) card that can be used to pay merchants. The regulations of the government does not allow for consumers to withdraw money from their savings or money market accounts more than six times a month or statement cycle. This is likely because the government is trying to protect the financial institutions from failing by losing too many of their assets due to excessive withdrawals made by consumers. If the financial institutions begin to fail then they will likely need bailout money or the government will have to use their money in order to protect the deposits of the consumers. This is because the FDIC and NCUA deposit insurance programs they promised are not free for them to provide to the consumers. Bailout money or money needed to provide the FDIC and NCUA deposit insurance programs are both considered forms of credit and may cause the national debt to increase, which will have to be paid through increased taxes on consumers because debt can never magically disappear. Similar to an interest bearing or money market checking account, a savings account has no risk and cannot lose money. Consumers can close their savings account but the financial institution may require that it remain open for a certain number of days before a consumer can close it without being imposed any fees. For example, if Natalia opened a savings account with Fifth Third Bank and the next day, she wants to close it. Fifth Third Bank may require for Natalia to keep it open at least for a month otherwise they will charge her a fee for closing it early. The reason why some financial institutions have this policy is because it costs them money to order a credit report and ChexSystems report at the time of the consumer opening the account. If they did not charge any penalty for closing the account early then it would mean all the time that the bank representative spent helping the consumer and processing the paperwork went to waste.

Money Market Account: An account that is sometimes called a **"money market savings account"** and it pays interest to the consumer, which causes the balance within the account to grow. Like all interest bearing accounts, consumers are not allowed to withdraw money from the money market account more than six times a month or statement cycle or the account could potentially be shut down and fees may be imposed. There is no risk associated because the money cannot be lost as long as the money market account is protected by the NCUA insurance of the credit union or the FDIC insurance of the financial institution.

Warning! Consumers should not open many checking, savings, and money market accounts; although there is no impact on the credit scores, it is going to raise questions to the financial institutions as to why a consumer is opening so many deposit accounts. It makes no sense to them and makes them think the information of the consumer has been compromised and the criminal has the intention of making all the deposit accounts negative. This will cause the financial institutions to have a business loss. Additionally, consumers need to be aware that there are usually inactivity fees accessed to deposit accounts when they are showing no activity taking place such as periodic deposits made by the consumer. This can cause the deposit accounts to become negative. The financial institutions charge these fees because they want the consumers to use their accounts so the financial institutions can make profit especially through the debit, ATM card, and check fees they would charge the merchants that whom conducted business with the consumers.

Certificate of Deposit Account: A certificate of deposit account can be abbreviated as a "**CD**," which is how most consumers refer to them. Some consumers refer to a certificate of deposit account as a "time deposit." This is because a CD locks the funds of a consumer into a fixed and permanent interest rate for a certain time period, which the consumer chooses. Example of locked time periods include three months, six months, one year, two years, three years, and so on. The financial institution discloses the time periods it offers for the CD and the interest rates. In most cases, the longer time period that the consumer chooses for the CD then the higher the interest rate is and a consumer cannot withdraw or add funds to the CD at any time during the time period otherwise the consumer will be charged a penalty by the financial institution. This is because when consumers get a CD then they agree to a contract with the financial institution and the funds within the CD become part of their assets that they can use to grant loans to consumers. The day at which the time period of the CD ends is considered the maturity date. This is the date that the consumer can keep all the funds within their CD along with the interest or let it automatically renew for the same time period at which it was originally locked. In some rare cases such as medical emergencies, preventing loans from becoming delinquent, or to save the house from a foreclosure, it may be worth paying the fee and accessing the funds within the CD. Depending upon how much interest is being made on the CD, the consumer may or may not have to pay taxes on it. They have to check with the financial institution or a tax advisor because the interest made on the CD or any type of interest bearing savings is reported by the financial institution to the Internal Revenue Services as income, which was made by the consumer. However, if a CD is part of an individual retirement account (IRA) then a consumer does not have to pay taxes on it. Certificate of deposit accounts that are part of IRAs are considered retirement certificate of deposits or IRA CDs.

Individual Retirement Account: This account is abbreviated as an **IRA** and to some extent, it is considered a deposit account because consumers can deposit up to $5,000 per year and not pay income taxes on that money or any earnings made because the tax that they have to pay is deferred. Deposits made by the consumer are considered **contributions**. However, when consumers reach 59 and a half then they must pay taxes on the withdrawals they make from the IRA account because the money then becomes part of their income. If a consumer were to declare a bankruptcy or debt settlement, the money that they have within their IRA is fully protected from financial institutions trying to claim it as a way for making up for their loan losses off of the consumer. The consumer loses the protection against bankruptcy or a debt settlement if they withdraw the money from their IRA before reaching the age of retirement, which is usually 59 and a half. If consumers claim the money within the IRA account at the age of retirement and then declare a bankruptcy or debt settlement then the money is at risk of being lost. For this reason, it is recommended that consumers faithfully pay all their bills and never declare a bankruptcy or debt settlement so they do not have to face such stressful problems. Consumers must claim the funds within the IRA at the age of 70 and a half otherwise they may have to pay tax penalties. 70 and a half is considered the maximum **distribution age**. There is a maximum amount of money that a consumer can deposit within any IRA account and the financial institution at which the consumer opens the IRA will disclose such information to the consumer.

If the IRA is established at a credit union then it should have NCUA insurance where as if the IRA is established at a financial institution such as a community bank, traditional bank, investment, or brokerage firm then it should have FDIC insurance. An IRA is composed with savings and investments. Only the portion of the money within the IRA account that is not being invested and is only in savings such as in savings bonds, certificate of deposit, money market, or savings accounts has the deposit account insurance protection. Consumers should not establish an IRA at a financial institution or brokerage company that offers no insurance on it. Some of the funds within an IRA are invested into municipal bond funds, stocks, and in some cases, junk bonds, depending upon how the consumer has structured their IRA. Savings bonds are when consumers lend their money to the government of the United States by purchasing a bond. The government uses the money for their social welfare programs, economic reforms, stimulus packages, and other government related programs that require spending and pays the consumer back on their bond with interest. The savings bond fund the amount of money that the government has access to and it is considered their credit limit. The savings bond has no risk because the money cannot be lost but the consumer receives little returns. Savings bonds can be purchased in amounts ranging from $50 to $10,000. Junks bonds offer the greatest return in interest but they also offer the greatest risk at losing a great deal of the funds. Consumers should not invest too much money into junk bonds unless they absolutely have zero debt. Municipal bond funds and exchange traded funds are mutual funds, which are groups of stocks, that offer little returns in interest but little or no risk compared to junk bonds. When a consumer purchases a stock of a company then they invest their money within that company to help them grow and make profit. In buying the stock, the consumer becomes the shareholder. When the company makes profit then the price of the stock increases and they share that profit with their shareholders.

The shareholders make money along with the company. However, if the company fails then the purchase price at which the shareholder purchased the stock drops then they lose money and get no returns. A stock is broken into shares. The more shares that a shareholder purchases then the more money they are investing into the company and the more risk they are taking. Sometimes, consumers are paid money by the company per share and this money is known as the **dividends**. Consumers can let the dividends continue growing within the stock and not pay any taxes or they can collect it but they must pay taxes. If consumers decide to sell a stock then they have to pay taxes and in some cases, a fee to the stockbrokerage company or the financial institution. Consumers buy stocks, mutual funds, and savings bonds through stock brokers. Some financial institutions have a division within their company that is in charge of stock broking and so, if consumers want then they can choose their financial institution to be their stock brokerage company. Consumers should not invest too much money into stocks or save too much money into their IRA to the point that they do not have enough money to pay their bills. Default interest, high insurance, and late fees will offset any returns consumers get back through stocks or the interest they make in their IRA. The funds along with the interest earned within an IRA account are accessed when consumers want to retire but consumers still do not pay taxes on it. Unless absolutely necessary, consumers should not access the funds within their IRA account early because they will have to pay about 10% in tax penalties, which defeats the purpose of trying to save money. The only situation that may be justified to access the funds within an IRA account is if consumers are trying to save their houses from a foreclosure or their vehicles from repossession. Repossession or foreclosure is the most negative piece of financial information that can appear on a credit report and employers will frown upon seeing it. Additionally, any down payment the consumers had made on the house or car will be lost if either of them are repossessed. Consumers with damaged credit may struggle to get a new house, apartment, or car considering the rough economic conditions have caused financial institutions to become very strict in granting credit.

Roth IRA: This is a type of IRA account that, if needed, allows for consumers to take the money that they deposited into the account before the age of retirement, which is 59 and a half, without paying a 10% tax penalty like they would on a traditional IRA. They cannot take the interest made in the Roth IRA before the age of retirement otherwise they will have to pay tax penalties.

For example, if a consumer has contributed $12,000 in their Roth IRA account and it made $200 in earnings then a consumer can take any amount up to $12,000 only. When consumers reach the age of 59 and a half then they can take all the money within the Roth IRA and they must pay taxes on the earnings because there is no way to escape paying taxes. Unlike traditional IRAs, if consumers want then they can also wait, let the money with the Roth IRA make more interest (earnings), and take all the money within the Roth IRA after the age of retirement such as 60, 70, 80, or above and still pay no taxes on that money. There is no maximum distribution age. Like any type of IRA, Roth IRAs have a maximum amount of money with which they can be funded, which is usually up to $5,000 a year. If consumers take out the money at any age and declare a bankruptcy or debt settlements then they run the risk of the money being claimed by the financial institutions. Another major difference between a Roth IRA and traditional IRA is that before depositing money into a Roth IRA, consumers have to pay taxes on their income. The money that is left over after paying the taxes can be deposited (contributed) into a Roth IRA. However, with a traditional IRA, consumers pay no taxes on the money that they want to deposit because they will have to pay taxes when they withdraw the money at the age of 59 and a half. Traditional IRAs are tax-deferred accounts meaning the consumer will pay taxes on their contributions (deposits) and earnings when they claim the money. In contrast, Roth IRAs are not tax-deferred accounts on the contributions because consumers have to immediately pay taxes on the contributions that they make to the Roth IRA before it goes into the account but the earnings, which can be considered the interest that they make, consumers will have to pay taxes on the earnings when they claim all the money within the Roth IRA. Only the earnings within a Roth IRA are tax-deferred.

Money on which tax has not been paid is considered **pre-tax dollars** whereas money on which tax has been paid is considered **after-tax dollars**. It is personally recommended that consumers, without paying fees, transfer most of the funds from their CD, savings, money market, traditional IRA, and 401(k) into a Roth IRA account in the event that a consumer needs to save their house or car from a repossession or pay for college expenses then they can claim the money within the Roth IRA without paying a 10% tax penalty. Consumers should open a Roth IRA immediately when they get a job and turn the legal age at which their state jurisdiction allows for a consumer to establish an IRA. Countries outside of the United States have a different retirement plan for its consumers.

Consumers will have to pay taxes on the earnings that are made within a Roth IRA when they claim the money at retirement. However, it is possible the earnings can be tax-free meaning the consumer never has to pay taxes on it when they claim the money if they can meet one or more of these conditions and they are 59 and a half or older.

1. The consumer is purchasing their first house.
2. The Roth IRA has existed for at least five years and the consumer has not taken the money they deposited into the Roth IRA during the time frame.
3. The consumer is disabled.
4. The Roth IRA belongs to a consumer who has passed away. The beneficiary will not have to pay taxes on the earnings that were made within the Roth IRA.

After consumers have reached the limit to which their company will match their contributions into the 401k or 403b plan then after paying the bills, they should contribute the rest of their money into their Roth IRA to the maximum amount so they do not have to pay taxes on their earnings and will have plenty of money for retirement. Before opening the Roth IRA, consumers should confirm with a credible representative of the financial institution that if they meet one or more of the conditions then their earnings will be free from being taxed.

Table shows legal ages at which an individual can open an IRA depending upon their state of residency. Source of information is TD Ameritrade.

Jurisdiction Age of Majority
Alabama 19
Alaska 18
Arizona 18
Arkansas 18
California 18
Colorado 18
Connecticut 18
Delaware 18
District of Columbia 18
Florida 18
Georgia 18
Hawaii 18
Idaho 18
Illinois 18
Indiana 18
Iowa 18
Kansas 18/16 if married
Kentucky 18
Louisiana 18
Maine 18
Maryland 18
Massachusetts 18
Michigan 18
Minnesota 18
Mississippi 18
Missouri 18
Montana 18
Nebraska 19

Nevada 18
New Hampshire 18
New Jersey 18
New Mexico 18
New York 18
North Carolina 18
North Dakota 18
Ohio 18
Oklahoma 18
Oregon 18
Pennsylvania 18
Puerto Rico 21
Rhode Island 18
South Carolina 18
South Dakota 18
Tennessee 18
Texas 18
Utah 18
Vermont 18
Virgin Islands 18
Virginia 18
Washington 18
West Virginia 18
Wisconsin 18
Wyoming 18 Non-Resident Aliens 19

401(k): This is a type of retirement and investment account which consumers can get through their employer. It is not FDIC or NCUA insured because the money can lose value. As allowed by the federal tax code set up by the government, a portion of the wage amounts of the employed consumers are invested into the **401(k)** and accumulate earnings, which is considered interest (earnings). The employer automatically withdraws some of the funds, the amount is specified by the consumer, from the wages of the employees to save into the **401(k)** account and the employer may use its own money to make contributions.

For example, Melissa works for the Microsoft Corporation and contributes $300 to her 401(k) account. Microsoft is going to match her contribution and deposit an additional $300 into her 401(k) account because it is her employee benefit. Melissa now has a total of $600 in her 401(k) account. When companies use their money to match the contributions of their employees, which is called company matching, then they get tax benefits from the government and they grow as a business, because their employees become more likely to stay with the company. Not all companies, especially small businesses, do company matching because they may not be making enough profits to do so. For the reason of wanting company matching is why consumers make contributions towards their 401(k) and if they withdraw all the money before reaching 59 and a half then they supply their 401(k) with money again. Consumers can potentially not make any contributions towards their 401(k) and they are not required to supply their 401(k) with money again if they withdraw it early, which is not recommended unless they are in a financial crisis and desperately need money.

Employees do not pay taxes on the funds within the 401(k) until they begin withdrawing the funds at the age of retirement, which is 59 and a half. Like a traditional IRA, a 401(k) is a tax-deferred account and if consumers take the money early then they have to pay income taxes on it and a 10% tax penalty. Additionally, consumers should not withdraw money from their 401(k) before retirement because if they lose their job then they are expected to pay all the money back within twos months or less in most cases. If consumers do not pay the money back then they could get into trouble with the Internal Revenue Services. They may not get any tax returns or be able to receive any tax benefits.

For such reasons, if possible, it is recommended that consumers do a rollover, which means transfer without taking any money, the funds from their 401(k) account into their Roth IRA only if their job is not secure and after the matching point of the company matching. Consumers will have to pay taxes on the money within their 401(k) account in order to do the rollover but it may be worth it because if consumers need to access the money within their Roth IRA to save their house from a foreclosure or car from a repossession then they will not have to the pay the 10% tax penalty no matter what their age is where as if they access the money within a 401(k) then they have to pay income taxes and the 10% tax penalty. 401(k) plans are usually offered by for-profit companies to their employees whereas non-profit companies offer their employees 403(b) plans. A 403(b) plan is similar to a 401(k) but it may offer more tax savings considering employees of non-profit organizations usually make less money than employees of for-profit organizations. Some employers do company matching on 403(b) accounts meaning if a consumer contributes $100 to their 403(b) account then a company will match that and will contribute an additional $100 to the 403(b) account of the consumer. Finally, like any IRA, the money within a 401(k) plan is protected from the financial institutions trying to claim it because the consumer has declared a bankruptcy or debt settlement. If the consumer claims the money at any age and declares a bankruptcy or debt settlement then it can be seized by the financial institutions possibly along with other assets of the consumer.

Roth 401(k): Some employers offer this type of 401(k) plan to its employees. They pull a certain amount of the wage of the consumer, which is specified by the consumer, and invest it into the Roth 401(k) plan. There is no limit to how much contribution amount can be made to a Roth 401(k) account. Like a Roth IRA, consumers pay taxes on the money that is deposited into the account and that money grows tax-free. Unlike a traditional IRA and traditional 401(k), a Roth 401(k) is not tax-deferred. Consumers will not have to pay taxes on the earnings (interest) when they claim the money at the age of retirement, which is 59 and a half, with the maximum distribution retirement age being 70 and a half. If they claim the money within a Roth 401(k) sooner than the age of retirement then they may have to pay tax penalties and income taxes on that money. Finally, a 401(k) or 403(b) in general, may be used as collateral, which can be considered a security deposit, if a consumer needs to get a loan in order to save their house from a foreclosure or car from repossession. This is different from withdrawing the money from a 401(k), which is usually more expensive considering there are more tax fees and penalties. Although there is no 10% tax penalty for taking a loan against a 401(k), there may be loans fees associated in using a 401(k) as collateral so consumers should only consider doing it if they need to save their house or car. The employer provides the loan money. Consumers that take a loan against a 401(k) should not lose their job because then they are expected to pay it back within two months.

**Note: A Roth IRA and Roth 401(k) may not always be the best for consumers that make over $90,000 income because it is possible their taxes will then become very expensive to the point that they will have difficulties paying their other bills. A traditional IRA and traditional 401(k) is better for consumers with such high income levels because it is likely when they retire then they will have less overall taxes they will have to pay to the IRS. Before doing any rollover or making contributions to an IRA, consumers need to make sure they understand what taxes they will have to pay. They can find out such information from the financial institution with which they have the IRA. For finding out what taxes a consumer will have to pay on a 401(k), consumers can find out this information from the finance department of their employer.

Warning! Consumers should not declare a bankruptcy or debt settlement after withdrawing money from any type of 401(k) or IRA at any age even at retirement because if they do then they run the risk of all their money being seized by the financial institutions.

Number one tip when establishing an IRA, 401(k), or 403(b)

Consumers should be careful when taking the investment advice of financial advisors or some brokers; because they usually charge a fee for giving advice, purchasing, or selling stocks and investments. They may advise consumers on what investments they should make, what types of stocks they should buy, what companies in which they should invest money, and simply how they should structure their investment accounts. It is likely the financial advisor is going to advise the consumer to invest in companies that have a special business relationship with the financial institution or stock brokerage company.

For example; Edward Jones or H&R Block, for whom employs the financial advisor. That company may pay a commission to the financial institution or stock brokerage company for getting a certain number of consumers to invest in their company. Truthfully, financial advisors do not know which investments will grow or decline. In order to do so, financial advisors would need the ability to see into the future. For this reason, consumers are best off using their own judgment as to what investments should make and with which companies they should buy stocks. Consumers worked hard to earn that money and so they have the only right to determine how it should be invested. It makes no sense to waste money paying financial advisors because they are not liable for any losses that occur with the investments even if the consumer accepts their financial advice. Consumers should however listen to the financial advisors about determining how much taxes they will have to pay for investing a certain amount of money. Financial advisors or tax advisors will not charge money for disclosing such information. Consumers never want to invest too much money that will cause their taxes to become too expensive.

Finance 101: The Whiz Kid's Perfect Credit Guide

Deposit Account Basics

Rewards Checking Accounts

Consumers need to look for certain factors when trying to decide on a financial institution; with which they should open a checking account. Consumers should get a free debit card rewards program; because such helps them save money on everyday purchases. They should not get a checking account that offers no rewards on debit card purchases; or fees just for having the checking account, unless they have a negative ChexSystems profile meaning they have bounded many checks and/or have had negative deposit accounts or in some cases, they have a bad credit profile. The business purpose behind debit and credit card rewards programs are to encourage the consumers to use their debit and credit cards because financial institutions make more profit than if consumers were to use paper checks, cash, or another form of payment.

Use Debit Card as Credit

When consumers receive their new debit card, in all scenarios, consumers should always use their debit cards as a credit, which means they are doing a "signature-based transaction" and do not need to enter a personal identification number (PIN) into the personal identification number machine, when making purchases. The chances of fraud happening with them are greatly reduced because there have been cases in which criminals have placed microscopic readers on the personal identification number machines. This machines will not be detected easily and will record the numbers that all consumers enter and will electronically send that data to the criminal. The criminal will then use the personal identification numbers of the consumers and clean out all the funds within their deposit accounts possibly making it negative. The consumer will not be able to get all the funds back and it will solely be their liability. Additionally, most financial institutions require that debit cards be used as credit in order to earn the rewards on the purchases. This is because the PIN based transactions when the debit card is used as a debit costs the financial institution more money to process the transaction because they have to pull money immediately from the checking account of the consumer. A PIN based transaction is the same difference as writing a check to a merchant and the financial institution has to pull money immediately and pay fees for processing of the check payment. For the reason being fees, financial institutions do not give rewards when consumers pay with checks or PIN based debit card transactions. Signature based transactions on debit cards save them money and they pass on these savings to the consumers.

ATM Cards Do Not Save Money

Deposit accounts, other than a checking account, do not offer rewards programs; such as a savings or money market account, which is why it does not save money when consumers use their ATM cards.

Free Overdraft Protection can Save Hundreds in Fees

Consumers need to get a checking account that offers overdraft protection but there is no monthly fee for the service. Overdraft protection is when the financial institution pays for the transactions; for which the consumers do not have enough funds, but the consumer must pay back the financial institution immediately; otherwise they will report the overdraft protection money that they paid for the consumer as an unpaid and past due debt to the credit agencies and ChexSystems. A transaction can be suggested as any purchase made by a consumer. The overdraft protection money that the financial institution pays for the transactions is considered loan money or in other words, a form of unsecured credit because the financial institution has nothing they can keep or repossess from the consumer in the event they decide not to repay the overdraft protection money.

Example
Nargis has $40.00 in her Bank of the Ozarks checking account. She opted-in for overdraft protection. She gets her hair done and it costs her $80.00, which she pays using her Bank of the Ozarks debit card. Bank of the Ozarks pays the additional $40.00 so the debit card of Nargis does not decline. For this overdraft protection service, Bank of the Ozarks charges Nargis a $15.00 service fee.

$80.00 (hair styling fee) + $15.00 (overdraft protection fee) = $95.00.
Nargis had $40 in her checking account and so she would subtract $95.00 - $40.00.
Nargis owes Bank of the Ozarks $55.00 because they paid the remaining money that was needed for the hair styling fee and they charged their own service fee.
If Nargis does not pay the $55.00 to Bank of the Ozarks then they will have a complete loan loss because they cannot repossess anything from Nargis or get any money out of her. They will however ruin her credit profile and ChexSystems profile. Nargis will struggle to open a new bank account and/or loan.

When the consumer opens the checking account, the financial institution will ask the consumer if they want to "opt-out" of the overdraft protection program; which means the financial institution will never pay for the debit card transactions for which the consumer does not have sufficient funds and the consumer will not endure any fees. They will not pay for their check transactions either, but bounced checks will always result in returned check fees. The merchant to whom the check is paid will receive the returned payment and charge the consumer a returned payment fee. For this reason, unless the overdraft protection has a monthly fee, then the best financial decision for a consumer is to accept the overdraft protection. If consumers accept the overdraft protection then the financial institution may, not always, pay for the check and debit card transactions that require more money. The financial institution may or may not, depending upon their policies, disclose the overdraft protection limit, which is the maximum amount of money they will pay for transactions needing more funds. Usually all consumers have the same checking account product with the same financial institution will have the same overdraft protection limit, regardless of their individual credit profiles. The financial institution provides the overdraft protection limit as a benefit for being a customer. Overdraft protection limits are most commonly provided by credit unions and community banks. When deciding whether or not to pay a transaction, the computer system of the financial institution automatically reviews the history of the checking account when the transaction takes place. If the checking account has had a history of several bounced checks or transactions that exceeded the amount of the current balance then it is unlikely the financial institution will pay for the transaction needing extra funds. This is because the history of the checking account suggests; the consumer is financially irresponsible, spends beyond their means, and is unlikely to repay the financial institution for the loan money they use to pay for the transactions. The financial institution may even think that the consumer is doing **check kitting**.

This is when consumers purposely write checks with amounts greater than the current balance in their deposit account such as the checking, savings, or money market account. To some extent, this is considered check fraud. Financial institutions check the history of deposit accounts because they do not check credit when deciding whether or not to pay for check and debit card transactions that require more money. If consumers unknowingly write a check to a merchant with an amount that exceeds or will exceed the current balance within the checking account and the consumer has no overdraft protection attached to the account then consumers need to immediately deposit more money into the checking account for the purpose of preventing the check from being bounced. If the bank or credit union branch office is closed then consumers can login into their bank accounts online. They can then deposit money electronically by transferring money from a bank account that they have with another financial institution into the bank account that needs more money. This called a **bank-to-bank transfer**, sometimes called a **wire transfer**. Bank-to-bank transfers sometimes require that consumers pay a fee for the service but the fee is worth paying rather than paying expensive and multiple overdraft fees.

Benefits of Overdraft Protection

Overdraft protection prevents the consumer from needing to worry about their deposit accounts becoming negative and having to do bank-to-bank transfers. Some financial institutions may not offer overdraft protection and will require that the consumer apply for a line of credit or credit card; that will serve as the overdraft protection, because it will be attached to their checking account.

For example, my mother banks with Wells Fargo Bank. She has a checking, savings, and credit card account with them. The checking account is linked to the credit card and if she wrote a check with an amount that exceeded the current balance in the checking account then the rest of the funds would automatically come from the credit card. The check would not be returned to the merchant and she would not be charged a returned check fee by the financial institution or returned payment fee by the merchant. Consumers have the option of connecting their checking account to a saving account and the funds within the savings or money market account will serve as the overdraft protection or if they use the savings or money market account more often then they can potentially connect the checking account to the savings or money market account to serve as its overdraft protection. They have to notify the financial institution of how they want the overdraft protection structured and not all financial institutions have the option of giving a money market or savings account overdraft protection but in most cases, they have the option of giving the checking account overdraft protection through some means. As another example, if my mother wanted, she could connect the savings account to the checking account to serve as the overdraft protection and if there were not enough funds in the savings account then the computer system of the financial institution will pull the needed funds from the credit card. Therefore, the checking account of my mother has two overdraft protection methods, one method is the funds within the savings account and the second method is the credit card.

With overdraft protection, the consumer will not have to face the embarrassment of the debit card being declined, checks being returned, and being charged outrageous overdraft fees for each denied purchase. According to the Federal Deposit Insurance Corporation, they found that the "overdraft fees ranged from $10 to $38" with the "median fee for overdrafts [being] $27." Consumers need to be aware though that whenever a financial institution uses overdraft protection to pay for any transaction regardless of where the overdraft protection money comes from such as the savings account, credit card, or the overdraft protection limit set by the financial institution, the consumer must pay a fee every time overdraft protection is used. Some financial institutions only charge a fee once to cover multiple transactions that need extra funds within a single day whereas other financial institutions may charge a fee for each transaction requiring extra funds no matter what day the transaction occurs. In connection to the financial profile of my mother, if Wells Fargo took money from her credit card or savings account to cover a transaction that needs more money in order to not be rejected then she would be charged a $10 fee for all transactions that occur on the same day. She would not be charged a $10 fee for each transaction but if she was with another financial institution then they may charge her a fee for each transaction. If overdraft protection money is taken from the credit card, line of credit, or the overdraft protection limit, then the consumer must pay back the financial immediately or if they wait too long to repay it then they will have to pay interest on the amount of overdraft protection money that was used just as they would pay on any loan. The interest rates are usually higher than average compared to the rates of other loans because overdraft protection should only be used in the case of emergencies and not all the time. Regardless of the overdraft protection interest and fees, overdraft protection is always cheaper than paying returned check fees, returned payment fees, and overdraft fees. The goal of overdraft protection is to prevent such fees. If there is no monthly fee for the service then consumers should always have overdraft protection set up on their checking or savings account, whichever account they use the most. Consumers should <u>never</u> pay monthly fees because there are financial institutions that do not charge monthly fees so it would be wise to switch their deposit accounts to them. As evidence, my mother pays no monthly fee for the overdraft protection she has set up to her checking account using her credit card.

Get Accounts that Offer Bonuses

Consumers should consider getting into business with financial institutions that are offering free bonuses just for opening a new account; such as checking, savings, money market, or a certificate of deposit, because it does not make money to open a deposit account with a financial institution that offers no bonuses. A free bonus can include a gift such as a free bag, chair, backpack, or simply any item. Either a gift or a free bonus can be cash such as the funds that will be deposited by the financial institution into the new deposit account or the financial institution will give the consumer a gift card. Consumers should aim to open deposit accounts with the financial institutions that are offering the greatest bonuses. Financial institutions may require in order to for the consumer to receive the bonus for opening the new account, they must use their debit card for a certain number of purchases, keep their account open for a certain timeframe, or set up direct deposit, which is when the consumer asks their employer to automatically and electronically deposit their paycheck into their deposit account every time they get paid. Direct deposit is a free and safe service offered to the consumer by the employer. Funds can never get lost. Consumers should not do direct deposit if their employer charges them a fee for the service then this defeats the purpose of trying to save money. Consumers can find the most current bonuses being offered by financial institutions for opening up new deposit accounts by going to www.ibankbonus.com, www.budgetcents.net, www.depositaccounts.com/banks/promotions, and www.ibankdesign.com. Consumers can also do an internet search by typing *"bank bonus," "checking bonus,"* or *"account bonus"* on the search bar and they will see all the financial offering promotions. Some credit unions and community banks, at certain times of the year, also offer bonuses for opening up accounts but consumers would have to call them to find out. Consumers can use the mentioned website to look up bonuses being offered by financial institutions for opening up a credit card. Consumers should not apply for credit cards for which they are unlikely to get approved because then their scores will drop for no reason due to the credit checks. Consumers can sometimes tell if they will get approved or denied for a credit card based upon if the majority of consumers with their individual credit profiles were approved or denied for the particular credit card. If a consumer has a similar credit profile to a consumer that was denied then it is more likely that they will get denied for the credit card whereas if a consumer has a similar credit profile to a consumer that was approved then it is more likely that they will get approved. Consumers can see the credit profiles of consumers that applied for the same credit card they want to apply for by going to www.financeglobe.com or http://creditboards.com/forums/index.php?autocom=creditpulls and typing in the name of the credit card on the search bar. The websites may also have information regarding which credit reporting agency the credit card issuer most commonly uses for the credit check. This is useful information for a consumer because if a consumer has a low score with that consumer reporting agency then they should not apply for the credit card. Consumers want to apply for credit cards with issuers that check the credit reporting agency with whom they have the best credit profile. This will raise the chances of the consumer getting approved. However, there is no guarantee regarding the accuracy of the information on the websites because the credit card issuers may have changed their policies such as which credit reporting agency they use to do the credit check on the consumer for the certain credit card product. The Finance Globe and Credit Boards websites keep a record of most credit cards that exist within the market and average percentage of consumers that applied for the credit cards and were approved or denied. It stands to reason that if a credit card has a high percentage of consumers that were approved then the consumer is more likely to get approved for it. In contrast, if a credit card has a low percentage of consumers that were approved then it is less likely that the consumer will get approved unless the credit profile of the consumer is significantly better than the credit profiles of the consumers who had applied and were denied.

Free Online Bill Pay Saves Time and Money

Consumers should get checking accounts with free online bill pay service so they do not have to spend money unnecessarily buying checkbooks. They can use the bill pay service to conveniently and securely submit payments to their bill issuers.

No Minimum Balance Requirements

Consumers should get deposit accounts with low or no minimum balance requirements so their chances of being charged fees are low. If consumers are charged any kind of fee, they should <u>always</u> contact the financial institution and ask for a refund as a one-time courtesy. Consumers cannot give up on getting fees refunded even if they are small amounts. Consumers work extremely hard to earn every penny and if they ignore the fees then they will add up to large amounts and thus, large losses.

Insured Deposit Accounts Only

Consumers should get deposit accounts that with financial institutions are FDIC insured or with credit unions, are NCUA insured. The insurance offered by the National Credit Union Association for consumers that have deposit accounts with credit unions are sometimes called "National Credit Union Share Insurance Fund," which is abbreviated as NCUSIF. According to About.com, FDIC and NCUA insurances offer up to $250,000 of protection thanks to the the "Emergency Economic Stabilization Act of 2008," which allowed for the government to provide bailout money to the financial institutions in the United States that were failing due to the 2000s mortgage crisis. The Emergency Economic Stabilization Act increased the amount of coverage consumers would get on their deposit accounts because it is likely, a greater number of consumers would deposit more money into their deposit accounts knowing they have more coverage. As a result, the financial institutions would be able to strengthen their assets using the deposits of consumers and be able to grant loans more easily and make up for their losses. The $250,000 coverage lasts on all deposit and retirement accounts until December 31st, 2013. After this date, depending upon the decisions of the government and current economic conditions, the coverage may remain the same amount or may change to the original coverage amounts of the FDIC and NCUA insurance, which were "$100,000 per individual, and $250,000 for retirement accounts." No matter what the amounts of the coverage's are, consumers are safe getting accounts that have some kind of coverage rather than no coverage.

No Fee-Based Accounts Ever

Unless they have a bad ChexSystems or credit profile, consumers should <u>never</u> get any kind of account with monthly maintenance fees. There are free accounts available so there is no reason why a consumer would get an account with a fee just for having it.

Get Competitive Interest Rate Accounts

Consumers should get deposit accounts that offer the high interest rates and this information can usually be found on <u>www.bankrate.com</u>. However, in some cases, consumers should be more concerned about getting a bonus for opening the account than they should about getting a high interest rate. This is because the bonus will award them more money than they money they would earn through getting paid interest. In some cases, consumers that make high income, with is considered $70,000 or more, should try and get accounts with financial institutions that are offering gift cards or gifts that have a high value such as for example, a digital camera. This is because gift cards and physical gifts are not reported to the Internal Revenue Services by the financial institutions as interest that the consumer gained on the deposit account. This means consumers will not have to pay income taxes on the account bonuses. If the financial institutions offer a bonus such as for example, $100, which will be deposited into the new deposit account, then the $100 will be reported as interest to the Internal Revenue Services. The consumer will have to pay taxes on the interest.

Denial for Deposit Account- Serious Issue

If consumers are denied for a free checking, savings, money market, retirement, or just any type of deposit account by the financial institution then this should be taken seriously because it means there is a deposit account under their social security number that is negative or one of their bank accounts was levied in the past meaning the financial institution did not get repaid for their loan and they had to clean out all the funds within the bank account to make up for the loan loss. Being denied for a deposit account could also mean that the consumer has bounced too many checks, debit card transactions, or a criminal has fraudulently opened deposit accounts under the social security number of the consumer and has made them negative. For these reasons, ChexSystems has negative information regarding the consumer. The consumer needs to freeze their ChexSystems report online and put a security alert on the report at https://www.consumerdebit.com/consumerinfo/us/en/victimidtheft.htm or call 1-800-428-9623. They need to order a copy of their ChexSystems report and contact the financial institutions at which fraudulent or negative deposit accounts exist. If fraud truly happened then the consumer needs to file a police report, freeze their credit reports with Equifax, Experian, TransUnion, and Innovis, and have their social number changed with the Social Security Administration by calling 1-800-629-0271. No matter what the situation, the consumer needs to negotiate with the financial institutions about making their deposit accounts positive because negative deposit accounts are considered debts belonging to the consumer. The consumer needs to deposit funds into the negative deposit accounts but there are special arrangements that need to be made with law officials about what to do with deposit accounts that were opened and made negative as a result of fraud. The consumer should request for the financial institutions to remove the negative information that they reported to ChexSystems and the credit agencies.

Loans

Recourse and Non-Recourse Loans

Being a recourse or non-recourse loan is a characteristic that is part of all loans. The terms, "recourse loan" and "non-recourse loan" usually refer to mortgages, but as a personal analysis, they can refer to any loan. If the consumer fails to make the payments on their recourse loan debt then the financial institution is at a loss. To make up for some of the loss, the financial institutions can potentially and legally use other means to get back their loan money, from the consumer.

This is considered the financial institution doing recourse against the consumer, and the legal term for recourse is called a **deficiency judgment**. Such means can include; suing the consumer in court, garnishing their wages, seizing the funds within their deposit accounts, and putting a claim (which is usually a non-consensual lien) on their property or other items worth of high market value, such as; an automobile or boat.

A claim is not the same as a foreclosure or repossession. A claim can be thought of as a warning to the consumer that if they do not repay the loan money to the financial institution, in a timely manner, then the financial institution can do the repossession. In a sense, a claim initiates the process that repossession will take place. Once repossessed, the financial institution will then sell the item or property to make up for their loan, loss but even after doing so; they may still try to get more money out of the consumer until the financial institution feels as though they have had minimal loan loss. There is no guarantee that a bankruptcy or debt settlement will protect the consumer from the adverse actions of the financial institutions who issued recourse loans to them. For this reason, consumers are best off working out payment plans with the financial institutions rather than having to pay high attorney and court fees for a bankruptcy, debt settlement, and having to deal with any legal actions taken against the consumer by the financial institution.

Common Types of Recourse Loans

Most unsecured loans such as credit cards, student loans, personal lines of credit, and unsecured personal loans are usually, not always, considered recourse loans. These loans do not require for the consumer to provide a collateral or security deposit in order for them to obtain the loan. However, it is also possible for secured loans; which are loans that have a security deposit or collateral, such as a mortgage, car loan, boat loan, or secured credit card to be a recourse loan debt depending upon the polices of the financial institution and the terms and conditions that were indicated, on the loan contact that the consumer had signed.

Most mortgages, in Florida, are recourse mortgages; because some of the money generated, from the real estate sales and property taxes that the consumers would pay on their houses help build tourist attractions. Tourist attractions help maintain a strong economy in Florida. Additionally, many consumers purchase houses in Florida for the purpose of using them as vacation homes or renting them to other consumers so the financial institutions cannot afford consumers to one day stop paying on those mortgages and walk away from the houses. For this reason, financial institutions in Florida have to structure the mortgages as recourse loans.

Common Types of Non-Recourse Loans

In contrast, non-recourse loans are usually secured loans; but they can also be unsecured loans meaning if the consumer stops paying on their loan then the financial institution will not do anything to try and get the loan money out of the consumer.

For example, if the consumer stops paying on their credit card and the contract they agreed to with the credit card company indicated that the credit card was a non-recourse loan; then the financial institution will simply ruin their credit profile, they may sell the credit card debt to a collection agency, and do nothing more against the consumer in terms of trying to make up for the loan loss. If the credit card was a recourse loan then the financial institution would ruin the credit profile of the consumer and possibly take them to court, sue them, garnish their wages, levy their bank accounts, or put a non-consensual lien (claim) on their house. For this reason, non-recourse loan debts typically have higher interest rates than recourse loans because non-recourse loans the mean greatest risk for the financial institution and so they are going to want to make the maximum amount of profit off of the consumer. Before agreeing to get a loan of any type, consumers should always ask the financial institution if the loan is considered a recourse or non-recourse loan but consumers need to be aware that even if a loan is a non-recourse loan, there is still no telling what adverse actions the financial institution will take if the consumer does not make the payments. As a personal analysis, a non-recourse loan simply lowers the likelihood that a financial institution will take adverse actions but does not completely prevent them from doing so. Ideally, consumers should not default on any loan in any case.

Signature Loans can be Expensive

Some unsecured debts are signature loans, which are sometimes called character loans or good faith loans. This is because they are debts that only require the signature of the borrower, but no collateral or security deposit that a financial institution can repossess in the event a consumer fails to make payments. Signature loans tend to be higher in interest than credit cards and borrowers usually get them when they are in great need of money for some purpose. Not all financial institutions offer signature loans because of the weak economic times. It is unlikely consumers will pay their signature loans and it is likely that financial institutions will have a loss. Signature loans, like all loans, can negatively affect credit if left unpaid. Consumers should check with the financial institution from whom they will get the signature loan that if they will report the positive payment history to the credit agencies because such will help raise the credit scores of the consumer.

Tax Anticipation Refund Loans

A tax refund anticipation loan is dangerous! It is a secured loan in which consumer can use their expected tax refund, as a security deposit, of the loan. The can borrow up to the amount of their tax refund and in the event that they fail to pay the loan; then the security deposit is kept by the tax anticipation loan issuer. Tax anticipation loans are offered to consumers by most tax firm agencies such as H&R Block or Jackson Hewitt. Most tax firms do not check the credit profile of the consumer for the tax anticipation loan because it costs them money to do so, and they usually do not report the payment history to the credit agencies, which hurts the consumer because there is no opportunity for their credit scores to improve.

Consumers have the option of making monthly installment payments on their tax anticipation loan. Like all loans, tax anticipation loans charge fees and interest. According to the National Consumer Law Center (NCLC), the average tax anticipation loan fee in 2004 was $32 and it is likely the current average fee of most tax firm agencies are similar to that amount. Tax anticipation loans are similar to car title and payday loans because they have been criticized for charging exorbitant interest and in this sense, taking advantage of consumers with low income levels.

According to the Center for Responsible Lending, most tax anticipation loans are "offered at interest rates ranging from about 50% to over 500%" in interest alone. This is because the tax anticipation loans are short-term loans, and the goal of the tax firm agencies is to make as much profit as possible off of the consumers during the term of the loan. It is possible most or all of the tax refund of the consumer will get consumed by the interest and fees. For this reason, consumers should avoid them because they are better off using a credit card or getting another type of low interest rate loan product, preferably a secured loan, from a community bank or credit union.

Microloans

Consumers making little or no interest within their deposit accounts such as money market or savings accounts may want to consider participating in microfinance. Microfinance is when consumers use their money to offer micro loans to entrepreneurs who want to start or expand upon their businesses. The consumer becomes the micro lender. The entrepreneurs repay the micro loans to the consumers with interest. Microfinance helps the economy because consumers are making more money on their money for retirement and entrepreneurs are creating jobs with their businesses. However, consumers should not invest too much money into granting micro loans because there is a risk the entrepreneur may not repay them and the loans are not insured in any way. Money Talks News recommended www.microplace.com, a website where consumers can learn more about how to grant micro loans and the risks in doing so.

Mortgage Tip

Consumers need to make sure any extra money they pay towards their mortgage is applied to the principle balance. They do not want the extra money used to pay interest; otherwise this will defeat the purpose of trying to pay off the mortgage quickly. Before sending in the extra money, consumers can call the mortgage company and indicate they want the extra payment to be applied towards principle. The same rule applies to car loans.

Loan-To-Value Ratio Suggests Likelihood of Defaulting

When consumers apply for secured loans, such as; car loans, boat loans, house loans, or simply any kind of loan, in which collateral is needed, financial institutions determine how likely a consumer is in defaulting on their loan by calculating the loan-to-value (LTV) ratio. This ratio can be thought of as a fraction, which is the loan money being needed over the value of the item that the consumer wishes to purchase.

For example, Philip wants to purchase a house that is worth $300,000, as indicated by the house appraiser, and is currently selling for $250,000. For this reason, he applies for a $250,000 mortgage (home) loan with Wachovia Bank. As part of the application process, Wachovia Bank calculates the loan-to-value ratio as being 83% rounded. The calculation was done by dividing the $250,000 loan money being needed by the $300,000 value of the house. According to *Dummies for Mortgages by Eric Tyson and Ray Brown*, when a loan-to-value ratio exceeds 80% of the property value then the financial institution is taking on great loan risk in granting the mortgage, to the consumer.

The financial institution cannot afford to grant so much loan money, to the consumer, without having some kind of insurance or guarantee; that the consumer will fully repay the loan, because the consumer is taking on a huge liability. For this reason, the financial institution will ask the consumer to pay some down payment money on the house, before they fully grant the mortgage for the purpose of bringing down the loan-to-value ratio below 80%. The financial institutions think that when a consumer provides a down payment then the consumer is less likely to stop paying on the loan because they would lose all their down payment money. The down payment helps the financial institution feel more secure in granting the loan because if the consumer stops paying then they can partially make up for the loan loss by keeping the down payment money in addition to repossessing the collateral, which in the case of Philip is the house. Not wanting to lose the down payment is another reason why consumers should remain motivated to pay off their loans.

Financial Institutions Asked for Little or No Down Payment

When the consumers could not sell or rent their houses; they simply stopped paying on their mortgages and left their houses. Some of these consumers did not care about the damage that would occur on their credit profiles and it is likely due to the fact; they did not pay enough or any down payment money, the consumers felt as though they would be having no loss by not paying the mortgages. Consumers also stopped paying on the credit cards they were using to pay for the maintenance of the house, such as; water, electricity, and other utilities. Many financial institutions suffered great loan losses and they could not fully make up for all of them, because there was great difficulty in selling the houses on which they had foreclosed. Trying to avoid the same financial crisis, almost all financial institutions require for the consumers to make a 20-25%, before the financial institution will grant them the mortgage. If the consumer has a bad credit profile then it is likely that the financial institution will require a larger down payment than what they normally would want from the consumer. Consumers with bad credit will likely have higher closing costs, which can be considered fees simply for getting the mortgage. Closing costs are similar to loan origination fees. Consumers with bad credit and high loan-to-value ratios can expect to be approved for higher than average interest rates. Consumers with bad credit are very likely to stop paying on the mortgage. For this reason, the financial institutions want to make the maximum profit amounts off of them for the purpose of offsetting the risks.

Federal Funds Rate

The Feds funds rate is set by the Federal Reserve and influences the interest rate, on variable interest rate mortgages, such as; the adjustable rate mortgages (ARMs), as well as, the interest made by consumers on their money within money market, savings, and other interest bearing deposit accounts. The Feds fund rate is added with 3%, to determine the prime rate.

For example, if the feds fund rate is 1% then added with 3%, the prime rate for adjustable rate mortgages within the United States becomes 4%. The total interest rate of an adjustable rate mortgage is usually 1%, 2%, or 3% higher than the prime rate. When the feds fund rate increases then it helps consumers make more money within their deposit accounts and it causes some growth with the stock market and businesses. The con with an increase of the feds fund rate is that it is likely the monthly mortgage payment of consumers with an adjustable rate mortgage will also increase because the minimum payment will demand more interest from the consumer. If the consumer cannot afford to make the higher minimum monthly payment, then their credit profile will be ruined, they will struggle to get a job, and the house will get foreclosed by the financial institution if they do not eventually receive a payment from the consumer.

For this reason, it is personally recommended consumers avoid getting adjustable rate mortgages. Consumers are always better off getting a fixed rate mortgage; because they know how much they are expected to pay every month and the amount never changes due to the fact the interest rate never changes. In the beginning, the interest rate of adjustable rate mortgages may be cheaper than fixed rate mortgages but consumers need to be aware that the interest rate of an adjustable rate mortgage can increase to a very high rate after the reset period is over especially if the economy is doing poorly. Some consumers have the attitude that they will sell the house immediately after the reset period, which is the time for which an ARM mortgage has a certain interest rate, but the real estate market is unpredictable. Consumers cannot depend on selling the house so they can avoid making their mortgage payments. For this reason, consumers should be safe and refinance their adjustable rate mortgage into a fixed rate mortgage always with a credit union. Credit unions will always offer the cheapest closing costs and fees.

Prime Lending is Best

Creditors called "prime creditors", specialize in "prime lending," which means extending credit to consumers with average or excellent credit histories. They may charge annual fees, on some of their credit products, due to their aggressive rewards programs.

For example, Chase is an example of a prime creditor and their Chase Sapphire Preferred credit card has an annual fee. This is because it offers consumers two points per dollar spent on certain purchases. The consumers can redeem the points for gift cards, account credits, airline tickets, and actual merchandise. The prime creditors are offering the rewards programs to get consumers to use their credit cards more often, so they can make more profit. They do not want to lose money on the rewards programs and that is why they charge an annual fee.

In some cases, rewards programs can help consumers save money, if they pay off their balances immediately; because they are not having to pay interest. However, consumers do not save money if they are carrying balances, because then they are paying interest along with the annual fee. This defeats the purpose of the rewards programs. The prime creditor has relationships with other companies to provide the rewards programs. It is likely the prime creditor, which is considered a financial institution, shares some of their profits made on the credit cards with those companies. Gift cards, merchandise, and airline tickets usually cause the consumer to spend more money at other companies, and in this scenario both the financial institution and other companies are making profits. In a sense, the financial institution is marketing products and other companies by providing the rewards programs.

Not all prime creditors charge annual fees on their credit products. Examples of prime creditors can include Discover Card, Citibank, American Express, or Barclays. Some creditors specialize in both prime and subprime lending; meaning they offer credit products for consumers with good credit and bad credit histories. Such creditors are considered to be both a prime and subprime creditor and examples can include Bank of America, Wells Fargo, and Fifth Third Bank. Prime creditors are usually able to offer better interest rates on their loan products than subprime creditors because prime creditors primarily get into business with consumers who are unlikely to default.

Subprime Lending is failing in Economy

An increasing number of financial institutions are trying to escape the subprime credit industry; because the government has been passing laws restricting financial institutions on how much interest and fees they can charge the consumers. An increasing number of consumers are developing bad credit. Subprime creditors need to impose, the higher than average, interest and fees; because the high-risk consumers to whom they grant credit are very likely to default. Due to the fees and high interest, some consumers think of subprime creditors as being "loan sharks." If the subprime creditors do not offset the risks involved in lending to high risk consumers, then as a company they are very likely to fail due to their weak business performance. The subprime creditors will not be able to make enough profits to pay their employees, create more jobs, expand to more locations, diversify, and keep their business running. For such reasons, consumers with limited or bad credit are finding it difficult to obtain credit because financial institutions are reluctant to get into business with them due to the fear of not being able to make enough profit. This is part of the reason why many small financial institutions failed and had to be shut down.

Think 6 Times before Cosigning

A consumer is considered a "secondary or joint account holder", when they cosign for another consumer, so they can be approved for a loan or service. The consumer, for whom the joint account user is cosigning, is considered the "primary account holder." The joint account holder is equally as responsible for making payments, on the loan or service, as the primary account holder. If the loans and services are not paid in a timely manner; than the credit profiles of the both the primary and joint account holders will be damaged, and there will be nothing that either of them can do to fix it. Consumers should be careful when cosigning for others including family members. In some cases, consumers that need cosigners have bad credit otherwise they would not need a cosigner. If a consumer is irresponsible enough to ruin their credit then it is likely they will ruin the credit profiles of others. For this reason, consumers should not let others do their finances and blindly trust them. It is getting increasingly common for spouses to ruin the credit profile of their partner.

Depending upon the rules of the financial institutions and the state where the consumers reside, if the primary account holder were to pass away or was unable to make payments then the secondary account holder would be required to make payments. If consumers want to help others build credit then they can add them as an "authorized user" to their accounts. Authorized users are not liable for any of the charges that take place on the account, unless indicated otherwise, by the financial institution. Some financial institutions do report the credit history of the primary account holder to the credit reports of the authorized users but consumers need to ask because not all financial institutions do so.

Consumers should not ask other consumers, who have a bad credit history, to add them as a joint or authorized user onto their accounts. This is because, if consumers get added onto accounts that have bad payment histories, then this will ruin their credit. If joint or authorized users feel as though the primary account holder will default; then they should immediately remove themselves from the account. If a husband and wife were not on accounts of each other; and one of them passed away then it is unlikely the living spouse will have to pay the debts of the deceased spouse. However, there have been situations in which debt collectors, using public records, have found out about the spouses or family members of their deceased customers. The family members or spouse were never on the accounts of the deceased customer. The debt collectors sent notices anyway, saying they must pay for the debts. In this situation, a consumer should see an attorney or if the debts are small then they should just pay them immediately rather than paying high attorney and court fees. Consumer cannot ignore the notices sent by debt collectors because they have ways of reporting the debts to the credit agencies as negative financial information about the consumer, taking the consumer to court, garnishing their wages, or putting claims on their properties. Debt collectors will do <u>anything</u> to get their money back from whomever they can.

Advice: Consumers who cosign for others; including spouses and their children, should monitor the credit accounts to ensure they are being paid in a timely manner. Consumers with bad credit should not cosign for others, because they are doing them more harm than good. This is because the consumer, for whom they are cosigning, will likely get approved for a higher than average interest rate and a low loan amount. If the consumer is planning on paying off the balance immediately; than a high interest rate does not matter. Consumers that are secondary account holders, on deposit accounts, such as; checking, savings, money market, or certificate of deposit need to monitor them; ensuring they do not become negative. Negative deposit accounts are reported as negative financial information, to the ChexSystems profiles, of all the account holders on the deposit accounts. Negative deposit accounts are potentially also reported as negative financial information to the credit agencies if the consumers do not make their deposit accounts positive in a timely manner.

Credit Reports do not Show Interest Rates of Loans

As of now, no credit report shows the interest rates consumers are paying on their loans; because the credit agencies do not collect such information. It may be a business weakness of financial institutions not to be able to see the interest rates consumers are paying when they review credit reports. This is because it is likely consumers who have high balances on credit accounts, with high interest rates, are at high risk of giving up on paying the debts. They will default, which results in a loss for the financial institution and increased costs on all consumers, such as; on loans and less interest paid on their deposit accounts. There have been cases in which interest rates on credit accounts were increased to the penalty rates due to too many returned payments. Credit reports do not reflect any information regarding the returned payments on credit accounts but if financial institutions can see the interest rates on credit accounts being 29% or more, which usually means the credit account is being charged a penalty interest rate, and then they may be able to determine that the consumer did not handle the credit account responsibly. The financial institution will be reluctant, as they should be, in extending credit to the consumer.

Interest Rates Appearing on Credit Reports would Protect Businesses

Seeing the interest rates that consumers are paying on credit accounts may help financial institutions better market their credit products, with lower interest rates, than what the consumers are currently paying. Consumers will be more likely to sign up for the new credit products so they can save money on interest. If financial institution can see the interest rates consumers are paying on their accounts; then they can better tell how successfully consumers are paying down their balances every month. It stands to reason that it is going to be more difficult for consumers to pay down the balances, of credit accounts, that have high interest rates. It is not a case in which a consumer is merely using their accounts aggressively until they are maxed out and that is when the consumer will stop paying. However, credit accounts that have low interest rates, should be easier for consumers to pay down. It should send a red flag to the financial institution that a balance on a low interest rate credit card is not dropping as fast as it should in relation to the income level of the consumer because low interest rates accounts such as 13% or below have lower minimum payments than high interest rate accounts such as 14% or above. The consumer may have the bad intention of not paying off the credit account. Finally, if the financial institutions can see the interest rates of accounts on which the consumer made late payments then they should deny the consumer a credit product that will have the same or similar interest rate because it is likely the consumer will default on it.

Have All Types of Credit

Although if consumers have had loans, besides credit cards, then they technically have an established credit history; it is considered weak and underdeveloped because financial institutions want to see how consumers handle different types of loans and credit for the purpose of best assessing their financial abilities. If consumers only have one type of loan showing on their credit report, then it may suggest to the financial institution that the consumer is financially weak and they could not handle other types of loans.

For example, if Manu only has a student loan showing, on his credit report, and he applies for a car loan then it is likely Manu will get approved for a high interest rate or he may get denied. It raises the question to the car loan lender why Manu never tried getting a credit card, home loan, or other type of loan. It is likely, due to the fact Manu has had only one loan and therefore, one credit type, which is an unsecured student loan; his credit scores are not as high as they could be with the credit agencies. This is because the credit scoring models calculate the scores taking into consideration that fifteen percent is influenced by the types of credit and loans that are being used by the consumer.

For this reason, consumers that have a home loan or car loan or both tend to have better credit profiles than consumers who have no home loan or car provided they have a perfect payment history established on the loans. Manu should try getting a credit card to improve his credit scores so he has a variety of loan and credit types showing on his reports. With an exception to credit cards, consumers should be careful when getting secured or unsecured personal loans because some auto, signature, student, and just any kind of loan has fees just for getting the loan. Such fees are called loan origination fees and most credit cards do not have these fees unless the consumer gets a credit card from a subprime creditor, because they have bad credit. Mortgages have loan origination fees, which are called closing costs.

Life Insurance Loan

Companies try to get consumers to purchase whole, universal, and variable life insurance policies; convincing them that the policy has a quick-cash loan option, meaning the consumer can get loan money using their policy. The total amount of payments that the consumer has made towards the life insurance policy, causes it to have a cash value. Consumers cannot take more loan money than their cash value and there is no credit check to get loan money. Consumers do not have to repay the loan money unless they choose to do so because this means their beneficiaries that are protected with the policy will get less life insurance money. However, the amount of loan money that the consumer has taken from the life insurance policy will get charged interest from about 5% to 9% and like a credit card balance, the interest will cause the life insurance loan balance to compound with interest. If consumers do not pay the interest then they will have to pay income taxes to the IRS on the interest that the loan accumulated as well as the amount of loan money they borrowed. The amount of money consumers pay towards their life insurance policy is not taxable but when they take it as a loan then it is taxable. For this reason, consumers should never take a loan using their life insurance policy and they should never get universal, whole, or variable life insurance policies. If consumers do get a life insurance policy loan then they should repay it immediately with whatever interest was charged on the balance so they can avoid paying taxes.

Criteria for Loan Approvals

Upon reviewing applications for credit, financial institutions consider a variety of factors that influence their level of confidence in the ability of the consumer to repay the loans and/or credit cards.

Income Score

The credit agency, Experian, created a business management product called the "Income Insight W2," which is an income score that can determine the estimated annual income of a consumer. An income score can be used, by financial institutions, to verify the authenticity of the income that the consumer is stating on the application. Unfortunately, some consumers purposely state incomes much higher than their actual income with the intention of getting a higher amount of credit than what they make for the purpose of being able to purchase anything. Such consumers are unlikely to pay back their loans and it raises concern to financial institutions as to why a consumer wants so much credit. For this reason, it is likely a financial institution will deny credit to a consumer; who overstates their income. The Income Insight W2 does an estimated income amount calculation, by analyzing the information on the credit reports, of consumers. It stands to reason, that if consumers are successfully paying their loans then they are likely making a certain income. Using the credit reports, the Income Insight W2, will look at the minimum payments required by the loans of the consumer, which are usually 3-4% of the primary balances, and then it will look at the balance changes that have occurred every month on the loans. The balance changes, such as if the balances were significantly going up or down and the "last payment amount," as reflected on the credit reports, may help determine if a consumer is paying above the minimum payment requirements. If the consumer is paying above the minimum payment requirements significantly every month on all or most of their loans; then it is likely the Income Insight W2 will view their stated income on the application as being more authentic. If the consumer is only making the minimum payments on the loans or has some late payments; then it is likely the Income Insight W2 will think of the stated income on the credit application as being inauthentic. The business will be more likely to ask the consumer for a copy of their pay stub or W-2 for the purpose of verifying the income. The Income Insight W2 only focuses on the wages of the consumer being received from their employer. Consumers should always state their truthful income on credit applications.

Household Review

Some financial institutions conduct a household review on consumers; that apply for credit or already have credit with them. A household review is when the financial institution reviews the financial information of all consumers living within the same household or property using the address that the consumer states on the application or has on the credit account. They may use the last name of the consumer to associate them with other consumers, in the household, that have the same last name or they will do a background check that will show their relationships to other consumers. They may already have financial data, on the consumers, because they have had accounts with the financial institution or the credit agencies had shared information about them; with the financial institution when the financial institution was trying to market its credit card and loan products to consumers of certain credit types. If a consumer lives in a household that has a majority of other consumers who have bad credit; then it is possible the financial institution may use such information against the consumer and depending upon their overall credit profile, may extend a low credit limit or high interest rate because they think the consumer has a potential for defaulting. The reason for this is because in the eyes of the financial institutions; it is common for consumers living within the same household to share their financial information with each other and make financial decisions; such as whether or not to pay bills. There have been situations in which one spouse may convince the other to not pay a bill, because they think it is not important to do so. This is why it is important to understand; why bills should be paid. It is possible parents may negatively influence their children by not paying the bills. Children may start thinking it is okay to not pay the bills, due to the conditioning; they have had in their environment. It is also possible teenagers may be negatively influencing each other expressing that it is okay to use credit and never pay the bills. Part of the purpose of doing a household review is because financial institutions do not want the consumer; whom they grant credit to lend their credit card to consumers that have bad credit because there is always a potential that a consumer can do so. The financial institution does not want the consumer, with bad credit, to have access to any credit until they start paying their bills. Usually, consumers that come from households which have a majority of consumers with good credit; are less likely to default in the eyes of the financial institutions; this is because it is likely all the consumers living within that household understand the significance of paying the bills and therefore, have healthy financial behaviors.

As an example, if two consumers are living in the same household; both of them have credit cards with Household Bank and one of them declares a bankruptcy. It is possible Household Bank may conduct a household review upon receiving the notification from the court or consumer regarding the bankruptcy. Specifically, they would do an account review on the consumer who did not declare the bankruptcy; for the purpose of evaluating how likely that consumer is to default on their credit account. Financial institutions assume if the majority of consumers living within a household are developing bad credit then it is likely their overall financial conditions are poor and too much spending is being done. For this reason, it is likely the consumer, who did not declare the bankruptcy, has more expenses to pay since the consumer who did declare a bankruptcy has little or no money or assets. It is assumed; if the consumer did have enough money, assets, or had a stable job then they would have had no reason to declare a bankruptcy unless they had low character and wanted to escape paying the bills. However, it is also possible the consumer who declared the bankruptcy has little or no money or assets because the creditors seized all of them during the processing of the bankruptcy.

Delinquency Ratio

A crucial factor all financial institutions focus on when reviewing credit reports, for the purpose of approving the consumer for all new loans or services is the delinquency ratio. This ratio is considered the number of past-due (delinquent) debts over the total amount of debts that are owed by the consumer. For the purpose of maintaining the delinquency ratio at zero percent, consumers never want to be late on any type of bill. The delinquency ratio is the heart of any credit profile that tells the company and employers whether or not the consumer is faithful in paying their bills. Companies that specialize in subprime lending; meaning they cater to consumers with bad credit profiles expect to see high delinquency ratios. In contrast, companies that specialize in prime lending mean they cater to consumers with average to excellent credit profiles expect to see low or zero percent delinquency ratios.

Delinquency ratio calculation example

Citibank credit card
Balance: $350.40
Paying on time

First Premier Bank credit card
Balance: $260.50
30 days late

Fairwinds Credit Union auto loan
Balance: $9,493.24
60 days late

BB&T home equity loan
Balance: $4,403.60
Paying on time

Delinquent debts: Fairwinds Credit Union auto loan and First Premier Bank credit card
$9,493.24 + $260.50 = $9,753.74
Current debts (debt on which the consumer has not been late): BB&T home equity loan and Citibank credit card
$4,403.60 + $350.40 = $4,754.00

Total debts amount: $14,507.74
$4,754.00 (current debts) + $9,753.74 (delinquent debts) = $14,507.74

Delinquency ratio = $9,753.74/$14,507.74 = 67% (rounded).
67% is considered a high delinquency ratio because it means more than half of the debts belonging to the consumer were or are currently late. A consumer will this delinquency ratio is very likely to be denied for credit or will be granted credit with a low loan amount and a higher than average interest rate and/or fees. This is because a high delinquency ratio means the consumer will not successfully repay all their debts. Such a consumer is likely to declare a bankruptcy or debt settlement and this means that the financial institution will have a loan loss.

To get a more accurate picture of the credit profile of a consumer, some financial institutions calculate a specialized secured debts delinquency ratio and an unsecured debts delinquency ratio, which are two different ratios. The secured debts delinquency ratio focuses on the amount of past due secured debts, which are debts that have a security deposit or collateral that the financial institution can seize in the event that the consumer fails to make payments. The secured debts delinquency ratio divides the amount of past due secured debts over the total amount of debts belonging to the consumer.

An auto loan is considered a secured debt because it has collateral which is the car. The car can be repossessed by Fairwinds Credit Union in the event that the consumer stops making payments on the auto loan. Similarly, the home equity loan is considered a secured debt because it has collateral which is the house. The house can be repossessed in the event that the consumer stops making payments on the home equity loan.

BB&T home equity loan
Balance: $4,403.60
Paying on time

Fairwinds Credit Union auto loan
Balance: $9,493.24
60 days late

Secured debts delinquency ratio is $9,493.24 (delinquent auto loan)/$14,507.74 (total debts) = 65% (rounded).

Financial may also calculate a secured debts delinquency ratio focusing only on the amount of past due secured debts over the total amount of secured debts.

$4,403.60 (BB&T home equity loan) + $9,493.24 (Fairwinds Credit Union credit card) = $13,896.84 (total amount of secured debts).

$9,493.24 (delinquent auto loan)/$13,896.84 = 68% (rounded). 65% and 68% are both high percentages of secured debt that is or was delinquent at some point in time and a consumer with such a financial profile is likely to get denied credit or be approved with a higher than average interest rate and/or fees because they cannot responsibly handle their secured loans. A secured loans delinquency ratio is calculated most often by auto loan issuers and car dealerships because some car dealerships have their own financing options for consumers.

The unsecured debts delinquency ratio divides the amount of past due unsecured debts over the total amount of debts belonging to the consumer. With an exception to secured credit cards (credit cards that require for the consumer to provide a security deposit), unsecured credit cards are unsecured debts because the financial institution has nothing they can repossess in the event that the consumer stops making the payments.

**Note: Consumers should never think simply because the credit card providers cannot repossess anything then the consumers should not pay them. The credit card companies have the power to take drastic actions against the consumer such as sue them in court, put a non-consensual lien on their house, levy their bank accounts, or anything if the consumer stops paying them. It is better to pay the credit cards than it is to take a risk and potentially get into trouble. Employers do not like seeing any type of unpaid debt on credit reports.

Citibank credit card
Balance: $350.40
Paying on time

First Premier Bank credit card
Balance: $260.50
30 days late

Unsecured debts delinquency ratio is $260.50 (delinquent credit card)/$14,507.74 (total debts) = 2% (rounded).
Financial may also calculate a specialized unsecured debts delinquency ratio focusing only on the amount of past due unsecured debts over the total amount of unsecured debts for the purpose of better understanding the credit profile of a consumer.
$350.40 (Citibank credit card) + $260.50 (First Premier Bank credit card) = $610.90, which is the total amount of unsecured debt.
$260.50 (delinquent credit card)/$610.90 (total unsecured debt amount) = 43% (rounded).

Overall, the financial institution is going to think the consumer is better at handling credit cards than they are at handling secured loans because the delinquency ratios with the secured loans are higher than the delinquency ratios with the credit cards. This may suggest that the consumer struggles to make payments on the secured loans for the possible reason that the secured loans have higher minimum payment requirements than credit cards due to the fact that the secured loans have higher balances. All financial institutions have their set lending guidelines as to what unsecured and secured delinquency ratios with which they feel comfortable in order for them to grant loans to consumers. Ideally, consumers want to have zero percent delinquency ratios by never defaulting on any of their loans or bills.

Debt-to-Credit Ratio

Many credit cards do not lower credit scores, but actually raise them. Having too many open or closed credit cards, with balances, hurt credit even if the balances are not past due. The balance is the amount of money a consumer must pay back, to the financial institution. It helps credit when a consumer has many open credit cards, does not carry balances on all of them, and is using a small portion of all the available credit by using only one or two credit cards daily and paying them off immediately. Available credit is the amount of loan money a consumer has available to spend because it has not been used. A high amount of available credit causes the debt-to-credit limit ratio to remain low, which helps raise the credit scores. This is the ratio that is created when the amount of total debt owed is divided by the amount of total available credit on all the credit cards. The debt-to-credit limit ratio is recorded by the credit bureaus and helps potential creditors understand the credit utilization level of the consumer. High credit utilization levels often lower credit scores.

Example of a consumer with a healthy debt-to-credit limit ratio: Josh.

Chase credit card
Credit limit: $10,000
Balance: $0

HSBC credit card
Credit limit: $5,000
Balance: $0

Barclay's credit card
Credit limit: $2,000
Balance: $0

Discover credit card
Credit limit: $6,000
Balance: $1,254.49

Josh, with his financial scenario, is likely to be considered low risk in defaulting. Josh is not using the full $23,000 credit and this suggests Josh is financially strong. The creditor is more likely to approve Josh and extend credit.

Credit limits: $10,000 + $5,000 + $2,000 + $6,000 = $23,000

Total available credit: $23,000

Balance (total debts that are not past due): $1,254.49

Debt-to-credit limit ratio: $1,254.49/$23,000

Credit utilization level = 5.5% (rounded)

Most financial institutions do not want to see a debt-to-credit limit ratio higher than thirty percent. This is because the financial institutions are reluctant to extend credit to consumers with high utilization levels. This suggests the consumers are heavily using all their credit cards, spending beyond their means, and the balances are close to the credit limits or have gone over the limit. In the eyes of the financial institutions, the consumers are irresponsible and are very prone to get into high levels of debt; that they will not be able to pay back. As a result, the consumers will declare a bankruptcy or debt settlement. The creditors will have a financial loss. The only situation, in which a consumer may have too much available credit, is when the amount of available credit exceeds their annual income. Financial institutions try to make sure they do not extend more credit than income. Part of the reason why financial institutions had major losses, which contributed to the recession, was because they had extended more credit than what the income of a consumer could support. Some consumers had no income but still had access to credit. This is because not all financial institutions were verifying the incomes of consumers before they were granting loans such as mortgages, credit cards, and auto loans.

Closure of Credit Cards = Not Wise

For the purpose of maintaining a low debt-to-credit limit ratio, do not close credit cards unless they have expensive annual fees that cannot be removed. Call the number on the back of the credit card; and ask customer service if the annual fee can be removed without closing the account. If this does not work then ask customer service if the credit card program can be converted into a credit card program that has no annual fee.

For example, the Delta Sky Miles credit card program issued by American Express has an annual fee. If a consumer wanted to get rid of their annual fee then they can ask American Express to switch their Delta Sky Miles credit card program to a Sky Blue or Blue Cash credit card program, which has no annual fee but less rewards.

Usually, switching programs requires no credit check but ask customer service if a check will be done and if they say yes then cancel the request because the credit check lowers the credit score. If customer service indicates that the annual fee cannot be removed from the credit card; then contact the corporate office of the bank or their credit department through mail or phone using the contact information that has been provided at the back of this book. If the contact information is not available for a certain financial institution then ask customer service for a fax number and put the attention to the executive department of the bank on the letter.

Do not switch the credit card program, if enough rewards have been established for a certain item; such as a free flight ticket, gift card, or account credit. Redeem the reward first and then do the program switch. There is no reason to pay an annual fee when there are credit cards that offer free rewards programs. The annual fee defeats the purpose of trying to save money through the rewards programs. Besides having an annual fee that cannot be removed, another reason why a consumer may have to close a credit card is when they have a joint credit card with a spouse or family member with whom they do not have the best relationship. This is because consumers are liable for any additional charges that are made by the joint user. Any current balances on the joint credit cards, both the primary consumer and joint consumer are responsible for paying those balances otherwise it will negatively affect their credit profiles. If possible, consumers should remove their names from all joint credit cards and ask the credit card companies if they are still liable for the balances. In most cases, the consumers will still be liable, but they will be protected in the event the joint user tries to reopen the credit accounts and make charges. Consumers should speak to an attorney, if their joint users are trying to somehow make them liable for additional charges; even though the credit cards have been closed. For the same reason, consumers should close joint deposit accounts such as joint checking accounts, because the joint consumer can make them negative. Closing a deposit account of any type has no impact on the credit scores. The last reason in which consumers need to close their credit cards is when their financial institution tells them they are worried that the consumer will plunge into too much debt. Not all, but some financial institutions think that consumers, usually the ones with a bad credit history, that have several credit cards; are prone to use them excessively and not be able to repay the debts. Financial institutions usually may tell high risk consumers to close credit cards when they are trying to get a home loan, because they are worried the consumers will use the credit cards to pay on the mortgage and other household expenses. In this sense, the consumers are not paying on their mortgages; but only building more debt that they are not planning on paying, but still get to keep their house for the months they make timely payments. If a financial institution requests for a consumer to close some of their credit cards; they can consider asking their credit card issuers to reduce their credit limits. This will have less negative impact on the credit profile of a consumer, than if they were to close their credit card. Consumers with good credit do not have to worry about being told to close their credit cards when they attempt to get home loans. It is unlikely the financial institution will worry about them using their credit cards aggressively, because they have proven themselves to always pay their bills. In a rare case in which a consumer must close a credit card, consumers should close the credit card that has the lowest credit limit and lowest time of history established compared to the other credit accounts. There may still be negative impact to the credit scores but they will not be as severe.

Closing a credit card can sometimes send the message that the consumer cannot handle the financial responsibility. Financial institutions will think that financial hardships caused the consumer to close their credit card because usually, that is the most common reason why consumers close credit cards. If consumers close a credit card due to their fear of getting into debt, this still is considered a financial weakness of the consumer in the eyes of the financial institution. When consumers apply for loans and financial institutions see short account history established on accounts then they could potentially deny the consumer for new credit. Another possibility is that the financial institution will approve the consumer but with a higher than average interest rate because short account history may suggest the consumer is likely to default. For this reason, they are going to want to make as much profit as possible off of the consumer for the time they are making timely payments. Closing a credit card causes the credit scores to drop, because the amount of total available credit has been reduced and mathematically, the consumer is using more of the credit that is available to them. Up to ten years of being a closed account, the credit card drops off the credit reports and it seems as though the consumer never had the account. The payment history of the consumer has disappeared and this has defeated the purpose of making timely payments. The closure of a credit account lowers the average length of history the consumer has established on their credit. Financial institutions want to see many years of history established on credit accounts such as fifteen or more years so they can better understand how a consumer handles their bills.

This is how the average length of history established on credit accounts is calculated
Barclays Bank MasterCard
Length of time the account was/is open: Five years and zero months (5.0)

Wachovia Bank Visa card
Length of time the account was/is open: One year and six months (1.6)

Commerce Bank MasterCard
Length of time the account was/is open: Five years and two months (5.2)

Dillard's card
Length of time the account was/is open: Two months (0.2)

Average length of history established on revolving credit accounts: 5 + 1.6 + 5.2 + 0.2 = 12 months, this is considered one year. One year is considered a short length of history established on credit accounts and it is likely a consumer with such a financial scenario will have low credit scores. The consumer may be looked upon by the financial institution with some risk in defaulting on their credit account because they have not fully proven themselves as to how successfully they handle all their bills for a long time period. For this reason, the financial institution is likely to deny the consumer or approve them with a low credit limit or loan amount and a higher than average interest rate.

Length of Credit History

Long history increases the credit scores too. Short history established on credit accounts can cause a consumer to be denied for credit in the future because they are considered financially weak and their credit scores are usually low. Consumers should be monitoring all their credit accounts making sure they are not being used fraudulently. Due to the fact closing a credit card, lowers the credit scores, consumers that are worried about fraud happening should be careful of how many credit cards they get throughout their lifetime. It is likely if a consumer has no delinquencies or high debts but many credit cards then they are unlikely to be denied for new credit. Depending upon the amount of available credit they currently have; they may be extended new credit cards with low credit limits but this does not affect their credit negatively. The credit scores increase due to the fact they have access to more available credit due to the opening of new credit accounts. The overall utilization level of credit drops which shows the consumer is financially strong because they are using a small portion of all the available credit.

Credit cards that are not being used regularly by their account owners are causing losses for the financial institutions. It costs them money to manage the accounts, check credit reports, and they need for them to be used so they can continue providing free customer service departments to help the account owners. To avoid the creditor from closing the credit card for inactivity, make a small purchase every six to seven months on all the credit cards and then pay it off the very same day it is used. This prevents the account from becoming delinquent. If an account is closed, always ask that it be reopened without a credit check so the history helps the credit scores. When the creditor closes the account, it is considered negative because the credit reports will say "closed by credit grantor," which may send the message that the consumer did not handle the account responsibly. Any closed account should always say "closed by consumer", on all credit reports belonging to the consumer. Finally, if consumers do not have access to any income; they should <u>not</u> use their credit cards but keep them open so their credits scores remain high and the credit cards continue building history. Even if a loan such, as a credit card, is not being used, it is still building positive history every month for the time it is open. This is because in the eyes of the financial institutions, they appreciate the fact the consumer is not using the credit card rather than using it and letting it become delinquent.

Example showing how the closure of a credit card negatively affects a consumer: Kirstin.

Closed Chase credit card
Credit limit: $0
Balance: $0

Closed HSBC credit card
Credit limit: $0
Balance: $0

Closed Barclays credit card
Credit limit: $0
Balance: $0

Open Discover credit card
Credit limit: $6,000
Balance: $1,254.49

Kirstin with her financial scenario is likely to be looked upon with some risk in defaulting. This is because Kirstin is using a large amount of their total available credit and the financial institution may think Kirstin is financially weak, which is why she closed some of the credit cards.

Credit limits: $0 + $0 + $0 + $6,000 = $6,000

Total available credit: $6,000

Balance (total debts that are not past due): $1,254.49

Debt-to-credit limit ratio: $1,254.49/$6,000

Credit utilization level = 21% (rounded)

Debt-to-Income Ratio

Carrying a balance on a credit card hurts credit, because thirty percent of the FICO credit scores take balances owed on accounts into the scoring calculation. Carrying a balance causes the debt-to-income and debt-to-credit limit ratios to be higher especially considering the balance is growing, due to the accumulation of interest. A debt-to-income ratio is when the unsecured debts are divided by the annual income of the consumer. It is not calculated by the credit bureaus, but by the financial institutions. Income is any money the consumer is using such as from their employment, child support, or savings to pay their debts and the annual income amount is asked, on the credit application. The financial institutions do not want the consumers to have access to more credit than they do income. Unsecured debts are caused by unsecured loans. They are debts that have no security deposits or collateral.

Examples of unsecured debts can include a credit card, unsecured student loan, or any loan or service that if the consumer does not pay it then the financial institution cannot repossess anything. For example, if a consumer spends five thousand dollars on their credit card and does not pay it then there is nothing the financial institution can take back from the consumer as a consequence for not paying the credit card bill. Thus, the financial institution has a complete financial loss.

In contrast, secured debts, sometimes called collateralized loans or collateralized debts, are debts that are accumulated only from secured loans. They are debts that do have security deposits, sometimes called collateral, such as a mortgage (house loan), auto loan (car loan), secured credit card, or any loan or service that if the consumer does not pay it then as a consequence, the financial institution has the power to repossess money or property.

For example, if a consumer stops paying on their mortgage then the financial institution can repossess the house as a consequence for not paying the mortgage bill. Thus, the financial institution has a partial loss because they will not be able to make as much profit as they would have if the consumer continued making payments on their mortgage. Some financial institutions may include the secured debts along with the unsecured debts when calculating the debt-to income ratio. This ratio is used to help financial institutions understand how much of the income is being used to pay debt and if a consumer will be able to handle new debts if a new loan is granted. According to www.Bankrate.com, most financial institutions do not want to see the debt-to-income ratio higher than thirty-five percent; otherwise it may indicate that the consumer is using credit excessively and eventually, the consumer will have more debt than income. If this happens then the consumer will be very likely to declare a bankruptcy or debt settlement and the financial institution will have a loss.

Example of a consumer with a healthy debt-to-income ratio: Jillian

Chase credit card
Credit limit: $10,000
Balance: $103.04

HSBC credit card
Credit limit: $5,000
Balance: $0

Barclay's credit card
Credit limit: $2,000
Balance: $23.69

Discover credit card
Credit limit: $6,000
Balance: $1,000

Jillian, with her financial scenario, is likely to be looked upon with low risk in defaulting provided none of the accounts, become delinquent and the balances are not being carried every month. This is because the consumer is not spending beyond what their income can support. The consumer is likely to be approved for new loans and receive low interest rates.

Unsecured debt balances that are not past due: $103.04 + $0 + $23.69 + $1,000 = $1,126.73

Annual income: $63,500

Debt-to-income ratio: $1,126.73/$63,500

Proportion of income paying debt = 2% (rounded)

Example of a consumer with an unhealthy debt-to-income ratio

Chase credit card
Credit limit: $10,000
Balance: $9,800

HSBC credit card
Credit limit: $5,000
Balance: $4,501

Barclay's credit card
Credit limit: $2,000
Balance: $1,235

Discover credit card
Credit limit: $6,000
Balance: $4,695

A consumer with this financial scenario is likely to be looked upon with high risk in defaulting. The credit cards are being used aggressively and are close to their credit limits. This means the consumer is using a large portion of their available credit and is spending beyond what their income can support. The consumer is unlikely to be approved for new loans or loans with decent interest rates and fees.

Unsecured debt balances: $9,800.00 + $4,501.00 + $1,235.00 + $4,695.00 = $20,231.00

Annual income: $63,500

Debt-to-income ratio: $20,231/$63,500

Proportion of income paying debt = 32% (rounded)

If the consumer has a poor payment history, on the accounts showing on their credit reports, then the financial institution may give less value to the debt-to-income ratio. This is because the consumer is unlikely to pay their new loan, no matter how much income they make.

For example, it is possible for a consumer to make $100,000 annual income, have $60,000 credit card debt, and have a very poor credit history. This consumer will be looked upon with high risk and is unlikely to be approved for a new loan or a loan with a decent interest rate.

Carrying Balances is a BAD Habit and Hurts Credit

Any balances being carried sometimes sends the message to the creditor; that the consumer is spending beyond their means and has a high likelihood of defaulting. Do not carry balances and pay the balances the same day that the credit cards are used, to avoid being late or pay them at the end of the month. Consumers should always pay earlier than the due date for the purpose of demonstrating financial strengths. The financial institution is more likely to grant a credit limit increase or interest rate reduction for rewarding such positive financial behavior. The credit limit increase improves the credit scores of the consumer because the debt-to-credit limit ratio has gone down. The amount of available credit has been increased and this shows financial institutions trust the consumer with more credit, which is spending power. It is a positive sign because it means the financial institution trusts the consumer with more loan money. However, the consumer should not use all the new credit because this action will lower the credit scores. The credit utilization level will increase from the extra spending and this is a negative sign.

Credit Denials

Do Not Just Accept Denial

Financial institutions can deny consumers credit for many reasons. Some reasons are minor and may be challenged by the consumer. They may ask for a **reconsideration** hoping that the denied application will be approved. In contrast, some reasons are major and there is very little that the consumer can do, because these reasons suggest that the consumer cheated the financial institution at some point in time and for this reason, are considered financially weak. Usually, any reason for credit denial that indicates that the consumer was past due on a credit account is a major reason.

The **credit analysts** and **officers** of the financial institutions are who review, decline, or approve the credit applications. They are subjective because they all have their own perspectives, as to what denial reasons they consider minor or major. The reasons for denials have numerical codes. These codes can be used by the consumer to determine how they can improve the reason for which they were denied for credit or understand the denial reason more in-depth. The codes usually appear in the computer systems of the financial institutions when they are processing credit applications. Financial institutions will also receive the reasons, if any, why they should approve a credit application. Consumers do not usually receive these reasons unless they ask the credit analyst.

Look for Letter of Reason for Denial

When consumers are denied credit, they should always receive a notification from the financial institution with the reasons for the denial. If they do not, consumers should always find out the reasons why they were denied. By not doing so, consumers are not using their rights and the credit checks that were done on them are going to waste. Hard inquiry credit checks always lower the credit scores. For this reason, consumers need to be ambitious in always getting approvals of their credit applications. The reasons below are just the reasons why financial institutions can potentially deny credit to consumers, but they are also factors that lower the credit scores. For this reason, when consumers check their credit scores then they may see some of the reasons listed below; unless they have solid and excellent credit.

Innovis is the fourth credit agency and they do not use a numerical coding system for their denial reasons, unlike the other three credit bureaus. Not all three credit bureaus have the same denial reasons because they all have different management systems. For this reason, some of reasons are listed as "N/A" underneath some of the bureaus on the list below. Finally, some of the reasons are similar but are worded differently and so consumers should follow the same advice for one reason as they would for another reason. The advice may be similar. Overall, if a consumer can maintain good credit then they will not have to worry about being denied credit, but if they are denied then they can fix the reason by continuing to maintain good credit. Good credit continues to strengthen as time passes and no delinquencies occur.

Note: The numerical code for the denial reason does not indicate its level of severity.

	Equifax	TransUnion	Experian
Amount owed is too high	1	1	1
Level of delinquency on account	2	2	2
Too few bank revolving accounts	3	N/A	3
Too many bank/national revolving accounts	4	N/A	4
Too many accounts with balances	5	5	5
Too many consumer finance company records	6	6	6
Account payment is too new to rate	7	7	7
Too many recent inquiries in the last 12 months	8	8	8
Too many accounts recently opened	9	9	9
Proportion of balances to credit limits is too high on accounts	10	10	10
Amount owed on revolving accounts is too high	11	11	11
Lengths of time revolving accounts have been established	12	12	12
Time since delinquency is too recent or unknown	13	13	13
Lengths of time accounts have been established	14	14	14
Lack of recent bank revolving information	15	15	15
Lack of recent revolving account information	16	16	16
No recent non-mortgage balance information	17	17	17
Number of accounts with delinquency	18	18	18
Date of last inquiry too recent	N/A	19	N/A
Too few accounts currently paid as agreed	19	27	19
Length of time since derogatory public record or collection is too short	20	20	20
Amount past due on accounts	21	21	21
Serious delinquency, derogatory public record, or collection filed	22	22	22
Number of bank or national revolving account with balances	23	N/A	23
No recent revolving balances	24	24	24
Number of revolving accounts	26	N/A	26
Number of established accounts	28	28	28
No recent bankcard balances	N/A	29	29
Time since most recent account opening too short	30	30	30
Too few account with recent payment information	31	N/A	31
Lack of recent installment credit loan information	32	4	32
Proportion of loan balances to loan amounts too high	33	3	33
Amount owed on delinquent accounts	34	31	34
Serious delinquency, public record, collection filed	38	38	38
Serious delinquency	39	39	39
Derogatory public record or collection filed	40	40	40

1. **Amount owed on accounts is too high.**
Consumers should not carry balances higher than 30% of the credit limits or loan amounts. They should pay them off immediately. High amounts owed raise the chances that the consumer will default because they are spending beyond their means and not paying enough

on the accounts. They are plunging themselves into too much debt and, in the eyes of the financial institutions, they are more likely to file for a bankruptcy or debt settlement. Additionally, even if a consumer heavily charges a credit card and pays it off, the credit agencies will record the highest balance achieved on the credit account as the "high balance." This information cannot be removed from the credit reports and will lower the scores. When future creditors review the credit report then they may deny the consumer thinking they are prone to heavily use the credit cards and in a sense, are desperate for loan money. Finally, high balances on credit accounts mean high utilization in the eyes of the credit agencies and this will further lower the credit scores.

2. Level of delinquency on accounts
Consumers should not be late or stop paying on ANY bill. A delinquency means a past due account. There are certain levels of delinquency, which are influenced by the time for which a credit account is past due. When an account is past due for 30 days then it is immediately reported as a delinquency to the credit reports of the consumer. When the consumer lets the credit account remain unpaid for 60 days; then the interest rate increases to the penalty interest rate. The monthly minimum payment requirement increases, because the payment amount required will be composed of a greater amount of interest and the consumer is very unlikely to continue paying on the credit account so the financial institution is going to want the maximum amount of profit for the time that payments are being successfully made on the credit account. Some consumers still do not pay on the credit account and let the level of delinquency increase. The credit account eventually becomes past due by 60 days, 90 days, 120 days, and finally, 150 days. After a credit account is past due for so long then the financial institution will give up on collecting the debt, from the consumer, and will likely sell the credit account to a collection agency. The credit account will become considered a charged-off account. The number of days for which the account was past due is reflected on the credit reports. The higher the level of delinquency a consumer develops on a credit account then the more their credit scores become low. Other creditors, of the consumer, will find out about the negative financial information of the consumer and possibly take adverse actions such as closing the credit accounts or increasing the interest rates. The financial institutions will become reluctant to reduce interest rates.

3. Too few bank revolving accounts.
Consumers should apply for credit carefully, get approved, and use the credit cards periodically. Any credit card of which a consumer is not required to pay the full balance at the end of the month is considered a "revolving account." Consumers need to have a variety of revolving credit cards including store cards such as Macys and major branded "bank revolving" cards such as Visa, Discover Card, American Express, and MasterCard. All bank credit cards are branded. To fix the credit denial reason listed above, consumers can ask the issuers of their store credit cards to upgrade their credit account to a bank revolving credit card account. For example, in the case of a consumer that has a Macy's store credit card, the consumer can ask the issuer of the Macys card, which is Department Stores National Bank, a division of Citibank, to upgrade the account to a Macys American Express credit card. If the upgrade is granted then the credit scores of the consumer should increase. Unfortunately, not all store card issuers offer upgrades, on their credit accounts. After one to two years of getting the last credit card, consumers can apply for new Visa, MasterCard, American Express, Discover, or another branded bank credit card to fix the denial reason and improve their credit.

4. Too many bank or national revolving accounts.
In general, consumers should be careful how many credit cards are opened, within a lifetime. As years of history are established, on credit accounts, then this reason will no longer negatively affect the consumer. Financial institutions view this reason as being minor unless the consumer has a bad credit history because then it is unlikely they will pay on all their credit accounts and so the financial institution does not want them to have many credit cards. It is never a crime to have many credit cards, as long as; the consumer is handling them all responsibly, not using them all aggressively, and paying them whenever they are used. Before asking for an account upgrade, consumers should freeze their credit reports so the financial institutions do not perform hard inquiry credit checks, which lower credit scores. The financial institutions should only do soft inquiry credit checks. Consumers can use these websites, addresses, and phone numbers to freeze their credit reports with the credit agencies. They should use the method that is most convenient but mailing requests can be dangerous unless the letters are certified. This is because the mail requests can be lost and this is dangerous because they have personal information about the consumer such as the credit report number. The credit report number must be mentioned on any mailed correspondence in order for the credit agencies to access and freeze the credit reports. Consumers wanting to freeze the credit reports of minors should also use this contact information.

5. Too many accounts with balances.
Consumers should not carry balances on multiple loans or credit cards, even small balances. In the eyes of the financial institutions, too many balances make it likely the consumer will default on one or more of the credit accounts. If carrying multiple balances, consumers should combine all the balances onto one low interest rate credit card or loan and make large payments on it. Such should improve the credit scores and overall credit profile. Financial institutions feel more comfortable lending to consumers that have a balance on only one to two loans rather than multiple balances even if they are small amounts in relation to the credit limits. Consumers should not close the extra loans or credit cards. Financial institutions will like that the consumer is using a small portion of all their available credit.

6. Too many consumer finance company records.
Consumers should not get too many mortgages (home loans), automobile loans, or loans to finance furniture or appliances. With an exception to credit cards, these loans are considered installment credit loans. Installment credit means making monthly payments with the intended goal of paying off the entire balance, which is the price of the item that was purchased.
There are two types of installment credit loans; Secured Installment Credit Loans and Unsecured Installment Credit Loans.
Secured Installment Credit Loans require collateral, which are items of value, which the financial institution can repossess in the event that the consumer fails to make the payments such as the boat, house, or car.
Unsecured Installment Credit Loans do not require collateral and so if the consumer fails to make payments then the financial institution has a complete loss. An example of an unsecured installment credit loan can be considered an unsecured government student loan subsidized (interest free until graduation) or unsubsidized (interest accumulates while in school). An example of a secured installment credit loan can be considered an automobile or house loan (mortgage).

In most cases, unsecured installment credit loans are more expensive than secured installment credit loans because there is no collateral or security deposit that the financial institution gets to keep or repossess in the event that the consumer does not pay on the unsecured installment credit loan. In the way that the credit agencies view the credit data, most but not all installment credit loans, unsecured or secured, are considered "**consumer finance company accounts**."

Financial institutions will classify their loans as to what types they are and so consumers have to ask the financial institution before getting the loan; if it will be reported to the credit agencies as an installment credit loan. Consumers should want some installment credit loans and their histories appearing on their credit reports because 10% of the FICO credit scoring model takes into consideration the types of credit and loans. If the consumer has no installment credit loans then their credit scores will not be as high as they can be; and as a result, financial institutions will view consumers as being financially weak. The loans on the credit reports will specify if they are installment credit loans or not.

Although similar to unsecured installment credit loans because they do not require collaterals or security deposits; unsecured credit cards, unsecured lines of credit, sometimes called revolving, pay day, or signature lines of credit, are still not considered unsecured installment credit loans. This is because unlike unsecured credit cards and unsecured lines of credit (excluding home equity lines of credit), unsecured installment credit loans give consumers a fixed and total loan amount at the time of the closing, which means finalizing, of the loan. The financial institution will write the consumer a check or will do a direct deposit all of the loan funds within their deposit account and the consumer starts getting charged on all the loan funds. When consumers pay back that loan amount, they do not have access to anymore loan money unless they apply for a new installment credit loan whereas with a credit card or line of credit, when the consumer pays off their balance then they have access to the entire credit limit amount again.

Consumers do not have to use the entire credit limit; they can only use a small amount and pay interest for only the amount that they are using. Credit cards and lines of credit do not have fixed monthly payments because they can be different every month depending upon the current balances whereas with installment credit loans, the monthly payments are the same every month, which means they are "fixed" because consumers can only pay down on them. For such reasons, installment credit loans may sometimes be cheaper in interest than credit cards and lines of credit.

Finally, most unsecured and secured installment credit loans have a fixed term in which all the loan money must be paid back to the financial institution by the consumer; such as 12 month, 24 month, 36 month, or longer depending upon the options provided by the financial institution. This is because installment credit loans are considered to be "closed-end credit." This is another reason why installment credit loans may sometimes be cheaper in interest because credit cards and lines of credit are "open-end credit" meaning the consumer can take as much time as they want to pay back the loans; such as for example, twenty years but they still have to make the minimum payments. The consumer chooses the loan term for the unsecured or secured installment credit loan and the longer that the loan term is then the more interest that the consumer will be charged even though the monthly minimum payments will be smaller.

Some signature (sometimes called good faith and character) loans may be considered an unsecured installment credit loan depending upon how the financial institution classifies the loan. Some financial institutions may call their; signature, good faith, or character loan products, an installment credit loan or vice versa. All financial institutions use different terminologies and this can sometimes make it confusing for consumers. Overall, in most cases, loans that are considered installment credit loans (auto loans, student loans, home loans, and home equity loans) will have fixed payments, no credit limits, fixed interest rates, possible prepayment penalties, and a fixed term to pay the loan.

Although still considered an installment credit loan, due to the fact, a fixed time term is established between the financial institution and student, in which the private student loan must be fully repaid, some private student loans have variable interest rates and variable interest rates mean payments that are not the same every month but similar. Government student loans have fixed interest rates and fixed payments. In contrast, all revolving credit loans (home equity lines of credit, lines of credit, credit cards) will have different monthly payments, no set time term to pay off the loans, credit limits, no prepayment penalties, and more likely, to have variable interest rates. Some credit cards only have fixed interest rates but they are still considered a revolving credit loan because there is no set time term to pay off the loan, different monthly payments, and a credit limit.

Consumers should pay off an installment credit loan, which is considered a consumer finance account, before getting a new one. For example, if they have the cash for a vehicle then it would be wise for them to get the auto loan, which is considered a type of consumer finance account, and just pay it off immediately; unless there are high loan origination fees. Consumers should negotiate with the financial institutions that they want to get and immediately pay off the auto loan for the purpose of improving their credit. They may cause the financial institution to waive all or some of the loan origination fees because the consumer is being faithful in paying the loan. They will not have to worry about the consumer defaulting and spending extra money to repossess the collateral, which is the automobile. Depending upon the amount of the loan origination fee, in some cases, it may be worth paying the fee because the consumer is less likely to be denied a house, credit card, or interest rate reduction on other loans.

7. Account payment history is too new to rate.
Consumers should not wait to build their good credit history. They should start building credit immediately when the legal age, depending upon the legislature of their residential state, has been reached. Credit history can be established by opening a loan or being added as an authorized or joint user on the account of another individual who has good credit. If consumers have little payment history established, on their credit accounts, then it is likely they may be denied or approved with a higher than average interest rate and/or annual fee. The financial institution cannot assume the consumer will maintain a positive and strong payment history for a long time frame. For this reason, the consumer should not close credit accounts but keep them open and build positive payment histories on them.

8. Too many recent inquiries in the last 12 months.
Consumers should not apply for credit aggressively. They should always monitor their four credit reports periodically and make sure companies are not doing multiple credit checks for the same credit application. This often happens when the consumer unknowingly submits duplicate applications by clicking "submit" multiple times on the websites of the financial institutions. Consumers should dispute the extra credit inquiries with the credit agencies and contact the companies to have them remove the inquiries. If consumers have too many hard inquiry credit checks then they should immediately freeze all their credit reports so they do not get tempted to apply for credit again.

When financial institutions with which the consumer already has credit, does an account review on their credit accounts and reviews their credit profile. The financial institutions will notice the freeze on the credit reports and may be more lenient if they take any adverse actions against the consumer for having so many credit checks. The credit freeze will suggest to the financial institutions that the consumer has taken the necessary actions to prevent their information from being compromised because in most cases, consumers that have too many credit checks are at high risk in having credit accounts fraudulently established under their name. Fraudulent credit accounts are considered liabilities for financial institutions because they have to pay for the fraudulent charges until the investigations have been completed.

9. Too many accounts recently opened.
Consumers should not open multiple loans or credit cards too quickly otherwise financial institutions will think the consumers are trying to get into large amounts of debt or that their information has been compromised. Opening two to three new credit accounts every two years is considered safe. It makes no sense why consumers would open so many credit accounts at once. To fix the denial reason, consumers should not open new credit accounts or close the new accounts. Instead, they should just allow for time to pass such as two or more years and establish a positive payment history on all the credit accounts. As time passes, the denial reason will go away.

10. Proportion of balances to credit limits is too high on bank revolving or other revolving accounts.
Consumers should not use credit cards or loans aggressively to the point that they are close to being maxed out or going over the credit limit. Consumers should pay off their balances the day that they use the credit account or at the end of the month. In the eyes of the financial institutions, consumers with high and growing debts are very likely to default on the credit accounts. To fix the denial reason, consumers can consider getting a low interest rate secured or unsecured loan from a community bank or credit union and combining all the debts onto that new loan. If given a worth offer with a fixed for life interest rate then consumers can consider doing a balance transfer in which all or most of the debts are transferred onto the one credit card that is offering the fixed rate. Consumers can use their savings to pay off the debts. Finally, consumers that own houses or condominiums can possibly consider getting a home equity loan and paying off all their debt. Consumers should not consider getting a home equity loan or any loan in general that has a higher interest rate than their credit cards or fees that would be much higher than interest charged by the credit card issuers.

Consumers should use their tax or social security refunds to pay the debts because any interest they make by putting it in a savings account will mean nothing. This is because the interest charged on the loans will overpower the interest made. Consumers that are in severe financial conditions and cannot get a new loan should consider doing credit counseling and can find a government approved credit counseling agency within their state by visiting this website: http://www.justice.gov/ust/eo/bapcpa/ccde/cc_a pproved.html. To get out of paying the debts, consumers should <u>not</u> consider doing a bankruptcy or debt settlement. In most cases, consumers that file for a bankruptcy or debt settlement have to pay attorney or court fees and their assets are seized by the financial institutions to which they owe money. Consumers are better off using their assets to pay the debts and working out payment plans with the financial institutions.

11. Amount owed on revolving accounts is too high.
Consumers should not build high balances. They should pay off the balances immediately or pay significantly above the minimum payment requirements on all loans and credit cards. They should call the financial institution every two-three months for a lower annual percentage rate because a lowered interest rate will always make it easier for a consumer to pay down their balance. Consumers should not be late on making payments because the late fees will cause the balances to grow despite the payments because the late fees themselves will accumulate interest. Consumers should stop using credit cards that have balances that are high in relation to the credit limit. Consumers need to pay off those credit cards and then, they can and should use them again but carefully so they do not repeat their mistakes of building up high debts.

12. Lengths of time revolving accounts have been established.
Consumers should not close credit cards otherwise the average length of history established on accounts will become short. If the credit cards have been closed then consumers should ask the financial institutions to reopen them because all the payment history will help increase the credit scores. If the credit card has a negative payment history then consumers should still reopen it because the goal should be to redeem themselves in the eyes of the financial institutions by making timely payments. Consumers just need to keep all their credit accounts open, pay them in a timely manner, and monitor them in order to fix the denial reason.

If credit accounts have annual fees then the consumers should contact the financial institutions to request for the annual fees to be removed or reduced. Consumers can often request to switch their annual fee based credit card program to a non-annual fee based credit card program without any negative impact to their credit, no credit check, and they keep all the account history. The only con is that the non-annual fee based credit card program may mean that the consumer will earn fewer rewards on their purchases. However, in some cases, the annual fees overpower the savings through rewards programs so it would be wise to get rid of them unless consumers have accumulated a great deal of rewards. Consumers should redeem the rewards such as points, miles, or cash back and then have the annual fee removed or the rewards will be lost. The rewards getting lost defeats the purpose of trying to save money by using a credit card.

13. Time since delinquency is too recent or unknown.
If consumers are late on a loan or credit card by thirty days or more then the financial institution will immediately report the credit card, as a **delinquency,** to the credit agencies. When the credit account is left past due for sixty days, then the financial institution can increase the interest rate to the penalty annual percentage rate. If a consumer were to apply for new credit quickly after a delinquency appeared on their credit reports then it is likely they will be denied for the reason listed above. Consumers need to get all or if not possible, then some of the delinquencies removed from their credit reports by disputing the with the credit agencies.

Consumers need to contact the corporate offices of the financial institutions that reported the delinquencies and negotiate with them to have the delinquencies removed. Consumers need to explain why they were delinquent on their credit accounts. There is no guarantee that the delinquency will be removed but trying to get it removed is always better than doing nothing. If the delinquencies cannot be removed; then consumers have to get a secured credit card, establish a positive payment history on it, and try disputing the delinquencies again after 7-8 months. Consumers should also ask a close family member who has little or no debt and a strong credit history to add them as a joint or authorized user, whichever the financial institution will allow, onto their credit accounts that do not have balances and have never been late. The positive payment history will boost the credit scores of the consumer who is being added onto the account. The financial institutions may be more likely to agree to remove the delinquencies because they will appreciate the fact that the consumer redeemed themselves by trying to establish a positive credit history.

14. Lengths of time accounts have been established.
Consumers should not close credit cards or let the financial institutions close them. To fix this denial reason, consumers need to reopen the closed credit cards without letting the financial institutions run hard inquiry credit checks on them. In some financial scenarios, a hard inquiry credit check may be worth getting the account reopened because the credit scores will greatly increase. This will overpower the credit scores becoming low due to the credit check. Credit check usually lower scores by up to five points. However, always suggest to the financial institution to run a soft inquiry credit check as such does not hurt the credit scores. Consumers need to keep their credit accounts open. When consumers close their credit accounts then the financial institutions think financial struggles is why they had to close the accounts and for this reason, they are financially weak to handle new credit accounts.

15. Lack of recent bank revolving information.
"**Bank revolving**" means carrying a balance on a Visa, MasterCard, American Express, Discover Card, or another major, branded credit card. However, this does not mean consumers should carry a balance on their credit accounts. Credit accounts can either be a revolving account, which means the consumer can carry a balance on the account without any penalties, or a **charge card**, which means the consumer, must pay off their balance by the end of the month or they may face penalties such as fees. It is the choice of the consumer whether they want a revolving credit card or charge credit card. Not all financial institutions offer both products and depending upon their policies, some financial institutions may have more requirements for a consumer to get approved for a charge card such as a pristine credit profile. This is because consumers can usually spend more money with charge cards than with credit cards. For this reason, charge cards usually have more aggressive rewards programs than credit cards and this costs more money for the financial institutions.

The rewards programs are why most charge cards have associated annual fees that the consumer must pay and so the consumer should not get too many charge cards because the fees can get expensive. Financial institutions cannot afford to grant charge cards to consumers who are unlikely to pay them. Consumers should get revolving credit cards and not just charge credit cards so they have a variety of loans showing on their credit and this makes their creditworthiness level stronger. Consumers must make sure the financial institutions are reporting all the credit cards to the credit bureaus. Consumers that have many charge cards should request for the financial institutions to convert some or all of the charge cards into revolving credit cards.

Note: The term, "*charge card*" should not get confused with the term, "*charge account*" or the term, "*charged-off account*." Charge account or just "charge**" may appear under the descriptions of credit accounts on the credit reports, which mean the credit account was a store account such as for example, Macys, Kohl's, and Old Navy. A charged-off account may appear next to the condition of the credit accounts appearing on the credit reports and this means that the credit card or loan was never paid by the consumer. The financial institution stopped trying to collect money from the consumer. This is considered to be very negative information on a credit report and will make the credit scores very low.

16. Lack of recent revolving account information.
The term, "**revolving**" is less specific than the term, "bank revolving." It means carrying a balance on any credit card including store cards; such as for example, Macy's, Kohl's, and Target. Financial institutions want to see a mix of credit account types showing on the credit reports. For this reason, they want to see both "bank revolving" and "store revolving" credit accounts. Store revolving credit accounts are also called "charge accounts" on credit reports.

Financial institutions want to see how a consumer would handle a bank revolving account such as Visa, MasterCard, Discover, American Express, or another major branded credit card; versus how they would handle a store account because bank revolving credit cards can be used anywhere and balance transfers as well as **cash advances** can be done on them. In contrast, store revolving credit cards can only be used in the store and any affiliated stores but balance transfers or cash advances cannot be done on them.

Unfortunately, there are high risk consumers who only pay the minimum payments on the bank revolving credit cards so they can use the cash advances to pay other bills such as other credit cards, use them for everyday expenses, or deposit the funds within IRA accounts because those funds will then be protected from bankruptcy. Consumers usually do so because they are trying to avoid paying the bills, and when all the credit is used then they will likely declare a bankruptcy or a debt settlement. They are less concerned about paying the store revolving credit cards. Financial institutions are trying to avoid granting any credit to such high-risk consumers. To have the best credit profile possible, it is personally recommended that consumers should get store and bank credit cards but not open them all too quickly because this will then damage credit.

Note: It is **highly discouraged that consumers do cash advances from credit cards, because it is a waste of money to pay fees and cash advance interest rates, which are usually above 19%. Almost all merchants accept credit cards and consumers should be skeptical about merchants, usually small businesses, which only accept cash. It is likely some of these merchants may be selling defective merchandise or have the bad intention of taking the money and running off without providing the promised service. There is nothing that the consumer can do to recover their lost cash funds, whereas with a credit card, they have protection to do a dispute on the charge.

As ensured by the Fair Credit Card Billing Act, the credit card issuer will refund the funds to the consumer and impose a **chargeback fee** to the merchant, for not providing the promised services or merchandises. The consumer has no loss. If consumers really need cash then they should withdraw money from their checking account, or savings account provided they are not exceeding the number of allowed withdrawals from a savings or money market account within a month. Currently, the Federal Reserve does not allow for consumers to withdraw money more than six times from a savings or money market account.

17. No recent non-mortgage balance information.
Consumers cannot stop using loans or credit cards even after they purchase a house. In order for consumers to purchase a house, they get a home loan that is called a **mortgage** from a

financial institution. Consumers must be carefully using credit and paying it off at all times. If consumers stop using credit after purchasing a house then their credit profile may become weak. This is because the financial institutions will report no usage on the credit accounts to the credit agencies or may even close the credit accounts for inactivity. When credit accounts are closed then it sends the message that the consumer could not handle financial institutions. It is similar to the case of a student when they are withdrawn from a class. The student is viewed as being academically weak just as a consumer is viewed as being financially weak.

Despite having a mortgage or car loan, consumers should have some usage on credit cards but pay them off immediately. This is to prevent financial institutions from thinking they are having financial struggles and cannot pay on the credit cards in the event they are used for expenses. Financial institutions may then start thinking that the consumer is likely to default on their mortgage. This may cause the financial institution to refuse doing a **refinance** for the consumer in the future, which is when the consumer requests for the interest rate on the mortgage to be reduced and/or for the loan repayment time to be stretched for the purpose of reducing the minimum payments.

A refinance can also be used to reduce the time length needed to pay off the mortgage, which would cause the minimum payments to increase with more of the payment amount going towards the primary balance rather than interest. This will allow for the consumer to pay off their mortgage faster provided that they are not late in making the payments because the late fees make the balance higher.

18. Number of accounts with delinquency.
This is considered a major denial reason, because it suggests that the consumer is high risk, to the financial institution because they have cheated many financial institutions. Many accounts with **delinquency** means the accounts have been past due by thirty days or more. This means the consumer is likely to default again on any new credit account and as a result, the financial institution will have a business loss. Consumers cannot ever be late on any bill or credit card. For the purpose of reducing the chances of becoming delinquent on any bill, consumers should set up automatic payments on all of them. Consumers should only use one credit card for everyday purchases because using multiple credit cards may cause the consumer to forget making payments on some of them. Consumers that have delinquencies should pay off the credit accounts if they still have balances, keep them open or reopen them, and request for the delinquencies to be removed from the credit reports. There is no guarantee that the delinquencies will be removed but financial institutions look at delinquent credit accounts without balances less severely than they do delinquent credit accounts with balances. This is because financial institutions will appreciate the fact that the consumer paid off the delinquent credit account rather than just let it become a charged-off account meaning that they never paid it and the financial institution could not collect the debt from them.

19. Date of last inquiry too recent.
An **"inquiry"** is referring to a hard inquiry credit check performed by a company or financial institution on one, or more of the credit reports belonging to the consumer. This happens when a consumer applies for credit. The denial reason usually occurs when a consumer is applying for credit aggressively. For example, if Arisa applied for a credit card on Wednesday and then on Thursday, she applied for another credit card; then Arisa is more likely to be denied for the second credit card, due to the reason listed above. It makes no sense to a financial institution why Arisa would be applying for a second credit card when she just applied for a new credit

card. It suggests to a financial institution that Arisa is trying to get into large amounts of debt or that a criminal is applying for credit under her name.

Consumers should not apply for credit aggressively. Credit scores become low too due to excessive credit checks or excessive new accounts. To fix the denial reason, consumers should dispute the inquiry with the credit agency that was used to pull the credit report. The consumer should also contact the financial institution that performed the credit check. The consumer must explain why they need the credit inquiry removed such as if they are doing a refinance on their house, buying a car, or just shopping for a low interest rate. The financial institution may be lenient and remove the credit inquiry because they will respect the fact that the intention of the consumer is not to have the credit inquiry removed so they can get approved for new credit accounts, use them, and never pay on them. Some consumers unfortunately have such bad intentions, which is why financial institutions are sometimes reluctant to remove negative information from credit reports or credit inquiries.

20. Too few accounts currently paid as agreed.
This is considered a major denial reason because it suggests the consumer is not being faithful in paying their credit accounts. When a credit account on a credit report indicates the status as **"paid as agreed"** then this is considered positive information because it means the consumer has never been seriously past due on making payments. In doing so, the consumer has never broken the contract with the financial institution they agreed to when they applied for the credit account.

When the account becomes past due by 30 or more days; then the status shows as a derogatory account. The greater the number of credit accounts that become derogatory; then the more likely the consumers is to be denied credit. This is because the number of credit accounts in positive status, if any, will become low. Consumers can fix the denial reason by paying off the balances on their delinquent credit accounts or making payment plan arrangements with the financial institutions. Paid off delinquent credit accounts raise the chances they will drop off the credit reports much faster, because it is possible the financial institutions will drop the accounts from their database systems. Not paying or paying late will never fix the denial reason.

21. Length of time since derogatory public record or collection is too short.
When an unpaid and past due debt; such as from a credit card, student loan, or utility bill is sold by the financial institution or service company to a collection agency. The credit account will be considered a **charged-off account** on the credit reports because the consumer never paid on it. The collection agency converts the unpaid debt from the credit account, utility bill, or just any bill into a **collection account**, which is immediately reported as negative financial information to the credit agencies. A collection account implies the message that a consumer has not paid their debt for a long time and the financial institution has given up on trying to collect it. Even if a consumer pays off the collection account then it still stays on the credit reports for up to ten years unless the consumer can negotiate with the collection agency and dispute the collection account from their credit reports.

However, consumers can best improve their credit profile by paying off the collection accounts because the credit scores may increase and the financial institutions will appreciate the fact that the consumer did not just let the collection account become a charged-off account itself.

Paying off a collection account may increase the chances it will drop off the credit reports faster. In any case, if a consumer applies for credit in close time proximity to when a collection account was reported to their credit reports then it is likely they will get denied.

Derogatory public records are negative information about a consumer that is available for the public to access that is usually reported by a county, state, or federal court such as bankruptcies, tax liens, judgments, wage garnishments, failure to pay alimony or child support, foreclosures, property evictions, and non-consensual liens. Public records such as a divorce or being sued do not show on a credit report. It is difficult to remove derogatory public records from credit reports but consumers should try disputing them with the credit agencies and negotiate with the courts to have some of the information removed. Derogatory public records lower credit scores.

22. Amount past due on accounts.

Although it may not erase the negative credit history, consumers need to pay the past due amounts on their credit accounts to satisfy the minimum payments. If possible, they should fully pay off the credit accounts that have the past due balances and keep the accounts open or reopen them. This is because financial institutions will like seeing past due accounts that were fully paid off rather than seeing past due accounts that were never paid off and became charged-off accounts. For this reason, consumers can possibly negotiate with them to remove the past due remarks on the credit accounts off of the credit reports. Although there is no guarantee that the financial institutions will agree to remove the derogatory remarks, paid off past due accounts help raise the credit scores, because the debts are no longer liabilities for consumers.

Consumers that lose their jobs can prevent the credit accounts from becoming past due by calling the financial institution, explaining the situation, the deferring the payment or working out a payment plan before the due date arrives or on the due date. Consumers can possibly avoid late fees. Consumers should never simply let the account become past due no matter what the circumstances. This can eliminate some payment relief options, which can protect the credit profiles of consumers. Financial institutions and employers would always prefer to see deferred payments or payment plans with credit accounts on credit reports rather than delinquencies. Additionally, the deferred payments and payment plans prevent the credit scores from becoming too low.

23. Serious delinquency, derogatory public record or collection filed.

Consumers that have a delinquency showing on their credit reports such as a 30 days, 60 days, 90 days, or longer level delinquent credit or collection account, should try to pay all of them off by using savings funds or consolidating all the debts onto a single new or existing loan such as a credit card which has the lowest interest rate among the other credit cards belonging to the consumer. They should focus on paying off the highest level delinquent accounts, which are usually 150 days and 180 days past due accounts. This is because these accounts have the greatest chances of becoming charged-off accounts and being sold by the financial institutions to collection agencies. The consumer should not want this to happen because collection accounts will further lower the credit scores and thus, damage the credit profile. Consumers should not let delinquent accounts increase in their level of delinquency.

For example, consumers should not let a 30 days delinquent account develop into a 60 days delinquent account because this will mean lower credit scores, more fees, and little or no respect from the financial institution. If consumers cannot pay on the credit accounts then they can notify the financial institutions regarding their hardships, defer the payments, and in doing so, they can protect their credit profiles because credit reports will show the consumers are doing payment plans. Consumers also have the option of doing credit counseling in order to prevent the level of delinquency from growing on credit accounts. The credit accounts showing on the credit reports that have the highest level of delinquency are considered "serious delinquencies."

Collection accounts that are 30 days, 60 days, 90 days, or more delinquent can at one point become charged-off accounts themselves. It is possible the collection agencies may take drastic actions against the consumer such as imposing anon-consensual lien on their property, taking them to court, garnishing their wage, or putting claims on some or all of their assets. Consumers should not take this risk. They should simply pay their collection accounts or negotiate with the collection agencies to create payment plans.

In some situations, not all, consumers can fix the derogatory public records. For example, if the consumer has a derogatory public record due to not paying child support or alimony then they should start paying it. Later, they can negotiate with the court to have the derogatory public record removed. Another example in which a derogatory public record could potentially be removed would be if a consumer has a repossession happen such as with their car. It may be possible to use funds from savings or another loan to pay the full amount of the car balance, reclaim the car, and negotiate with the car loan issuer to remove the derogatory public record of the repossession. If consumers are told they will not receive the vehicle back even after they agree to pay the remaining car loan balance then they should consult with an attorney.

Consumers should aim at getting the vehicle back since they are paying for it. The same advice applies to consumers whose houses are repossessed. In most cases, consumers cannot pay the remaining mortgage balance but they should make an offer to the financial institution such as a large upfront amount that they can pay using another loan or their savings and agree to pay the rest of the mortgage balance in monthly installment payments. Consumers should offer other incentives to the financial institution so they feel comfortable in doing business with the consumer again and this may cause the financial institution to allow the consumer to live in their house again. Consumers could mention offering their certificate of deposit, savings, or automobile as an additional collateral to the financial institution that they can repossess along with the house in the event that the consumer fails to make their payments. The financial institution may agree to this offer because in their eyes, it is unlikely a consumer would offer an additional collateral if they were not planning on paying their mortgage. In order to get back the repossessed house or car and have the derogatory public record removed, consumers could mention agreeing to pay a higher interest rate loan. Finally, for consumers that have a close family member such as a spouse, father, mother, daughter, or son with a strong credit history and source of income. With the consent of the family member, consumers can offer putting them as a secondary on the loan. This means they will be responsible for repaying the loan in the event that the primary consumer fails to do so. The financial institution may agree to this and will release the repossessed house or car. Additionally, it may be wise for the primary loan consumer to get life insurance with sufficient coverage from a reputable company. This is because in the event that the primary loan consumer passes away, the secondary consumer will not have to repay all or most of the loan debt.

Unfortunately, other derogatory public records such as bankruptcy cannot usually be removed until time passes. For this reason, consumers need to avoid filing for bankruptcies and debt settlements.

24. Number of bank or national revolving accounts with balances.
Consumers need to avoid building and carrying balances on loans and credit cards because the balances will start compounding with interest and fees. As the balances grow then the credit scores of the consumer will begin to decrease because the consumer is plunging themselves into more debt. In the eyes of the financial institutions, they are plunging into so much debt that they will likely default on one or more of the credit accounts and get themselves into a bad situation that they will strongly consider doing a bankruptcy or debt settlement. If necessary, consumers should only carry a balance on one credit card. To fix the denial reason, consumers should consolidate their debts onto one low interest rate credit card or loan such as a personal installment loan or home equity loan. In order to avoid building balances on multiple credit cards, consumers should shred the credit cards they are not using and just monitor them on the internet or review the statements they get in the mail.

It is recommended consumers only keep two credit cards with them for everyday purchases so in the event one credit card declines for whatever the reasons may be, consumers have a second credit card as backup and protection. However, ultimately, consumers should use all their credit cards including store cards and charge cards at least once every six months for the purpose of avoiding having the financial institutions close them for inactivity and the credit scores dropping. Consumers should make small purchases and then immediately pay off the credit cards.

25. No recent revolving balances.
To achieve and maintain the best credit profile possible, consumers should not carry balances on credit cards or loans at any time but they should periodically use their credit cards and not just use debit, prepaid, ATM cards, or cash. When consumers use credit cards and pay them off immediately, the balances that they had along with the payments are immediately reported to the credit agencies and this shows positive activity is taking place on the credit accounts. Some consumers may have the misconception that they need to carry balances in order for the credit agencies to acknowledge that the credit cards are being used and paid successfully. This is never true and actually lowers the credit scores because it is suggesting the consumers are in debt that they cannot repay easily. Financial institutions will think consumers that are carrying a balance, especially multiple balances, have spent beyond their means. Consumers do not want to give them this impression because it is possible then the financial institutions could increase the interest rate on the credit account, impose an annual fee, or close down the credit account because the consumer is at high risk of defaulting. For this reason, the financial institutions are going to want to make as much profits as they can off of the consumers for the time they are successfully making payments.

26. Number of revolving accounts.
Consumers need to be careful not to get too many credit cards and loans throughout their lifetime and not open up too many credit accounts within a short time proximity. However, as a consumer, it is going to be natural to open up credit accounts when large purchases such as furniture, jewelry, and computers are made in order to finance them and save money through discounts. For this reason, it is recommended consumers only up a credit account if they are going to get a significant discount such as a savings of $50 or more, and can pay off the balance immediately in order to avoid getting charged interest by the financial institution. Minor savings such as $15 or less are not worth establishing credit accounts. After paying off the credit account that was established by the consumer to make the purchase, they should not close it but just monitor it, make small purchases, pay them immediately, not build a large

balance, and let the history grow. No matter how many credit accounts a consumer gets, they should follow the same advice and this should fix the denial reason. There is no set number of how many credit accounts a consumer can have but they all must be handled responsibly. This will cause the credit scores to increase. There is a misconception that consumers with many credit accounts are financially weak. This is not true because as long as all the credit accounts do not have balances and have never been delinquent then the financial institutions will respect the fact that the consumer is able to handle so much momentum. They are considered financially strong and unlikely to default. In a sense, having many credit accounts and handling them all responsibly is the same difference as a student taking many classes within a time frame and performing academically well in all the classes. The student is considered academically strong unless they earn a poor grade in one or more of the several classes. Similarly, if a consumer defaults on one or more of the many credit accounts then they will be considered financially weak.

27. Number of established accounts.
Consumers need to be careful not to get too many loans or credit cards at once or build large balances on new or multiple credit accounts. To fix the denial reason, consumers need to allow for time to pass because the positive history will gradually grow on the credit accounts. Consumers should not close the credit accounts or their average length of history established credit accounts will decrease and this will lower the credit scores. They should never be delinquent on the credit accounts. If they lose their jobs then they should still not close the credit accounts and simply use savings to make the payments, defer the minimum payments, or create a payment plan with the financial institutions.

28. No recent bankcard balances.
To fix the denial reason, consumers need to make sure there is positive activity taking place on their major branded bank credit cards such as the Visa, MasterCard, American Express, and Discover cards. This means making small purchases at least once every six months, not carrying balances, and paying them off immediately. They cannot always use debit, prepaid, ATM cards, or cash because they are not strengthening their credit history. Financial institutions sometimes think that if consumers are not periodically using their credit cards then they are having financial struggles, which is why some financial institutions may close down their credit accounts. They are worried that the consumer will one day aggressively use their credit card to the point that they cannot pay it.

29. Time since most recent account opening too short.
After opening a loan or credit card, consumers cannot immediately open another loan or credit card. It raises the question to the financial institutions as to why a consumer would be getting another loan or credit card immediately after recently opening one. They may think that the consumer has the intention of plunging into large debts that they will not be able to pay or will choose not to pay. To fix the denial reason, consumers simply have to let time pass such as one to two years after the opening of the last credit account and not let it become delinquent or build a high balance before opening a new credit account or loan.

30. Too few accounts with recent payment information.
Consumers need to make sure all their credit accounts and loans are reporting the payment histories to all the credit agencies. On the credit reports, on the payment history section with each account, there should be a checkmark underneath each month. If there is no checkmark for a month then this likely means that the payment history for that month was not reported

by the financial institution. The consumer would need to contact the financial institution and request for them to report that the account was satisfactorily paid for the month missing the checkmark unless the account was past due. Additionally, consumers need to make sure that they have credit accounts and are periodically using and paying them off. Not having and using credit never helps improves the credit profile and this increases the chances of getting denied for an apartment, house, car, utility service, job, or simply anything.

31. Lack of recent installment credit loan information.
Consumers need to get secured and unsecured installment credit loans under their name such as a house loan, car loan, boat loan, signature loan, student loan, personal loan, or home equity loan. Most installment loans have the same or similar monthly payments, a fixed interest rate, no credit limit, and a fixed loan amount that will be released to the consumer at the closing, which means finalizing, of the loan. The consumer can use the funds to make the purchase such as a car, house, boat, college expenses, or another major expense. Before getting the loan, consumers should ask the financial institution if they will report the loan as an installment loan to the credit agencies otherwise the consumer is wasting their time and money getting the loan because it will not fix the denial reason. It will be most beneficial, if possible, to immediately pay off the installment loan unless the financial institution indicates there will be prepayment penalties. The consumer will potentially save thousands paying interest and their credit scores will increase immediately because the credit reports will reflect a paid off installment loan that was never delinquent.

32. Proportion of loan balances to loan amounts is too high.
Consumers cannot build high balances on loans and they cannot spend beyond their means otherwise they will never be able to pay off their debts. To fix the denial reason, consumers need to pay down their loans using the funds they get through employment; tax refunds unemployment funds, or savings. They need to pay the balances in full or pay above the minimum payment requirements. Some consumers use one loan to pay another loan and this does not fix the denial reason but only results in higher debt amounts with interest compounding every month.

33. Amount owed on delinquent accounts.
To fix the denial reason, consumers need to immediately pay off the amounts owed on past due credit accounts. If they cannot pay off the balances then they should pay above the minimum payment requirements and keep the accounts open or reopen them because such will improve their credit scores. They can possibly negotiate with the financial institutions for a lower annual percentage rate. The penalty interest rate on a delinquent credit card will go down to the original purchase interest rate if the consumer manages to make timely payments for at least 6 months. If consumers do not have enough funds to pay off the balances on the delinquent credit accounts then they should consider transferring the balances from the delinquent credit accounts onto a low interest rate credit card or loan because usually the minimum payments due every month will be small. However, before doing the transfer, consumers should ask the financial institution for an estimation of how much the minimum payment will be every month and then consumers can determine whether or not they can afford to pay it. Consumers should not let the balances on the delinquent accounts left unpaid otherwise the level of delinquency will continue growing and the credit scores will continue decreasing. After so long, the delinquent credit accounts with balances will become charged-off accounts meaning the financial institution has ruled that the consumer will not pay them at all and they will stop trying to collect the debt from the consumer. Consumers without

any funds need to consider doing credit counseling to pay off the balances on the delinquent credit accounts or can work out a payment plan with the financial Institutions directly and defer the payments.

34. Serious delinquency and public record or collection filed.

Consumers should pay off the balances on the delinquent credit or collection accounts, contact the financial institutions, negotiate with them to remove the negative credit data from the credit reports, and then dispute the delinquent accounts with the credit agencies. Through internet, phone, or writing, consumers can request for the credit agencies to put a note under each delinquent credit account and collection account indicating the reason as to why the account was delinquent, how it originated, or what is being done to pay it. The note is known as the "consumer statement." The consumer statements will not have any impact on the credit scores. There is no guarantee that the financial institutions will even look at them but it is better to have the consumer statements because there is still a small chance. The financial institutions may look at the statements and take them into consideration when determining if a consumer should be approved or denied for credit. The consumer has the option of putting a consumer statement with each derogatory public record as to how it originated or what is being done to help resolve the issue. Consumers will need to dispute the derogatory public records with the courts that reported them and with the credit agencies. They may need an attorney to do so. Consumers need to be careful not to get outrageously expensive attorneys because in some cases, they are scams and do not promise what they deliver. Attorneys or just any business that expresses it is reputable because it has a positive rating with the Better Business Bureau does not always mean it is not a scam. This is because any business can get listed with the Better Business Bureau by paying fees. In some cases, businesses that have listings with the Better Business Bureau means they will charge higher than average costs for their services and merchandises to consumers because they have to pay money to the Better Business Bureau in order to maintain their listing. They also have to make profits for themselves being a business.

35. Serious delinquency.

Consumers cannot let the level of delinquency increase on credit accounts by not paying them. For example, a consumer should not let a 30 days delinquent credit account grow into a 60 days delinquent credit account. Consumers need to reopen or keep the delinquent credit accounts open because the credit scores will not drop as heavily as they would if the delinquent credit accounts were closed. This is because it sends the message that the consumer has given up in trying to pay off the delinquent credit account by closing it. Consumers need to pay off the delinquent credit account in full or above the minimum payment requirements. Consumers should use any funds to which they have access with an exception to the funds in an Individual Retirement Account (IRA) or 401(k) because they then have to pay heavy tax penalties to the IRS. The funds will no longer have protection against any bankruptcy that the consumer chooses to do. If consumers do not have any funds or limited funds then they should consider doing credit counseling or contacting the financial institutions, working out a payment plan with them, and deferring the current payment that is due. Credit counseling should always be a last option because credit counseling agencies, even if they are non-profit organizations, usually charge fees for their service. Consumers are better off using the funds they would use to pay the credit counseling fees; they should instead pay the credit card and loan issuers.

36. Derogatory public record or collection filed.
Consumers need to avoid taking risky actions that may cause the courts to report negative public record information about them to the credit agencies. Such examples can include not paying alimony or child support, not paying service contactors who then impose a non-consensual lien on the property of the consumer, and declaring a bankruptcy or debt settlement. If consumers do such actions then they will have to pay the consequences by paying fees to attorneys in order to get the negative public records information removed from their credit profiles. They have to do everything possible to get the negative public records information removed otherwise they could face getting denied for a job, credit, and having to pay high insurance premiums. Collection accounts need to be fully paid off and then the consumer can negotiate with the collection agencies to remove the collection accounts off of the credit reports. Consumers can also dispute the collection accounts off of the credit reports with the credit agencies. However, there is no guarantee that the collection accounts will drop off but financial institutions would rather see them with no balances than with balances. They will honor the fact that the consumer paid them off because it is possible that consumers will never pay the collection accounts. Collection accounts can always be avoided if consumers pay all their bills and take them seriously. Consumers need to remember that any bill under their name if left unpaid can become a collection account such as a movie rental, ticket fine, hospital bill, utility bill, and a credit card bill.

If consumers are denied for credit, especially for minor reasons such as too short of history established on credit accounts, then they must be persistent in getting the credit application approved and request for a **reconsideration**. If consumers do not ask for reconsideration then their credit scores would have dropped for no reason because whenever a consumer applies for credit then hard inquiry credit checks are done on them by the financial institutions

The opening of a new credit account will eventually cause the credit scores to increase provided the consumer is never late on making the payments or does not aggressively use the credit card. The only reason why a consumer should not both trying to get the credit application reconsidered is if they were denied for having too many delinquencies, collections, bankruptcy, or a debt settlement. Such reasons are considered major by most financial institutions. Below is contact information that consumers can use to contact the credit or executive departments of the financial institutions via mail or phone for reconsiderations, credit limit increases, interest rate reductions, or to remove late payments showing on credit reports. Consumers should not contact the back of the credit card because from personal experience, the customer service representatives of some financial institutions will express that there is nothing that can be done about getting the denied application approved or will not know what to do about it. Regular customer service agents are not trained to handle the issues regarding the approval or denial of credit applications or credit reporting issues. They will say anything to get the consumer to hang up the phone because it costs the financial institutions money when too many consumers are on the phone lines or are calling. My mother was denied for an Air Tran Airways credit card due to "insufficient history established on revolving accounts" because she was closing too many credit cards too quickly, which negatively impacts credit. Such is considered a minor credit denial reason because it does not imply that my mother cheated any bank or ever defaulted. On the behalf of my mother and as a joint account applicant, I had called the regular customer service department of the bank on their website to ask for a reconsideration of the application. They told me nothing could be done to approve the application and she would have to reapply for the credit card, which would mean another credit check. I was able to call the credit department of Barclays Bank who is the issuer of the credit card, and convince them to approve her application without doing additional credit checks. They were able to use the credit report that their systems had originally pulled, which was a TransUnion report.

Consumers should use certified mail when sending letters because they must put their account number or social security number on the letter or it will let get lost. For this reason, <u>always</u> indicate "please make a note on my credit application [or account] that this letter was received" and sign the letter. Consumers always need to make financial institutions feel confident as much as possible that the consumer is unlikely to default and so consumers should always indicate somewhere on the reconsideration letters "I do not cheat banks of their loan money. Please approve my application. If I were to default then please garnish my wages, put a claim on my house and car, or take me to court." They should also express this confidently in phone conversations because it is unlikely that consumers who are planning on defaulting would say such comments. Finally, consumers should always mention any current or previous positive relationships, if any, that they have had with the financial institution such as a checking or savings account that has very rarely become negative or checks have been bounced and previous or current loans or credit cards on which the consumer has never been delinquent.

Here is a letter format consumers can send to creditors that denied them for credit or for a cheaper interest rate, which is considered a refinance.

Bank name:
Attention: Executive department
Corporate office address:
Date:
Application identification number or social security number: Address of consumer that was on the credit application:

To Whom It May Concern:

I applied for an Air Tran Airways credit card (name of the loan or credit card) on January 10, 2011 (approximate date that application was submitted) and regretfully, was denied due to short length of history established on revolving accounts (state the reason for the credit denial). My intention for getting the (loan or credit card) was to earn the bonus miles promotion (state the legitimate purpose as to why the loan is wanted or needed and elaborate on it so the financial institution does not think the intention behind getting the loan is to use all the loan money and not pay it). My plan was to make small purchases, earn rewards, pay off the balance immediately, and save money (consumers should explain how they plan on handling the loan).

Although I have short history on my revolving accounts (reason for denial) because I was closing credit cards too quickly and not building long history on them (state the cause for the credit weakness), this reason is still minimal. From now on, I will not close credit cards but instead, keep them open, use them very lightly, and pay them off the day that they are used (how a consumer can fix the credit denial reason). Please reconsider my application and approve me for the credit card. I assure you by granting me credit, Barclays Bank (state the name of the financial institution or company) will not have a loan loss because my credit report reflects no delinquencies, over 30 credit accounts in good standing, a variety of credit with several banks, and very few inquiries (consumers should establish their financial strengths and elaborate on them because this shows they are confident about paying their loans). In fact, Barclays Bank can perform any background check or a credit check with the other consumer reporting agencies and they will still find no negative credit information on me.

I have never cheated any bank of their loan money by not paying them or declaring a bankruptcy or settlement and will never do so. For this reason, I do not appreciate the denial for credit because my credit score decreased due to the credit check (consumers are encouraged to include these statements on their reconsideration letter because it shows more confidence in being able to repay the loan). In the event I did not pay on my credit card, Barclays Bank can garnish my wages, take me to court, or put a claim on my assets or house (consumers are encouraged to include consequences that the financial institution can take against them in the event that the consumer fails to repay the loan).

Please make a note on the application that this letter was received (consumers must include this statement with the reconsideration letter otherwise the financial institution can say that they never received the letter). If possible, please simply approve the credit application. I am willing to accept a low credit limit and after establishing a strong payment history, I will ask for a credit limit increase (consumers should include this statement because financial institutions are less likely to think that consumers that want a small credit limit have the bad intention of defaulting on the credit card). I would greatly appreciate a phone call at (407) 496-6005 to discuss the reconsideration of the loan application (consumers should indicate a phone number at which the financial institution can contact them). If I am unavailable then please leave me a voice message and I will promptly return your call. I greatly appreciate your assistance with the situation (consumers should be courteous because the bank representative is less likely to help rude consumers).

Thank you,
(State first and last name that was indicated on the credit application so the financial institution knows the legitimate consumer mailed them the reconsideration letter and not a criminal)

Here is a letter format that is focused on getting a cheaper interest rate on the loan, specifically a credit card.

Bank name:
Attention: Executive department
Corporate office address:
Date:
Application identification number or social security number:
Address of consumer that was on the credit application:

To Whom It May Concern

I have been a customer with Bank of America for about five years and have maintained checking and savings accounts that have never become negative; I am currently paying about 18.24% on my Bank of America World Points credit card and was hoping that my account could be reviewed for a lower interest rate (state the problem and what solution is desired). I was hoping for a rate closer to 9% (Considering the rough economic times, 10% or below for a credit card is considered a cheap interest rate so consumers should always make this statement). I have credit cards with other financial institutions and the Bank of America credit card I have has the interest rate among all of them.

I have never been late on the credit card or with any loan or credit card with any other financial institution in all the years I have had access to credit. I have no intention of defaulting, declaring a bankruptcy or settlement, or cheating the bank and am planning on periodically using the credit card again after repaying my debt. For such reasons, I feel as though Bank of America should value my relationship and grant me a lower interest rate. If it in the event I were to default on the credit card or my credit profile becomes negative then Bank of America can sue me in court, garnish my wages, or put a claim on my assets or house so they can make up for their loan loss.

I am not asking for a lower interest rate because I am in a financial struggle, but simply because I want to save money and pay the principle down much faster. Paying down the balance faster will cause my credit scores to increase.

Please make a note on my credit card account that this correspondence was received. I would greatly appreciate a phone call at (407) 496-6005 so we can discuss a solution. If the interest rate can be reduced then you have my authorization to reduce it. I greatly appreciate your assistance in the situation.

Thank you,
 (State first and last name that was indicated on credit application)

No-Income Verification Loans

Creditors that were giving mortgages, which are home loans, to consumers with bad or limited credit histories are considered "subprime mortgage lenders." Countrywide Home Loans is an example of a company that was a major subprime mortgage lender. The 2000s mortgage crisis that took place in America mostly hurt the subprime mortgage industry because most of those subprime mortgages that were given to some consumers did not require the verification of income and may have been more lenient in approving consumers with negative credit histories. Mortgages and other loans that do not require the verification of income, which are granted mostly by subprime creditors, are known as "no-income verification loans." Unfortunately, the no-income verification loans resulted in the most losses for financial institutions because the subprime creditors gave loans to consumers whose income could not support those loans and as a result, the consumers defaulted on the loans. However, it should not be thought that all consumers who were granted no-income verification loans defaulted on them because there were consumers that handled them responsibly due to their motivation and limited spending on luxuries.

The no-income verification loans were beneficial to consumers that wanted houses or other items but could not get approved for traditional loans in order to purchase them due to their income. They may not have been able to make high income due to lack of work experience, low economic demand for their degree or work skills, or just factors that were out of their control. In fact, my mother was granted a no-income verification mortgage but till this day, she has never defaulted on it or any bill. The majority of consumers did default and for this reason, very few financial institutions are offering no-income verification loans or mortgages. Many subprime mortgage lenders that only offered no-income verification mortgages or subprime mortgages were bought out by other financial institutions or shut down. Countrywide Home Loans was bought out by Bank of America Home Loans.

Here is an advertisement that once existed for a "no-income verification mortgage."

Source of image: http://njmch.com/NewJerseymortgages.html

Business Risks of Subprime Lending

An increasing number of financial institutions are trying to escape the subprime credit industry because the government has been passing laws restricting financial institutions on how much interest and fees they can charge the consumers. An increasing number of consumers are developing bad credit. Subprime creditors need to impose the higher than average interest and fees because the high risk consumers to whom they grant credit are very likely to default. Due to the fees and high interest, some consumers think of subprime creditors as being "loan sharks." If the subprime creditors do not offset the risks involved in lending to high risk consumers then as a company, they are very likely to fail due to their weak business performance. The subprime creditors will not be able to make enough profits to pay their employees, create more jobs, expand to more locations, diversify, and keep their business running. For such reasons, consumers with limited or bad credit are finding it difficult to obtain credit because financial institutions are reluctant to get into business with them due to the fear of not being able to make enough profit. This is part of the reason why many small financial institutions failed and had to be shut down.

Finance 101: The Whiz Kid's Perfect Credit Guide

Credit Rights

Through the Fair Credit Reporting Act

Consumers are allowed to place free fraud alerts on their credit reports, if they want to maximize their protection against fraud and identity. The fraud alert will have a phone number, which all financial institutions must call and verify that the authentic consumer has applied for credit, before approving the credit application. Depending upon the preferences of the consumer, the fraud alert can remain up to 90 days on all the credit reports or longer if the consumer so chooses. The consumer can permanently remove the fraud alert if they choose to do so. Additionally, consumers are allowed to freeze their credit reports but unless their state of residency provides special rights or if they have evidence such as a police report that verifies they were a victim of fraud then they have to pay a small fee for the security freeze. A credit security freeze prevents any financial institution from checking credit and for this reason, with a credit freeze, no credit account can be established under the name of the consume unless they remove the credit freeze from all their credit reports. Before applying for credit, consumers have the option of permanently removing the credit freeze or temporarily removing it otherwise the credit application will immediately be denied. If consumers choose the option of having the credit freeze temporarily lifted then they must set up a time frame for long it should remain lifted. After the time frame that is set by the consumer runs out, the credit freeze will be automatically reinstated on the credit reports by the credit bureaus.

Active Duty Alert Prevents Fraud

Consumers who join the United States Armed Services are allowed to place an active duty alert on their credit reports, with the intention of protecting their credit profile, while they are on duty. This is because it is possible that the information of consumers could be compromised and they will usually not notice this until returning home from serving; because they have limited access to computers and postal mail to check their financial activities. Similar to how a financial institution would treat a consumer with a fraud alert on any of their credit reports, if they check the credit report of a consumer and notice the active duty alert then they will perform extra methods of verification such as ask the consumer for personal documents that verifies their identity. This can include a driver's license, pay stub, proof of residence, or a financial statement of some type such as a bank or credit card statement.

Fair Debt Collections Practices Act

Ideally, consumers should pay their debts because the financial institutions have to be successful as a business. and consumers who do not pay their debts are not being fair to consumers who always pay their debts. When consumers do not pay their debts, they get phone calls and letters from angry debt collectors. The debt collectors are usually collection agencies or financial institutions with whom the consumer has an unpaid loan or service. Debt collectors are legally not allowed to harass consumers about repaying their debts. Some debt collectors become extreme and make threats or say other harsh comments towards consumers. If debt collectors do this then they are breaking the law, because they are violating the Fair Debt Collections Practices Act. This act protects consumers from being mistreated by the debt collectors and financial institutions. Consumers have protection rights against the debt collectors. However, it does not protect the credit profiles of the consumers from being ruined by the debt collectors nor does it prevent the debt collectors from putting claims on the assets and properties belonging to the consumer. If consumers are being harassed then they should take the following steps so they can file a legal case.

1. Consumers should identify the debt collector, collection agency, or financial institution and record this information.
2. In writing, consumers should send a letter to the debt collector explaining that they cannot pay the debt, why they cannot pay the debt, and for the debt collector to stop harassing them or the consumer will take legal action against them for violating the Fair Debt Collections Practices Act. Consumers can mention in the letter that they can only pay a partial amount of the debt. Consumers should sign the letter and keep a second copy of it before mailing it.
3. Consumers need to make arrangements to repay the debt. Suggestions can include taking a loan against a 401(k) or 403(b), getting a low interest rate loan from a credit union or community bank, borrowing money from a family member, and if the debt collectors are trying to collect unpaid credit card debt then seeking credit counseling with a non-profit agency is ideal for consumers.
4. Consumers who are permanently disabled and cannot work may consider filing for a bankruptcy or debt settlement, but this should be the absolute last option because it costs money to do a bankruptcy or debt settlement, the insurance premiums of the consumer may increase, and any open credit cards of the consumer will be shut down by the financial institutions. Bankruptcy or debt settlement will prevent the debts from continuing to grow because it will eliminate them. Before declaring a bankruptcy or debt settlement, if possible, consumers are advised to put all or most of their money and assets into an IRA account, preferably a Roth IRA account because the consumer can withdraw the money at any time without paying the 10% tax penalty. The reason why consumers should put their money into an IRA account before declaring bankruptcy or a debt settlement is because it protects the money from being seized by the financial institutions and the debt collectors. When a consumer declares a bankruptcy or debt settlement, the companies to whom they owe money try to collect all the assets of the consumers. Consumers need to be aware that if they try to earn a job then the bankruptcy or debt settlement may be used against them by the employer.

Information that Shows on the Credit Reports

Employment: Financial institutions will know whether or not the consumer is employed. If no employment is showing on the credit reports then they will likely ask for proof of income or their employment. New employers can use the employment information on the credit reports to verify the authenticity of the resume and will know that the consumers did not make up random employers and job positions.

Credit inquiries: Financial institutions and employers will know if the consumer is aggressively applying for loans or credit cards. They will look at the consumer with high risk if there are many credit checks.

Personal information: Addresses at which the consumer has resided, full name, social security number, date of birth, spouses, and phone numbers they have had during their lifetime will show on the credit reports.

Finance 101: The Whiz Kid's Perfect Credit Guide

Innovis Background Information (The 4th Credit Bureau)

The company was started in 1970 called the "Associated Credit Bureau Services" and is considered the fourth credit agency. The name was changed to "Innovis Data Solutions" in 1997. Like all the credit agencies, they collect the financial information of consumers but they specialize in selling this information to the financial institutions so they can send credit card and other loan product offers to consumers using mail and email. Innovis has no business relationship with the Fair Isaac Corporation or the credit agencies.

Pay Attention when Reading Credit Reports

When consumers are reading credit reports; then they need to pay attention to certain details that may be lowering their credit scores and resulting in consumers paying, higher than average, insurance premiums. Consumers would need to dispute these details with the credit agencies and contact the companies who reported the information.

No accounts, on the credit reports, should say "closed by credit grantor", as a remark; because it raises the question as to why a financial institution would close the credit account, of a consumer. This remark does not lower the credit scores; but it is considered content that will be questioned by future financial institutions and may result in the consumer getting denied for credit or their current accounts getting closed, which will lower the credit scores.

If accounts are open but the credit reports indicate they are closed, then the consumer needs to contact the financial institutions immediately and request for them, to report the correct information. This will cause the credit scores to increase; because open credit accounts give the credit scores more strength than closed credit card accounts.

An account status should <u>never</u> say "settled", but only "paid off", on the credit reports; because this is significantly lowering the credit scores. Settled accounts send the message that the consumer cheated the financial institution of their loan money.

There should be no multiple inquiries (credit checks) from the same creditor, for the same loan, with the same credit bureau. This lowers the credit score with that agency. For example, if Jillian applies for a Nordstrom credit card; and her Equifax credit report is showing two credit checks from Nordstrom then she needs to inform Nordstrom about this error. To an employer and financial institution, it looks like Jillian applied for two Nordstrom credit cards and it raises the question why she is applying for so much credit.

Consumers need to make sure all their credit accounts and loans are reporting to all the credit bureaus unless the creditor does not report to all agencies. If a credit report is not showing a loan or credit card belonging to the consumer then they need to inform the financial institution and have it reported. Consumers should not make this request if the missing credit account was ever delinquent because then it will lower their credit scores if they appear on the credit reports.

Consumers need to make sure the amount reported as the "high balance" or "high credit," which was the highest amount charged, is not higher than the credit limit on each loan or credit card otherwise it seems as though the consumer spent beyond their means. Credit cards and loan balances that went over the credit limit lower the credit scores of the consumer. Example—**Credit Limit/Original Amount: $1000. High Balance: $1359 (over the limit by $359)**

Credit Agencies and Trade Lines

Credit accounts and their payment histories, along with other personal data, such as; the social security number, date of birth, employment, and addresses; are reported monthly to one or more of the consumer reporting agencies in the United States; Equifax, Experian, TransUnion, and some lenders use, Innovis. Such information creates the credit reports of consumers.

All credit accounts, on credit reports, are considered **trade lines**. Consumer reporting agencies are also called "credit bureaus" or "credit agencies." The credit bureaus are private companies that are not owned or funded by the government. They make their money by selling credit reports and credit related information to companies and consumers. They are monitored by the Federal Trade Commission, which helps maintain the rights of consumers such as information that they can dispute from their credit reports. It is possible different countries may have different credit bureaus that their businesses and consumers use. This may hurt financial institutions and be unfair to consumers; because high risk consumers may negatively abuse the system. They may ruin their credit, in the United States, by cheating financial institutions and migrate to another country where they could potentially get loans. There will be no record of their bad credit history. This is not fair to consumers who work day and night to make sure all their bills are paid in a timely manner.

Purpose of Needing Credit

The purpose of credit is to show companies the strong financial capabilities, of the consumer. Credit is not about needing money or getting into debt. Companies will not lend consumers their services, such as; cable, phone, water, insurance, or loans; unless they know they are not at high risk of being cheated of their money. They cannot lend services blindly because there is always the chance they will send the bills to the consumers and the consumers will never pay them back. As a result, the company has had a financial loss. There is no way they can get back their money. Companies are trying to avoid having losses, which is why they are checking the credit reports of consumers. Besides credit, there is no other way for them to determine if they will be cheated. For this reason, it is very difficult for a consumer to get a house, apartment, car, insurance credit card, utility services, phone, or anything without having a strong credit history. In fact, some car rental companies are now performing credit checks on consumers who use debit cards to rent a car. If a consumer has poor credit then the car rental company will not rent the car to the consumer or may require a large security deposit.

Free Copy of Credit Report is a Right upon Denial of Credit or Service

Whenever a consumer is denied for credit, an apartment, insurance, or an adverse action is taken against them then consumers have the right to view a free copy of their credit report with each credit agency. Credit scores are not free. Adverse actions can include a credit limit reduction, the credit card is closed by the financial institution, they are denied for a job or their insurance premium or credit card interest rate is suddenly increased.

Transunion
P.O. Box 1000
Chester, PA 19022
http://annualcreditreport.transunion.com/tu/disclosure/currentSituation.jsp
1-800-888-4213

Experian
P.O. Box 9556
Allex, TX 75013
http://www.experian.com/reportaccess/
1-888-397-3742

Equifax
P.O. Box 740241
Atlanta, GA 30374
www.equifax.com/fcra
1-800-203-7843

Innovis
Attn: Consumer Assistance
P.O. Box 1689
Pittsburgh, PA 15230-1689
https://www.innovis.com/InnovisWeb/pers_orderCreditReport.html
1-800-540-2505

Just Being Rich is Not Enough

Some consumers think that as long as they make high income and investments, they will be financially strong. This is not true, because bad credit will mean high interest and fees that will consume any high income and profits made from investments. Additionally, companies do not value how much income a consumer makes, as much as they do, their credit profile. This is because even if a consumer makes high income, that does not mean they will use their income to pay the bills. It is possible for a consumer to use all the loans and services, not pay anyone, and keep the income. For this reason, some consumers and companies feel as though paying the bills is a moral decision.

Companies view Consumers with Bad Credit as Low in Character

The reason why some consumers stop paying their bills is not always because of financial struggles, but due to having low character. For this reason, some companies view consumers who have good credit also have good morals and are unlikely to default. In contrast, consumers who have bad credit are looked upon as having bad morals and are likely to default.

Abuse of Credit in Relationships

Bad credit suggesting bad morals is supported by the evidence; that some consumers with bad credit use the credit profiles of others including their girlfriend, boyfriend, or family member to obtain credit and eventually leave them, with all the bills. For this reason, some single parents, especially single pregnant women, have to work excessively; because in most married families, one consumer handles the finances and the other consumer trusts them.

To better explain this, the consumer handling all the finances can be considered "consumer A" and consumer fully trusting consumer A can be considered "consumer B."
"Consumer A" has the opportunity to do financial damage to "consumer B". It is possible "consumer B" could be left homeless, with their children; because "consumer A" caused "consumer B" to develop such a bad credit profile, that it is almost impossible to get approved for an apartment, house, or car.

There are other cases, in which consumers may decide to form relationships, with other consumers, for the sole reason of using their credit. The intention is to use the credit to buy whatever they want and one of the consumers will be liable for all the charges. Often consumers, with such bad intentions, will refuse to pay any of the bills so they can save all their money. With the same bad intentions, a consumer may marry another consumer and later divorce them, with the desire of wanting **alimony**. Alimony is usually court ordered; it is when one spouse is required to send money to the other spouse. It is also possible a consumer will purposely bear kids with another consumer with the bad intention of wanting to get child support. Not paying the alimony or child support could potentially ruin the credit profile of the consumer.

Creditworthiness is Trustworthiness

The level of trustworthiness a consumer has in paying back credit or simply any bill. When a consumer applies for credit, the financial institution checks the credit reports and credit scores with one or more of the consumer reporting agencies to determine how creditworthy the consumer is considered. Usually, a score of 655 or higher suggests a consumer is at low risk for defaulting. Higher credit scores can suggest higher levels of creditworthiness. Lower credit scores, usually below 655, can suggest lower levels of creditworthiness. A person with a high level of creditworthiness can be thought of as an A or B school student. In contrast, a person with a low level of creditworthiness can be thought of as a D or F student. Just as A or B students are very likely to academically succeed in the eyes of their teachers, consumers with high levels of creditworthiness are very likely to financially succeed in the eyes of their financial institutions. Similarly, just as D or F school students are unlikely to succeed in the eyes of their teachers, consumers with low levels of creditworthiness are unlikely to financially succeed. Consumers that are likely to fail financially means no profit for the financial institutions, and they do not want to get into business with such high risk consumers.

Annual Fee is Profit Strategy

An annual fee is a yearly fee the creditors impose, on some of their financial products offered to consumers, such as credit cards, lines of credit, and personal loans. Annual fees are usually imposed on open credit accounts and not closed accounts. The annual fee can be considered paying interest, because if the consumer does not pay off the annual fee immediately; then it will be carried in the balance and accumulate more interest that will make the balance higher. Some creditors called "subprime creditors" charge annual fees to consumers with poor or limited credit histories so they can make more profit. This is because consumers with poor or limited credit histories are very likely to stop paying on the loans, and the subprime creditors are trying to make as much money as they can for the time that payments are successfully being made. Subprime creditors specialize in "subprime lending," which means granting credit to consumers with poor or limited credit histories. In charging the annual fee, the subprime creditor is offsetting the potential of risk by lending to the high risk consumers. Examples of subprime creditors can include HSBC, Capital One, First Premier Bank, and First Bank of Delaware.

Business Management of Credit

As a way of monitoring growth and successful lending standards; the financial institutions keep record of the credit profiles, of the consumers, to whom they grant credit. The institutions record average credit scores, debt amounts, delinquencies, ages, incomes, and other financial related information of the consumers. The financial institutions break their customers into groups; and each group contains customers with similar credit profiles. Financial institutions usually have special computer software to do such calculations; because it saves them time and money. If they did not use software, then they would have to hire more employees or give more tasks to current employees, which mean the financial institutions would have to pay them more money. Employees doing calculations will make it likely there will be errors with the lending performance data. The financial institutions will have to pay more money to the employees for spending more time trying to redo the calculations. This will mean increased costs on financial products for consumers.

An example of special risk management software used by financial institutions would be the Business Intelligence program created by Microsoft. Business risk management programs allow for financial institutions to statistically keep track of the groups and observe which group develops the highest number of customers that default on their accounts. This group is considered to have the most high risk consumers. The financial institutions will want to reduce the number of high risk consumers who are being granted credit. This is because such consumers are bringing a bad reputation to the institution; and it suggests their lending standards are weak and are causing them loss. For the future, the financial institution may limit granting credit or will extend credit with higher than average fees and interest rates to consumers with similar credit information to that of the high risk group. The financial institution will focus on improving their business performance, by lending credit more often, to the group with the lowest number of consumers that are defaulting on their accounts. The risk management software will recommend granting higher loan amounts and credit limits to credit healthy consumers. This means the company is trying to produce more as a business and increase its **productivity function** and **cash flow** levels.

The cash flow is the amount of money a business is spending on its products such as the loans, and receiving from the profits made off of consumers. The profits are considered income. The cash flow is weak when a business is spending more money than its income level. The productivity function is the rate of producing, which in the case of financial institutions, consists of its rates of lending and paying interest to consumers on their deposit accounts. For the purpose of maintaining a strong productivity function level, financial institutions must increase the interest rate on a credit card whenever a consumer is significantly late in making their payment because if they do not then consumers will become careless in making their payments and as a business, they will endure more losses.

The institutions will use the average financial information, of the credit-healthy group; and make modifications to their credit applications processing systems to be more prone to approve future consumers with similar financial and credit information, as well as market more credit card offers to them. In doing so, the financial institutions are hoping to lower risk and make more profits, which will allow for them to hire more employees for their lending departments and grant even more credit. Higher volumes of employees are needed because they will be responsible for monitoring all the new lending. More lending will result in more employees needed to market the credit products. In fact, there is business management software available that financial institutions use to determine television networks, radio stations, newspapers, and any other forms of media most popular among consumers within certain geographical locations. The financial institutions will likely use those popular media forms to advertise their own products. They will be able to save money and make profits because they will not waste time advertising their credit products on unpopular media forms and stations. Finally, a feature of business risk management software is that it reports data to the credit agencies regarding the payment histories and balances on the credit accounts of the consumers.

There are some weaknesses of business risk management software; when managing and analyzing the data of a company as well as that of consumers. For this reason, financial institutions will going to alternate and use software created by different companies. They are likely going to make a business relationship, with the company; whose risk management software allows for them to achieve the most productive and profitable business performance. When consumers submit credit applications, the business risk software evaluates the credit application for authenticity by using public records and any prior stored data, if any, that the financial institution has on the consumer; pulling the credit reports and scores from one or more of the credit agencies, and then the software flags an application if it needs to be reviewed by a credit analyst. If there is no review needed, then the risk management software will approve the credit application and will assign the consumer a credit limit based on their level of creditworthiness.

There have been cases in which the business risk software did not properly analyze the credit reports of the consumers and missed detecting some of the negative credit information such as delinquent credit accounts, excessive credit checks, or collection accounts. Thus, some consumers, with bad credit profiles, were approved for credit for which they should not have been approved. Some of these consumers were unsuccessful in repaying their credit accounts and the financial institutions reviewed their credit reports that were used to approve them in the first place.

The financial institutions then realized that their business risk software had flaws; because it extended credit to consumers who were unlikely to repay the financial institutions due to their bad credit. In fact, the software may have extended credit limits that were too high in relation to the debt, income, and liability levels of the consumers. When this has happened, the financial institutions made modifications to their software so high-risk credit consumers are less likely to be approved for credit. This means that financial institutions are more likely to be able to achieve higher levels of productivity when the risks they take are low. If a financial institution notices the business risk management software still has flaws because it is creating too much risk for the financial institution by approving too many consumers with bad credit profiles or failing to detect consumers who already have credit accounts but fail to pay on loans with other companies, or consumers who use bogus information to try to fraudulently obtain credit, then it is likely that the financial institution will going to use the management software made by another company. Trying to find suitable management software is why credit analysts and officers monitor them; because they do not want too much risk created for the financial institution. That would likely lead to the failure of the financial institution. There is no guarantee that any business risk management software will be flawless. The goal of the financial institutions is to find the software that has the least number of flaws so they maintain the safest and most profitable lending standards.

Behavior Score suggests Profit

A behavior score is calculated, by the business management software that the financial institution uses to determine if lending to a consumer would bring them profit based upon how much money the consumer is depositing and withdrawing from their deposit accounts, such as; checking, savings, and money market. Credit bureaus do not calculate a behavior score; because they do not have the ability to see the deposit account activities of consumers. Besides credit scores, a behavior score is another factor financial institutions take into consideration when deciding whether or not to grant credit and how much credit to a consumer. If a consumer is depositing more money than he withdraws, then it is likely the financial institution may target that consumer to grant credit. Such a consumer is likely to have a high behavior score. However, if a consumer is withdrawing more money than he deposit, or if his employer's direct deposit stops or gets reduced, this might be a sign of a financial weakness. Such a consumer would have a low behavior score. For this reason, consumers who are charged NSF fees and overdraft fees due to overly using their deposit accounts may be denied credit because the financial institutions may review their deposit account activities and will think they are not responsible. The computer and business software of financial institutions have own behavior score scales, and such information is likely unavailable to consumers. Consumers who score high on the behavior score scale are likely to be granted high credit limits and loan amounts.

Consumers with good credit and are within the age range of 59 ½ to 70 ½ are likely to have high behavior scores, and for this reason they are likely to be granted high amounts of loan money and credit. This is because financial institutions know if a consumer has a job; because their credit reports will reflect their employment information. Financial institutions assume that most consumers have a 401(k) with their employers. Consumers must start withdrawing money from their 401(k) before they surpass the age of 70 ½, otherwise they could face tax penalties. Such money, along with the funds that are withdrawn from an Individual Retirement Account, is considered extra income that the consumer can use to spend. Financial institutions view that these consumers are more likely to be successful in repaying their loans, and they want them to use their loans often so the financial institutions can make high levels of profit. For this reason, it is likely that employed consumers within the certain age range are going to be granted credit limit increases on their credit cards.

USA Patriot Act

George W. Bush, signed the Patriot Act into law on October 26, 2001; to strengthen the overall defenses of America. The United States was on full alert, after the terrorist attack on the twin towers, on September 11th, 2001. For financial institutions, till this day, it requires for them to obtain and verify all pieces of information consumers put on applications for credit or bank accounts to prevent potentially granting financial services to terrorists. For this reason, financial institutions may ask for a driver's license, passport, bank statements, or any other document; that verifies the consumer and all the information that the consumer has provided. Part of the Patriot Act was expected to help lower the amount of money laundering taking place within the United States. Money laundering is when criminals or terrorists get money through illegal sources, such as the sales of drugs or counterfeit money. They then somehow try to make their transactions seem legitimate, in the eyes of financial institutions, when they review the transactions, of the terrorists on the bank statements. It is possible a criminal or terrorist may even use credit to purchase illegal drugs or weapons, and the Patriot Act is trying to prevent such from happening. The purpose of verifying identity is a reason why financial institutions ask for social security numbers from consumers. Verifying all pieces of information, also helps financial institutions save money; because in the event they need to contact the consumer, they are less likely to get returned mail and waste money on postage and save money on the phone bills because they will not be calling wrong or disconnected phone numbers. Employees will not be wasting their time. The savings of the financial institutions are passed on to consumers because it is more likely consumers can get paid more interest on their deposit accounts and pay overall less interest and fees on loans.

Utility Bills are Important

All bills must be paid, in a timely manner, and cannot be left unpaid; even if they are not reporting payment histories, to the credit bureaus. Any bill that is not paid has a potential of being reported, as negative information to credit agencies. When bills such as utilities, insurance, movie or video game rentals, newspapers, memberships, or any miscellaneous expenses are left unpaid for a long time; even if the amounts are small, the companies will usually sell the debts to collection agencies. In doing so, the businesses are able to get a partial amount of the unpaid debts. Collection agencies are responsible for collecting the unpaid debts from the consumer. The unpaid debts are now "collection accounts," which means they are debts that the consumer has refused to pay for a long time and such accounts are immediately reported to the credit agencies. They ruin the credit reports and scores of consumers; because in the eyes of financial institutions and the credit agencies, collection accounts send the message that the companies were cheated and the consumer is financially weak. Some companies may have their own collection departments handle the collection accounts; and continuously contact the consumers through phone or mail until the debts have been paid. Collection accounts stay on credit reports for up to ten years. Even if the collection accounts are paid in full in a timely manner, they will still be viewed negatively. However, the collection accounts will not be viewed as negatively as they would if they were never paid. Depending upon the rules of the collection agency, some collection accounts do charge interest for the time the debt amounts are being carried every month. The interest rate is determined by the collection agency and they may or may not use the credit profile information of the consumer to determine the interest rate because it costs them money to order the credit reports. It is also possible the collection agency may have a set interest rate on all collection accounts.

Example: If Alexis rents a movie from Blockbuster and never returns it, Blockbuster would then send Alexis a notice indicating she must pay for the movie or return it and pay the late fee. Alexis refuses to pay the bill for a month. Blockbuster will sell the bill to their collection agency and Alexis will have a collection account reported to her credit reports. Even if Alexis pays off the collection account in full, it will still remain on her credit profile for up to ten years as negative information. Blockbuster had a financial loss because their movie was never returned.

Unfortunately, companies, such as; Blockbuster get risky consumers, such as; Alexis, and for this reason they always ask for a driver's license, social security, and other personal information as a business safeguard. They will be able share this information with the collection agency and report the unpaid debt to the credit bureaus. If the collection accounts are never paid then they become "charged-off accounts." A charged-off account is one of the most negative pieces of financial information that can be reported to the credit agencies. Consumers can still pay on the charged-off account and the credit reports will reflect the payments and say "charged-off/

paid" but they will show all the negative history behind the accounts. In the eyes of the financial institutions, the credit account should never have been past due to begin.

Advice: Do not take any bill lightly. Consumers have an equal level of liability for all bills. Unfortunately, some consumers spend excessively beyond their means to the point that they choose to pay one bill and not pay the other. This can result in credit being damaged and the late fees will cause the bill amounts to double. Small bill amounts will become big bill amounts. Such will make it more difficult for consumers to pay future bills. Pay the bills immediately to avoid late fees and do not take risks by delaying on paying.

Paying Bills in a Timely Manner is Not Enough

The payment history composes the greatest portion, of the FICO credit score, which is thirty-five percent. For this reason, a consumer must pay all their bills on time and it is the key to a strong credit history. However, just paying everything on time does not guarantee the best credit possible. This is because there are other factors financial institutions take into consideration. Some of these factors can even make a credit score low. Financial institutions and all credit scoring models look at balances owed on accounts. Carrying balances on credit cards that are close to credit limits are viewed negatively; even if they are paid in a timely manner. This is because it makes financial institutions think a consumer is spending beyond their means and is likely to get into so much debt that they will not be able to pay. It is likely consumers with high balances have a high debt-to-income ratio, which is higher than thirty-five percent and a high debt-to-credit limit ratio, which means they are utilizing too much credit. Financial institutions may approve consumers for new credit due to the fact they are being faithful in paying the bills but it is likely they will approve them with higher than average interest rates and low credit limits. For this reason, it is best to pay off the entire balance on any loan or credit card immediately. There is no reason to let balances continue growing and accumulate interest.

Income has No Relationship with Credit

Income never guarantees that consumers will pay their loans. Financial institutions ask for income so they can calculate the debt-to-income ratio, for their own purposes of maintaining high lending standards, and running a successful business. Consumers should never think just because they make low income; then they will not financially succeed. It is possible to be retired or have a low income level such as thirty-five thousand and have a better credit profile than a consumer with a high income level such as one hundred thousand or more. Consumers need to have motivation in paying the bills and be proud whenever they are granted credit. This is because unfortunately, there are consumers out there who live on credit, buy whatever they want, never pay back the loans, and financial institutions will not approve these high risk consumers for new credit or services. All consumers have an equal chance at being granted credit based on their individual qualifications thanks to the "Equal Credit Opportunity Act" of 1974, which is maintained by the Federal Trade Commission. Creditors cannot discriminate against consumers.

Advice: Consumers need to be confident and never think badly about themselves no matter how low of income they make. It is possible for wealthy consumers to develop bad credit. In this regard, being wealthy means nothing because bad credit is not honorable as viewed by financial institutions. The credit agencies do not record any data related to the income level of a consumer because income is not part of the credit scoring models. Income does not influence credit scores.

Bad Credit means Many Problems

Unfortunately, some consumers give up on paying their bills and debts; or use credit without any intention of paying the financial institutions. Many consumers do not understand the many dangers in paying late, not paying at all, or filing for a bankruptcy or a debt settlement; even if they already have a house, automobile, or job. Such is considered poor financial behavior, which leads to bad credit. Bad credit is becoming increasingly common among consumers especially in the current economy. Consumers need to understand that bad credit makes everything more expensive and so in this sense, they are doubling the amounts of the bills they are not paying, which will <u>never</u> disappear.

Please understand the consequences when developing bad credit. Also, please use such consequences as motivation to always maintain excellent credit. In regards to the pros with bad credit, guess what? There are <u>no</u> pros.

Companies may lose respect for consumers who are late in making their payments or do not pay at all. Companies are less prone to refund fees, reduce interest rates, or increase the spending power in the event that the consumer needs access to more credit. In the eyes of some companies, consumers that do not pay or pay late are stealing from them. Companies will make numerous calls, send letters, and take drastic actions until they have been paid.

Companies may increase interest rates or apply fees to the credit accounts. There will be nothing that the consumer can do.

Companies may close the credit accounts due to bad credit history, and such activity lowers credit scores and can be considered negative content on the credit reports. This is because the accounts will report as "closed by credit grantor." Potential creditors in the future may question consumers on why the previous creditors closed their accounts. It may be considered risky information to the creditors. Closed accounts should always say "closed by consumer." An account that says "closed for inactivity" as its status is not considered negative, but it is not the best status possible.

If possible, consumers should contact the issuer of the account to see if the status can be changed to "closed by consumer." This is because it is possible that future financial institutions may see that status and think they cannot make much profit off of the consumer. Instead, they will have a financial loss because the consumer is somewhat unlikely to use the credit account heavily, and it costs money for the financial institutions to maintain a credit account within their databases especially when they have to pay fees for periodic credit reports during account reviews. If too many credit accounts have the "closed for inactivity" status, then the financial institution may grant the consumer a low credit limit because consumers who are unlikely to use their credit accounts are more likely to not notice when their accounts are fraudulently used, and this will result in a loss for the financial institution. The financial institution is likely to approve the consumer with a higher than average interest rate with the intention of trying to make as much profit as possible off of the consumer for whatever little purchases they make using the credit account. When creditors close accounts, they do not immediately inform consumers, and so the consumer will have to face embarrassment when they use a credit card that has been closed. The card will decline. Consumers with bad credit will face more embarrassment when they apply for a credit card and are denied.

Bad credit guarantees paying thousands in interest and fees and higher minimum payments. More companies will require security deposits from consumers before extending services. Creditors may approve consumers that have bad credit with higher than average interest rates and annual fees. This makes it harder for consumers to save money for retirement, children's expenses, college education, and other expenses. High interest and fees increases the likelihood of the consumers becoming late on their credit accounts in the event that they cannot afford the minimum payments. Consumers will be living in debt for longer time periods because most of their payments will be going towards high interest and not the principle amounts. High interest and fees increases the amounts owed on the credit accounts. High amounts owed and debts lower the credit scores.

Due to the severe economic conditions and competitive job market, many employers seek only well-qualified candidates for their jobs. For this reason, employers are checking the credit reports and credit scores of the candidates. In the eyes of the employers, a candidate with bad credit takes away credibility from their college degree. This is because if the candidate was educated enough to earn the degree then the employer begins to wonder why the candidate would not be educated enough to earn and maintain perfect credit. Bad credit suggests the candidate is irresponsible and no employer wants to hire an irresponsible candidate. Employers may deny jobs to candidates with bad credit. Bad credit sends the employers a bad message about the candidates. Candidates may also be dismissed from their job due to bad credit because employers will often conduct periodic reviews on their employees and such involves checking their credit and background. Consumers will either be jobless or have to get jobs that do not make enough incomes to cover all the expenses. This will increase the likelihood of the consumers becoming late on their accounts and being hit with numerous late fees and default interest rates.

Bad credit can mean being denied for a house, car, insurance, apartment, or _anything_ a consumer can purchase. As a result, consumers cannot live the decent lifestyles that they desire and are more likely to become stressed. Bad credit is part of the reason why some consumers are homeless. Some consumers that live in apartments do so because their credit is not strong enough to be approved for a mortgage- home loan. Some consumers that drive obsolete cars or are always taking the bus are because their credit is not strong enough to be approved for auto loan (car loan). Some consumers that are always using debit cards or cash is because their credit is so poor that no company wants to extend credit to them. They need a credit card especially when trying to rent a car or get extra protection on merchandise they purchase. Additionally, credit checks performed by companies cause the credit scores of consumers to drop. Such credit checks are known as "hard inquiries." Inquiries stay on the credit reports for two years and many inquiries make it more difficult to be granted credit or get low interest rates. This is because, in the eyes of the creditors, many inquiries indicate that the consumer is trying to get into large debts, may be financially unstable, and may be desperate for credit. For such reasons, the creditors feel as though they are at high risk because the consumer has a high likelihood in defaulting on their credit accounts.

Subprime creditors specialize in granting credit to consumers who have bad credit because such consumers cannot get traditional credit cards with decent interest rates. Consumers will be granted low credit limits such as three hundred dollars. Low credit limits make it more likely for the consumers to spend over the credit limit and be charged fees for doing so. Often times, subprime creditors will charge additional fees such as when they increase the credit limit, a fee to process the credit application, monthly maintenance fees, fees for using their website, and fees to activate the credit card. Subprime creditors charge these fees because there is high risk that the consumers with bad credit will stop paying their bills. The subprime creditors are trying to make as much profit as they can from the high risk consumers for the time that the consumers continue to make the payments on the credit accounts. Consumers should not develop bad credit so they can avoid having to do business with the subprime creditors.

Consumers with bad credit will have a difficult time trying to get free traditional checking and savings accounts. Some financial institutions may check credit when consumers want to open up deposit accounts such as checking or savings accounts. Bad credit may cause them to get denied because in the eyes of the financial institutions, consumers with bad credit are considered financially weak and are more likely to make their deposit accounts negative by overdrawing them. As a result, the financial institutions have a loss because they cannot recover their funds. It costs financial institutions money to maintain the deposit accounts and so they cannot afford to have checking accounts become negative or pay written checks with amounts needing more than the funds in the accounts. Such checks are "bounced." Bounced checks can also be called "returned checks." If the financial institution does grant the consumer with bad credit a checking or savings account then it is likely the accounts will have monthly service fees. The fees will make it difficult for consumers to save money in their deposit accounts, which means less money for retirement and paying bills.

Consumers who do not pay their bills or service contractors to whom they owe money may have a "non-consensual lien" imposed on their house or personal property as a way for the companies to get back some of their lost money. The companies can keep or sell the house or property. There is nothing that the consumer can do to have the non-consensual lien removed unless they negotiate with the company and pay them the owed debt. A non-consensual lien is a derogatory term, which means when a property has strict financial restrictions placed on it by a business to which the consumer owes money. In this sense, the business has a claim on the property. The consumer cannot refinance, keep, or sell their house with the lien. In fact, if the lean is not removed quickly it may reflect as negative information on the public records of the consumers, which can be reported as negative financial information to the credit agencies. The credit profiles of the consumers will be ruined. Liens always suggest that a consumer is unlikely to pay on their credit accounts. Liens can also be imposed on properties by the Internal Revenue Services, which is abbreviated as the IRS, when consumers do not pay their taxes.

Finally, although more consumers and financial institutions would call it a claim rather than a non-consensual lien because a lien usually refers to a claim on a property, it is possible for a financial institution to put a claim on an automobile or boat. This is not as common as placing non-consensual liens on properties because in most cases, automobiles and boats have less value than properties or houses due to **depreciation**. The financial institutions and service contractors are trying to get as much money as possible from the consumers because it costs them money to file for liens and claims. For this reason, they will use the public records to see how much value the boat or car has compared to the market value of the property. Depending upon the market values of the automobile, boat, property or house and how much debt the consumer owes, the financial institution or service contractor may impose a claim on everything until they have been paid. The value of such assets is considered cash equivalence. If the automobile or boat has little or no market value then it is likely only a non-consensual lean will be placed on the property belonging to the consumer because it has a low level of cash equivalence. For consumers who do not own any property, house, automobile, or boat and owe debts then it is possible the financial institution or service contractor will take them to court and sue them. The court may order that the wage and any assets of the consumer be **garnished**, which means they will be taken by force and there is nothing that the consumer can do. There is another financial term that is called a "consensual lien" but it has a different definition and it is not considered derogatory. A consensual lien would be placed on any product such as a house, property, or car by the lien holder when the consumer agrees to get a loan in order to buy it. The lien holder is simply the loan issuer. The consensual lien means the product is not fully considered to be owned by the consumer until they have paid off the loan. A consensual lien allows for the lien holder to repossess the product in the event the consumer fails to make payments.

Some creditors may sue consumers in court for the money that the consumers did not pay them back. If the creditor wins the case then the consumers will have to also pay the lawyers of the creditor. The court events may show on the credit reports as negative information.

Bad Credit causes some Financial Institutions to "Blacklist" Consumers

Bad credit is not honorable, in the eyes of companies, employers, and some family members, such as spouses. According to A Society of Human Resources Management (SHRM) survey conducted in 2010, it is reported that about 60% of employers check the credit profiles of employee applicants. Bad credit stays on credit report for up to ten years. Financial institutions and employers may save copies of past credit reports with the negative credit information and such may be used against the consumer even after ten or more years pass. There is no guarantee that the past negative financial information cannot be used against the consumer because their computer databases will recognize negative financial information that is associated with the social security number and/or address listed on the records of the consumer. In this, the bad credit profile is causing the consumer to be blacklisted with the employer and financial institutions. In fact, it is possible employers can check the credit profiles of current employees when evaluating the performance levels of employees. There is nothing legally that prohibits a current employer from checking credit. An employee cannot prohibit their employer from checking credit, because it raises the question what the employee is hiding from the employer. Finally, for the ten year range in which the consumer has bad credit, that will mean ten years of paying thousands on high interest and fees guaranteed. This hard-earned money could have been saved by the consumer.

Do Not Pay Thousands to Credit Repair Agencies

Companies that advertise on the radio, television, internet, or just any means indicating that they can repair the credit profile of a consumer or help them establish credit are scams. They always want a fee for their services, usually $1000, $2000, $3000, or more; but what they do is trivial. This is because consumers can fix their own credit by disputing the negative information, with all the credit agencies, contacting the corporate offices of the financial institutions that issued the credit accounts on which they were delinquent to have them removed, and getting a secured credit card to improve their credit scores. Companies claiming that they can erase a bankruptcy, debt settlement, or delinquent accounts off of the credit reports are exaggerating because that would mean they would be trying to falsify information on the credit reports. The credit agencies and financial institutions will notice this fraudulent activity and may take adverse actions against the consumer, such as putting a negative comment on all their credit reports that the consumer is trying to purposely dispute accurate information with the means of fraudulently getting approved for credit. The credit repair companies have no liability for this and will not refund the consumer their fees. Only the financial institution has the ability to remove negative information off of the credit reports. In most cases, consumers cannot remove negative information until seven to ten years have passed depending upon its severity level. For example, it is more likely a consumer that has one delinquency can get it removed than the likelihood of a consumer with multiple delinquencies getting them all removed. Consumers cannot ever develop bad credit and rely on unrealistic factors such as credit repair agencies to fix their credit.

Freezing Credit Reports will Not Hide Information from Companies

Consumers can never hide information from any employer or company. The company or employer will perform a soft inquiry credit check, on the consumer, and the security freeze will not prevent them from doing so. The soft inquiry credit check will allow for the company and/or employer to view the negative credit information. Security freezes are only effective when consumers apply for credit and the financial institution has to do a hard inquiry credit check. If financial institutions or employers want to see a more detailed version of the credit profile of the consumer then they will ask the consumer to remove the security freeze because they may get the impression that the consumer is trying to hide information from them. Financial institutions specifically do hard inquiry check credits because they want other businesses and financial institutions to see the fact that the consumer recently obtained a loan, which is why a credit check had occurred on them. When a financial institution grants credit, they do not want other companies immediately granting more loan money to a consumer because this raises the likelihood of the consumer using all the loan money and putting themselves in a bad financial position in which they cannot repay anyone. As a result, all the companies have had a business loss. For this reason, the credit agencies have structured their credit scoring model to lower the credit scores whenever hard inquiry credit checks occur on the consumer. Soft inquiry credit checks can only be viewed by the consumer and they do not affect credit scores because soft inquiry credit checks are not done when a consumer applies for credit but only hard inquiries.

Good Credit means a Good Life, Good Future, and No Cons

Please avoid all the cons by always paying your bills in a timely manner. There are never any cons to achieving and maintaining excellent credit. There are only pros, no stress, and unlimited financial success.

Excellent credit <u>ensures</u> the lowest interest rates, no fees, and little or no security deposits. Companies feel comfortable granting their services to consumers with excellent credit because the company is at low risk of losing their money. As a result, the consumers can save thousands and put the savings towards retirement, their children, college expenses, a house, and a car.

Excellent credit <u>ensures</u> the approval of credit applications, including approvals for mortgages (house loans), auto loans (car loans), credit cards, insurance, utilities, cell phone, and <u>anything</u> a consumer could imagine. Consumers are more likely to get approved for the loan amounts that they need to purchase the houses and cars that they want such as a brand new Mercedes. Consumers will face no embarrassment as they would if their applications were denied or were approved for less than the needed loan amounts. In this situation, a consumer would most likely need to get a used car, house, or in some cases, may need to live in an apartment and without a car.

Excellent credit <u>ensures</u> the respect of creditors. Creditors are more likely to waive fees, permanently remove annual fees, extend the time length needed to pay off the loans, reduce interest rates, less likely to close accounts or do credit limit decreases, and offer better rewards programs- saves money. Creditors are more likely to offer refinancing options on cars and houses and this means lower interest rates and payments. In the unexpected event that the consumer needs more time to make a payment then companies are more likely to extend the due date without penalties to consumers that have always been faithful in paying their bills.

Excellent credit <u>ensures</u> cheaper insurance costs. Consumers should try calling their insurance providers and mentioning that their credit has become stronger. For this reason, they should request that the insurances companies offer them lower premiums. This is because the consumer is less likely to not pay the insurance bills and cheat the companies.

Excellent credit increases the likelihood of being able to get checking, money market, certificate of deposit, and savings accounts without monthly fees. Some financial institutions have fees set on certain deposit accounts and there is nothing that the consumer can do to avoid them besides going to a different financial institution. The reason why financial institutions have set fees such as on their debit cards is because they are trying to get the consumers to use their credit cards more so they can make more profits. Such profits will allow for financial institutions to make up for their losses on their loans. For this reason, too many consumers cannot default on their loans otherwise it is possible all financial institutions will start imposing fees on all deposit accounts.

In the eyes of the employers, excellent credit adds credibility to the educational degrees of the candidates. Therefore, the likelihood of being granted a job is increased. The employers will be confident that they are hiring responsible candidates. Getting jobs quickly will make it less likely for consumers to be late on their bills and be attacked by late fees as well as penalty interest rates, which are usually above twenty-nine percent. Consumers that are not late are able to protect their credit from being damaged.

Excellent credit increases the likelihood of being granted credit limit increases, which increases the buying power of the consumer. This positively influences a credit report and credit scores because the credit limit increases will show underneath the accounts. They will list the original credit limit and the new increased credit limit. Credit limit increases raise the credit scores due to the fact the debt-to-credit limit ratio of the consumer is becoming less. This shows they are utilizing less of their available credit, which suggests they are financially stronger. Credit is utilization and low utilization is a positive financial sign. In addition, credit limit increases show the creditors trust the consumers more with their loan money. The business purpose of credit limit increases is that financial institutions are trying to get consumers to use their credit cards more often so they can make more profit.

Excellent credit makes it more likely that consumers will be approved for credit cards with the best rewards programs with a small or no annual fee and the lowest interest rates. Consumers will be able to save more money on every day purchases when they use their credit card and pay off their balances immediately. The rewards will gradually grow and can be redeemed for gift cards, account credits, cash back, merchandise, and airline tickets. For example, the Discover More credit card is granted to consumers with an excellent credit profile. They are able to get five percent cash back certain months of the year on the money spent on gas. In fact, credit card issuers often send their customers coupons, which do save money as long as the consumer does not carry balances.

Consumers that want to start businesses are more likely to get approved for the loans they need because the financial institutions may want to check their personal credit. In the eyes of the financial institutions, if consumers are successful with their own finances then are more likely to be successful with their business finances. Consumers that are approved for business loans allows for them to create new jobs for other consumers when they expand their businesses. This will have a positive impact on the economy. For this reason, it is likely when the majorities of consumers have good credit then society as a whole will economically benefit.

Excellent credit lowers the chances of a consumer developing bad credit by defaulting because consumers with excellent credit tend to have cheaper bills than consumers with bad credit. Consumers with excellent credit are less likely to have their houses foreclosed and their vehicles repossessed.

Denied for Credit? Do Not Give Up!

Financial institutions can deny consumers credit for many reasons. Some reasons are minor and may be challenged by the consumer if they ask for **reconsideration,** hoping that the denied application will be approved. In contrast, some reasons are major and there is very little that the consumer can do because these reasons suggest that the consumer cheated the financial institution at some point in time and for this reason, are considered financially weak. Usually, any reason for credit denial that indicates that the consumer was past due on a credit account is a major reason.

The **credit analysts** and **officers** of the financial institutions are who review, decline, or approve the credit applications. They are subjective because they all have their own perspectives as to what denial reasons they consider minor or major. The reasons for denial have numerical codes. These codes can be used by the consumer to determine how they can improve the reason for which they were denied for credit or understand the denial reason more in-depth. The codes usually appear in the computer systems of the financial institutions when they are processing credit applications. Financial institutions will also receive the reasons, if any, why they should approve a credit application. Consumers do not usually receive these reasons unless they ask the credit analyst

Look for Denial Letter with Reasons

When consumers are denied credit, they should always receive a notification from the financial institution, with the reasons for the denial. If they do not then consumers should always find out the reasons why they were denied. By not doing so, consumers are not using their rights; and the credit checks that were done on them are going to waste. Hard inquiry credit checks always lower the credit scores. For this reason, consumers need to be ambitious in always getting approvals of their credit applications. The reasons below are just the reasons why financial institutions can potentially deny credit to consumers but they are also factors that lower the credit scores. For this reason, when consumers check their credit scores then they may see some of the reasons listed below unless they have solid and excellent credit. Innovis is the fourth credit agency and they do not use a numerical coding system for their denial reasons unlike the other three credit bureaus. Not all three credit bureaus have the same denial reasons because they all have different management systems. For this reason, some of reasons are listed as "N/A" underneath some of the bureaus on the list below. Finally, some of the reasons are similar but are worded differently and so consumers should follow the same advice for one reason as they would for another reason. The advice may be similar. Overall, if a consumer can maintain good credit then they will not have to worry about being denied credit but if they are denied then they can fix the reason by continuing to maintain good credit. Good credit continues to strengthen as time passes and no delinquencies occur.

Reconsideration helps Credit

If consumers are denied for credit, especially for minor reasons such as too short of history established on credit accounts, then they must be persistent in getting the credit application approved and request for a **reconsideration**. If consumers do not ask for reconsideration then their credit scores would have dropped for no reason because whenever a consumer applies for credit then hard inquiry credit checks are done on them by the financial institutions.

Account Approval helps Credit

The opening of a new credit account will eventually cause credit scores to increase, provided the consumer is never late on making the payments or does not aggressively use the credit card. The only reason why a consumer should not both trying to get the credit application reconsidered is if they were denied for having too many delinquencies, collections, bankruptcy, or a debt settlement. Such reasons are considered major by most financial institutions. Below is contact information that consumers can use to contact the credit or executive departments of the financial institutions via mail or phone for reconsiderations, credit limit increases, interest rate reductions, or to remove late payments showing on credit reports. Consumers should not contact the back of the credit card because from personal experience, the customer service representatives of some financial institutions will express that there is nothing that can be done about getting the denied application approved or will not know what to do about it.

Do Not Give Up on Getting Approval

Regular customer service agents are not trained to handle the issues regarding the approval or denial of credit applications or credit reporting issues. They will say anything to get the consumer to hang up the phone because it costs the financial institutions money when too many consumers are on the phone lines or are calling.

My mother was denied for an Air Tran Airways credit card due to, "insufficient history established on revolving accounts", because she was closing too many credit cards too quickly, which negatively impacts credit. Such is considered a minor credit denial reason because it does not imply that my mother cheated any bank or ever defaulted. On the behalf of my mother and as a joint account applicant, I had called the regular customer service department of the bank, on their website, to ask for reconsideration of the application. They told me nothing could be done to approve the application and she would have to reapply for the credit card, which would mean another credit check. I was able to call the credit department, of Barclays Bank who is the issuer of the credit card, and convince them to approve her application without doing additional credit checks. They were able to use the credit report that their systems had originally pulled, which was a TransUnion report.

Use Certified Mail to Send Reconsideration Letters

Consumers should always use certified mail when sending letters because they must put their account number or social security number on the letter, or it will let get lost. For this reason, always indicate "please make a note on my credit application [or account] that this letter was received" and sign the letter. Consumers always need to make financial institutions feel confident as much as possible that the consumer is unlikely to default and so consumers should always indicate somewhere on the reconsideration letters "I do not cheat banks of their loan money. Please approve my application. If I were to default then please garnish my wages, put a claim on my house and car, or take me to court." They should also express this confidently in phone conversations because it is unlikely that consumers who are planning on defaulting would say such comments. Finally, consumers should always mention any current or previous positive relationships, if any, that they have had with the financial institution such as a checking or savings account that has very rarely become negative or checks have been bounced and previous or current loans or credit cards on which the consumer has never been delinquent.

Here is a letter format consumers can send to creditors that denied them for credit or for a cheaper interest rate, which is considered a refinance.

Bank name:

Attention: Executive department

Corporate office address (consumers can find this information by doing a Google.com search) or the address from which the denial letter was received:

Date:

Application identification number or social security number:

Address of consumer that was on the credit application:

    To Whom It May Concern:

    I applied for an Air Tran Airways credit card (name of the loan or credit card) on January 10, 2011 (approximate date that application was submitted) and regretfully, was denied due to short length of history established on revolving accounts (state the reason for the credit denial). My intention for getting the (loan or credit card) was to earn the bonus miles promotion (state the legitimate purpose as to why the loan is wanted or needed and elaborate on it so the financial institution does not think the intention behind getting the loan is to use all the loan money and not pay it). My plan was to make small purchases, earn rewards, pay off the balance immediately, and save money (consumers should explain how they plan on handling the loan).

Although I have short history on my revolving accounts (reason for denial) because I was closing credit cards too quickly and not building long history on them (state the cause for the credit weakness), this reason is still minimal. From now on, I will not close credit cards but instead, keep them open, use them very lightly, and pay them off the day that they are used (how a consumer can fix the credit denial reason). Please reconsider my application and approve me for the credit card. I assure you by granting me credit, Barclays Bank (state the name of the financial institution or company) will not have a loan loss because my credit report reflects no delinquencies, over 30 credit accounts in good standing, a variety of credit with several banks, and very few inquiries (consumers should establish their financial strengths and elaborate on them because this shows they are confident about paying their loans). In fact, Barclays Bank can perform any background check or a credit check with the other consumer reporting agencies and they will still find no negative credit information on me. I have never cheated any bank of their loan money by not paying them or declaring a bankruptcy or settlement and will never do so. For this reason, I do not appreciate the denial for credit because my credit score decreased due to the credit check (consumers are encouraged to include these statements on their reconsideration letter because it shows more confidence in being able to repay the loan). In the event I did not pay on my credit card, Barclays Bank can garnish my wages, take me to court, or put a claim on my assets or house (consumers are encouraged to include consequences that the financial institution can take against them in the event that the consumer fails to repay the loan).

Please make a note on the application that this letter was received (consumers must include this statement with the reconsideration letter otherwise the financial institution can say that they never received the letter). If possible, please simply approve the credit application. I am willing to accept a low credit limit and after establishing a strong payment history, I will ask for a credit limit increase (consumers should include this statement because financial institutions are less likely to think that consumers that want a small credit limit have the bad intention of defaulting on the credit card). I would greatly appreciate a phone call at (407) 496-6005 to discuss the reconsideration of the loan application (consumers should indicate a phone number at which the financial institution can contact them). If I am unavailable then please leave me a voice message and I will promptly return your call. I greatly appreciate your assistance with the situation (consumers should be courteous because the bank representative is less likely to help rude consumers).

Thank you,
Danny Singh (State first and last name that was indicated on the credit application so the financial institution knows the legitimate consumer mailed them the reconsideration letter and not a criminal)

Here is a letter format that is more focused on getting a cheaper interest rate on the loan, specifically a credit card.

Bank name:
Attention: Executive department
Corporate office address (consumers can find this information by doing a Google.com search) or the address from which the denial letter was received:
Date:

Application identification number or social security number:
Address of consumer that was on the credit application:

Danny Singh

To Whom It May Concern:

I have been a customer with Bank of America for about five years and have maintained checking and savings accounts that have never become negative (consumers should express their past or current positive relationships with the financial institution). I am currently paying about 18.24% on my Bank of America World Points credit card and was hoping that my account could be reviewed for a lower interest rate (state the problem and what solution is desired). I was hoping for a rate closer to 9% (considering the rough economic times, 10% or below for a credit card is considered a cheap interest rate so consumers should always make this statement). I have credit cards with other financial institutions and the Bank of America credit card I have has the interest rate among all of them (even if the credit card on which the consumer is wanting a cheaper interest rate truthfully does not have the highest interest rate compared to their other credit cards, consumers should still make this statement because the financial institution will likely feel more focused on getting the consumer a cheaper interest rate due to the fear of losing their business).

I have never been late on the credit card or with any loan or credit card with any other financial institution in all the years I have had access to credit. I have no intention of defaulting, declaring a bankruptcy or settlement, or cheating the bank (consumers should indicate their financial strengths) and am planning on periodically using the credit card again after paying it down (consumers should mention that they will use their credit card again lightly but not to the point that they will default on it so financial institution has an incentive in reducing the interest rate and pleasing the consumer). For such reasons, I feel as though Bank of America should value my relationship and grant me a lower interest rate. If it in the event I were to default on the credit card or my credit profile becomes negative then Bank of America can sue me in court, garnish my wages, or put a claim on my assets or house so they can makeup for their loan loss (consumers should mention the adverse actions that the financial institution can take against them because the financial institution is more likely to think that the consumer will not default on the credit card and thus, they deserve to be granted a cheaper interest rate). I am not asking for a lower interest rate because I am in a financial struggle but simply because I want to save money and pay the principle down much faster (consumers never want to give the impression that they need a lower interest rate because they are having financial struggles otherwise the financial institution may close down the credit account and this will hurt the credit scores). Paying down the balance faster will cause my credit scores to increase (financial institutions are more likely to help financially responsible consumers that want to achieve the most success with their credit profile because it is unlikely they are a business risk).

Please make <u>a note on my credit card account that this correspondence was received</u> (consumers can call the financial institution and will be able to verify that the letter was received and not lost because the representative will see the note on the account). I would greatly appreciate <u>a phone call at (407) 496-6005</u> (consumers need to provide a strong phone number otherwise the bank representative cannot help them and thus, the letter has gone to waste) so we can discuss a solution. <u>If the interest rate can be reduced then you have my authorization to reduce it</u> (financial institutions need the permission of consumers before making any changes to their credit account). <u>I greatly appreciate your assistance in the situation</u> (courtesy is the most important aspect for anyone to show during verbal or written communication).

Thank you,
<u>Danny Singh</u> (state first and last name that was indicated on credit application)

Loan Modification

Some consumers, struggling to make their mortgage payments and cannot get approved for a cheaper mortgage interest rate and/or lower monthly payment; which is considered a mortgage refinance, are doing what is called a loan modification. Loan modification can also be referred to as mortgage forbearance. A loan modification is when the consumer pays an expensive fee; anywhere from $700 and up, to a third party company or individual to negotiate with their mortgage company to lower the monthly mortgage payments, to an amount that will be specified by the consumer. The consumer may also request for the loan modifier to get their mortgage interest rate reduced. The loan modifying company or individual will usually have their attorney, or someone who works in the legal services, contact the mortgage company of the consumer to handle all the proceedings.

Consumers do not need to hire third parties because they are usually scams; since they want high fees and may exaggerate about being accredited in the legal services. Consumers can negotiate with the mortgage company themselves simply by walking into their branch office or calling them and requesting that their mortgage be modified, so they can better afford the monthly payments. If the mortgage company does not help the consumer then the consumer is encouraged to contact the corporate office explaining that they need a loan modification done.

Regardless of how the loan modification process is initiated, the mortgage company will then contact the consumer to inform them if the mortgage payment and/or interest rate can be lowered and if the loan modification is temporary or permanent. If the loan modification is temporary then this means it is considered a **trial loan modification;** meaning the mortgage company will monitor the equity value of the house belonging to the consumer, income of the consumer, the overall conditions of the economy, the credit profile of the consumer, and whether or not there is a high number of consumers purchasing real estate near the location of the house. It is likely the mortgage company will only grant a permanent loan modification if there is a low number of consumers buying real estate, which means property, near the area of the house and if they think the consumer is very likely to successfully pay off the mortgage, because it will cost the mortgage company more money to foreclose on the house than it would to lower the monthly payments. For this reason, the consumer will need to have an average to good credit profile with a stable source of verifiable income. The mortgage company will be able to make more profit through the consumer by lowering their monthly payment, because it is unlikely another consumer would purchase the house if they foreclosed on it and by lowering the monthly payment, they are able to increase the principle balance of the mortgage. This means the mortgage company will be able to charge more interest even though the monthly payment has been lowered.

During a trial loan modification, for a certain number of months, the consumer will have to pay the lowered mortgage payment that has been established. The mortgage company may or may not reveal the number of months for which the trial loan modification will last. The consumer must find out such information from them, because after the trial period, the mortgage payment amount will be the original amount that was being paid by the consumer, before the loan modification or potentially higher, if the consumer did not maintain a perfect payment history. The danger behind a trial loan modification is that the amount by which the monthly payment has been lowered is being deferred. This means the amount will be added to the loan and likely still accumulate interest, until the mortgage company makes a final decision on whether or not the loan modification will be permanent. The amount by which the mortgage payment has been reduced does not magically disappear.

Example

The monthly mortgage payment of Steven with Bank of America Home Loans is $1,405.49. Steven contacts a loan modifying company whose legal person then contacts Bank of America Home Loans. After two to three weeks, Steven gets a letter from Bank of America indicating his monthly mortgage payment will now be $993.58. His mortgage interest rate remains the same because with most trial loan modifications, the interest rates do not change but only the monthly payment.

$1,405.49 - $993.58 = $411.91. This $411.91 is being deferred every month and accumulating with interest for however long the trial loan modification lasts.
Steven calls Bank of America and they inform him the loan modification will last for six months. This means Steven will have a payment for $993.58 for six months. This also means that the $411.91 will be deferred six times.

$411.91 x 6 = $2,471.46.

$2,471.46 + Mortgage interest = The amount of money Steven must pay Bank of America at the end of the six months along with the $1,405.49 to satisfy the mortgage payment for the month at the end of the six months unless Bank of America indicates they will make his loan modification permanent.

$2,471.46 + $1,405.49 = $3,876.95 + Mortgage interest that accumulated on the $2,471.46 worth of six deferred payments. If Steven does not pay all this to Bank of America then they will foreclose, which means repossession, on his house.

If Bank of America had decided that the loan modification of Steven will remain permanent then his payments will be $993.58 for the life of the loan assuming his taxes will not increase and he has a fixed rate mortgage. The $2,471.46 (six deferred payments of $411.91) plus the mortgage interest that it accumulated will be added back to the principle mortgage balance and Steven will have to pay compounded mortgage interest on it again. When interest combines itself with the principal balance then this is considered capitalization because it causes the principal balance to increase instead of decrease. As Steven was deferring his monthly mortgage payments as part of the loan modification program, he was capitalizing on his mortgage. Capitalization is bad.

In addition, loan modifications, whether they are temporary or permanent, damage credit. This is because there is no telling what kind of payment history data the mortgage company will report to the credit agencies during the time in which the mortgage of the consumer is in the loan modification program. They may report that the payment was late for each month that the consumer was paying a lowered payment amount. In they case of Steven, his credit report would possibly reflect six late payments that occurred on his mortgage because Steven had six months in which he was making reduced payments. The longer that a mortgage is part of a loan modification program; then the credit scores of the consumer continue to lower. If the mortgage company determines that the loan modification will be permanent, the time in which the loan modification was temporary and late payments were reported to the credit reports of the consumer during that period will still not be removed or disappear. The months after the day that the mortgage company notified the consumer that the loan modification will remain permanent will not reflect late payments on the credit reports provided that Steven does not become late in making the payments of $993.58. This is because a permanent loan modification means a new loan contract has been established with the consumer with more suitable payment terms.

Another possibility is that the mortgage company may not report that the mortgage was late but instead, that the consumer was doing forbearance, which is what a loan modification is considered. This information will usually show next to the "remarks" section of the mortgage on the credit reports. Future financial institutions with whom the consumer applies for credit or insurance providers, when they check the credit reports of the consumer and see the late payments or the forbearance that the consumer did with their mortgage then they will think that the consumer is financially weak and is unlikely to pay on new bills and loans.

Developing bad credit is a con behind getting the mortgage payments reduced. This is because by the consumer requesting for the mortgage payment to be reduced, they are in a sense, breaking the original contract to which they agreed to make a certain monthly payment amount when they obtained the mortgage (home loan) to purchase the house. Late payments imply the idea that the consumer broke the contract with the financial institution about paying their loan. The mortgage company is having a financial loss by lowering the monthly payment of the consumer because there is always the possibility that the consumer may bankrupt their home loan debt and leave their house. The financial institution does not know the intentions of the consumer. The financial institution will not be able to get any profit out of the consumer for the deferred payments in which the house was in the loan modification program.

It is not recommended that consumers do a loan modification because in most cases, the loan modification is not permanent and when the consumer is notified of this by the mortgage company then the consumer cannot afford to pay them all the deferred payments. The mortgage company forecloses on the house and a foreclosure reflects on all the credit reports of the consumer. The consumer will struggle to get a job and get approved for new loans with decent interest rates. Many consumers do not understand that the purpose behind a trial loan modification is to delay a foreclosure from happening but during the time in which the payments have been reduced, the consumers are supposed to save money so they can pay the mortgage company in the event that they say that the load modification will not be permanent. Consumers have to be prepared for this scenario and cannot assume the loan modification is permanent.

Loan Modification Warnings and Tips
Applies to all the Loans of Consumers; Not Just Mortgages

1. Consumers should **never** listen to **any** mortgage company, individual, banker, or lawyer that says the consumer should stop paying on their loan. This guarantees that the party that is working with the consumer is a scam or has no idea what they are doing. Consumers should not get fooled by their inauthentic accreditations, if any; because it is likely the party does not care about having good credit and they have no liability when the consumer develops bad credit. Not paying loans will **always** damage credit and eliminate any payment relief options of the consumer because the financial institutions are not going to want to work with consumers

that have done them wrong by not paying the loans. The business risk software of the credit card companies of the consumer will detect the negative changes in the credit profile and this will possibly cause the credit analysts to close down the credit accounts, reduce the credit limits, or increase the interest rate because in their eyes, the consumer is very likely to stop paying their credit cards. Consumers may soon find that all or most of their credit cards will decline when they try and use them at the stores to make purchases.

2. There are options which are financially healthy that a consumer has if they cannot afford their mortgage payments.

   A. Consumers can refinance the mortgage with a credit union or community bank. They are usually more flexible than traditional banks in helping consumers that have bad credit.
   B. Consumers can rent out their house, save up money while living in apartment, and later, reclaim their house. This has no negative impact on their credit.
   C. Consumers can use the money that they deposited, not the earnings (interest), in their Roth IRA to catch up on their mortgage payments and save their house from a foreclosure. Taking money from a Roth IRA has no 10% tax penalty and the consumer does not have to pay income taxes on that money. For this reason, consumers should try and rollover most of their assets that are within a CD, savings account, money market account, 401(k), and traditional IRA into the Roth IRA. Doing so may require for them to pay taxes on some or all of that money but paying taxes but they will not have to pay taxes on it again when they claim it at the age of retirement or earlier from the Roth IRA. There is no way to escape paying taxes. In contrast, when consumers withdraw money from the traditional IRA or any 401(k) then they have to pay income taxes on the money and a 10% tax penalty. The funds within CDs, savings, money market accounts, and checking accounts are likely not protected against bankruptcy or debt settlement. This is another reason why consumers should put the funds of these accounts into a Roth IRA.
   D. Consumers that have a close and trustworthy family member, such as; a mother, father, spouse, son, or daughter, that have a source of income and no delinquencies on their credit profile should ask that family member if they would be willing to cosign on the mortgage. If the family member agrees then the consumer should contact the corporate office of the mortgage company and mention to them that if the person is added onto the mortgage then can the mortgage payment be reduced. Personally, if my mother needed me to be added onto her mortgage for the purpose of saving the house from a foreclosure; then I would agree to do it because doing so is better than the option of becoming homeless. It would be wise for consumers that have added on a secondary loan consumer to their loan to get term life insurance, because if the primary loan consumer passes away then the secondary loan consumer will not have to repay all or most of the debt by themselves depending upon the amount of coverage that the primary loan consumer had purchased. Term life insurance is usually the most reasonable in terms of monthly payments compared to variable, universal, and whole life insurance policies. Term life insurance lasts for a certain time period that is specified by the consumer such as a certain number of years. Consumers do not need to get life insurance forever especially if they have strong assets such as in an IRA or 401(k). Consumers can name the person who cosigns for them as the beneficiary on their assets. A beneficiary is the person who will be granted the money or real estate of the deceased person. Consumers can also have a legal will made by an attorney in which the cosigner gets all the funds of the primary loan holder if they were to become

deceased. Consumers have to make sure that their cosigner does not end up paying for all the debts. For this reason, they need to save plenty of money in their investments on which the cosigner is named as a beneficiary.

E. Consumers can use a fixed interest rate home equity loan that they would get from a community bank or credit union and use the loan money to pay as much as possible on their primary mortgage for the purpose of saving the house from foreclosure. This can be beneficial because in some cases, the fixed interest rate of a home equity loan may be cheaper than the interest rate that the consumer is paying in their current mortgage. Consumers need to be aware that if they use the home equity loan to pay their mortgage, unless they pay off the entire mortgage, consumers will have to make two monthly payments. One payment will go towards the home equity loan and another payment will go towards the mortgage. Consumers can deduct some or most of the interest paid on the home equity loan and mortgage on their taxes up to a certain amount. The amount will be specified by the tax advisor or the IRS on their website, which is www.irs.gov/publications/p936/ar02.html.

F. Consumers should consider getting two or more jobs for the purpose of being able to afford their mortgage payments and all their bills. This is much better than doing a loan modification guaranteed.

G. Consumers can take a loan against their 401(k) but this option can be dangerous. There is no credit check to get the loan and the payment history is not reported to the credit reports of the consumer. Consumers should only consider doing this option if they feel as though their job is secure and the company is doing well as a business. This is because if the consumer takes a loan against their 401(k), there is no 10% tax penalty or income taxes that they have to pay but if they lose their job then they are expected to pay the loan back within two months. If not, then the consumer will get into trouble with the Internal Revenue Services and may not get any tax refunds. Additionally, it is possible that the consumer has paid taxes on some or all of the money that is placed back into a 401(k) as the consumer is repaying the loan. When the consumer claims the money at the age of retirement then it is likely they will have to pay taxes on some or all of the money that they obtain from the 401(k). In this sense, the consumer is facing double taxation because they may have to pay taxes twice on the same money. There is controversy on the internet that double taxation is a myth but it is better to be safe than sorry because there is no way to know which financial experts are correct and incorrect. Consumers should only take a loan against their 401(k) unless it is their last option to save their house or automobile.

H. If consumers cannot afford the monthly mortgage payment and the financial institution will not allow for them to defer the payment or refinance the mortgage. If the financial institution accepts credit cards as a payment method then the consumer can use a credit card from a credit union to make the monthly payment. Consumers should make the minimum payments or more on the credit cards. There are credit unions that offer credit cards that have interest rates in the range of 7% - 9% with no annual fees. If possible, consumers should try and get one of these credit cards and use them to make the payments until they can quickly get a second job or use some other means to get caught up on their mortgage payments. Building up a high balance on a credit card is dangerous due to the interest that the consumer will be charged but it is better than defaulting on the mortgage payment or doing a loan modification and possibly losing the house. Federally chartered credit unions cannot increase the interest rate on the credit card above 18% even if the consumer is late on making the payments but damage will occur with their credit profile. Credit cards from traditional financial institutions are dangerous because most of them can increase the interest rate to about 30% if the consumer is late on making the payment usually by sixty days or more. Due to the fact credit cards from credit unions offer the best terms compared to credit cards from banks, consumers should not close them. If consumers were to move from away from the location of the credit union, their credit card will still not be shut down because the credit union wants to keep the business of the consumer.

I. There is extreme fraud happening with mortgages all over the United States and to some extent, such did contribute to the severity of the 2000s housing crisis. Consumers that see signs on the road, advertisements on the internet, and hear advertisements on the radio that all indicate they can help the consumer save their house from foreclosure, can get the mortgage debt settled, save the house without bankruptcy, or any message that implies an action can be taken with the house which the consumer did not think was possible, are scams in most cases. Consumers should always be skeptical of the advertisements. The intention of these companies is to get the consumer to sign over the house to them so they can sell the house, make profit, and lie to the consumer about doing so. The companies will convince the consumer that they will handle all their payments. There have been cases in which the companies took all the equity out of the houses and then the consumer was liable for paying all the equity back to the financial institutions along with the mortgage payments. When the consumers could not make the payments then the financial institutions would levy, which means claim, all their bank account funds and assets. Consumers should only conduct their financial matters at a credit union or well-know bank. Even if the financial institutions will not help the consumer with their issues, they still should not go to companies of which they have never heard. Anytime a consumer gets into business with a company, the consumer should always do a complaints search of the company on Google.com. Companies that claim they are safe because they are part of the Better Business Bureau does not always mean they are safe because any company can pay for a listing with the Better Business Bureau. If companies can afford to pay for such listings then it is likely they are making high profits off of consumers. This can possibly mean but not always that the prices of the company for the merchandise and services they sell to consumers may be overpriced. Additionally, in many cases, companies that claim to have multiple certifications are inauthentic. For this reason, the consumer should always try and verify their certifications.

J. Consumers should not stop paying their credit cards and other loans because then it is less likely that the financial institution is going to work with them to make the monthly mortgage payments more affordable. If consumers have no job or not enough funds to make payments on all their bills without defaulting then consumers are encouraged to get a credit card at a credit union and transfer the balances of all or most of their debts to the credit union credit card. This is because credit union credit cards tend to have the cheapest interest rates compared to the credit cards of traditional banks. Consumers with weak financial conditions are discouraged from getting secured loans such as home equity loans or secured personal loans because if they default on such loans then they can lose their collateral, which in most cases, is their house, car, or assets. If consumers cannot get approved for any new loan from the credit union then they should immediately seek to do credit counseling with a non-profit and well-known credit counseling agency before letting the bills become delinquent. These credit counseling agencies will be members of the National Foundation for Credit Counseling (NFCC). Consumers can go to www.nfcc.org to find the nearest NFCC member credit counseling agency near their house location. Not all credit unions are good and for this reason, consumers should conduct a Google.com search with the name of the credit union for the purpose of looking up any complaints against them. Credit counseling agencies have payment options for consumers with low income levels or no income. Credit counseling may damage the credit profile of the consumer because it is likely the financial institutions that issued credit to the consumer may close down their accounts and this lowers the credit scores because the closure of a credit account lowers the amount of available credit to which a consumer has access, lowers the average length of history established on the credit accounts, and sometimes, the closure of a credit account signifies that a consumer could not handle the financial responsibility. The credit reports may reflect that the consumer was in a credit counseling program, which may suggest potential financial weakness to future financial institutions. Credit counseling is still a better option than bankruptcy or a debt settlement and will not cause severe damage. Employers are more likely to hire consumers that have done credit counseling in contrast to hiring consumers that have bankruptcy, a debt settlement, or delinquencies on their credit reports. Mortgages cannot be included with the credit counseling programs but it is likely the consumer will save enough money to make their mortgage payments. This is because the credit counselors request for the companies to reduce or eliminate the interest rates on the credit cards and/or collection accounts.

K. Companies that claim to "guarantee" to do some act for the consumer such as save their house from a foreclosure, save them from bankruptcy, reduce their payments, eliminate credit card debt, or actions that do not seem realistic should send a red flag to consumers that the company is a scam. No company can guarantee to do anything because they do not know how the financial institutions of the consumer will work with them. The companies will increase the financial troubles of the consumers and will likely cause huge damage to their credit profiles. The consumers will be in danger of losing their houses, cars, and assets. If any company says they can "settle" a debt then they are likely referring to doing a debt settlement and consumers should throw a rock at them because doing such will ruin the credit profiles of the consumers and the financial institutions or companies to whom they owe money will take drastic actions against the consumer.

L. When seeking financial help, consumers should not contact random companies whose contact information they would find in the phone book, internet, or on the signs consumers see on the grass fields near the roads. There is no guarantee if the companies are running legitimate businesses and for this reason, it is too dangerous for consumers to trust them with their personal financial problems. There is no telling what the company will do once they have acquired the personal information of the consumer. Any individual can start bogus websites on the internet, post signs near the road, and put advertisements in the phone claiming they are companies that can help consumers. Consumers should only work with well-known financial institutions and credit unions.

M. For whatever reasons consumers have for hiring a third party to handle their mortgage issues, consumers should always contact their district attorney with the name of the company to verify if there are any complaints against the company and if the company is legitimate. The district attorney is the legal officer of the state. A consumer can find out who their district attorney is and their contact information by going on the governmental website of their residential state.

N. Consumers that cannot afford to make their mortgage payments should go to http://www.makinghomeaffordable.gov or they can call 1-888-995-4673. The Making Home Affordable Program is regulated by the government and they are helping consumers keep their houses by arranging payments plan with them including load modifications. Before agreeing to a payment plan, consumers should ask if the new and reduced monthly payment that they will be required to pay is permanent or temporary and how this payment plan will affect their credit profile. Consumers should not do a payment plan if it will result in their credit profile getting damaged because then they will struggle to get a job and no job means no money to make the monthly payments. Consumers should always get a permanent reduced monthly payment. If they do a loan modification then it should be a permanent loan modification. Consumers should never do temporary loan modifications.

All Things Auto

Cash is Great but a Car Loan Is Better

Unless consumers already have some type of secured installment credit loan, with a positive payment history; showing on their credit reports, they should consider getting a car loan with a credit union or community bank, for the purpose of purchasing an automobile. This is because a car loan is a type of secured installment loan, meaning it has collateral, which is the car. The financial institution can repossess the car, in the event, that the consumer stops making payments on the car and the monthly payments; along with the interest rate are the same or similar every month. Unlike credit cards and loans that have no time frame, in which the entire loan must be repaid, due to the fact they are **open ended credit**. Installment loans must be fully repaid, within a certain time frame; such as 24 months, 36 months, 48 months, or longer. A secured installment loan helps the credit scores to be higher, because it helps the financial institutions understand; the consumer is financially strong. In their perspective, a secured installment loan, with a positive history, suggests the consumer does not default on their credit cards and unsecured debts; for the purpose of paying the installment loan due to the fact the financial institution can repossess the collateral. Some consumers quit paying their credit cards because they want to pay off their auto loan and house. The financial institutions do not want to grant credit to such consumers. Financial institutions like seeing the consumer has experience paying different types of credit; which are installment credit and revolving credit. The installment credit loan or revolving credit loan being secured or unsecured is considered a characteristic, of the loan.

The different auto loan month terms for new and used cars
24 months (2 years)
36 months (3 years)
48 months (4 years)
60 months (5 years)
72 months (6 years)
84 months (7 years)
**Note: Due to the credit crisis, 84 months for an auto loan is granted by few financial institutions and credit unions.

Get the Longest Loan Term Possible

72 months is usually the longest auto loan term a consumer can get for a new car whereas 60 months is usually the longest auto loan term a consumer can get a used car. The longer that an auto loan term is then the more interest that the financial institution will charge because as time passes then the likelihood of a consumer defaulting on an automobile increases. This is because the automobile depreciates in value as the years pass and some consumers may lose motivation, in making payments on an automobile; that is worth very little. This can support why some financial institutions and credit unions are reluctant to grant 84 month auto loans; unless the consumers have excellent credit. In 7 years, the car will have depreciated significantly in its market value. The interest paid on auto loans cannot be deducted from taxes. It is recommended that consumers, especially consumers with other debts; such as credit card debt, student loan debt, and mortgage debt; get the longest auto loan term possible, for the purpose of having the lowest monthly payments. If consumers want to avoid paying interest and pay off their car faster; they should make payments above the minimum

payment requirements, every month; or pay off the entire auto loan balance. Doing so will also cause their credit scores to quickly increase; because their overall level of debt is decreasing. Most auto loans do not have prepayment penalties, but consumers should check with the financial institutions for the purpose of being safe. Consumers, unless they have zero debts, should not get short term auto loans anywhere from 24 to 48 months because although there is less interest, the monthly minimum payment requirements will be high and if the consumer cannot afford the monthly payments, due to their other expenses or emergencies then their car will be repossessed. The repossession of the car will ruin their credit profile and chances at getting a job. It is better to pay more interest and have a long term auto loan such as 60 months or longer.

Good Credit means Cheap Insurance

Getting a secured installment loan means the consumer will be more likely to be granted a cheaper car, health, life, and home owner's insurance premiums; because all insurance providers check the credit profile of the consumer. It is the only way for them to know that the consumer has a low likelihood; of stopping payment of their insurance.

The car insurance company cannot make up for the loss; they had because it costs them money to provide coverage, for the automobile for the number of months it was ensured. If a consumer has cash for a vehicle then they should still get an auto loan and negotiate with the car loan provider; to waive some or all of the loan origination and dealership fees. Consumers should explain that they want to pay off the car loan; the same day that they are granted the loan. By paying off the loan immediately, the consumer will boost their credit scores and there is no need for the dealership, to charge extra fees, because they are guaranteed to get paid by the consumer. If consumers already have secured installment loans showing on their credit reports; and have saved up enough money to purchase an automobile then they should use their credit card; which has the highest rewards program, to make the car purchase, and then pay off the credit card immediately to avoid paying interest.

The rewards program saves money such as cash back, up to a certain percentage of the purchase amount or points. Consumers can redeem the rewards for actual cash, gift cards, merchandise, or airline tickets. For consumers that do not have credit cards; then they should use debit cards that have rewards programs, but no fees; otherwise the purpose for trying to save money is defeated. The advantage a credit card has that a debit card does not; is that if the consumer is deceived by the car dealer and is sold a defective or damaged car; then the consumer has special dispute rights with the credit card company. The credit card company will work with the consumer to resolve the issue; with the car dealer. If the car dealer does not cooperate, then the credit card company will do a chargeback against them and reimburse some or all of the money; that the consumer paid towards the car. Debit cards make less profit for the financial institutions and for this reason, debit cards offer less resources such as the dispute rights for a consumer compared to a credit card.

Family Member as Cosigner

For consumers that have weak or limited credit profiles; they should consider asking a close family member with a strong credit profile, to cosign for them. However, if the consumer that needs a cosigner has weak assets; then they should consider getting a term life insurance policy, from a credit union or community bank. This is because with term life insurance, if the consumer dies then the cosigner will not have to repay the remaining car loan debt. The consumer who obtains the life insurance money does not need to pay taxes on it, because it is considered **nontaxable income**. Term life insurance is usually much cheaper than whole, variable, and universal life insurance policies and a better financial investment. Whole, variable, and universal life insurance policies last forever and for this reason, they are very expensive but life insurance is not needed forever. If the consumer has strong assets matching or exceeding the amount of the car loan debt then they should not get any life insurance but instead, name their cosigner as the beneficiary. This way, the cosigner can use the asset funds to pay off; the remaining car loan debt, in the event that the primary consumer dies. For consumers that get term life insurance, when their assets exceed or match the amount of the remaining car loan debt; then they should use the asset money to pay off the car loan debt or cancel the life insurance and put their cosigner, as the beneficiary on the asset accounts such as the retirement accounts. Life insurance is not needed, when the assets of the consumer are strong; or if they have no family members.

"Bad Credit Car Dealerships" = Death of Thousands of Dollars!

Consumers should not purchase cars from car dealerships that claim to cater to consumers, with bad credit profiles; or get auto loans from companies, that cater to consumers with bad credit. These companies usually make advertisements on the internet, radio, television, and just any form of media indicating; they can give a car to a consumer that has a limited or bad credit profile including a credit profile that reflects a bankruptcy or debt settlement. Companies that claim they do not check the credit profile of the consumer to grant the consumer a car are equally as dangerous. Such advertisements should send a red flag to consumers, that the company is a scam because their intention is to charge the consumer exorbitant fees; before giving them the car and a higher than average interest rate that the consumer will pay towards the car in their monthly payments to the company. The fees are paid, by the consumer, with their down payment money and not all the down payment money goes towards paying the principle balance, of the car. Depending upon the policies, of the bad credit car dealership companies, consumers may be able to get a cheaper interest rate if they make a significant down payment towards the car. The interest rates offered by bad credit car dealership companies such as Drive Time Automotive Group range from about 10% to 25% or more depending upon how severe the credit conditions of the consumer are and the price, at which the car dealership is selling the car. There is no cap on the amount of interest and fees a bad credit car dealership can charge a consumer.

There are two business methods, which bad credit car dealerships, can use to determine the interest rate and/or fees of the consumer.

- Some of the bad credit car dealerships tend to give higher interest rates and upfront fees to consumers that want to purchase cars; that are selling for low prices because they think the consumer is going to be able to pay off the car quickly. They want to make the maximum amount of profit, through charging interest. It is likely if the consumer pays off the car early; then they will have to pay prepayment penalties, because then the car dealership cannot make a great deal of profit, through interest.

- Some bad credit car dealerships; may charge the same, higher than average, interest rates and fees to all their consumers regardless, of what car they purchase.

No matter what method is used to charge the consumer; even if a consumer pays for the entire car with cash, in most cases, they still cannot escape paying the outrageous fees, of the bad credit car dealership.

Bad Quality Cars

Additionally, all the cars being sold by the bad credit car dealerships; are used. They are old; by a certain number of years, and the cars have many miles on them, up to 100,000 miles or more. The bad credit car dealerships sell these automobiles, almost three times, if not more, than their market value.

For example, a car that is worth $4,000. The bad credit car dealership will sell this car for $17,000 or more. It makes no sense for a consumer to waste so much of their, hard earned money on such cars. The bad credit car dealerships, often over exaggerate about their cars being inspected or certified for safety and reliability. For this reason, consumers can expect to pay a great deal of money, on car repair and maintenance. It is unlikely the consumers will be able to return the cars, because the dealerships will not accept them. As evidence, consumers can review the many complaints, some of the bad credit car dealerships have on the internet, by consumers who have purchased automobiles from them. The bad credit car dealerships are not going to thoroughly inspect their cars; or make any improvements with them, before selling them because they do not want to spend money on doing so. Their goal is to make the highest amount of profit off of the consumers, due to the fact, that they have a bad or limited credit profile. In this sense, they are taking advantage of consumers, because even consumers that may not have the best credit history do not deserve to pay excessively high interest and fees. Many bad credit car dealerships try to convince consumers to purchase cars from them, because doing so will help improve their credit scores. This is not necessarily true; because some bad credit car dealerships do not report any payment history of the consumer on the car to the credit agencies because it costs them money to do so. If the consumer stops paying on the car then the bad credit car dealerships will report the negative payment history to the credit agencies, for the purpose of trying to get the consumer to pay on the car. The negative payment history is considered a warning to the consumer. Eventually, if the bad credit car dealership does not receive any payments then they will repossess the car and report that car repossession took place to the credit agencies.

Alternatives to Buying an Automobile from a "Bad Credit Dealership"

1. Consumers should dispute the negative marks they have on their credit with the credit agencies (Equifax, Experian, Tran union, and Innovis) and if they have any debts; that are charge-offs meaning, they stopped paying on the loans. Consumers should contact the companies and make arrangements, to pay off the loans. The consumers should get the companies to report; that the credit accounts are now being paid by the consumer in a timely manner. The negative history will not disappear on the credit reports, but the fact that the consumer is paying the accounts will help raise the credit scores. If the consumer does not have enough funds to pay the credit accounts; then they should consider doing credit counseling, specifically a debt management program. Until the consumer has the negative marks on their credit reports, they should walk, take a taxi, ride a bike, or have a family member drop them off, to their desired locations. Consumers should get a cheap secured credit card from a credit union or community bank for the purpose of rebuilding their credit profile. There is no way to escape using

credit cards. Another option is that the consumer can have their close family member; such as a son, daughter, grandparent, or spouse with a strong credit history, add them as an authorized user onto a credit card. Most credit card companies, not all, report the payment history on the credit card to the credit reports, of the primary user, the joint user, and any authorized users. However, if consumers do this, then they must and should be prepared to make payments; in the event that the primary user cannot do so. It is true that authorized users are not liable for the credit card debt on which they are a user; but that will not stop the credit card companies from reporting negative credit history to them, due to the irresponsibility of the primary user. If the primary credit card holder dies, then the authorized users should remove their name from the credit cards immediately; by calling the financial institutions for the purpose of being safe. Although it is unlikely, the financial institutions may somehow make the authorized users liable for the debt, that was accumulated on the credit cards and as a result, it will ruin their credit profiles. After removing their names, the authorized users should inform the financial institutions that the primary credit card holder is deceased. If current authorized users are getting phone calls from debt collectors trying to collect the debt of the primary card holder then the authorized users need to contact the corporate offices of the financial institutions immediately, inform them that it is not their debt, and it should not affect their credit profile.

2. Consumers have the option of taking a loan against their 401(k), to buy a car from a regular dealership. Consumers must repay their 401(k) loan, usually within five years if they are using it to pay off credit card or any unsecured debt so they can avoid paying the 10% tax penalty. If consumers use the loan against the 401(k), to make a down payment on a house, use it to make mortgage payments, or use all the loan money to fully buy a house then they have up to 15 years to repay the loan. If consumers quit or are dismissed from their jobs, then they must repay the 401(k) loan immediately, usually within two months. Consumers do not leave their jobs if they take a loan against their 401(k) because if they do not pay it then it is possible they will get into trouble, with the Internal Revenue Services.

3. If consumers have a family member such as a son, daughter, or spouse with an average to excellent credit profile, with a verifiable source of income, then the consumer should ask the family member to cosign on the car loan. However, if the consumer does have strong assets; on which they can name the family member as the beneficiary, then they should purchase a term life insurance policy from a credit union or community bank. Term life insurance policies have cheap monthly payments and when the assets of the consumer become strong then they can use them to pay off the car loan debt and then cancel the term life insurance. Term life insurance lasts for a certain number of years and protects the cosigner from the car loan debt; if the primary consumer dies. In the situation of parents cosigning for their children; if the parents make high income, are financially stable, and can pay off the car loan debt, in the event that their children pass away then it is unnecessary for the children to get term life insurance. Instead, the children should pay on their student loans or save up for college.

4. If consumers have student loan money, with a fixed and cheap interest rate, then they should use that loan money to buy an affordable and safe automobile. A recommended and well known car dealership to purchase used cars is CarMax. Consumers that have equity on their houses and are not paying private mortgage insurance can consider

obtaining a home equity loan from a credit union or community bank to purchase the automobile. Home equity lines of credit are dangerous, because most of them have variable interest rates.

Finance with Credit Unions and Not Dealerships

If possible, consumers of all credit types should avoid doing the auto loan financing, with any car dealership. This is because the car dealerships have relationships with financial institutions, to which they forward consumers seeking to purchase automobiles. The financial institutions will likely pay a commission or some type of incentive, to the car dealerships for forwarding them the consumers. As a result, the financial institution is going to make up for the commission that they paid by charging the consumer a higher than average interest rate; and/or auto loan origination fees, sometimes called the closing costs. Before purchasing the automobile, consumers should go to a community bank or credit union to get the auto loan, because in most cases, they will offer cheaper interest rates and loan terms. After approving the consumer and the consumer decides on which automobile they want, the car dealership and credit union or community bank will then communicate about how much loan money is needed for the purchase. The financial institution will release the loan money to the car dealership and the consumer is free to take their car. Consumers need to be careful of car dealerships; they will try their best to convince the consumers to do the auto loan financing with them; due to the fact they make much more profit.

0% Promotion—Does It Really Save Money?

Consumers need to be careful of the 0%, no payments, until a certain month and year, and cash back financing offers that they have on television, the internet, the newspapers, or hear on the radio stations. These offers sometimes have schemes that will allow for the car dealerships to make high profits; off of the consumers. The car dealerships announce these offers with the intention of luring consumers, to their dealerships. It is likely a greater number of consumers will agree to do financing with the dealership, because they will be eager to purchase a car after test driving it. The financial promotions are not available on all vehicles; they are only available on certain models and this is likely because those particular automobiles are being sold for, higher than average prices, than what consumers would normally pay for an automobile. By selling those particular car models, the car dealerships will be able to make the same amount of profit, if not more, as they would if they sold another automobile to a consumer; with an average auto loan interest rate. Another reason why certain promotions may be offered on particular automobile models is because those models are not selling quickly and it is costly too much money for the car dealerships to pay for the maintenance, of those cars. Certain car models do not usually sell quickly, because they have higher than average insurance costs consumers; would have to pay or the consumer reviews of the models are poor. For this reason, consumers need to check with their insurance company and ask what the monthly insurance payment of the car would be, if they purchased it. Consumers should go to http://www.edmunds.com/car-reviews/ for the purpose of reviewing the flaws, if any, associated with the particular car model. If a consumer purchases a car that has bad reviews then the consumer may struggle in selling it; if they choose to do so in the future. Consumers cannot get fooled into purchasing an automobile; that will be too expensive for them to afford considering there will be a monthly auto loan and insurance payment otherwise they run the risk of the automobile being repossessed thus damaging their credit profile and their chances at getting a job.

Some car dealerships, offering the 0% interest promotion, may want that the consumer pay an expensive upfront fee, for the financing such $500 or more. In this sense, the car dealership is asking to get paid interest upfront; so they will not bill the consumer extra interest throughout the course of the auto loan. Consumers should only agree to the 0% promotion offer if it lasts through 60 months or longer; and only if there are no upfront fees, that they have to pay in order for them to get the promotion. Finally, consumers should not fall prey to the auto loan promotions indicating there are no payments required, for a certain number of months. Consumers should make payments anyway on their auto loans because the intention of the car dealerships is to make a great deal of profit through charging interest, which will compound more aggressively if the consumers do not make payments during the promotional time frame in which no payments are required. Making payments early will help raise the credit scores of the consumer because the overall levels of debt will be decreasing and in the eyes of the financial institutions, this lowers their likelihood of defaulting on the loans. The debt-to-income ratio and liabilities of the consumer are dropping by making payments on the loans; even when no payments are required. As a result, consumers can potentially get cheaper insurance premiums and interest rates, on their current and future loans; such as credit cards.

Repossessed and Used Cars = Risky Purchases

Consumers should be very careful when purchasing used or repossessed cars. Some financial experts think used cars are financially smarter to purchase because they already depreciated meaning they fell in value and for this reason, they are cheaper compared to most brand new cars. Used cars can have cheaper insurance premiums than brand new cars, because it costs less money for the insurance companies to replace or fix the parts of the used car and pay the consumer the value of the used car in the event it is completely wrecked. In some cases, used cars can eventually become more expensive than brand new cars, due to the fact some car dealerships over exaggerate about their used cars being in stable condition or being fully functional. Their only goal is to make a sale, because consumers cannot return the car after purchasing it. The consumers may end up paying money several times to get the used car repaired. Used cars, depending upon how old they are, can be more dangerous to drive than new cars because they do not have the most up-to-date security features. Such increases the likelihood of getting into an accident, which will result in the consumer paying expensive medical bills. Before purchasing a used car, consumers should always check its history on www.carfax.com using the vehicle identification number (VIN) of the car. The website will present a report that shows any accidents in which the vehicle was involved, any repairs or modifications that were made to the vehicle, and all the previous owners. Consumers cannot assume that the car dealer telling them; that the used car is in great condition, is the truth. Honestly, consumers do not know how the used cars were maintained; and the car dealers or current owners are going to say anything to sell the cars. They want to make money. Credit unions often sell used and repossessed automobiles, as well as boats, and so consumers should check the deals with them before going to car dealerships, because they also give extra financial incentives; such as a low auto loan interest rate.

For consumers that get an auto loan, used cars tend to have higher interest rate; than auto loans for new cars, because the used cars usually have a low market value, which means if the financial institution repossessed the used car in the event the consumer stopped making payments then they could not significantly make up for their loan loss. They have to sell the repossessed car cheaper; than the amount of loan money that the previous consumer borrowed to purchase it.

Example:
Jasmine has a Hyundai Sonata on which she owes an $18,583 auto loan. The auto loan is issued by Wells Fargo Bank. Jasmine stops paying and Wells Fargo repossesses the car. The market value of the Hyundai Sonata is about $12,000, which is the price at which Wells Fargo would need to sell the car or a price that is close to it. $18,583 auto loan - $12,000 market value = $6,583.00 is the amount of loss Wells Fargo has had due to Jasmine and they cannot make up for this loss.

For this reason, the financial institutions need to make the maximum amount of profit available off of the consumers; that purchase used cars and they can only do so by charging high interest rates. Another reason why financial institutions charge higher auto loan interest on used cars, than they do on new cars, is because they think due to the fact the used cars are not worth a great deal of money; then the consumer is more likely to one day stop making payments on the used car, because they will not have a major loss if the used car is repossessed. For this reason, some financial institutions and car dealerships may grant cheaper auto loan interest rates; to consumers who make a large down payment on the used car, because they are less likely to stop paying on the auto loan. This is because if they stop paying then they lose the car and all their down payment money. Consumers that get auto loans for used cars; should make large down payments if the financial institution or dealership will give them a discount and if there is no additional fee then the consumer should use their credit card to make the down payment so they save money through the rewards program and then immediately pay off the credit card. If the dealership or financial institution will not accept a credit card; or the consumer has no credit card then a debit card is ideal because most debit cards also have rewards programs. If there is no interest rate discount for making a down payment; then the consumer should use the money, they would have used to make a down payment and instead, make a payment on the auto loan. Their credit scores will increase due to the fact they have less debt; and interest will compound less aggressively, which will allow for the consumer to pay off the car much faster. Consumers should not put the money into a bank account; they will not make a great deal of interest and it will be offset by the amount of interest that will be charged, on the auto loan. Due to the better reliability and safety, consumers should always try to purchase a brand new car because for the protection of life, paying more money for a new car than a used car is worth it. Depreciation is not a good reason for consumers to purchase used cars and have a greater risk of losing their lives or getting injured.

Negotiate for Cheaper Costs <u>Always</u>!

To save the maximum amount of money in purchasing a car, consumers have to give the impression they are working with a limited amount of funds; for the purpose of trying to get the car dealer to lower the price at which they are trying to sell the car. Consumers should always aim at getting a "steal deal" and they have to be ambitious in getting the car at the cheapest price. The car dealers are going to want to negotiate cheaper prices because they want to do everything possible to earn a sale out of the consumer. They make large profits and they do not want to waste their money; on the maintenance of the cars. Consumers should always make an offer on the car that is about $1,000 to $1,500 cheaper than the price at which the car is being sold. If the car dealer will sell it at that price then it is a guaranteed sale. If the car dealer or individual refuses to sell it at that price; then consumers should say they will go to another car dealership and simply walk away. Consumers should contact other car dealerships that are selling the same car and should make the offer price. Consumers should also contact car dealerships outside their residential city because in some cases, car dealerships outside the city will be cheaper than car dealerships within the city. They usually will deliver the car to the location of the consumer. Consumers should seek to purchase an automobile that has a long term warranty included; with it as part of a promotion without having to pay extra money. Some consumers are not concerned about the warranty, because they think the insurance will cover the damages. Car insurance only provides the money to repair the damages to an automobile; when an accident occurs and it will not provide money to repair any defects with the car, if no accident occurs. For example, if the power seats stop working then the insurance company will not pay for them to get repaired. However, the car warranty will pay for the repair of the power seats. If an automobile has a defect, such as the power seats not working, before an accident occurs, then the insurance company will not pay for the damages because they already knew about that defect. This is because insurance companies ask for an inspection of the automobile; when the consumer first purchases it or they will have one of their representatives conduct an inspection, on the automobile themselves.

Multiple Cars

Consumers should not purchase multiple cars. It will be expensive for their maintenance such as oil changes, tire changes, and engine repairs, and individual insurance premiums. Consumers should not trade in or sell their current automobile. If their new car breaks down then consumers have a second car they can immediately use to drive to work or school. The consumers will not have to argue with the insurance companies about paying for a rental car while the new car is being repaired. Additionally, despite depreciation, consumers are having a financial loss by selling or trading in their old car due to the fact they have paid over thousands of dollars on it for its maintenance, insurance, and car loan interest. *AAA's Your Driving Costs* reports the average cost to operate a vehicle in the United States is now $8,946 annually. Such is almost $9,000 a year that a consumer has spent on the maintenance of their car. Compared to this amount, they are getting very little or no money for trading or selling the car. Keeping the old car and new car is especially beneficial for consumers with large families, because their kids or spouse are one day going to need the second car. Keeping the old car is cheaper than having to buy a second new car sometime in the future. The only case in which a consumer may consider trading or selling their old car is when; it is not running at all.

When consumers purchase a second car, if possible, they should transfer the driver's license tag from the old car to the new car for the purpose of saving money because it is unlikely the consumers will drive the old car as often as they would the new car. It is much cheaper to do a transfer of the driver's license tag than it is to purchase a brand new driver's license tag. If consumers are going to drive the old car just as often as the new car then they should not do a driver's license tag transfer but instead, purchase a new driver's license tag. The Department of Motors and Vehicles (DMV), if not the dealership, should be able to assist the consumer in purchasing or transferring the driver's license tag. Consumers can find the nearest DMV office near them by going to http://www.dmvlocator.com/.

Returning a Car

If a consumer purchases a car; and later decides to return it; they need to ask the dealership if they can get a full refund. When a consumer drives off the new car then it begins to depreciate, which means decrease in its market value. According to Sylvia Cochran, in *4 Expensive New Car Depreciation Facts You Should Know Today*, most cars depreciate by about 11% when they leave the dealership. This means if Vikram purchased a Ford Fusion for $19,994.39 and left the dealership then he lost almost $2,200 because the value of the Ford Fusion is now about $17,794.39. The Ford Fusion will continue to depreciate between 15% and 25% every year.

It is very likely the consumer will not get a full refund, if they return the car because the car dealerships cannot assume; that the consumer did not extensively use the car. For this reason, they have to charge the consumer some money for using the car otherwise consumers will take advantage of car dealerships, use the cars, and return them possibly even damaged. As a result, the car dealerships will have major financial losses considering they must pay for the maintenance of the cars. The dealerships also cannot refund the consumer any fees; for doing the financing of the vehicle or for doing its tag, title, and insurance registration paperwork. Unless damage was caused on the car due to the fault of the car dealership or for some reason, the consumers cannot afford the monthly payments, consumers should not return the car to the dealership otherwise they will face a financial loss. Some car dealerships will not allow for the consumer to return the car. They may only allow for a consumer to sell the car back to them at a cheaper price than what the consumer had paid. Although they will not get all their money back, selling the car back to the dealership is best for consumers that cannot afford to make the payments compared to a repossession taking place someday; and damaging the credit profile. The consumer will have to make arrangements with the financial institution to pay off the remaining debt. They should not "settle" the debt meaning they only pay half or a small portion of the remaining car loan debt and this will damage their credit profile.

Caution about Gap Insurance

Car dealers offer gap automobile insurance to consumers that finance their vehicles, by getting an auto loan. When consumers drive off the vehicle from the car dealer then it loses value.

For example, if Yogi buys a $40,000 car, then the next day, it may be worth $37,000. If on that same day, the entire car gets wrecked then the car insurance company will pay Yogi $37,000. Yogi has a loss of $3,000. However, if Yogi has gap automobile insurance then the insurance company will pay him $40,000.

Gap automobile insurance requires for the insurance company to pay the consumer the amount of money that was the original value of the car at the time that they purchased it. However, the insurance company will only pay this money if the car is completely wrecked. For this reason, consumers should avoid getting cap automobile insurance because it is unlikely the entire automobile will be destroyed. For whatever reason, if a consumer wants gap automobile insurance then they should get it with a credit union and not the car dealer.

Repossession of a Vehicle

When the automobile or any item, of the consumer, is repossessed then they need to do everything possible to get it back and never lose their motivation to do so no matter how much time has passed; because in most cases they are still obligated to repay the debt. They deserve to get something for paying the debt. Consumers can potentially discharge the debt in a bankruptcy and this causes the financial institution to have a loss so they will appreciate consumers that negotiate with them to repay the debt.

This is supported by the fact, as a business, financial institutions make more profit when they get paid by the consumer whose vehicle they repossessed. It costs them more money to pay for the maintenance and advertising of the repossessed vehicle, as well as money to check the credit reports of consumers to whom they could sell the vehicle. They cannot sell the vehicle for a high price due to the fact it depreciated. For this reason, if consumers get a bill after the vehicle has been repossessed then they should pay it in a timely manner so their credit scores begin to grow again and the financial institution is more likely to negotiate with the consumer. Consumers should call the corporate office of the financial institution, if the customer service department is useless, and negotiate with them to return the vehicle and pay them whatever money is owed on the vehicle.

Here is a letter format consumers should use when sending correspondence to the auto loan provider using certified mail

>Attention: Name of company
>Corporate mailing address of company
>Date letter was written
>
>Name of consumer
>Social security number or auto loan account number of consumer (Financial institutions need this number in order to pull up the records on the consumer)
>Address of consumer
>Phone number of consumer
>
>To Whom It May Concern:

My 2010 Ford Fusion (name and year of car) was repossessed on October 9th, 2010 (estimate the date as to when the vehicle was repossessed). I was in the hospital from September 4th until October 7th (consumers need to indicate the legitimate reason(s) as to why they could not make payments on the auto loan) due to the fact I was severely ill and have provided documentation from the Florida Hospital verifying my hospitalization (consumers need to provide some kind of evidence that verifies the reasons they could not make the payments has truth to them, otherwise the financial institution may think the consumer is making up random and untrue reasons). For this reason, I could not make payments and I greatly apologize for not doing so. The repossession has ruined my credit profile (consumers need to sound convincing that they are worried about their damaged and want to fix it because it is unlikely financial institutions are going to want to help consumers that do not care about their credit profile; because it stands to reason they will default again on loans in the future) and I do not want Chase Bank to feel as though they have been cheated by me. I am willing to pay the full loan amount of $14,695.39 only if Chase agrees to return my vehicle (most important sentence of the letter in which consumers must state the remaining loan balance and that they are willing repay it provided that the vehicle is returned).

    I understand Chase is upset with the fact I did not send in the payments but there are consumers who bankrupt their car loan debt and I am not doing such (consumers need to make financial institutions realize that they are motivated about repaying the car loan debt otherwise they would be declaring a bankruptcy) so I feel as though Chase should honor my request. Being hospitalized and ill was a circumstance that was out of my control (consumers need to express that the circumstances that caused them to become delinquent on their car loan debt were out of their control). Additionally, since I am repaying the debt, I would appreciate it if Chase could report the auto loan as "paid in full" to the credit agencies (consumers want all credit accounts on their credit reports to indicate "paid in full" otherwise employers and insurance providers will think they cheat banks by not paying their bills) because I want my credit scores to increase.

      I can be reached at (407) 496-6005 (consumers should put a strong contact phone number) and I am willing to make the payment over the phone. If Chase <u>does not agree to return my vehicle then I feel as though it is unfair to repay the full loan debt but only a partial amount</u> (consumers must pay money for the time that they were using the vehicle, if the financial institution does not agree to return the vehicle to them). <u>I am willing to take this issue to court</u> (consumers need to have a strong attitude about repaying the car loan debt to the point they are willing to attend court for the purpose of reclaiming their car) Chase does not agree to work with me.

      Thank you,
      Danny Singh

Note: Consumers should include documents, with the letter, that verify the hardships they faced and as a result, they could not make payments on the auto loan. The purpose behind this is so the financial institution does not think they are making up excuses for not paying the bills and refuses to help them. The most common hardships are unemployment and hospitalization. Consumers could provide a copy of their unemployment checks that verifies their unemployment. For hospitalization, consumers could get documents from the hospital where they received treatment and include it with their letter. The documents should indicate the dates for which they were hospitalized and what illness was being treated.

Use Retirement Account to Save Automobile

Consumers should take a loan against their 401(k) or 403(b) plan and/or rollover, which means transfer, all the money from their IRA and other assets into a Roth IRA; pay the necessary taxes, and take the money to pay the car loan provider, as much as possible. Roth IRA has no 10% tax penalty.

If for whatever reason, a consumer does not have access to any retirement account, then they should borrow money from a family member or see if they can get a home equity loan or other type of low interest rate loan from a credit union or community bank, for the purpose of paying the car loan provider. Consumers should explain the situation to the credit union or community bank. Students have the option of using their student loan money and/or grant money to repay the car loan provider. If none of the options work then the consumer will have to work two jobs and save up the money to fully repay the car loan provider. If the consumer cannot accumulate enough money to repay the car loan provider, then consumers should ask the car loan provider if they would be willing to accept a partial amount and still return the car. Consumers can mention they are willing to continue sending payments even after paying the partial amount until the loan is fully repaid.

Attorneys to Help with Repossession Case

If the car loan provider still refuses to return the car despite the fact the consumer has the money to repay them; then the consumer needs to seek out a credible attorney. For the purpose of paying the least amount of attorney and court fees, consumers should ask their family members, employers, and friends if they have any connections to attorneys. Despite not having the car, consumers should make the monthly car loan payments, to protect their credit profile, as best as possible. If the auto loan provider agrees to return the car then the consumer should pay them immediately and keep a record of the check. Consumers should tell the car loan provider to report to the credit agencies that the car loan is paid in full and if possible, remove the information indicating the car was repossessed. Consumers cannot let the financial institution keep the vehicle and do nothing about it because if consumers do so then they lose all the down payment money they made on the vehicle, money they spent on maintenance, as well as the insurance payments.

Umbrella Insurance is Ideal for Risky Drivers

Consumers have a limited amount of protection with their homeowners and auto insurance, if an incident that caused injury to another consumer is found to be their fault.

For example, if a consumer is driving, after they drank alcohol, and they crash into the automobile of another consumer then it is likely the injured consumer will have many medical expenses worth $20,000 or more. The injured consumer could potentially submit a lawsuit such as a personal injury case against the consumer and the amount of money that the injured consumer will be awarded by the lawyer will not be fully paid for by the insurance company if they even pay any money at all. The consumer will have to use the money they live on to pay the injured consumer and this could cause the consumer to become homeless because they will not have enough money to pay their own bills such as the mortgage.

For this reason, all consumers should have umbrella insurance, which provides extra protection in addition to the coverage provided by the homeowners and auto insurance policies. According to About.com, umbrella insurance can add an additional one to five million dollars in liability protection. Consumers will need this amount of protection because if the injured consumer cannot work then the consumer who caused the accident will have to give them money for their everyday living expenses in addition to paying for their layer and court fees. The beauty behind umbrella insurance is that it is very cheap. Umbrella insurance can be used by the consumer anywhere in the world where they cause an incident. Ideally, consumers should not take risks such as drinking shortly before driving or launching explosive fireworks from their household near the household of another consumer. When such incidents happen then the insurance premiums of the consumers increase regardless whether or not they have umbrella insurance and these incidents could result in ending the life of another consumer. The consumer who is responsible for the incidents may end up in jail.

Vehicles can Develop Negative Equity like Houses

Automobiles can develop negative equity because they depreciate in value, which may cause consumers to struggle in selling them or trading them for a new car.

Example
Jose wants to trade in his 2011 Toyota Corolla so he can purchase a 2012 Ford Fusion.
The Toyota Corolla has a $14,405 auto loan debt against it.
The car sales person tells Jose that his Toyota Corolla is worth $11,000.
$14,405 debt - $11,000 value = $3,405 negative equity. There is more debt against the Corolla than what it is worth.

In order for Jose to trade in his car, he must pay the $3,405. Depending upon the guidelines of the financial institution and his credit profile, they may allow for him to include this negative equity debt with the new car loan he would get to purchase the Ford Fusion.

Jose needs to get a $19,589 car loan in order to purchase the Ford Fusion.

$19,589 auto loan + $3,405 negative equity from the Toyota Corolla = $22,994 total loan amount needed.

If possible, it is recommended that Jose pay the $3,405 by himself without the loan because a $22,994 car loan is going to compound with more interest than a $19,589 car loan. This will likely mean that Jose will need more time to repay the car loan in full and this may negatively affect his credit scores because he will be in debt for a longer time frame.

For consumers who cannot afford to make their car loan payments and have negative equity, they should negotiate with the financial institution to stretch out their payments and make the loan term longer. This will mean paying more interest but this is better for the credit profile than a repossession taking place with the car. It is more likely consumers will be denied for jobs when the employers see that the consumer has repossession on their credit reports. Although it is rare, the financial institutions may be willing to accept the negative equity as a loss and let the consumer sell the car but for doing this, it is likely the financial institutions will report negative information to the credit reports of the consumer. However, the negative information will be less severe than repossession showing on the credit reports. Consumers should not buy cars and then immediately sell them because they are wasting their money on negative equity. Additionally, in most cases, when consumers purchase cars, they get car loans, and this means that credit checks are done on the consumer. If consumers are always buying and selling cars then they credit scores can potentially become low because of the excessive credit checks and short history established on the installment credit accounts. Future financial institutions may question why a consumer kept buying and selling cars and will wonder if it was due to financial weaknesses and they could not make the monthly payments.

Car Refinancing

Despite the fact that the consumer has a fixed interest rate on their auto loan, they can always ask for the financial institution or a credit union to grant them a cheaper fixed interest rate provided that they have an excellent credit profile or it has improved from the time that the consumer purchased the automobile. Consumers need to be aware some financial institutions charge closing costs to refinance the automobile so if the closing costs are high then the consumer should not do the refinance unless they are greatly in need of a cheaper monthly payment and want to protect their credit profile from a delinquent auto loan. Consumers cannot deduct any interest paid on auto loans from their taxes. Consumers should offer to make a down payment to the financial institution because down payments always suggest the consumer is less likely to become delinquent on the auto loan and so the financial institution can trust them with a cheaper interest rate. Consumers should not apply for an auto loan refinance with many financial institutions otherwise the many credit checks will damage their credit profile.

Other ways in which Consumers can save Money with their Auto Loan

1. Sometimes a home equity loan interest rate is cheaper than an auto loan interest rate so consumers should consider getting a home equity loan to pay off their car loan debt unless the closing costs for getting a home equity loan from a credit union are outrageous or the house does not have enough equity.

2. Consumers should look for a fixed interest rate for life credit card and transfer the balance from the auto loan and onto the credit card. I did this myself for my mother's automobile and got the auto loan balance onto a 3.99% for life credit card. There may be a balance transfer fee that the credit card issuer will charge to do the transfer but it is worth paying because the consumer will save money on interest. Initially, doing the transfer will cause the credit scores to drop but as the balance is being paid off then the credit scores will begin to increase again. However, consumers should never do the transfer if their source of income or unemployment is weak because if they are late on making the credit card payment then the auto loan balance will start being charged a 30% penalty interest rate by the credit card issuer. If consumers have never been late on making their auto loan payment then it is unlikely they will be late in making their credit card payment but to be safe, consumers should ask the financial institution how much the monthly payment will be on the credit card if they transfer the auto loan balance onto it. If the consumer cannot afford the monthly payments then they should not do the transfer.

Escrow: Some of the money that the consumer pays towards mortgage payments, closing costs, down payment and other fees in getting the mortgage is held in an escrow account. If the consumer leaves the house or the financial institution forecloses on the house then they would keep the money within the escrow account for the purpose of trying to make up for their loss and use some of it to pay for the house taxes and insurance until the house is sold again.

Insurance Brokers and Agents

An insurance broker and insurance agent are similar, because they both sell different types of insurance to consumers, such as; home owner's insurance, pet insurance, RV insurance, automobile insurance, health insurance, and life insurance. However, they are two different occupations.

An insurance broker works for an insurance agency, which has business relationships with multiple insurance companies. The insurance agency collects information from the consumers and forwards them to all its partner insurance companies. The partner insurance company pays the insurance agency a fee for forwarding them a consumer. The insurance broker collects a portion of the fee money.

For example, Wells Fargo is an insurance agency. Anyone who needs car insurance coverage could call them at 1-866-294-2571 or go onto their website; which is https://www.wellsfargo.com/insurance/. If the consumer chooses to call Wells Fargo then an insurance broker would answer the phone. Regardless whether online or over the phone, Wells Fargo would collect the information of the consumer, such as; their driver's license number, social security number, address, date of birth, and other personal information for the purpose of performing a credit check on them, background report, and checking their driver's license profile information. Wells Fargo would then electronically submit this information to the insurance companies with whom it has a business relationship such as Geico, All-State, Progressive, and State Farm. The insurance companies would individually respond back to Wells Fargo with an estimated amount that the consumer would pay for car insurance every month with a certain amount of **coverage**, which is the amount of money that the insurance company will pay for the automobile repairs. This information is considered the quote. Wells Fargo would then share the quote received from each insurance company with the consumer. The consumer would choose the quote that satisfies their budget and how much coverage they want for their automobile. If the consumer picked Geico then Wells Fargo would get the consumer set up with Geico or whichever insurance company from whom the consumer desires insurance.

Insurance agencies make their money by forwarding consumers to insurance companies that pay them a fee or some type of commission. Insurance agents work for insurance companies such as Progressive, All-State, Geico, and State Farm, and not insurance agencies. If a consumer wants to get insurance from Progressive and calls them then they would speak to an insurance agent. Unlike an insurance broker, the insurance agent would only tell the consumer the quote from Progressive. They would tell the consumer the quotes from other insurance companies that are considered the competitors of Progressive otherwise the run the risk of losing the business of the consumer. When consumers are seeking insurance of any type then they should contact an insurance agency and not any company directly because consumers have a greater chance of being able to save money when they are working with quotes from multiple companies. Consumers do not pay any money to the insurance agency or the insurance broker. However, insurance agencies do not have a business relationship with all the insurance companies in existence. For this reason, consumers should contact the insurance companies from whom the insurance agency did not get a quote because they do not have relationship with those companies. In some cases, insurance companies that do not have a relationship with insurance agencies may be cheaper for consumers than insurance companies that do have relationships. This is because the insurance companies without any relationships are able to save more money because they do not have to pay a fee to the insurance agency. They pass this savings onto the consumers by offering them cheaper insurance premiums.

A personally recommended insurance company for all types of insurance is Esurance. I have my car insurance with this company and they offered me the same coverage as the other insurance companies but for a much cheaper premium, which is the cost of the insurance. Esurance can be contacted on their website http://www.esurance.com/ or on their 24/7 customer service number, 1-800-378-7262. However, before going to Esurance, consumers should get a quote from an insurance company with whom they already have some type of insurance such as homeowners insurance or health insurance. This is because insurance companies often give discounts to consumers with whom they already do business when consumers desire multiple insurance products.

For example, my grandfather has his car insurance and homeowners insurance through All-State because he gets a discount. Consumers should mention they are a student attending a college or high school; because insurance companies give discounts to students. It is encouraged that all consumers take a driver's education safety and drug course; because insurance companies will also give discounts to consumers for passing the course. In fact, I took the driver's education course with Florida Virtual School and as a result, I am getting a discount on my car insurance. Consumers should be able to take the course any time they wish and to find out at what locations or credible websites the course is being taught, consumers can contact their local Department of Motors and Vehicles office. Some high schools offer the DMV course to their students. Consumers should not take the driver's education course at a website that has no credibility and only wants to collect high fees from the consumer. Consumers should only take the course at the website or location recommended by the DMV. If consumers can pay it off at the end of the month then they should use a high rewards level credit card to pay for their insurance products in advance such as 6 months worth of insurance payments because the insurance providers will give discounts for paying ahead of time. This is because they are at less risk of having a business loss. Some consumers get the insurance providers to pay for the damages and when the insurance bill comes then the consumer chooses not to pay the bill. The deductible alone is not enough money for the insurance company to make profit and run a successful business because they usually spend more money than the deductible to get the damages repaired. Consumers should not pay for the insurance and then carry a balance on the credit card because the interest will offset the savings given by insurance providers. If consumers cannot pay in advance then they should use a high rewards level debit card to make the monthly payments. The rewards will help save money. The last step to save the most money on any type of insurance is to get a bank or store credit card, not build a balance, use it lightly, and pay it off at the end of the month or the day that it is used for the purpose of establishing an excellent credit profile. All insurance companies check the credit profile of the consumer using their social security number before granting the consumer the insurance product. They have to do so because there is no way for them to know whether or not the consumer is trustworthy enough to repay them. If the consumer has a bad or limited credit profile then they have to assume that the consumer is very likely to one day stop paying them and for this reason, they have to make high profits off of the consumer so they can compensate for the potential loss they will face someday. They will charge consumers with bad and limited credit profiles a high insurance premium. This means if currently, consumers have insurance but little or no credit history showing on their credit reports then it is likely they are paying too much money towards insurance. Consumers will excellent credit profiles will be able to save large amounts of money on insurance. After getting a credit card and establishing at least 6 to 8 months of excellent payment history on it then consumers should call their insurance provider and ask for a cheaper insurance premium notifying them that their credit profile has become stronger since the time they first obtained the insurance product. If the insurance company refuses to lower the insurance premium for the same amount of coverage then the consumer should call other providers and get quotes from them. After finding a quote that is cheaper than the amount of money that the consumer is currently paying to their insurance provider then the consumer should immediately accept the insurance offer and cancel their insurance product with their current provider. Consumers should never cancel their insurance products before getting insured with a new provider. Consumers should always look over the policy and have attention to the details because often, the insurance companies charge consumers for services they do not need especially if consumers do not drive their vehicles very often and/or do not use drugs shortly before driving, which significantly lowers their chances of getting into an accident. It may be wise to show the insurance policy to an attorney for the purpose of determining what services are needed.

Consumers need to be aware; they must have insurance on their car. According to www.ehow.com, every state in the United States has a law that requires every person that drives a vehicle to have automobile insurance. It is illegal to drive without insurance and most financial institutions, for consumers that get an auto loan to purchase the vehicle, require that the vehicle be protected with insurance. In fact, the financial institution will not even grant an auto loan without the consumer first getting insurance and if the consumer removes the insurance after getting the car; then the insurance company will notify the financial institution, who will then warn the consumer about getting insurance otherwise they may repossess the car or take other adverse actions against the consumer. Consumers must the exact amount of car insurance coverage, if not more, that will be specified by the financial institution. The financial institution must protect the collateral.

Unfortunately, statistics show there is about 1.5 million people in the United States that drive without insurance. If consumers get into an accident, regardless if it is their fault or not, and the law official finds out that they have no insurance then their driver's license could potentially get suspended and the consumer will be required to pay a heavy fine. If the consumer owed any money to the financial institution for the car then they will be very upset with the consumer because the vehicle is considered the collateral of the auto loan and if the vehicle is damaged then the collateral has little or no money value. There is nothing that the financial institution can repossess if the consumer stops paying on the auto loan balance. For this reason, they are at high risk, of the consumer defaulting, on the auto loan balance and so they may take drastic actions against the consumer such as garnishing their wages, taking them to court, levying their bank accounts, or putting a non-consensual lien (claim) on their property.

If the consumer had insurance on their vehicle then they could have had the vehicle repaired. As a result, the financial institution and the consumer would have had no financial loss. If for whatever reason, a consumer gets into an accident with a vehicle that has no insurance then they need to make arrangements with the financial institution to repay the auto loan debt or they will have to use their own money to get the vehicle repaired and this will not be cheap. Consumers may have to take a loan against their 401k or just a loan in general to get the vehicle repaired. Despite the vehicle becoming wrecked or damaged, this does not free the consumer from the debt.

Similar to how financial institutions want the vehicles insured for which they are providing financing, they also want houses to be insured. A financial institution will not grant a consumer a mortgage (home loan) unless they first get homeowners insurance for it. If the consumer removes the insurance after getting the house then the homeowner's insurance company will notify the financial institution that the house is no longer insured. The financial institution will warn the consumer to get the insurance otherwise they will repossess the house or put a claim on it. The financial institution will do so because if the house burns down or is severely damaged due to bad weather conditions such as a hurricane then the financial institution will have a major loss. This is because there is no collateral or collateral worth of little or no value that they can repossess if the consumer stops paying on the mortgage. No collateral or collateral worth of little value raises the likelihood that the consumer will default on their mortgage. Unless the consumer makes arrangements with the financial institution to pay off the mortgage debt or uses their own money to get the house repaired, the financial institution may take adverse actions against the consumer such as take them to court, garnish their wages, put a claim on the house, repossess it, or do anything possible to get the maximum amount of money from the consumer before the house gets damaged. To avoid all this, consumers should always have their house insured. For Florida and Texas home owners only, a personally recommended homeowner's insurance company is Cypress Property and Casualty. When I refinanced my mother's mortgage, I also made her homeowner's insurance cheaper by switching to this company but keeping the same amount of coverage. They are small because they only grant insurance to home owners in Florida and Texas and do not have as many expenses as other insurance companies do and so they pass on the saving to consumers. Their website is http://www.cypressig.com/ and their number for Florida customers is 1-888-352-9773 whereas their number for Texas customers is 1-888-892-9773. After the consumer pays off the house then it is their choice whether or not they want to keep homeowners insurance. It is recommended that consumers always have homeowners insurance because all the money they used to make mortgage payments will go to waste if the house is damaged especially during hurricane seasons or due to a fire. It will cost consumers thousands of dollars to get the house repaired. Consumers can get discounts on their homeowner's insurance if they get a security system installed within their household. In some cases, especially if the area in which they are living has a high level of crime, then getting a security system for their house is worth paying money.

There are special types of homeowners insurance such as hurricane insurance, flood insurance, and earthquake insurance, which pays more money for house repairs than regular homeowner's insurance. Depending upon their polices for each state, financial institutions may require that the consumer also have the special types of insurance if the state where the house is located often experiences earthquakes, floods, or hurricanes. It is the choice of the consumer if they want to keep the special types of insurance after the house is fully paid. If consumers were to rent their house to someone then they must switch their insurance type from regular homeowners insurance to homeowner's rental insurance. After consumers reclaim their house then they must switch the homeowner's rental insurance type to the regular homeowner's insurance type. Consumers do not need insurance for their condo or apartment. However, for apartments, they can and should get apartment renter insurance if they live in an area where robbery and crime is dominant because the insurance of the landlord, who is the owner of the entire apartment complex, will not compensate consumers of the value of all their stolen and/or damaged possessions. Similarly, with condos, the insurance of the condominium complex owner will not compensate the consumer of all their losses in the event they are robbed or their possessions are damaged. If consumers own a condo in an area that has a high crime rate then they should get special condominium insurance.

Insurance

Health and Dental Insurance

Health insurance, vision insurance, and dental insurance are not the same. Health insurance will pay for most of the costs involved with visiting the doctor's office and any treatments. Dental insurance will cover a large extent of the costs involved, in maintaining healthy teeth. Vision insurance will cover a large extent of the costs involved in maintaining healthy eyes. Consumers need health insurance, vision insurance, and dental insurance for themselves, as well as, their family members.

Employment Discounts on Insurance

Consumers may get discounts on these insurance types through the connections of their employers, with insurance companies. Most employers provide their employees with health insurance. However, most small business owners do not provider their employees with workers' compensation, which is a type of insurance, not health insurance, that pays for the treatment of consumers if they are injured while doing their job tasks or if they contract a disease at the location of their job. For this reason, consumers, especially consumers that work for small businesses, should get life and health insurance plans with sufficient overages.

CIGNA is an Ideal Insurance Company

A personally recommended health, vision and dental care insurance company is CIGNA and they can be contacted using www.cigna.com or through phone, 1-866-877-1128. Consumers can explore the costs of getting all kinds of insurance from different companies using http://www.ehealthinsurance.com/ or by calling them at 1-800-977-8860. Consumers may get a discount if they mention that they are a student.

Medicaid

Consumers that cannot afford to get health insurance should apply for Medicaid using the governmental website of their state of residency. This is a government funded health care program, in the United States, that pays for the medical expenses of financially unstable consumers, as well as, their children. The government uses the money paid by consumers in taxes to fund the Medicaid program. Florida residents would apply for Medicaid using www.myflorida.com/accessflorida.

Medicare

Consumers, over the age of 65, should apply for the Medicare program, even if they are not ready to retire, using the website of the Social Security Administration, which is www.ssa.gov/medicareonly/. This is a health care program for seniors and pays for their medical expenses. The government partially pays for Medicare using the tax money and the rest of the costs are paid for by the seniors. In a sense, they are getting a discounted health care program.

4 Insurance Policies to Avoid

Credit Life Insurance
This insurance pays off a certain debt such as a car loan or mortgage in the event that the consumer passes away.

Life Insurance Policy on Children
It makes no sense why consumers would purchase income on their children, because their children make no money and the consumers do not depend on them.

Insurance on Rental Cars
Consumers should use a credit card to rent a car because the credit card company offers free insurance to cover any damages that occur with the car. It is a benefit for being a credit card customer. The car rental stores make high profits off of rental car insurance.

Disease Insurance
Unless consumers have bad health insurance policies that do not cover all the expenses and consumers are always getting ill, disease insurance is not necessary.

Snapshot Auto Insurance Discount
Sometimes called auto safety device or snapshot insurance discount, this is for consumers who drive their vehicle very little and have excellent driving skills. This insurance is when the auto insurance company puts an electronic device into the car which monitors the driving performance of the driver. It will record information such as the number of miles the consumer drives every day, what times of the day they drive, and the highest miles per hour point that the consumer reaches every day. According to Money Talks News, if the insurance company feels as though the driver is safe, then they will offer a discount on the insurance policy up to 30% compared to regular auto insurance. However, not all insurance companies offer pay as you drive insurance in all states, so consumers should seek out credible insurance companies that do offer it. Consumers have little or no privacy with pay as you go insurance but for saving money, it is worth it. Consumers should not get this insurance if they have a habit of driving after midnight or are always getting traffic tickets; otherwise it could cost them much more money than regular auto insurance. To get even more savings, consumers should maintain a good credit profile and should pay all their traffic tickets. Unpaid traffic tickets can sometimes become collections accounts and such accounts are immediately reported as negative information to the credit reporting agencies.

Health Savings Account

Consumers with severe illnesses, little income, many children; or consumers that want to reduce their health insurance premiums should consider getting a health savings account, abbreviated as an HSA, from a credit union or community bank. An HSA is a FDIC-insured or NCUA-insured savings account in which consumers can save money, deduct the amount of money they save within the HSA from their taxes, and use the money whenever needed to pay for medical expenses only without paying a 10% tax penalty or ordinary income taxes.

The money grows within the HSA tax free, meaning no taxes are charged on the interest being made.

For example, if Natalia deposits $1.00 into her HSA account then she can deduct that $1.00 from her taxes and if that $1.00 makes an additional $1.00 then Natalia does not have to pay taxes on the additional dollar that was earned. Medical expenses can include paying for medicines, hospital treatments, ambulance services, some dental expenses, doctor's fees, and consumers can talk with the financial representative at the financial institution for more qualified medical expenses. Consumers can access the money within their HSA account using a debit card and this is safe to pay for medical expenses versus paying with a check or cash. The amount of money that the consumer can contribute (deposit) into the HSA has a limit and this limit is determined by the Internal Revenue Service; so consumers do not abuse the system and contribute as much money as possible with the intention of wanting to pay the least amount of money in their taxes. The contribution limit keeps the financial world fair. A health savings account is personally recommended due to all the tax savings and the money is not lost or charged taxes if the consumer changes their health insurance or their employer. Some consumers have a flexible spending health account and that is different from an HSA because the money within a flexible spending health account must be used within a year so the consumer can save the money from being charged taxes. The money within an HSA does not have to be used by a certain time. The money grows with interest tax free for as many years as desired by the consumer. If possible and without paying any tax penalties, consumers should convert their flexible spending health account into a health savings account. Consumers that are a dependent on the tax return of another individual, enrolled in Medicare, or are receiving veterans medical benefits may not qualify to open a health savings account so they should call the financial institution and confirm whether or not they are eligible before they attempt opening the account. Consumers should not establish an HSA at a financial institution that charges them a monthly fee just for having the account.

Finance 101: The Whiz Kid's Perfect Credit Guide

Real Estate

Apartments and Houses

Apartment and Condo Hunting

The first step to get an apartment or condo is to establish a strong and positive credit profile; by getting a credit card, using it lightly, and paying off the entire balance immediately. This is because apartment and condo landlords check the credit profile of the consumer. There is no way for them to know if the consumer will stay for a certain number of days; and when they receive the bill then they will simply take off to stay at another place. This will result in a loss for the apartment or condo landlord; because they need to make money for allowing the consumer to stay at the complex.

If consumers have a positive credit profile, then the apartment owner will likely ask for little or no security deposit money from the consumer; because they are unlikely to not pay the bill. A little or no security deposit means the consumer can save more money; and can pay their other bills more easily. In contrast, if consumers have a bad credit profile then it is very likely that the apartment or condo landlord will ask for a higher than average security deposit because the consumer is very likely to not pay the bill and it costs money for the apartment and condo landlords to get evictions. They have a financial loss in doing so, which they will try to avoid by checking the consumer's credit profile.

Real Estate Agents can find Great Deals

After establishing credit, consumers should always talk to a licensed real estate agent when they are seeking to rent an apartment or purchase a condo. The real estate agents are usually very familiar with the area and keep a listing of all the available apartments and condos. They can also advise the consumers of areas where they should not get an apartment or condo due to the fact there are high levels of criminal activity, within those areas. Consumers can find a real estate agent using www.realtor.com.

Consumers should not aim towards living in an apartment for a long time frame because over time, an apartment can get more expensive than a house. This is because consumers have to make payments on apartments forever whereas they make payments on a house or condo until it is fully paid.

Roth IRA can help Save Money Faster

The best way to save up money for an apartment is for employed consumers to open a Roth IRA, with a credit union or community bank and consumers should contribute as much money as possible towards it. The money within a Roth IRA will make the most earnings compared to the earnings (interest) it would make in interest bearing savings and money market accounts. Consumers have to pay taxes on the money before contributing (depositing) it towards a Roth IRA and they can claim the money, not the earnings, before age 59 ½ without paying a 10% tax penalty. If consumers work for an employer that does company matching meaning they deposit an equal amount of money into a 401(k) or 403(b) that the consumer had deposited then consumers should contribute as much money as possible towards that account and later, rollover the money they contributed only and not the employer from the 401(k) or 403(b) into a Roth IRA and claim the money for the apartment without paying the 10% tax penalty or additional income taxes. Consumers can only take the money that the employer contributed towards their 401(k) or 403(b) plan when they reach the age of retirement. For an emergency, consumers can take a loan against their 401(k) or 403(b) for the purpose of getting an apartment.

Mortgage Prepayment Scams

Consumers may receive a notice from their mortgage provider that the term to repay the mortgage can be cut.

For example, a 30 year mortgage can be reduced to 22 years, and consumers get the impression that this program will save them money. It will not save them money, because mortgage providers often charge extra fees for these programs that claim to help them. If consumers want to pay off their mortgage faster, they should pay above the minimum payment requirements.

For example, if the minimum payment is $1,000 every month, then consumers should pay $1,100 or as high as possible without letting other bills become late or building high balances on credit cards. Consumers can pay extra money to their mortgage provider at any time free of charge so it makes no sense to sign up for the fancy prepayment and other programs and pay hundreds of dollars in fees. The programs that claim to help consumers are designed to help the financial institutions make more profit. The financial institutions are not going to offer programs for free.

Pay down Student Loans before getting Apartment

Consumers, that have student loan debt, should not get an apartment; but instead, they should focus more towards making payments on the student loans. This is because the student loan debt will never go away but instead, they will continue growing with compounded interest and fees. Student loans cannot be discharged in bankruptcy or debt settlement and if students default on them then it will not matter if they earned a Ph.D., employers will be reluctant to grant them jobs.

As a result, the consumers will be evicted from their apartment. When the student loans are significantly paid down then the consumers can consider renting an apartment and some apartment complexes give discounts to students and this is information that the real estate agent would know. If their parents want them to move out, then consumers can show them this book and explain that their future will be jeopardized if they do not use their money to first pay down their student loan debts. It is unlikely any parent would want for their children to have bad futures due to having dangerous debt. Consumers that have financial aid such as grants and scholarship money paying for their dorm rooms are better off living at the college than getting an apartment unless they can use the financial aid money to pay for an apartment by depositing the money into a bank account.

Housing Crisis of 2000s: Mistakes of Congress and the Federal Reserve

A possible cause behind the 2000s housing crisis was a series of poor decisions made by the Federal Reserve and Congress. The Federal Reserve is the central bank, of the United States, that manages interest rates and monetary policies that regulate the rates; at which consumers can obtain loans, mostly mortgages, and financial institutions can grant loans. The Federal Reserve has about twelve branches throughout the United States and their goal is to ensure the United

States is able to maintain a healthy inflation rate, employment rate, cash flow, and ultimately, a healthy economy.

The Federal Reserve was keeping interest rates low on loans and deposit accounts during the years of 2004 through 2006. Low interest rates may have added severity to the 2000s housing crisis; because financial institutions had weak assets. This is because not many consumers were depositing all their funds within deposit accounts. Consumers would not get paid lots of interest and so they had little or no incentives to do deposits. Instead, more consumers were spending their money and creating debts that they could not pay. The strength of the assets of the financial institutions depends upon the amounts of deposits they are receiving from consumers. Weak assets meant that the financial institutions could not do very much lending. According to Dr. Gary Becker, professor at the University of Chicago and founder of the Chicago School of Economics, despite the weak assets, Congress, who is the group of governmental lawmakers in the United States consisting of the Senate and the House of Representatives, was encouraging the financial institutions to lend greatly to consumers of all credit types and income levels and not discriminate against them. It is likely Congress thought that the profits made off of the loans would allow for the financial institutions to strengthen their assets, grant more loans, and consumers could expand on their businesses using the loans and in doing so, create new jobs. Congress thought spending, which is considered the aggregate demand, would cause the economy to progress. For this purpose, Congress was greatly pushing the Community Reinvestment Act of 1977 during the 1990s and 2000s. This act encouraged financial institutions to lend all types of loans, not just mortgages, to consumers without being strict about their financial profiles. As evidence, Dr. Gary Becker had expressed the 2000s as a great expansion of credit in the United States.

By granting loans, the financial institutions were spending money, and some financial institutions were spending more money than what could be supported by their assets. In doing so, the financial institutions created deficits, which are amounts spent above their planned budgets. The deficits were increasing because some financial institutions were borrowing money from government sponsored private investors such as Fannie Mae and Freddie Mac. Financial institutions had to borrow money from them because they did not have enough assets to grant loans themselves to consumers. Fannie Mae and Freddie Mac had lending policies that they wanted the financial institutions to follow such as the average income and credit profile that the consumers possess but it is unlikely all the financial institutions adhered to their guidelines because they wanted to sell real estate aggressively.

Many consumers purchased houses and condominiums due to the low interest rates, which meant low monthly payments. Low minimum payments may have made consumers not worried about possible financial struggles happening and so they confidently took equity, which is loan money based on the property value, out of the properties in order to make large purchases. Some financial institutions were granting consumers a higher amount of equity than the value of the real estate with the intention of making high profits off of the consumer. This is because a higher amount of equity being borrowed means a higher loan balance, which results in higher interest being charged to the consumer. Financial institutions granting loans, consumers purchasing houses, and then using equity to make more purchases were causing a boom within the United States because growth was happening immoderately.

As part of the boom-and-bust cycle, which is the alternation between economic growth and economic decline, the bust was beginning to develop. When equity is taken out of a property then its market value drops. Depending upon the conditions of the economy, the market value of a property can increase again and as a result, the consumer may not have as great a loss because the market value increase will offset the decrease that occurred when the consumer took out equity from the property. Unfortunately, due to the fact so many consumers were taking equity out of their properties and getting into debt on which they were defaulting, the economy declined, which is when the bust occurred. The market values of the properties decreased more and this made it difficult for the consumers to sell their houses. Consumers did not want to purchase real estate with decreasing market value, as the consumers would lose money because the amount of money they would pay for a house or condominium would be worth less. The property-owning consumers now had to pay their mortgage balances, which were significantly higher than the value of the house, and all the equity they borrowed. The equity they borrowed is considered a second mortgage that they must pay otherwise the property will be repossessed by the financial institution and their credit profile will be ruined. In this sense, the consumers had to pay two mortgages on one property. For this reason, some consumers had to clear out all the funds within their savings and other deposit accounts and this hurt financial institutions because their assets further weakened and they had to begin limiting how much credit they could extend. Despite using all their assets, some consumers still failed to make the payments on their mortgages and as a result, the houses were foreclosed by the financial institutions. This is because many consumers had variable mortgages, sometimes called adjustable rate mortgages, or interest-only mortgages because their intention was to wait for the houses to increase in equity values and sell the houses for prices much higher than what they originally paid.

Due to the recession that was happening, the financial institutions along with some influence from the Federal Reserve and Wall Street Journal made the mortgage rates high so they could make up for the losses they were having and because there was a decline in the number of consumers purchasing real estate. Increased mortgage rates caused the minimum payments for consumers to increase beyond what could be supported by their incomes. As more consumers were failing to make their payments, an increasing number of financial institutions were having more losses and some of them became bankrupt because they did not have enough money to pay back their private investors from whom they borrowed money. For this reason, Freddie Mac and Fannie Mae were having losses. The government had to provide bailout money to help make up for some of their losses in addition to the losses of the financial institutions. The government had passed a savings tax credit because they were trying to get more consumers to deposit all their funds within deposit accounts. The government did so with the intention of trying to strengthen the assets of the financial institutions. To this day, many financial institutions are trying to make up for the loan losses they are having and it is likely for this reason, an increasing number of financial institutions are charging increased interest rates on unsecured loans such as credit cards and student loans. Financial institutions are reducing loan amounts and/or credit limits because they think by doing so, consumers are more likely to pay more towards their loans so they have access to more loan money for the purpose of spending it. More consumers now have to pay fees simply for using their debit cards or deposit accounts.

The Credit Crisis in Relation to the 2000s Housing Crisis

Bad credit is influencing the housing crisis. A major economic issue in many states is the growing number of house foreclosures. Florida has one of the nation's highest foreclosure rates. A possible cause behind this could be the increasing number of consumers developing bad credit because nationally, an increasing number of consumers are being laid off from their jobs, being victimized by identity theft, and are overextending themselves by creating excessive debt. These consumers are struggling to pay back their loan obligations, which can include credit cards, auto loans, and other types of personal loans. For this reason, many consumers are becoming delinquent on their loan accounts and this is creating a credit crisis. As required by the "Fair Credit Reporting Act," which was passed by Congress on October 26, 1970, the lenders may report this negative information to the consumer reporting agencies. Such has a negative impact on the credit bureau scores of the consumers because they can become low, which will cause lenders to view them as high risk borrowers. This may cause lenders to give such borrowers higher interest rates, fees, low loan amounts, and larger minimum payments on their loan products because the borrowers have a high potential of not paying back the loans. Lenders must follow the credit history data they receive from the consumer reporting agencies and take into consideration the income of the consumer to determine their "creditworthiness," which is the level of trustworthiness in paying back a loan.

In the past, lenders were not as strict in determining how creditworthy a consumer was, and they had major losses as a result. Mortgage losses were especially abundant during the late 2000s housing crisis. With the goal of trying to avoid a similar catastrophe, the lenders are trying to accumulate as much profit as they can from the borrowers for the time that they are successfully making payments on the loans. There is also the possibility that the lender might deny the consumer for the loan product, which can make any future loans more expensive for the consumer to obtain because their credit score might have gone down from the credit check. Due to the credit crisis, consumers are paying high interest on their loans, which is causing them to struggle making their mortgage payments and as a result, an increasing number of consumers are likely to have their houses foreclosed.

The increasing unemployment rate is another reason why consumers are defaulting on their loan products and as a result, their credit profiles are becoming damaged. In fact, some employers may check credit and deny an applicant a job because the negative credit history may suggest that the applicant is irresponsible. This makes it difficult for consumers to obtain new loans or loans with low interest, which is contributing to the failing credit industry. Whenever consumers apply for loans, the lender checks the credit report as well as the credit score of the consumer with one or more of the consumer reporting agencies, Equifax, TransUnion, Experian, and Innovis. This generates an inquiry on the report. The inquiry may lower the credit score by less than five points and when other lenders see that inquiry, they will know that the consumer applied for a loan. Too many inquiries will damage the credit profile of the consumer because it will suggest to the lenders that the consumer is aggressively seeking for many loans and in doing so, is trying to plunge into a large amount of debt that will be very difficult to pay back. Due to becoming default or late on previous loan products from being unemployed, it is likely that lenders might deny the consumer the loan because the consumer has a low credit score and is very likely not to pay the loan back. Despite the denial, the inquiry will stay on the credit report of the consumer for up to two years and it may prevent the consumer from getting a loan with low interest and low fees. This is because the unemployment damaged the credit profile of the consumer since there was no or very little income to pay the loans. It is likely when the consumer becomes late on making the payments on the loans, their annual percentage rates will increase to the default rates.

Having loans with high interest default rates will ultimately increase their balances and cause consumers to fall into more debt. Now, the lenders will be more likely to approve the consumer with high interest loans, which will make it more difficult for the consumer to successfully pay on their mortgage. Additionally, if offered by the financial institution, some consumers may choose to sign up for the "payment protection insurance" for the time that they are unemployed and cannot make payments on the loan. Payment protection insurance, sometimes called credit protection or credit insurance, will cancel the minimum payments for up to twelve months on the loan but it does increase the balance owed because the financial institution will charge more monthly fees in addition to interest based upon the balance of the loan. They are charging fees because they are trying to make profit and the financial institution may report to the consumer reporting agencies that the consumer has signed up for payment protection insurance. This can harm the credit profile of the consumer and make it difficult for the consumer to be approved for loans with low interest rates and fees because the fact that the consumer needed payment protection insurance may cause potential lenders to think of the financial capabilities of the consumer as being weak. The consumer may be at high risk for not paying back the loan. The payment protection insurance, depending upon the policies of the financial institution, may be reported to the credit profiles of the consumer with the credit agencies. Such suggests that the payment protection insurance can do more damage than good for the consumer. Therefore, unemployment raises the likelihood of a foreclosure happening with the house because a consumer has a higher chance of becoming late on making the payments and feeling the need to sign up for payment protection insurance. Becoming late or signing up for the payment protection insurance increases the debts of the consumer and makes it more difficult for the consumer to make payments on the mortgage. Consumers should not get into so much debt that they cannot pay it all off in the event that they lose their job.

Identity theft is contributing to the credit crisis as is one of the main causes damaging the credit profiles of consumers. In 1997 alone, 19,270 victims reported ID theft to the Federal Trade Commission. The number of victims is continuing to increase. It can take years for a consumer to clear their credit profile of all the negative information that was reported due to the ID theft. Such negative information can include excessive inquiries and excessive new accounts because it is common for ID theft criminals to try and establish numerous new credit accounts. Anytime the ID theft criminal tries to open an account, the lender will check the credit of the victim who identity they are using, which will result in an inquiry. Afterwards, they will attempt to charge the new accounts and not make the payments, which will result in delinquent credit accounts reported to consumer reporting agencies. The delinquencies can remain up to ten years from the date of the initial missed payment. The consumer will be liable for the debt until some type of negotiation can be made with the lender confirming that the consumer was a victim of fraud.

It is possible that the consumer might not even find out about some of the accounts that were established under their name until they become "charged-off accounts," which are debts that the consumer never paid. This is because not all companies report to the consumer reporting agencies due to their policies. Finally, the consumer closing all the newly opened accounts can severely hurt a credit score because the lenders will view those accounts with a short credit history and may even think that the consumer could not handle the financial responsibilities. The credit history influences fifteen percent of a FICO credit score. In some cases, closing accounts can significantly reduce the amount of total available credit that the consumer has available and this can negatively influence the credit profile. This is because when the consumer has a low amount of available credit compared to the balances on accounts then that may seem like the consumer is greatly utilizing the total available credit. Lenders can consider a consumer that is greatly utilizing their available credit to be irresponsible. In addition, financial institutions where the ID theft victim already has credit may take negative actions.

This is because their systems are monitoring the credit profile of the consumer to detect any drastic changes, which may suggest that the consumer is a high-risk borrower. It is likely that their systems will detect that several new accounts are being opened under the name of the consumer and either the consumer or the financial institutions are closing the accounts quickly. The systems may also detect many new inquiries are being generated on the credit reports, and accounts are being charged aggressively or becoming delinquent. For such reasons, the financial institutions may review the accounts of the consumer and decide to close them, reduce the credit limit or loan amount, or raise the annual percentage rate. Such can negatively influence the credit profile of the consumer and make it difficult for the consumer to obtain new loans or loans with low interest and fees. This will contribute to their likelihood of becoming default on a mortgage. Despite the ID theft, lenders cannot ignore or pay less attention to the negative information on the credit profile to determine the creditworthiness of the consumer unless they have some kind of police report or documentation verifying which accounts were opened or became delinquent as a result of fraud.

Adding severity to credit crisis, consumers are overextending themselves by greatly utilizing credit and plunging themselves into a large amount of debt. This supports that the average American carries more than eight thousand dollars in credit card debt. Even if a consumer manages to pay the debt off, the lender records the "high balance" of the credit account, which is the highest amount of credit that was utilized. Credit is a type of loan and lenders do not like seeing consumers utilizing a large amount of credit in a short time frame because it suggests weak financial capabilities. Furthermore, they do not like seeing more than thirty percent of the loan amount utilized because it suggests that the consumer is more likely to max out the entire loan or utilize other available loans. Later, the consumer will be unsuccessful in paying back any of the loans. For this reason, consumers utilizing more than thirty percent are vulnerable to have decreases in their loan amounts or have their accounts closed down, which can harm their credit scores. This is because they are having a decrease in their total available credit. Additionally, having high balances on several loan accounts influences the debt-to-income ratio of a consumer and lenders consider it risky when more than thirty-six percent of income is going towards paying debt. This suggests that the consumer is more likely to file for bankruptcy, which is when the consumer legally declares to all the lenders that he or she cannot pay back the debts. Finally, the amounts owed on accounts comprise the second largest portion of a credit score by thirty percent. Therefore, carrying high balances can severely harm the score and lowers the creditworthiness level of the consumer. For such reasons, consumers with high debt will have a difficult time in finding new loans with low interest or fees. Some lenders might deny the consumer a loan and so the credit profile will deteriorate even more from excessive inquiries. Having high balances along with high interest will make the consumer more vulnerable in becoming default with their mortgage and the house becoming foreclosed. The increasing number of house foreclosures is becoming a major economic issue. It is suggested that in order for the housing crisis to improve, the credit crisis must also improve.

The credit crisis can only improve when the majority of consumers are using loans and successfully paying off their balances immediately for there to be positive impacts on the economy. Consumers will not be getting into high debts and will be more likely to save their money in interest bearing deposit accounts. This will benefit financial institutions because then they will be able to grant more loans at cheaper interest rates. They will be able to make profits because there will be less need for them to close credit accounts due to the low number of high risk consumers and whenever the consumer uses their credit card then the financial institution collects a credit card payment processing fee from the store. It is likely **aggregate demand**, which is the level of spending within an economy, will not be too high or too low but balanced. A healthy aggregate demand level will likely keep the **cash flow** healthy and strong, which is the movement of money being made and spent within an economy. All of such will make it less likely that the economy will fall into a **recession**, which is when there is a decline in overall economic activity.

Loan-to-Value Ratio in Relation to the 2000s Housing Crisis

A negative factor that contributed to the severity of the 2000s housing crisis, in America, was that many financial institutions granted mortgages, with high loan-to-value ratios, and they did not ask enough down payment money, if any, from the consumers. They were overly confident that the consumers would repay their mortgages, due to encouragement, from the government. When the bust occurred in the economy, the majority of houses fell in value. The consumers could not sell them at a higher price than what they had paid because other consumers could not qualify for mortgages due to their damaged credit profiles or they did not want to purchase houses that were significantly decreasing in value.

For example, it makes no sense for a consumer to purchase a house for $100,000 if it will one day be worth $75,000. The consumer has had a loss of $25,000 because they paid for a house that was not worth the amount of money that they paid. If consumers are planning on living in their houses forever, then it is less likely they will be concerned about the decreasing value of the house.

Be Careful of No Closing Costs Mortgages!

Financial institutions that advertise little or no closing costs and other fees for getting a mortgage (home loan) are likely scams; because they intend to charge the consumer a higher than average interest rate. They are going to make money anyway possible.

Property Taxes

Property taxes increase when the value of the house increases; but when the value of the house decreases, then so do property taxes. If consumers notice that the value of the house has dropped, but their property taxes are the same or have become higher then they need to realize a possible mistake has been made by their county government of residence. Consumers need to do a property tax appeal. Consumers will get a document called "notice of assessed value" in the mail that indicates all the characteristics of their property; that is determining the price of the property taxes. Consumers should make sure all the information is correct such the size of the property and square footage. If the document is indicating the value of the house is too high compared to other homes within the area then consumers should hire a credible house appraiser.

Credit Disclosure Notice

Whenever consumers apply for a mortgage (home loan), despite if they are approved or denied; the lenders are required to provide them with a Credit Disclosure Notice. This document would have the credit agency that was used by the mortgage lender to do the credit check on the consumer, the credit score of the consumer, the scoring brand model that was used such as FICO or Vantage Score, credit score ranges, and the negative and positive factors regarding the credit profile of the consumer. The Credit Disclosure Notice will help consumers because then they will know that the mortgage lender did not discriminate against them when making the loan decision and the actions that the consumer can take in order to improve their credit with the intention of getting an approval or cheaper mortgage interest rate.

Private Mortgage Insurance is a Money Killer

Besides high interest rates and high closing costs, another business safeguard financial institutions have taken to offset the risks in lending to consumers, that want mortgages with high loan-to-value ratios above 80% or have bad credit profiles is that the financial institution will require for the consumer to pay **private mortgage insurance**, which can be abbreviated as PMI. Private mortgage insurance is sometimes called **lenders mortgage insurance**, which can be abbreviated as LMI.

Private mortgage insurance is when the consumer pays extra money to the financial institution because the consumer is very likely to stop paying on the mortgage someday considering they made a little or no down payment on the house or have bad credit. For this reason, the financial institution needs to make as much profit as possible off of the consumer. The private mortgage insurance makes the monthly mortgage payment more expensive, and there are no benefits behind it. If the consumer does not agree to pay the private mortgage insurance then the financial institution will not grant them the mortgage. The amount of money that the consumer paid towards the private mortgage insurance can be deducted from their taxes. After the consumers has made enough payments towards their house that has decreased the loan-to-value ratio below 80% and/or their credit profile has improved then the consumer can and should contact the financial institution to remove the private mortgage insurance off the mortgage. Most financial institutions want to see at least 22%, if not more, equity that is available on the house. Consumers will know when their loan-to-value ratio has become below 80% when they divide the current debts against the house such as the mortgage, home equity loan, and home equity line of credit over the current estimated value of the house that they can find on www.zillow.com or hire a house appraiser. Consumers should ask their financial institution to direct them to a credible and accredited house appraiser because some house appraisers consumers would find on Craigslist or a random internet search may over exaggerate about having any certifications. Consumers should only hire a house appraiser when they feel confident that the loan-to-value ratio is low because it is a waste of money to keep hiring house appraisers only to find out that the low-to-value ratio is still not low enough to remove the private mortgage insurance.

Consumers must Request for Removal of Private Mortgage Insurance

Consumers cannot assume that a financial institution will automatically remove the private mortgage insurance, because they have billions of mortgages, as well as, loans they are managing and it is unlikely they will pay attention to every detail of the mortgages. Additionally, the private mortgage insurance is allowing for the financial institution to make more profits off of the consumer. Removing the private mortgage insurance will allow for the consumer to save money; because the monthly mortgage payment amount will become less, it is less likely they be late on any bill, and as a result, they will have more money to put into their retirement and other investment accounts.

For consumers that are currently paying private mortgage insurance, it is not recommended that they take more debts against the house such as by getting a home equity loan, home equity line of credit, or doing cash out refinances. By doing so, they are increasing their loan-to-value ratios and in the eyes of the financial institutions. They are taking on more debts, liabilities, and increasing their chances of defaulting. The financial institutions are going to be less prone in agreeing to remove the private mortgage insurance. Consumers that currently have mortgages, are not paying private mortgage insurance, and are considering doing a refinance should not do it; if they know that there are significantly more debts against the house than what it is worth. This is because it is likely upon reviewing everything; the financial institution will require that the consumer pay private mortgage insurance in order to be granted the refinance. The purpose of a refinance is to lower the monthly payments and/or reduce the interest rate and having to pay private mortgage insurance defeats this purpose. By trying to do the refinance, the consumer is also letting their credit scores become low for no reason at all because the financial institution is going to do a credit check on them and the consumer is going to reject the refinance once they find out that they have to pay private mortgage insurance.

It should send a red flag to consumers if they are being required to pay private mortgage insurance; even after they have made a significant amount of payments on the house. For example, it would be unusual if a consumer is being required to pay private mortgage insurance when they have good credit, their house is worth $100,000, and they owe $33,000 to the financial institution, on their mortgage. This means their loan-to-value ratio is only 33% because $33,000 mortgage debt/$100,000 house value = 33%. 33% is considered a low loan-to-value ratio and it suggests the consumer is very unlikely to stop paying on their mortgage, because they have already made so many payments on it. If they stop paying and lose the house then the consumer loses all their money. In such a financial scenario, the consumer needs to contact the corporate office, of the financial institution, to have the private mortgage insurance removed if they are unsuccessful in getting the customer service department or one of the branches belonging to the financial institution to remove the private mortgage insurance. They may need the help of an attorney to get the private mortgage insurance removed. If the consumer is successful in getting all their money that they paid towards private mortgage insurance refunded every time they filed their taxes and are not struggling in making the mortgage payments then it may not be worth hiring an attorney, house appraiser, and paying them expensive fees. In some cases, the company that is making the consumer pay private mortgage insurance despite the consumer having a low loan-to-value ratio and good credit profile may suggest that the company is a scam. The consumer needs to report the company to the Better Business Bureau and the office of their attorney general.

Mortgages and Grace Period = Warning!

Not all financial institutions, but some, charge extra interest when consumers make the monthly payment on their home loan (mortgage) during the grace period because more days are included with the billing cycle. When consumers have more time to pay the bill then the financial institution charges them more interest. Another reason why financial institutions charge more interest is because they are offsetting for the potential of risk to their business. In their eyes, consumers making the monthly payment during the grace period are more likely to default otherwise it raises the question why the consumer would not make the payment early during the billing cycle.

Mortgage Lenders are More Consumer Friendly than Brokers

Consumers should only work with mortgage lenders and try their best to avoid mortgage brokers. A consumer would work with a mortgage lender when they want to get a mortgage from a bank, such as; Wells Fargo, but if consumers contacted a random mortgage company they found on the internet or phone book; then they would work with a mortgage broker. The representative will identify themselves as a mortgage broker, but the consumer should ask this if they do not identify themselves. Mortgage brokers buy loan money from mortgage lenders, for a cheap price and sell the loan money as mortgages to consumers at expensive interest rates and closing costs. As personal advice, mortgage brokers are only beneficial for consumers that have bad credit profiles but before going to a mortgage broker, consumers of all credit types should go to a credit union or community bank.

Mortgage Types

Consumers are going to see adjustable-rate and fixed-rate mortgages with fancy names and they should never get a mortgage type if they do not understand what its name means

Hybrid mortgage

This is considered both a fixed-rate and adjustable-rate mortgage, because the interest rate is fixed on the hybrid mortgage for about the first three to ten years of the mortgage. After this time frame, depending upon the feds fund rate, the hybrid mortgage interest rate will go up or down one time and it will remain that interest rate for the life of the mortgage. Hybrid mortgages are meant for consumers that want to sell their houses quickly but they are risky and they are personally not recommended.

Balloon mortgage

For three to ten years, consumers make low monthly payments because their interest rate is low. After this period, consumers will reach their maturity date on which they must pay off the entire remaining mortgage balance otherwise the financial institution will foreclose on the house and ruin the credit profile of the consumer. Balloon mortgages are dangerous but it is unlikely the consumer will have enough money by the maturity date to pay off the entire mortgage. If consumers have a balloon mortgage then they should significantly above the minimum payment because if they can pay off their mortgage before the maturity date then they have no worries and their credit scores will reflect a high increase.

Jumbo mortgage

A jumbo mortgage is taken; when a consumer needs to buy a very expensive house and for this reason, they need a large amount of mortgage loan money. The amount of mortgage loan money needed exceeds the maximum limit set by the Federal National Mortgage Association. In 2001, the limit they set was $275,000 and so if a consumer was trying to get a mortgage larger than this amount then they would be getting a jumbo mortgage. Due to the fact the loan amount needed is so large, jumbo mortgages usually have much higher closing costs and average interest rates than other mortgage types. If consumers are thinking about buying a house that requires for them to get a jumbo mortgage then consumers should **really think** about buying a cheaper house because it makes no sense to get into so much debt. Consumers have to think about their other expenses especially if they have children and saving for their retirement. A jumbo mortgage can have a variable interest or fixed interest rate depending upon how the consumer and financial institution structure the mortgage account.

Assumable mortgage
The mortgage allows for the future buyer of the house to take over the monthly mortgage payments, of the current homeowner. The mortgage account will be immediately transferred to the new homeowner along with the exact same interest rate and monthly payment amount that the previous homeowner was paying to the financial institution. If the previous homeowner had a variable interest rate then the new homeowner will pay a variable interest rate. However, if the previous homeowner had a fixed interest rate then the new homeowner will pay a fixed interest rate. Assumable mortgages can be awesome because if the feds fund rate is very high and the previous homeowner has a cheap interest rate then the new homeowner will be able to save a great deal of money whereas if the new homeowner obtained a regular mortgage then they would have to pay a high mortgage interest rate.

For this reason, assumable mortgages may help homeowners sell their houses much faster if they mention to the potential buyers that they have an assumable mortgage. However, before accepting the assumable mortgage, the buyer should show the mortgage contract and other paperwork to an attorney and get their input.

Reverse mortgage
When consumers become age 62 or older and have fully paid off their mortgage, but do not have enough money on which they can live and pay their other bills then they have the option of getting a reverse mortgage. A reverse mortgage is very similar to a home equity loan or home equity line of credit because it allows for the consumer to access all the equity, within their house, based on its market value. The financial institution will pay the consumer loan money every month or they will pay it all at once based on the preference of the consumer. The consumer has to repay the reverse mortgage to the financial institution usually with a variable interest rate based on the feds fund rate otherwise they will repossess the house. The financial institution begins asking for payments after a couple years pass and may repossess the house if the consumer passes away. This would be bad for the spouse of the consumer and their children living within the house. I do not recommend reverse mortgages to any consumer because the closing costs and other fees are very expensive and they will compound with interest themselves because they will go back into the loan balance. It makes no sense why a senior would need so much loan money that they need to get a reverse mortgage. The only pro about reverse mortgages is that in most cases, they are non-recourse loans meaning if the financial institution forecloses on the house then they will not hunt down the consumer to pay them any money but they will ruin their credit profile.

Financing through the seller: The seller of the house makes payment arrangements for the house with the buyer; instead of a financial institution; the buyer would pay the monthly payments to the seller or current homeowner of the house; This is dangerous because it is possible the buyer will pay the seller lots of money and after paying it all then the seller will still say it is their house or may run off to another country with the money. As a result, the buyer has lost of all their money. Consumers must talk to an attorney before doing financing with the seller. They need to be assured the house will be theirs after they are done paying all the money.

Mortgages for Consumers with Financial Struggles
Although these mortgages may be granted to the consumer, they should **not** accept them if they do not have enough money for a down payment. This is because as the 2000s housing crisis showed, if consumers do not have enough money for a down payment or their credit profile has

scars; then it is unlikely the consumers will be successful in repaying their mortgage and this will result in a major economic collapse for all of America. The financial institutions will have major mortgage losses and the government will have to pay them money to help them compensate for those losses. This will likely result in the national debt increasing along with the amount of money consumers will have to pay in taxes. The consumers will put themselves into a hole by accepting a mortgage they cannot afford and walking away will not be a solution because the mortgage may be a recourse loan so the consumers that do not pay will be hunted.

FHA mortgage
The Federal Housing Administration (FHA) is a governmental organization that helps consumers with limited funds or bad and limited credit profiles to get approved for mortgages. Financial institutions and other private investors provide the mortgage loan money to consumers and the government assures them that if the consumer defaults on the FHA mortgage then the government will repay them all. The government will do so using taxpayer money. FHA mortgages require only a 3.5% down payment from the consumer and the consumer can get a FHA mortgage with a fixed interest rate or variable interest rate. The loan terms for FHA mortgages are 15, 20, 25, or 30 years. Consumers are usually not allowed to have multiple FHA mortgages and in most cases, they are required to pay private mortgage insurance with their monthly mortgage payment due the fact the down payment they are making is so small and raises their likelihood for defaulting. The money that the consumer pays towards the private mortgage insurance helps the financial institution partially compensate for their loss.

Veteran's Administration mortgages (VA mortgage)
VA mortgages are available to veterans, active duty personnel, reservists, military members, and their eligible family members. VA mortgages usually have the cheapest overall costs than other mortgage types and are available with a fixed or variable interest rate. VA mortgages are available with terms of 15 or 30 years. Consumers do not have to get private mortgage insurance and are not required to make any down payment but personally, it is still wise to make a down payment for the purpose of not being in so much mortgage debt. Consumers with bad credit profiles may be eligible to get a VA mortgage.

Community Home Buyer's Program (CHBP) mortgage
CHBP mortgage is offered through the Federal National Mortgage Association (Fannie Mae) and only requires a 5% down payment from the consumer. 2% of this down payment can come from family members or friends. In order to be granted a CHBP mortgage, a consumer must first attend educational courses regarding personal finances and mortgages.

Fannie Neighbors mortgages
The Federal National Mortgage Association (Fannie Mae) grants fixed interest rate Fannie Neighbors mortgages to consumers; that purchase houses within certain areas that Fannie Mae designates. Fannie Mae hopes to boost the economic growth within these areas by selling houses. Fannie Neighbors mortgages do not require a large down payment and have cheap overall costs such as closing costs.

Beauty of owning a home! Property taxes such as the state and local real estate taxes along with the interest paid on any type of mortgage with any loan term is up to 100% tax deductible. This will allow for consumers to save money on their taxes.

Negative Amortization (NA loans)
Consumers need to be on high alert about negative amortization loans, specifically, negative amortization mortgages and avoid them at all costs! Amortization means reducing debt by making payments on the balance. Negative amortization happens when the monthly minimum payment is only paying the interest of the mortgage and not enough towards the principle balance. Consumers are fooled into getting negative amortization loans because they think the loans are a good deal because the monthly payments are so low and they have more money to invest within their retirement and savings accounts. Negative amortization loans are going to cause the consumer to struggle in paying off their mortgage quickly and they cannot deduct all the interest from their taxes or rely on selling the house quickly. The credit scores of the consumer cannot increase because the high mortgage debt will be viewed as a risk by future financial institutions.

Example:
Luisairis get a 30 years fixed interest rate negative amortization mortgage. The balance is $100,000 and the interest rate is 6%. The financial institution tells her that the monthly minimum payment will be $600.00. This means $500 of this payment will go towards interest and only $100 will pay the principle balance. After her first payment, the mortgage balance will be $99,900. At the end of the 30 years, she is still going to have a mortgage balance of about $64,000 provided she was never late in making the payments, and is going to be in debt for a long time.

It is possible for negative amortization loans to have variable interest rates and if Luisairis had a variable rate then she would likely be in much more debt than just $64,000 at the end of the 30 years loan term and her monthly payments could have skyrocketed at any time. Consumers need to be aware of the term, "teaser rate," which means the interest rate they will pay in the beginning; but it will gradually begin to increase as time passes. Another danger about negative amortization loans is that some financial institutions and companies structure the loan so only a small portion of the interest is being paid every month; and almost none of the payment is being applied towards the principle balance. In the case of Luisairis, if her mortgage payment was only $300.00 a month then nothing would pay the principle but only towards interest. The $200 worth of remaining interest would be added into the mortgage balance and it would compound with interest itself. Interest is being charged on interest, which is capitalization. If consumers currently have a negative amortization loan then they need to refinance their house immediately with a credit union and scream at their mortgage company for scamming them.

Caution About Mortgages

Financial institutions that advertise little or no closing costs and other fees for getting a mortgage (home loan) are likely scams because they intend on charging the consumer a higher than average interest rate. They are going to make money anyway possible.

Buying a house

Buying a house is the most important financial decision a consumer makes in their life. It is a decision that can forever haunt them, if; they spend beyond their means, develop or already have bad credit, and accept mortgage types, which offer low minimum payments. Low minimum payments usually mean high interest is being charged. Besides the monthly mortgage payment, maintaining a house is expensive due to the maintenance, insurance, and taxes.

With an exception to trying to pay current debts and college expenses; consumers should not use the equity in their house to get into a high level of debt using a home equity loan or home equity line of credit; because if they cannot pay it then their house will be repossessed, their credit profile will be ruined, they will struggle to get a job, and the financial institutions will still hunt for them to repay some of the mortgage debt if it was a recourse loan. In most cases, consumers that are using equity are getting into so much debt that they will not be able save any money for their retirement, the college education of their children, or do anything in life and this is a nightmare that many consumers lived during the 2000s housing crisis in America.

In fact, many consumers are still living this nightmare. As evidence, consumers can see all the foreclosed houses within their area using foreclosure.com; before buying a house, consumers need to establish the best credit profile possible and save the most money possible within a Roth IRA. They can later use the money to make a large down payment. If consumers do not have the money to make a down payment then they should not purchase a house regardless if the financial institution approves them for the mortgage because if they do not have sufficient funds to make a down payment then how do they expect to make the monthly mortgage payments and other expenses of maintaining a house. The consumers will put themselves into a deep hole and they will not appreciate the fact they purchased a house. Their families will suffer too. Consumers should not take a loan against their 401(k) or 403(b) to make a down payment on a house because if they lose their job then they must repay that money back into the account immediately and just the fact that the consumer is having to take a loan to make a down payment suggests that they will not be successful in making future mortgage payments.

Vital factors to Consider before buying a house

20% - 25% down payment- This will save the consumer paying a large amount of interest and other costs such as closing towards the mortgage. The financial institution will feel more comfortable to grant the consumer a cheaper interest rate because if they are paying a large down payment then it is less likely they will default and the financial institution will have a loss. A cheap interest rate means affordable monthly mortgage payments and a stress free life. If possible, consumers should pay at least 30% as a personal recommendation rather than put the money into interest bearing accounts. Paying off a house will always be a bigger gain than the amount of interest made within a deposit account. A paid off house will result in the credit scores dramatically increasing and various cheaper insurance premiums.

10 months emergency fund- The consumer needs to be prepared to make the mortgage payment and the other expenses of their house in the event that they lose their job or source of income. The financial institution will not tolerate the mortgage becoming delinquent because in their eyes, they feel as though they are being cheated and the consumer is living at the house for free. The IRS will not tolerate the consumer not paying their property taxes and they will both take adverse actions against the consumer even if the consumer just leaves their house.

No credit card or student loan debt- Consumers should not buy a house if they currently have any credit card or student loan debts; This is because these debts will cause the financial institution to approve the consumer for a high mortgage interest rate and this means high monthly mortgage payments, which raises the likelihood of the consumer defaulting and their house getting foreclosed. The financial institution may even deny the consumer for a mortgage if they see on their credit reports that they are carrying high debts of any type because they think that the consumer will use their credit cards to pay for the mortgage payments, all household expenses, and one day, try to bankrupt all their debts. This is often why some current homeowners have bad credit. The financial institution will have a major loss if they grant the mortgage to consumers with high debts. Consumers need to pay off their debts before buying a house.

Consumers should never buy a house at a location that has a high level of crime, is too far from their job location, or has other inconveniences because consumers should never put themselves into a situation in which they feel the need to sell the house and move. It is expensive to move from one house to another because consumers have to pay for the costs of getting the house cleaned, storage houses for the furniture, advertising costs to get the house marketed, gas, airline tickets, mortgage payments until the house is sold, and a moving truck. Consumers are better off putting the money that they would spend on moving into a retirement account or towards their current mortgage payment. Some consumers give away their televisions and furniture before they move to their new house. The money they spent on those items is lost. The credit checks that the financial institution performed on the consumer will go to waste and their credit scores went down for no reason at all.

Consumers should never call random mortgage companies on the internet and phone book because there is no way to know if they are credible and they may try to convince the consumer to get dangerous mortgages such as the negative amortization loans and charge them high fees and closing costs. Consumers should always get a mortgage from a credit union or community bank because they are likely to be the most ethical in their lending practices. Consumers are given a good faith estimate by the financial institution before being granted a mortgage which shows them the monthly payments, type of mortgage, and the interest rate they will be paying. The good faith estimate should always be shown to an attorney before making a commitment to get the mortgage.

Steal of a Deal

Consumers should always aim at getting a steal of a deal on a house meaning if a house is selling for $110,000 then consumers should convince the realtor or house company to sell it to them for $80,000 or less. If consumers are not offered a good deal then they should walk away because there will always be house companies and realtors that are going to do whatever it takes to sell their houses.

Cash-out Refinance

A cash-out refinance is when the consumer takes extra mortgage loan money in addition to changing their mortgage interest rate and/or mortgage loan type.

Example
If Devin is refinancing his $100,000 fixed-rate mortgage from a 5% mortgage into a 3% mortgage and wants to do a cash out refinance, because he wants $5,000 to pay off his credit card debt then his mortgage balance will become $110,000.

Consumers like Devin should not do a cash-out refinance to pay off debts such as credit cards, student loans, and other bills because his monthly mortgage payments will become higher to the point he may not be able to afford them and the house will be foreclosed. Due to the fact a cash-out refinance causes a higher mortgage balance then the closing costs will become higher and they will compound with interest themselves within the mortgage balance because usually 6% of the mortgage balance is used to determine the closing costs. In the case of Devin, if Devin did a cash out refinance of $110,000 then his closing costs would likely be $6,600 and combined with the mortgage balance, the total new balance would be $116,600 and this balance would get charged a 3% interest rate. The amount of money consumers pay in closing costs is not worth paying to do a cash-out refinance. Consumers should use this money and just pay their debts directly or negotiate with the companies for cheaper interest rates. Consumers also have the highly recommended option of doing a balance transfer of the debts to a credit union credit card because credit unions cannot increase the interest rate at any time higher than 18%.

Closing Costs Tips

Consumers should always be persistent in trying to get the financial institution to reduce some of the closing costs.

For example, if a consumer is told that they will have to pay $4,000 in closing costs then they should say that they are only going to agree to get the mortgage; if the closing costs are reduced to $3,000.

Buying a House with Cash

Buying a house with cash is smart because then the consumer does not have to get a mortgage and pay closing costs and other fees. They do not have to worry about making a mortgage payment. However, consumers should ask realtor or the company that is trying to sell them a house if they can pay using a credit or debit card. If possible, consumers should use a high level rewards credit or debit card to pay for the house; because the rewards program will save money.

If a Stannon were buying a house for $50,000 and their credit or debit card gave them 1% cash back on all purchases then Stannon could save up to $500 and this money can go into a retirement account and make earnings.

Alternative to Refinancing with No Fees

Consumers can lower other expenses of their house such as the homeowners insurance. Some consumers include their homeowners insurance monthly payment with their monthly mortgage payment whereas other consumers pay their homeowners insurance separately. It is the choice of the consumer how they wish to pay it. Consumers should call several different insurance brokers and see if they can get a cheaper price for the same coverage. I did the same task when I was trying to refinance the mortgage belonging to my mortgage and although, it was not a major savings, her monthly payment dropped by $75 and this was more money that could be contributed towards her retirement accounts. There are no hard inquiry credit checks done on consumers when they are exploring the insurance costs with different companies so their credit scores are protected. However, the insurance companies will perform soft inquiry credit checks so the consumer should make sure all their high debts such as credit card are paid before they go looking for a cheaper homeowner's insurance premium.

Mortgage Classifications

Fixed-rate mortgage

The interest rate that the consumer pays on the mortgage is the same every month throughout the life of the loan. The payment due every month is the same and the consumer knows what is expected of them. The reason why some consumers do not get a fixed-rate mortgage is because if the feds fund rate set by the Federal Reserve decreases then the interest rate of the fixed-rate mortgage does not change nor do the monthly payments decrease. However, the beauty of a fixed-rate mortgage is that if the feds fund rate increases then the interest rate of the fixed-rate mortgage does not change and the monthly payments do not increase. Consumers can pay points, which is paying interest upfront, if they want to have a cheaper monthly mortgage payment. One point is one percent of the total mortgage balance. The consumer is safe with a fixed-rate mortgage, which is why my mother, grandfather, and uncle have fixed-rate mortgages themselves.

Fixed-rate mortgage terms- Expected time frame in which mortgage will be fully repaid.

15 years

30 years

40 years

50 years

The longer mortgage term that is chosen by the consumer then the lower their monthly mortgage payments are because the financial institution is able to charge more interest. Despite this, consumers should get the longest loan term possible such as 30, 40, or 50 years for the purpose of being best prepared for emergency expenses. It is unlikely the consumer will default on the mortgage because the monthly payment due every month is low. If consumers have zero debts and emergency expenses then they should pay significantly above the minimum payment so the mortgage does not aggressively compound with interest and the loan amount does not double or triple. Consumers should not pay just the minimum payments because then their credit scores will become low from excessive mortgage debt and their insurance premiums will not decrease but increase. If consumers pay above the minimum payment every month then they can pay off the mortgage much faster than 30, 40, or 50 years. Short loan terms such as 15 years have high monthly minimum payments so they are risky and personally, I do not recommend them.

Adjustable-rate mortgage (ARMs)

All adjustable-rate mortgages have a variable interest rate and variable monthly payments that can change at any time depending upon the feds fund rate. Some consumers are fooled into getting an adjustable-rate mortgage because its beginning interest rate is cheaper than the interest rate for a fixed-rate mortgage, the monthly payments are cheaper, and they think they are saving money by getting an ARM. Other consumers get an ARM because they think they can sell the house quickly because the value of the house will increase after the purchase it. These consumers cannot rely on real estate market because it is always unpredictable. By relying on the real estate market, the consumers will pay the consequences with damaged credit profiles because this means no job and lives filled with debt. Unlike with fixed-rate mortgages, consumers do not have to pay points on ARMs if they want to get the monthly payment down because it all depends on the feds fund rate.

Common types of ARMs
7/1 ARM
Interest rate is locked for seven years and cannot change. After the seven years, the interest rate can change meaning it can go up or down every year along with the monthly payments.

1/1 ARM
The interest rate along with the monthly payment changes every year for the life of the loan based on the feds fund rate.

3/3 ARM

Interest rate is locked for three years and cannot change during this period. Every three years, the interest rate will increase by two percent levels, but it cannot exceed 6%. 6% is the lifetime interest rate cap of the ARM no matter what happens with the feds fund rate. However, consumers should always confirm the lifetime interest rate cap with the financial institution before getting any ARM because it may have changed from the time that this book was written.

Adjustable rate mortgages have a permanent payment cap limit meaning the monthly payment cannot exceed this amount during the life of the loan. However, a permanent payment cap is different from a temporary payment cap. A temporary payment cap means the monthly mortgage payment cannot exceed a certain amount for a certain number of months. Consumers need to pay special attention to the temporary payment cap because if the monthly payment increases and they cannot pay it then they are in trouble.

For consumers with **very** little or no debts, strong employment, strong retirement accounts, a 10 months emergency fund, term life insurance, health insurance, dental insurance, vision insurance, and enough down payment money then an adjustable-rate mortgage may help them save money compared to a fixed rate mortgage because if the feds fun rate goes down the mortgage interest rate of the ARM goes down along with the monthly payment.

Consumers have the option to refinance their ARM into a fixed-rate mortgage or vice versa but consumers should not do this unless they are going to become delinquent on the future mortgage payment and thus, need a cheaper payment because there are always closing costs when a consumer does a refinance. Closing costs include fees to pull the credit reports of the consumer, fees for the financial institution for doing the mortgage, taxes, application fees, and other miscellaneous fees. According to Quicken Loans, average closing costs range from $2,500 to $5,000 or about 6% of the mortgage loan amount needed. Consumers should never develop bad credit or high debts because then the financial institution will refuse to do the refinance for the consumer. Consumers will struggle to refinance their house if they have many debts against it such as a home equity loan or home equity line of credit and to do the refinance, they may be asked to pay private mortgage insurance with the monthly payment because the financial institution thinks the consumer is very likely to default with there being so many debts on the house despite their credit profile. For this reason, it is encouraged consumers try their best not to get those loans and high levels of debt. Consumers should make their credit profile perfect by paying off debts before applying for a refinance because the fees they pay to initiate the refinance process such as application fees will not be refunded even if the consumer is denied for the mortgage. Consumers should not refinance an adjustable-rate mortgage into a fixed-rate mortgage if they are planning on selling the house quickly because they are paying closing costs and having their credit checked for no reason at all.

Number one rule of refinancing! No matter what financial institution with whom the consumer currently has their mortgage, they should always go to a credit union or community bank because in most cases, they will be offered a cheaper deal. If the refinance is successful then the credit union or community bank will send a payoff check to the current financial institution with which the consumer has their mortgage. Same rule applies to refinancing a car.

If consumers have a bad credit profile but they have found a house that is very cheap in a safe area then it would be a good financial decision to rollover the money from their traditional IRA and traditional 401(k) into a Roth IRA, pay the necessary taxes, and take the money that they contributed towards the account and not the earnings so they can avoid paying the 10% tax penalty. Consumers should fully purchase the house and then afterwards, start saving money for retirement again. This is beneficial because consumers are taking advantage of house prices while they are low and they will not have to worry about making monthly mortgage payments. Consumers should not use money from their retirement accounts if they are close to reaching age 59 and a half.

Mortgage Tip in Paying Down Balance

Consumers need to make sure any extra money they pay towards their mortgage is applied to the principle balance. They do not want the extra money being used to pay interest otherwise this will defeat the purpose of trying to pay off the mortgage quickly. Before sending in the extra money, consumers can call the mortgage company and indicate they want the extra payment to be applied towards principle. The same rule applies to car loans.

Save House from Foreclosure

Regardless of having good or bad credit, consumers that are in danger of losing their houses should ask the financial institution if the option is available to do a short refinance. A short refinance is sometimes called a short payoff. A short refinance is when the financial institution pays off the current mortgage balance and grants the consumer a new mortgage loan amount that is less than the original mortgage balance with the same or cheaper interest rate and the same or reduced monthly payment amount. In a sense, the financial institution has forgiven some of the interest and fees that may have been charged on the original mortgage balance. The amount that was forgiven by the financial institution may be taxable, meaning consumers will have to pay taxes on that amount, so consumers should talk to a tax advisor as to how to process should be handled. The reason why some financial institutions grant a short sale because it allows for them to make more profit than it would for them to foreclose on the house especially if the economy is doing poorly. The danger behind a short refinance is that the financial institution will report to the credit reports of the consumer that they did a short refinance, which will suggest to the future financial institution that the consumer is financially weak. The short refinance will lower the credit scores but this is still better than a foreclosure appearing on the credit reports. Consumers need to be aware that their insurance premiums may increase and they may struggle to find a job if the short refinance reflects on their credit reports. Before doing a short refinance, consumers should get a legal document from the financial institution indicating they will be allowed to keep their house as long as they are successfully making payments in a timely manner. Consumers should never do a short refinance with some random company they find on the internet or the phone book. They should only do the short refinance with their financial institution.

Home Equity Loans

Homeowners have more options to pay their debts, thanks to their houses. All houses have what is called **equity**, which is the amount of how much a house is worth in the market if it were to be sold. Having equity is the same difference as having access to loan money that can be used.

How the Amount of Equity is Determined

Houses have physical features, such as; a balcony, attic, being one, two, or more stories high; these features, along with the conditions such as if they are new, old, or damaged; cause the houses to be popular. Depending upon the popularity level and physical conditions of the house, along with the conditions of the economy, it can be sold at a higher price than its equity value. This helps the current homeowner, whereas similarly, it can also be sold at a lower price than its equity value, which hurts the current homeowner because then they are losing money. They are selling a house for less than what it is worth. Homeowners and companies are sometimes forced into selling the house at a cheaper price than its equity value, because if the majority of consumers dislike that house then the house will never be sold and it will cost the company or homeowner money to maintain it.

For example, Target sells a brand new plasma television that has a built-in DVD player is worth $300. Think of the $300 as being the equity value. It is costing Target $2 a day to pay for electricity to power that television, because it is on the display. If no consumer is buying that television because they do not like it or the economy is in a recession; it is likely that Target will mark down the price to $150 and it will be sold at that price. This sale has caused Target to lose $150. Considering Target had purchased the television from their vendor for $180 then they actually lost more than $180 because they also spent money on the electricity to power the television on the display stand.
$180 price of vendor to Target - $150 sale price = $30 loss.
$300 television value + $30 loss = $330.
$330 loss - $150 sale price = $180 loss.
$180 loss + $10 (five days of electricity at $two per day) = $190 total loss.

If Target did not sell the television for $150 then they would have continued to pay $two everyday on electricity. If the economy were not in a recession then it is more likely Target could have sold the television for $300 or more and they would have made a profit because $300 is more money than what Target had paid for the television from the vendor. For the reason of trying to avoid losses due to maintenance of the items and trying to make space for new items, retail stores will sell their unpopular items at clearance prices. Similarly, companies must sell houses so they can move themselves into new areas, build houses, and sell them. They cannot spend too much money on maintenance such as hiring lawn mowers, property taxes, fees to keep the interior and exterior clean and miscellaneous expenses. When homeowners purchase the house then they agree to take over all these expenses and for this reason, in some financial scenarios, it is better for a company to sell the house at a reduced value. Current homeowners may be rushed to sell their houses and have to sell it at reduced values because they can no longer afford to make the monthly mortgage payments. If they do not sell their houses quickly then they will default on the loan and their credit profiles will be damaged. They will struggle trying to get a new and more affordable house or apartment.

House Appraisers help Determine Equity

Equity can be found by subtracting the market value of the house, which is determined by a **house appraiser**, and the debts against the house, which are usually the mortgage balance and any other loans against it such as a home equity loan or home equity line of credit. As consumers are paying down their mortgage, home equity loan, or home equity line of credit then they are adding equity to their house, because they are getting access to more loan money, which can potentially be used by the consumer. Paying down a mortgage and having access to a greater amount of equity is the same difference as paying down a credit card and as a result, having access to more credit.

Lacey has a house that she purchased for $189,590, which is now her mortgage balance that she must pay back. Lacey made payments on the mortgage and now the mortgage balance is $171,104. Lacey wants to know the value of her house. She calls a house appraiser who indicates the house is worth $200,000. To determine how much equity Lacey has access to, she would subtract the appraised value with the current mortgage balance. $200,000 - $171,104 = $28,896 is how much equity Lacey currently has available to her.

The Thinking of House Appraisers

House appraisers take many positive and negative factors into consideration when they are trying to determine the market value of a house including the conditions of the community such as if there is a great deal of crimes being committed, if there are schools and other useful facilities such as banks and grocery stores nearby, and the average equity values of nearby houses. They inspect the house too to understand its physical conditions such as the number of rooms it has, what types of rooms it has, and any extra features the house has such as a patio, fireplace, or attic. House appraisers can be considered subjective because they all have different perspectives and for this reason, one house appraiser cannot be considered correct over another appraiser. For this reason, financial institutions may require that consumers use one of their house appraisers and none from outside parties. This is because the house appraisers that the financial institutions choose have certain certifications that add to their credibility and make their house appraisals more legitimate. If consumers want to know a rough estimate of the market value of their house then they can go to a website called http://realestate.yahoo.com.

Financial Institutions Spy on Consumers' Assets

When consumers apply for credit then some financial institutions may check the equity value of their house using the residential address that the consumer puts on the credit application. Financial institutions will use the public records to do so. This is because consumers that have houses worth high equity value are less risky for the financial institutions when they extend credit. In the event a consumer does not pay on their loans then the financial institution has the ability to put a claim on their house and in doing so, they may be able to make up for some of their loss. Financial institutions take into consideration that consumers that have houses are less prone to declare a bankruptcy or debt settlement because they can get loans using the equity. This can support why having a house that has equity can be considered an asset. It can be considered more risk to a financial institution when they grant credit to a consumer that has a house worth low equity value because it will cause them more loss than profit by putting a claim on it. Submitting claims for are not free. Financial institutions may also use the public records to see what vehicles and boats the consumer owns and if they have a high collateral value based on how much they can be sold for in the market. It is possible for consumer to use such items and get secured loans to pay off their debts. Consumers are better off doing so because they do not want for the financial institutions to put claims on them. In most cases, financial institutions focus more on the value of the house than they do the value of other possessions belonging to the consumer. This is due to the fact automobiles and boats usually **depreciate** faster than houses due to usage and the fact that technology is always improving. Depreciation is when items lose value. For example, when consumers purchase a new or used boat or automobile, they begin to depreciate the minute that the consumer starts using it. Houses are more likely to **appreciate**, which means gaining value over time. This benefits the consumer and the financial institution because then either of them can potentially sell the house for a price higher than what the consumer paid and make profit. Houses appreciate usually when overall economic conditions are strong, resources are built within the community such as nearby playgrounds, gates and swimming pools, and extra features are built within the house such as for example, a balcony, patio, or porch are built.

However, some financial institutions may have a different perspective regarding if the ownership of property and possessions are assets depending upon the credit profile of the homeowner. If the homeowner has an overall bad credit history then they may get the impression that the consumer no longer cares about their credit or being responsible due to the fact they already have a house and automobile. The financial institution may think the consumer feels as though that there is no need to have a strong credit profile. Financial institutions will refuse to grant credit to such consumers or offer them cheaper interest rates on their current loans.

Home equity loan: A secured installment credit loan in which the amount of the loan is influenced by how much equity, which is considered the value of the house, is available on the house. When consumers say, "second mortgage," then they are usually referring to a home equity loan. The consumer can attempt to get a loan amount up to a certain percentage such as for example, 75%, of the appraised value of their house but in most cases, they cannot exceed the percentage. If the financial institution allows a consumer to take a greater amount of equity than the percentage such as for example, 80% or more, then it is likely the financial institution plans on charging extra interest and fees for the purpose of making more profit. The percentage of the equity within a house that can be accessed by the consumer is considered the loan-to-value ratio, which is abbreviated as a LTV ratio.

For example, Sara has a house worth $110,000 as indicated by the appraiser. Her mortgage balance is $50,000.
Sara wants to take 50% of her appraised value and get a home equity loan from Trustco Bank because she wants to pay off her student loan debt. 50% is considered the LTV ratio because 50% is how much loan money Sara wants based on the value of her house.
$110,000 appraised value x .5 = $55,000.
She now must subtract $55,000 - $50,000 mortgage debt = $5,000 available equity, which is the maximum and potential amount of loan money Sara can access through a home equity loan. There is no guarantee that the financial institution will grant her the full $5,000 unless she has an average to excellent credit profile.

Credit Profile determines Amount of Loan Money
The amount of loan money that will be granted to the consumer depends upon their level of creditworthiness. For this reason, the consumer may or may not be able to access all the available equity on their house. A consumer seeking a high amount of loan money means they are going to pull a high percentage of the equity money out of the appraised value of the house. A high percentage of equity money means that a consumer is taking on a high loan-to-value ratio. They are using most of the equity value that is available on their property for the purpose of obtaining the loan and this creates a high risk for the financial institution. This is because if the consumer does not repay the home equity loan, which results in the financial institution repossessing the house. They still cannot fully make up for their loan loss. This is because, in most cases, after a consumer obtains a home equity loan, the equity value of the house drops and in a sense, the consumer has obtained loan money that is higher than the value of the house. For this reason, consumers seeking LTV percentages of 50% or more are going to be expected to have excellent credit with little or no negative information. Consumers that have some negative credit information may be asked to provide a certain down payment amount before they are granted the home equity loan for the purpose of bringing down the loan-to-value ratio. Down payments will help the financial institutions feel as though the consumers are less likely to stop paying on the home equity loan because if they stop paying then they will loose their down payment.

Be Careful of Recourse Loans
Additionally, it is more likely financial institutions are going to grant consumers that need high LTV home equity loans as recourse loans. The term, "recourse" by itself means the right of the company to demand money or some form of repayment from the consumer. A recourse loan means if the consumer stops paying on the home equity loan then the house of the consumer will be repossessed because the house is considered the collateral. In addition, the financial institution may use other means to get the loan money out of the consumer so they can makeup to the greatest extent for their loan loss. Provided that they have an average to excellent overall credit profile, financial institutions will be less strict about approving consumers that seek low loan-to-value ratio home equity loans because the financial institution is taking on little risk. Low loan-to-value ratios would usually be considered percentages of 40% or less of the appraised house value.

Finalizing of Loans
At the finalizing, also called the **closing**, of the home equity loan, the funds are given to the consumer usually in the form of a check. Consumers can use the money to pay for home improvements, credit card debts, wedding expenses, or catch up on payments with the first mortgage of the house, or simply any type of expense. Before using the home equity loan money, consumers should deposit the money into their bank account and if possible, use a credit card to pay for the expenses because a credit card offers the most protection against fraudulent purchases and scammers. Additionally, the rewards program helps save money. After paying the expenses, the consumers should then use the home equity loan money and pay off the credit card. If consumers do not have a credit card then they should use a debit card that has a rewards program and has no monthly or annual fees. Consumers should never write checks or pay any merchant with cash because doing so offers the least amount of protection for the money and the merchant can potentially run off with the money. If a merchant has already provided the service or merchandise then it is safe to pay them with a money order

or cashier's check because they do not have account numbers listed on them. It is dangerous to pay merchants in advance unless it is for an apartment, house, or if the merchant is well known. An example of a well known merchant would be Wal-Mart whereas a merchant that is not well known would be a merchant that a consumer found off of a random Google or Craigslist search.

Handle Payments Wisely

Most home equity loans are granted at a fixed interest rate using the prime rate published in the Wall Street Journal and will have fixed monthly installment payments. For this reason, they will appear as an installment loan on the credit reports of the consumer. Consumers are given the option to make interest-only payments on the home equity loan but it is recommended that consumers make payment amounts above the minimum payment requirements so they can pay down the principle loan amount and as a result, their credit scores increase because they are in less debt. This increases the chances consumers will be approved for a cheaper insurance premium, a potential reduction in the interest rate of the loan that is considered a refinance, and better chances at being able to get a better paying job. If consumers choose to make interest only payments then they are taking on great risk because before getting a home equity loan or equity line of credit, financial institutions set a **loan maturity date** with the consumers. The farther that a maturity date is from the day that the consumer is granted the home equity loan then this means the financial institution has more freedom to charge more interest because the consumer has more time to repay the loan. A loan maturity date that is close to the day that the consumer had obtained the home equity loan means the financial institution will charge less interest because the consumer has less time to repay the loan. On the maturity date, the consumer must pay back the entire principle loan amount, which is considered the **balloon payment**. If consumers want then they can pay the entire principle loan amount earlier than the maturity date as long as the financial institution does not have any **prepayment penalties**, which are fees for paying early. Consumers that want to pay early should ask for the financial institution to waive the prepayment penalties. If consumers do not pay the loan balance on the loan maturity date then their credit profile will be ruined, they will be charged late fees, and their house will be repossessed by the financial institution. Consumers that make payments above the minimum payment requirements are less likely to face such a financial catastrophe because the principle they will have to pay, if any is left, by the maturity date, will be very low and affordable.

Tax Benefits of Home Equity Loans and Home Equity Line of Credit Products

Consumers have the option of **deducting**, which means subtracting, the interest paid on the home equity loan or line of credit off of their taxes. A tax deduction is not the same as a **tax exemption**. A tax exemption helps a consumer pay fewer taxes on their income due to the fact they are supporting a family such as their spouse and kids. The spouse and kids are dependents on the consumer because the consumer financially supports them. For this reason, the IRS is going to require that the consumer pay less tax on their income for the purpose of continuing to support the spouse and kids. Therefore, the consumer is receiving a tax exemption thanks to their dependents. A tax deduction occurs when a consumer is deducting money that they paid on tax deductible expenses such as student loans, home equity loans or equity lines of credit, mortgages (home loans) or some major contributions they made to an educational facility such as a public elementary school. The government allows for tax deductions to occur on such items because they are trying to encourage consumers to purchase houses, attend college, and contribute money towards education. These items cause a boost in the economy.

Benefits of Home Equity Loans

Provided the closing costs and loan origination fees are cheap meaning $500 or less, home equity loans may be ideal for paying off other debts such as credit cards, especially delinquent credit cards that have an interest rate of about 30%, and student loans, depending upon the current average interest rates of home equity loans which can be found on http://www.bankrate.com/home-equity.aspx. Consumers should compare the interest rates that they are currently paying on their credit card and/or student loan and if the average interest percentage they are paying is higher than the average interest percentage of a home equity loan then it may be beneficial for a consumer to obtain a home equity loan, consolidate all the debts, raise their credit scores, and pay off the debt much faster due to the fact they have a cheaper interest rate. Consumers that consolidate their debts should not close their credit cards because doing such will lower their credit scores due to the fact closing a credit card lowers the average length of history established on credit accounts. Home equity loans may be cheaper than car loans or boat loans and so a consumer may want to consider getting a home equity in order to purchase a car.

Tax Deduction Limitations

Consumers can deduct the interest that they pay on the home equity loan or home equity line of credit off of their taxes but there is no guarantee that they will be able to get all the interest deducted because they may need to have certain qualifications to do so such a certain income level, and usually, there is a cap as to how much interest can be deducted from the taxes. As reported by Bankrate.com, Thomas Langdon is a certified financial planner and tax professor at The American College in Pennsylvania. Langdon expresses that "for home equity, [consumers] can deduct the interest on a loan up to $100,000." This statement likely means that consumers may not be able to deduct more home equity interest than $100,000 off of their taxes. It is unlikely consumers will be able to deduct late fees from their taxes so consumers should always submit payments in a timely manner but if they are late then they should ask the financial institution to waive the late fee as a one time courtesy. In addition, high interest rates can mean the consumer will have high monthly minimum payments and in the event an emergency happens such as a reduction in salary or medical expenses, consumers have a high chance of defaulting on their payments. For this reason, consumers need to focus on getting the cheapest and fixed interest rate home equity loans and equity lines of credit. Community banks and credit unions will usually offer the cheapest interest rates on all loans. The number one tip consumers need to follow is that any home equity loan money they did not use should be immediately paid back to the financial institution without paying prepayment fees. In doing so, consumers will be able to save interest because a lower loan balance always means lower interest. A lower loan balance causes the credit scores to increase because the overall level of debt belonging to the consumer has decreased.

Home equity line of credit: Like a home equity loan, a home equity line of credit uses the equity value of the house to determine the loan amount, which is considered the credit limit, and allows for consumers to deduct up to $100,000 in loan interest off of their taxes. The house is the collateral of the loan. In the event that the consumer stops paying on the loan then the financial institution has the freedom to repossess the house. In most cases, like home equity loans, home equity lines of credit are granted as recourse loans to consumers meaning even after the financial institution repossesses the house, they can still take other adverse actions against the consumer such as garnishing their wages in order to get back their loan money and in doing so, make up for their loan loss. Finally, similar to a home equity loan, a home equity line of credit allows for consumers to make monthly interest only payments but they can and should make higher payment amounts than the minimum payment requirements for the purpose of paying on the principle amount. This is because if consumers arrive on the loan maturity date, which is considered the due date, then they are expected to provide a balloon payment that pays off the entire balance. If the consumer fails to pay the entire balance then they may be allowed to refinance their loan and extend the loan maturity date but if they have bad credit then it is unlikely the financial institution will agree to extend the loan maturity date. The credit profile of the consumer will reflect a late payment on the home equity line of credit or home equity loan.

Be Careful when Closing Home Equity Line of Credit Products

The major difference between a home equity loan and home equity line of credit is that a home equity line of credit is structured more like a credit card because consumers only use the line of credit when they need it. On the credit report, the home equity line of credit will be reported as a revolving credit line because the consumer is carrying a balance and credit limit whereas a home equity loan will report as an installment loan since home equity loan has no credit limit. Due to the reason, the home equity line of credit is revolving credit, like a credit card, if a consumer closes it they no longer have access to the available credit, which is loan money they can use and this causes their credit utilization level to be higher.

For example, Andre has $3,500 in total debt. This is because he has a credit card with a balance of $1,000 and a credit limit (spending limit) of $2,000. He also has a home equity line of credit with a balance of $2,500 and a spending limit of $5,500.
Currently, the debt-to-credit limit ratio of Andre is $3,500 (total debts)/$7,500 (total available credit thanks to the spending limits of the home equity line of credit and credit card)
$2,000 credit card spending limit + $5,500 home equity line of credit = $7,500, which is his total available credit.
Debt-to-credit limit ratio = $3,500/$7,500, which is about 47% (rounded). Although a 47% debt-to-credit limit ratio may be considered high, it is still good because it shows Andre is using less than half of all his available credit. Financial institutions will not think Andre has a high chance of defaulting provided he has not been late in making all his previous payments.

If Andre closes the home equity line of credit then here is the bad financial situation he will face.
Debt-to-credit limit ratio: $3,500 (total debts)/$2,000 (total available credit) = 175%
Closing the home equity line, which had a spending limit of $5,500, caused the amount of total available credit to decrease from $7,500 to $2,000.
The credit scores of Andre have become low because his debt-to-credit limit ratio has become extremely high. It suggests Andre is utilizing too much credit and is very likely to default. It makes no sense to a financial institution why Andre would be using so much credit and they may get the impression that he is living on loan money because he has little or no money of his own and this means he will not be able to pay them.

As shown in the case of Andre, by closing or reducing the spending limit of a home equity line of credit, it looks like the consumer is using a large portion of their total available loan money and is more likely to default because in the eyes of the financial institutions, they are using too much loan money. When a home equity line of credit is closed then it lowers the average length of history established on credit accounts and this makes it harder for financial institutions to understand the financial capabilities of consumers in paying their bills. After 7 to 10 years, the home equity line of credit and its payment history will fall off the credit report and there will be no record that the consumer ever paid the loan or had it. Financial institutions want to see that the financial responsibilities of paying the bills in a timely manner were maintained by the consumer for a long time. For these reasons, closing a home equity line of credit lowers the credit scores as would if a consumer closed a credit card. Just like how a credit limit reduction, which means reduction with the amount of available loan money to spend, on a credit card hurts the credit scores so would a reduction in the credit limit of the home equity line of credit because it raises the question why the financial institution had to lower the amount of loan money a consumer can spend and this often happens because they think the consumer will not be able to repay the loans due to the fact negative information is showing on their credit reports. If the house loses too much value due to the bad economic conditions then the financial institution can shut down the home equity line of credit or reduce its spending limit. Such will lower the credit scores and for this reason, to some extent, consumers are taking a risk by taking a home equity line of credit. In most cases, any loan that a consumer is given that has a spending limit, which is a credit limit to which a consumer has access, if they close or its limit is reduced then the credit scores will always go down. The purpose of revolving credit, which is loans that have spending limits, is to show to financial institutions that consumers are not using all their available credit and for this reason, are considered strong financially.

Distribution of Home Equity Line of Credit Product Money

Unlike a home equity loan, which has no spending limit, consumers are not given all the loan money at once. They are usually given a plastic debit card that will pull money from their home equity line of credit whenever they need money. It depends on the guidelines of the financial institution if they offer any rewards on the purchases made using the debit card. Such rewards would help consumers save money. If consumers have little or no expenses then a home equity line of credit may be cheaper for them than a home equity loan because if they use little loan money then there is little or no interest, the consumer can pay off the loan debt immediately, and the credit scores will not become too low due to high loan debt. With a home equity loan, the entire loan balance becomes the debt of the consumer and this lowers the credit scores. The consumer has to pay interest on the entire loan balance. In contrast, with a home equity line of credit, consumers have an equity credit limit and so they do not need to pull more loan money than what they need. Consumers do not pay interest for having the access to the equity credit limit.

Example
Home equity loan
Home equity loan amount that has been given to the consumer: $6,000
Interest rate: 6.55%
The full $6,000 is being charged the 6.55% interest.

Home equity line of credit
Home equity credit limit to which the consumer has access to use: $6,000
Interest rate: 6.55%

Kristi has only used $500 of her home equity line of credit. Thus, only $500 is going to be charged the 6.55%

In this financial situation, it is likely Kristi will have a higher credit score with the home equity line of credit than she would the home equity loan because she is in less debt. It is also likely, as long as the interest rate on the home equity line of credit is fixed and she is not late, she will pay less money on interest with the home equity line of credit than she would on the home equity loan.

Dangers of Home Equity Line of Credit Product- Very Expensive

There are two dangers behind a home equity line of credit that are not found with a home equity loan. After approving the home equity line of credit, financial institutions will use their own means and monitor any major decreases with the equity value of the house belonging to the consumer that was used to get the home equity loan. A significant decrease with the equity value will usually occur if there is a major decline in the overall economy, specifically a decline with the real estate and banking industries. If such happens and the consumer does not have the most excellent credit profile possible then the financial institution may close the home equity line of credit immediately and the consumer will not know this until their debit card declines when they try and make a purchase or when the consumer receives the notice from the financial institution. The reason why the financial institution has closed the home equity line of credit is because in simplest terms, the consumer has access to more loan money than what their house is worth. Financial institutions cannot afford to take this loan risk because if the consumer does not repay the loan and they repossess the low valued house then they cannot significantly make up for their loan loss.

Variable Interest Rate of Home Equity Line of Credit = Problems

The second danger behind a home equity line of credit is that most, not all, home equity lines of credit have variable interest rates. Like most variable rate private student loans issued by financial institutions, they can increase at any time up to 16%, 17%, or 18% depending upon the prime rate that is published by Wall Street in their journal. It is likely when the economy is doing poorly then Wall Street will publish a high prime interest rate so the financial institutions can make more money, create more jobs, do more lending, and hopefully, the economy can improve. In contrast, when the economy is doing well then it is likely that Wall Street will publish a low interest rate in their journal because the conditions of the economy are elevated for the most part and there is not as great a need to make high profits. The prime rate is used by most financial institutions to determine the total interest that the consumer will pay on their loan that has a variable interest rate. Fixed interest rates are not affected by the changes with the prime rate. The total interest rate combines the prime rate plus the additional interest rate that will be determined by the financial institution. If Wall Street suddenly increases the prime interest rate then consumers can likely expect to see an increased minimum payment requirement than what they normally would see on their home equity line of credit because the minimum payment requirement will consist of a larger amount of interest that must be paid. Larger minimum payment requirements can be dangerous because they increase the likelihood of a consumer defaulting on the loan if they cannot afford to make the payment. Additionally, some financial institutions charge an annual fee, which is a fee paid every month by the consumer, just to have the home equity line of credit. Overall, if consumers need a large loan amount or cannot get a fixed interest rate home equity line of credit then they are best off getting a home equity loan. For whatever reason a consumer may have for wanting to get a home equity line of credit, it is recommended they have zero or little debt and they should get the home equity line of credit at a community bank or credit union because it is most likely, most credit unions and community banks will have the least amount of fees or no fees such as prepayment penalties and the least amount of interest compared to the home equity line products of traditional banks. Consumers should **never** get home equity loans or home equity lines of credit for the purpose of investing the loan money into stocks.

The Abuse of Home Equity Loans and Equity Line of Credit Products

During the 2000s housing crisis, some consumers were investing the equity loan money they were getting out of their houses thinking they would be able to sell the houses for higher prices than what they paid for them when the house values increased. For this reason, some consumers thought it was wise to invest the equity money. The house values had dropped and the consumers had losses with their investments, and could not afford to pay the mortgage and/or the home equity loan or home equity line of credit.

Warnings about Home Equity Loans and Home Equity Lines of Credit

Avoid "no closing costs" home equity loan or home equity line of credit products because this means their interest rates will be high so the financial institutions can make the same, if not more, amount of profit if they had charged closing costs. Consumers are discouraged from taking home equity or equity line of credit loans if they are planning on selling their houses within close time proximities. This is because the values of the houses can drop at any time even after the consumer obtains the home equity loan or home equity line of credit depending upon economic conditions. If the amounts of the debts that are using the house as collateral are higher than the value of the house then this means the consumer has **negative equity**. The debt amounts are overpowering the value of the house. When houses have negative equity then they are usually considered to be "under water." Being under water may also mean that a consumer is in bad financial conditions. Negative equity may cause the consumer to struggle in selling the house because they may not be able to pay the financial institution all the loan money that was obtained using the house. Consumers cannot refinance their house or get a home equity line of credit or home equity loan if they have negative equity on their house.

Example
Stephanie has a house that has an appraised value of $66,500 according to the house appraiser.
She has a mortgage balance of $40,000.
$66,500 appraised value - $40,000 mortgage balance = $26,500 available equity, which is considered loan money, Stephanie can use if she wants to do anything such as buy a car.
Stephanie takes the full $26,500 equity out of her house by getting a home equity loan. The home equity loan is considered her second mortgage that must pay.
Stephanie now has debts totaling $66,500 against the house.
One month later, depreciation occurs with the house due to the weak conditions in the economy and its appraised value drops to $60,000.
$66,500 debts against the house - $60,000 reduced appraised value = $6,500 negative equity.
Stephanie now wants to sell her house but she is going to struggle doing so because it is unlikely a consumer is going to want to pay more than $60,000, which is the current value of the house. They are going to want to pay $60,000 or an amount underneath that for the

purpose of saving their money. If Stephanie sells the house for such an amount then it raises the question of how she is going to pay the bank $6,500, which is the amount of negative equity on her house.

Negative Equity is Bad

The negative equity is considered loan money that Stephanie must repay or the financial institution will have a loss and they can potentially use other means to get the loan money out of Stephanie such as garnish her wages, take her to court, or put a claim on her assets. Stephanie will have to negotiate with the bank as to how she can repay the $6,500 unless she gets a house buyer that wants to pay $66,500 or more for the house. She would use the money that the house buyer gives to pay her mortgage with the financial institution.

Short Sales

Short Sale is Better than a Foreclosure

In this financial situation, if Stephanie cannot afford her monthly mortgage payments then she needs to immediately negotiate with her financial institution and be honest with them about it, because they do not want to have to foreclose on her house. A foreclosure results in a financial loss, for the financial institution, because until they can sell the house; they do not know what to do with it and have to pay for its maintenance such as house insurance. Stephanie has to get the permission from the bank to do a **short sale**, which means the house buyer will buy the house for $60,000 and the full or partial $6,500 will be absorbed as a loss by the financial institution. There is no guarantee that the financial institution will agree to do a short sale and if they do, they may or may not collect all or some of the $6,500 debt from Stephanie. Stephanie would need to find out such information from the financial institution. Furthermore, Stephanie would need to find out how the financial institution will report the mortgage to the credit reports of the consumer. Stephanie does not want that the financial institution report the mortgage as "settled," "paid partially," or any message that implies that the consumer was not faithful in paying off the entire mortgage. In most cases, the financial institution will report to the credit agencies that a short sale occurred with the mortgage. This may lower the credit scores of the consumer but this is less credit damage than the damaged that would be caused by a house foreclosure appearing on the credit reports. A house foreclosure lowers the credit scores more than a short sale. For this reason, consumers that cannot afford their mortgage payments should consider doing short sales but they should never get themselves in such a bad financial position by taking out so many loans.

Short Sales during the 2000s Housing Crisis

Part of the reason that added severity to the 2000s housing crisis in America was that many consumers had to do short sales because they had taken so many loans using their houses. The consumers were planning on selling the houses once they increased in value. Sadly, the houses fell in value, developed an increased amount of negative equity, and the consumers could not afford the monthly payments nor could they easily sell the houses.

If Stephanie can afford the monthly mortgage payments, Stephanie should wait before selling her house. She should wait for the economy to improve and sell it when an increase occurs with the house value, which is the idea of appreciation.
If the economy improved and the house for example, increased in value to about $70,000 then it would be wise for Stephanie to sell the house immediately because it is likely a house buyer would pay an amount near the $70,000 range. The increase in value means the house has appreciated.
Stephanie would make a profit from the selling of her house.
If a house buyer paid $70,000 for the house then $70,000 amount paid - $66,500 debts against the house = $3,500 profit for Stephanie.

The majority of consumers that own houses right now are hoping that they increase in value so the consumers can sell them and make profit. This is because they will likely be selling the houses for a higher amount that what they had paid.

Mortgage Score

CoreLogic

CoreLogic is a company similar to the credit agencies and the Fair Isaac Corporation that specializes in creating products such as computer software for businesses. Such software helps businesses better analyze data related to consumers and make decisions with the intended goals of reducing costs, risks and increasing profits.

As of 2011, there have been news reports indicating CoreLogic is working with the Fair Isaac Corporation to develop a **mortgage score**, which will help determine how likely a consumer is to default on their home loan. The Fair Isaac Corporation currently has their own "FICO eight Mortgage Score" but they are hoping to analyze the weaknesses of their scoring model, which are causing some businesses to grant loans and services to high risk consumers. CoreLogic and the Fair Isaac Corporation hope to prevent these weaknesses from happening with the newly advanced mortgage scoring model, which will be calculated using a new credit report brand of CoreLogic called the "CoreScore credit report."

The CoreScore credit report is different from other credit reports because it is more detailed regarding the financial situations of consumers.

Unlike other credit reports that consumers can order from the consumer reporting agencies (Equifax, Experian, TransUnion, and Innovis), the CoreScore credit report has information about… Loans I Hate

Payday loan: Short term secured loans also known as "cash advance loans," which are very expensive with many upfront fees because most payday loan lenders do not check the credit reports of consumers. Payday loan lenders do not check credit because it costs them money to do so and they want to make as much profit as possible.

Payday loan lenders do verify employment by asking the consumer for a recent pay stub or W-2. Either document verifies the amount of income belonging to the consumer. The W-2 shows the amount of income that was reported to the Internal Revenue Services (IRS). However, some payday loan lenders, especially the online lenders, do not verify income, which usually means they will charge more fees and interest to offset the high risk lending. According to www.paydayloaninfo.org, interest rates on payday loans range from 390% to 780% and for this reason, some consumers feel as though payday loan lenders are practicing **usury**.

Usury is the idea of granting loans with higher than average interest rates and doing so for the purpose of taking advantage of the consumers. Consumers with bad or no credit usually get payday loans when they need money immediately. In the eyes of the financial institutions, such consumers are more likely to default on any loan because they are financially weak otherwise they would have had no need to get a payday loan. Most financial institutions do not grant payday loans due to the laws of their individual states and the fear of developing a bad reputation in the eyes of consumers. Consumers usually have to go to "payday loan stores" or "cash stores" to get a payday loan or car title loan. Depending upon the rules of the individual payday loan stores, consumers must provide their checking or savings account numbers and sign a contract. The contract will indicate the payday loan store will withdraw the entire loan amount due along with the fees and interest on the day that the consumer gets paid from their source of income such as their employer, alimony, or child support.

This is risky because if for some reason, the consumer did not get paid then the payday loan store would still try and take the money from the bank account. As a result, the financial institution will return or accept the attempted payment depending upon their guidelines, charge the consumer an overdraft fee, and the checking account will become negative. A negative checking account is considered a debt a consumer must pay back to the financial institution. If the payment is returned to the payday loan store then they will charge additional fees and interest to the consumer because the fees accumulate more interest. Some payday loan stores will continue trying to take the money from the bank account until they are successful in getting their loan fully paid. Unless the consumer does supply the money within the bank account then this will mean an overdraft fee will be charged everyday the payday loan store attempts taking money. The payday loan balance will continue increasing and interest will be compounding everyday. Additionally, if the consumer does not supply the money into the negative bank account then the financial institution may close the account and report it as negative financial information to ChexSystems.

For the future, the consumer will be less likely to be approved for free checking, savings, and money market deposit accounts. In some cases, the financial institution may even sell the debt to a collection agency. The collection agency will convert the checking account debt into a collection account and this will be immediately reported as negative financial information to the credit reports of the consumer with the credit agencies. Some collection agencies also run credit checks on consumers to verify the correct consumer is being held liable for the collection account. Such ruins the credit profile of the consumer. If consumers notice credit checks from collection companies then they should immediately contact and pay them before the actual account appears on the credit reports. Some payday loans do not ask for bank account information. Instead, they ask the consumer for a signed postponed check with the loan amount including the fees and instead they must pay on the due date. When the due date arrives then the payday loan store will cash the check. If there is not enough money in the bank account of the consumer then they will get charged a returned check fee, which is considered a type of an overdraft fee. Some payday loan stores ask for some kind of collateral, which is an item worth high or the same value in relation to the loan amount that the consumer needs. Such an item could be a car, boat, and in rare cases, a house. The consumer would sign over the title to the payday loan store. The payday loan store would get ownership of the collateral in the event the consumer fails to pay the loan. Finally, some payday loan stores ask for a security deposit, which is money. They will ask for an amount that is close to the loan amount that the consumer is seeking.

For example, if Joey wanted a payday loan for $500 then the payday loan store may ask him for a security deposit for $350. If Joey fails to pay the payday loan then the loan issuer gets to keep the $350 and in this sense, they do not have a full loss but they will still try to recover all the loan debt from the consumer. Most, payday loan issuers do not report credit history to the credit agencies because it costs them money and payday loans are not needed to establish or strengthen credit. In order to get the business of the consumer, payday loan issuers may over exaggerate that they do report the payment history of the consumer to the credit agencies because some consumers may want to get a payday loan so they can improve their credit history. However, if a consumer did not pay their payday loan then it is possible that the payday loan issuer will pay the costs and report negative financial information to the credit bureaus in the hopes that the consumer may pay it. This is because as more days pass by in which the payday loan is left unpaid then the more the credit scores of the consumer drops.

Note: Unsecured loans or just any loan indicating it is not a payday loan, it is a loan for consumers with bad credit, or it is a loan of which the funds will be deposited into the bank account of the consumer **must be avoided. In most cases, they are scams, especially the loans advertised on the internet by small companies. Such loans are payday loans but the company does not want to call them the term, "payday loan," because they do not want to scare away consumers.

Here is an advertisement from Western Sky Financial for a loan targeted mostly for consumers with bad credit

Source of image: http://img.youtube.com/vi/v9mhlRp8DzI/0.jpg

Loan Product	Borrower Proceeds	Loan Fee	APR	Number of Payments	Payment Amount
$10,000 Loan	$9,925	$75	89.68%	84	$743.49
$5,075 Loan	$5,000	$75	116.73%	84	$486.58
$2,600 Loan	$2,525	$75	139.22%	47	$294.46
$1,500 Loan	$1,000	$500	234.25%	24	$198.19
$850 Loan	$500	$350	342.86%	12	$150.72

Example
Loan amount with fee: $5,075
Number of monthly (installment) payments: 84, which means 84 months because there will be a payment due each month.

Monthly payment amount: $486.58
$486.58 x 84 months = $40,872.72.
A $5,075 loan amount has resulted in the consumer paying a total of $40,872.72.
$40,872.72 - $5,075 = $35,797.72 is how much the consumer paid in interest alone.

The interest rates are exorbitant! If a consumer gets such a loan for whatever the reasons may be, they must pay it back immediately otherwise the company will take advantage of them through interest. If the consumer cannot pay back the high interest loan immediately then they should immediately contact a credit union or community bank, explain the situation, and see if they can get another loan to which they can transfer the balance of the high interest rate loan. If possible, the consumer should use savings to pay off the high interest rate loan or transfer as much as they can of the balance from the high interest rate loan to their credit card. Even a credit card with a penalty interest rate is cheaper than the interest rates of most loans for consumers with bad credit.

Car title loans: A car title loan, sometimes called an auto title loan, which is considered to be a type of payday loan. Unlike a payday loan, it is a type of secured credit because the consumer offers their automobile as collateral that the company can keep in the event that the consumer fails to make their payments and in this way, the company does not have as great a loss. The car title loan issuers have their own rules as to how old an automobile can be that can be used as the collateral and usually, they require for the automobile to have protection through insurance. Due to there being a collateral, although most all car title loans have exorbitant interest rates like payday loans, consumers may be able get a cheaper interest rate on a car title loan than they would a payday loan.

According to the National Consumer Law Center, most car title loans "[have] APR[s] that exceeds 36%." "APR" stands for the annual percentage rate, which is the rate of interest that the consumer will be charged on the loan. In personal experience, car title loan APRs can go higher than 100% especially if they are variable rates. In order for consumers to get a car title loan, they transfer the title of their paid off automobile, to the name of the car title loan company. The automobile cannot currently have any debts against it such as an auto loan because then the car title loan issuer will be liable for that debt and they do not want to be liable for that debt. Similar to the payday loan store or issuer, the car title loan issuer does not check the credit profile of the consumer because it costs them money. The loan amount which the consumer is granted is based off of the market value of their automobile. The car title loan issuer will determine the market value of the automobile by having their automobile appraiser evaluate it or use a website that suggests the market values of automobiles such as the Kelley Blue Book website, which is www.kbb.com. If the value of the automobile is not high then it is likely that the consumer will not be granted a high loan amount. Similarly, if the value of the automobile is high; then it is likely that the consumer will be granted a high loan amount. Consumers can borrow money up to the market value of the automobile. Unless the company is charging upfront fees, then it is unlikely that a consumer will be able to get a loan amount higher than the value of the automobile depending upon the policies of the car title loan issuer.

In most cases, car title loan issuers need a court order in order to repossess the automobile. In the United Kingdom, car title loan are sometimes called "logbook loans" or "pink slip loans." The major aspect in which a logbook or pink slip loan can be considered different from a car title loan is because most loan issuers who provide these loans do not require a court order to repossess the automobile. In general, consumers need to be careful of any car title loan because there have been cases in which the loan issuer took the automobile anyway even after the consumer managed to repay the loan. Similar to payday loans, car title loan issuers may over exaggerate about reporting the payment history to the credit agencies so they can win the business of the consumer but in reality, they will not report the payment history because it costs them money to do so.

In some cases, some consumers abuse or misuse the payday loans, tax refund loans, car title loans, pawn shop loans, or just any type of loan with exorbitant interest because they may use them to pay other loans such as their mortgage, credit cards or car loans. It makes no sense why consumers would do so because they are building up more debt. Some consumers use the exorbitant interest rate loans to make only the minimum payments on the credit card and make high purchases using the credit card in relation to their payment amounts. Once the credit card is completely maxed out then the consumer declares a bankruptcy, debt settlement, or simply lets the credit card become a collection account.

Finally, some consumers contribute all the loan money that they get into their Individual Retirement Account (IRA) with no intention of paying the loan issuers. The consumer then declares a bankruptcy or debt settlement thinking that their money is safe because all money that is within a 401(k) or IRA is protected from being seized by the loan issuers of the consumer. When financial institutions review the CoreScore credit report and see the exorbitant interest rate loans that the consumer has taken then they take into consideration all the potential abuse and misuse of the loans and look at the consumer with increased risk in defaulting on any new loans. Financial institutions can sometimes determine that the consumer has bad intentions because they will look at the dates on which the payday or car title loans were taken and will look at the balance histories on the other loans of the consumer. In the eyes of the financial institutions, if the overall balances on the other loans are increasing from the date that the consumer obtained the exorbitant interest rate loans then it is possible that the consumer is using the loan money from the exorbitant interest rate loans to make the minimum payments so the credit cards will not decline when they use them to make more purchases. Financial institutions will also question why a consumer had to get several exorbitant interest rate loans such as car title loans, payday loans, pawnshop loans, or tax refund loans. It makes no sense why a consumer would get several loans that have interest rates up to about 800%. They cannot deduct the interest from their taxes. For whatever reasons consumers have for needing such loans, they are better off rolling most or all of the funds from their assets such as their 401(k), savings, money market, saving bonds, certificate of deposit that is about to mature, and checking account into a Roth IRA, paying any necessary taxes, and then taking the money, not the earnings (if any), out of the Roth IRA so they can avoid paying the 10% tax penalty. If a consumer cannot get a Roth IRA then they should take a loan against their 401(k). A loan against a 401(k) is not taxable as long as it is repaid within 5 years. If the 401(k) loan is not repaid within this time or the consumer leaves their job then the amount of money that was taken through the loan will be considered a 401(k) withdrawal. This money will then be reported as income to the IRS on which the consumer will have to income taxes and a 10% tax penalty. If a consumer does not have a 401(k) and cannot get a Roth IRA then taking out the money from a traditional IRA is still the best option. This is because paying the 10% tax penalty and income taxes are still cheaper than getting exorbitant interest rate loans. Consumers are not required to put money back into an IRA because an employer only makes contributions, which are deposits, into a 401(k). This is why consumers have to repay their 401(k) accounts. Taking money out of a 401(k) and IRA should be the absolute least option for consumers and they should not get themselves into a bad financial position where they need to take that money.

Rental records: If a consumer has a history of being late on the rent payments then this will suggest that the consumer is financially weak. This raises the chances that the consumer will be late on any loan including a home loan. For this reason, the financial institution will be more likely to deny the consumer for credit or impose a higher than average interest rate or fees because the consumer is very likely to one day stop paying on the bills. The financial institution needs to make as much profit as possible off of the consumer. Unless left unpaid, rental companies and apartment management teams do not report payment history to the credit agencies because it costs them money to do so.

Property liens: Consumers that have had non-consensual property liens on their houses raises a red flag for financial institutions. A lien can be thought of as a claim. When service contractors such as the ones who install carpet, fix roofs, or just provide any service in general are not paid by the consumer then they will impose a lien on the property on which they performed the service and have the right to evict the consumer. In some cases, financial institutions may also be able to impose a lien in the event that a consumer fails to pay on their loans. No matter what the case, a lien implies that a consumer has cheated a company or individual.

Evictions: An eviction is when a consumer is forced to leave the property at which they reside. This usually happens when a consumer violates the contract they agreed to with an individual or company when they took ownership of the property. Although there can be many reasons for contract violations, a common reason they occur is when a consumer fails to make payments for staying at the property. In the eyes of the financial institution, this raises a red flag. Evictions are considered negative financial information and raise the chances for the denial of credit because a consumer is unlikely to pay on newly accumulated debts.

Child support judgments: This type of court judgment happens when consumers are required to make child support payments. Their adopted or biological children get the money to use for food, shelter, school, and medical expenses. In the eyes of some financial institutions, if consumers do not make their child support payments in a timely manner then they are considered financially weak and in some regards, low in character. If the child support payments are being made in a timely manner then the financial institution will still consider the child support to be a liability for the consumer but they will not hold it against the consumer more severe than if they were not making the child support payments. Child support payment obligations cannot be discharged in a bankruptcy or debt settlement. There has been arguments that some parents who receive child support do not use it to financially support their children and that the government needs to do a better job ensuring that the child support is supporting the child and is not being used in other means.

Court records: Financial institutions will be concerned lending to consumers that have had problems obeying the law and as a result, they have had to appear at court hearings. It will cause financial institutions to think if a consumer is always getting into trouble with law officials then they are not trustworthy enough to pay back loans especially considering consumers that are appearing at court are usually spending a great deal of money on lawyer fees. For this reason, financial institutions will review the court records carefully and understand for what reasons a consumer had to appear at court. Financial institutions are very likely to deny consumers for credit that have been accused of committing crimes such as robbery, felony, or fraud. Additionally, financial institutions may think if a consumer is prone to get into trouble with the law again and get convicted to jail then it is unlikely they will pay on their loans.

It is unsure if many financial institutions will use the CoreScore credit report or the new mortgage score because they have not yet established much popularity. However, the consumers should still check them periodically before getting a home loan because there is no way to tell what scoring model or credit report brand the financial institution will use. As permitted by law, consumers can get a free annual copy of their CoreScore credit report by calling 1-877-532-8778. Consumers should dispute any inaccurate information from the report otherwise it could result in them getting denied.

Finance 101: The Whiz Kid's Perfect Credit Guide

Fraud

Phishing

Phishing is the illegal and fraudulent act of criminals trying to obtain the personal information of consumers such as their credit card numbers, social security numbers, bank account numbers, and other personal information with the intention of stealing money from them. To do so, criminals send out fake emails, create fake websites, and make phone calls to consumers pretending to be legitimate banks. The email messaging systems of Yahoo, Google, Outlook, and many others cannot always detect the fake emails. This is supported by the fact that the Federal Trade Commission reports more than 9.9 million adults are victims of fraud within the United States and this number keeps growing exponentially.

Here is an example of phony email I received from a criminal pretending to be Bank of America. Phony emails look very similar to legitimate emails.

From: Bank Of America <RiskDept@aol.com>
Subject: Online Account Notification

Dear Valued Customer,

Bank of America Online Service has been receiving complaints from our customers for unauthorized use of the Bank of America Online Accounts. As a result we are making an extra security verification on all of our Customers account in order to protect their information from theft and fraud. How ever we would temporarily restrict access of those accounts which we think are vulnerable to the unauthorized use.

Due to this, you are requested to follow the provided steps and confirm your Online Banking details for the safety of your Accounts We have sent you an attachment which contains all the necessary steps in order to restore your account access.
Download and open it in your browser.

However, Failure to do so may result in temporary account limitation and restrictions. Please understand that this is a security measure intended to help protect your account.We apologize for any inconvenience.

Sincerely

Bank of America Corporation. All rights reserved.

There are several ways a consumer can determine if an email they receive is phony as shown in the analysis of the email. Phony emails are referred to as **hoax emails**.

From: <u>Bank Of America <RiskDept@aol.com></u> (Notice the "O" in "Of" is capitalized, which is a grammatical error. All phony emails have grammatical errors because if they were legitimate then a financial institution would never send their customers emails with grammatical errors because it is unprofessional to do so and brings a bad reputation to the company. Additionally, consumers should notice this email is coming from an American Online account, which is why the return address says "@aol.com." A financial institution would never use a third

party emailing system to messages to consumers because the information is too confidential within emails and financial institutions have to use their own email systems to send out the information)
Subject: Online Account Notification

Dear Valued Customer, (A financial institution would always address their customer by their name in any form of communication such as phone, email, or postal mail)

Bank of America Online Service has been receiving complaints from our customers for unauthorized use of the Bank of America Online Accounts (notice the repetition and wordiness within the email. Legitimate emails would be concise). As a result (no comma) we are making an extra security verification on all of our Customers (unnecessary capitalization of a noun) account in order to protect their information from theft and fraud. How ever ("however" is one word and there should be a comma after it because the word in the sentence is being used as an interjection) we would temporarily restrict access (fake emails always threaten the consumers that a negative action will be taken against them such as suspending their account because the criminal is trying to scare them so they are more likely to provide their personal information) of those (the sentences are broken up and it looks like one word is being used in a sentence) accounts which we think are vulnerable to the unauthorized use.

Due to this, you are requested to follow the provided steps and confirm your Online Banking (unnecessary capitalization) details for the safety of your Accounts (unnecessary capitalization) (no period) We have sent you an attachment (a financial institution would never send consumers an attachment and fake emails have viral attachments that will disable any antivirus software on the computer so the consumer is taken to bogus websites without the computer detecting them) which contains all the necessary steps in order to restore your account access. Download (financial institutions would never tell consumers to download any type of file considering the information is personal) and open it in your browser.

However, Failure (unnecessary capitalization) to do so may result in temporary account limitation and restrictions (a financial institution would never warn the consumer using an email, if they are so concerned with security then they would call the consumer immediately). Please understand that this is a security measure intended to help protect your account.We (there is no space between the period and "We") apologize for any inconvenience.

Sincerely (no comma)

Bank of America Corporation. All rights reserved.

Criminals will also place small electronic and wireless card number readers at gas station pumps and inside of small stores. When consumers swipe their debit or credit cards then the readers will record the numbers and electronically transmit them as data to the criminals which will be stored data within their computer systems. After stealing the personal information of consumers, criminals will attempt to clean out the bank accounts of all its money possibly to the point that they become negative. In addition, criminals will open up credit cards and take out loans using the social security number of the consumer. The consumers must pay the fraudulent charges that are made by the criminals unless they can immediately contact the financial institutions and file police reports but doing all of this is a time consuming struggle and consumers are out of their money until they have fully recovered from the fraud. If consumers have little or no money then their chances of becoming delinquent on bills is greatly increased. To avoid being victimized by fraud, protecting money, and minimizing its effects, consumers need to follow these tips.

1. Consumers should never click on the links provided on emails because the links will take them to the fake websites created by the criminals.
Example
"Click here to log into your Chase account"—Do **not** click on any such link on any email!
The websites will ask for personal information such as the bank account login information that consumers would use when they log into their bank accounts using the internet. The websites may also ask for other information such as full name, date of birth, social security number, and account numbers of all accounts held with the financial institution claiming it is part of their security measures.

2. Consumers should never open the fake emails from criminals pretending to be financial institutions, especially if they are in the spam folder of the email system, nor should they download the attachments of the email. The attachments will have viruses that will disable the anti-virus and other protective programs of the computer. In doing so, the consumer will be on bogus websites claiming to be legitimate financial institutions and the computer will not detect the illegitimacy. The consumers will unknowingly submit their personal information and their financial future will be ruined. Consumers should delete the fake emails immediately but before doing so, they can also forward the fake emails and websites to the financial institution. Financial institutions have a special email address to which consumers can forward fake emails and websites and the financial institutions will be able to inform all their customers of the danger. Consumers would have to call the financial institution to obtain their special fraud prevention email address. For example, the fraud prevention email address to which consumers would forward fake Citibank emails and websites created by criminals to emailspoof@citigroup.com.

3. Fake emails and text messages from criminals claiming to be financial institutions will often have several grammatical errors within their messages as well as warnings to consumers that if they do not click on the link or download the attachments of the message then their accounts will be restricted or suspended. All of such messages should be forwarded to the financial institution along with the phone numbers showing on the caller ID so the consumer can protect other consumers. If consumers are not sure if the message is legitimate then they should call the financial institution immediately to verify if they sent that message. Consumers should never call the financial institution using the phone number, if any, that is showing on the email or text message because there is no guarantee if it is legitimate. Mailing addresses on the messages may be fake too so consumers should not use them to send correspondence.

4. If consumers get phone calls from individuals claiming to be a financial institution and they ask for personal information such as the account number then consumers need to write down the phone number from which the call is coming and is appearing on their caller ID, hang up the phone, and call the legitimate financial institution. The consumer needs to report the incident because the financial institution must get law enforcement involved for the purpose of tracking down the criminal who is making the fake phone calls with the intention of committing fraud.

5. Consumers must pay attention to the website addresses showing on the internet search bar and the spellings of the content showing on the websites. Bogus websites will always have

several grammatical errors and their font sizes as well as styles may be unusual. If the website address has unusual or extra words within it then it is likely the website is fraudulent and was created by a criminal so the personal information of the consumer can be stolen.
Example
Authentic website: https://www.citibank.com.
Fraudulent website: https://www.zeo.citibank.com.
Fraudulent website: https://www.citibank.baya.com.
Fraudulent website: https://www.citibank.com/geo.

6. If consumers feel as though their information has been compromised then they need to immediately freeze their bank accounts with the financial institutions and consumer reports with Equifax, Experian, TransUnion, Innovis, and ChexSystems. Consumers need to be aware when the report with one agency is frozen then this never means the consumer reports with the other agencies are frozen and the criminal can access them. Consumers need to add a "fraud victim statement" to all their consumer reports so no financial institution grants credit to a criminal using the information of the consumer. In addition, consumers need to change their social security number immediately by going to their nearest social security office that can be found on https://secure.ssa.gov/apps6z/FOLO/fo001.jsp. Calling the social security administration can be annoying because their hold times are long; but their phone number is 1-800-772-1213. Finally, consumers need to inform their credit card companies that fraud has occurred so the financial institutions do not think they are at high risk of the consumer defaulting on the credit accounts. They will notice fraud occurring on the credit reports during an account review and financial institutions need to be assured they will not have a loan loss.

Equifax
P.O. Box 105788
Atlanta, GA 30348
1-800-685-1111
https://www.freeze.equifax.com

Experian
P.O. Box 9554.
Allen, TX 75013
1-888-397-3742
https://www.experian.com/freeze/center.html

TransUnion
P.O. Box 390
Springfield, PA, 19064
1-888-909-8872
https://freeze.transunion.com

Innovis
Attn: Consumer Assistance
P.O. Box 26
Pittsburgh, PA 15230-0026
1-800-540-2505
https://www.innovis.com/InnovisWeb/pers_placeSecurityFreeze.html

ChexSystems
Attention: Consumer Relations, 7805 Hudson Road, Suite 100
Woodbury, MN, 55125
1-800-428-9623 or 1-800-887-7652
https://www.consumerdebit.com/consumerinfo/us/en/victimidtheft.html

7. Consumers need to file a police report at a local law enforcement agency and submit a complaint to the Internet Crime Center using their website that is www.ic3.gov. For the next 1-2 years, consumers need to monitor their ChexSystems report to ensure no fraudulent deposit accounts are established under their name because criminals will try to make them negative even if they have no money within them.

Note: If it is a close family member such as a son, daughter, or spouse that committed the fraud then it is personally not recommended that a police report be submitted; otherwise the family member could be incarcerated, their background profile will be ruined, and it will ruin their chances at being able to earn a job or do anything successful in life. Unfortunately, if consumers do not submit a police report then it is likely they will be liable for paying the charges that were made by the family member. If the family member continues making poor decisions then consumers must submit a police report otherwise the family member will get themselves into huge trouble.

Review ChexSystems Report to Prevent Fraud and Financial Crisis

Consumers should periodically review their ChexSystems report. Due to the Fair and Accurate Credit Transaction Act (FACTA); they are allowed one free report every year on www.consumerdebit.com. Criminals that compromise personal information will try and open not just credit accounts; but also checking, savings, money market, and simply any kind of account and use it. It is possible for criminals to use deposit accounts; that have no money in them and make them negative. This is because at times, financial institutions will allow for transactions to go through; but will still charge the account overdraft fees for excessive debit card use and NSF fees, for excessive amounts written through checks. Fraudulent and overdrawn accounts will damage the financial profile, of the consumer. If consumers become a victim of fraud, then they should freeze their Equifax, Experian, TransUnion, Innovis, and ChexSystems consumer reports. It is unsure, if all countries besides the United States use ChexSystems. Some high risk consumers may take advantage of this by purchasing whatever they want and letting their deposit accounts become negative. They will not bother funding the deposit accounts to make them positive again and may migrate to another country. The financial institutions will be cheated. They will not be held accountable for their negative financial behavior in the United States because there may not be any record of it.

Bankruptcy and Debt Settlement

Many commercials on the television, radio, and internet claim debt settlement companies can free consumers of their debts. The offers are not as healthy as they seem because most companies will encourage the consumers to file for a bankruptcy or debt settlement. There will be expensive fees from $1,000 or more that the company will collect from the consumer for handling the paperwork and the processing of the case. For this reason, the debt settlement companies will make the offers seem attractive. Most companies that claim to offer debt elimination services are scams and often have bad consumer reviews. Consumers are better off using the money they would pay to the debt settlement or bankruptcy companies and instead, pay the financial institutions and companies to whom they owe money. This protects their credit, lowers their likelihood for being denied a job, and does not cause their insurance premiums to increase.

Bankruptcy: When consumers legally declare, usually in court, that they cannot pay their debts. As a result, the consumer is no longer liable for the specific debts that they discharged. The financial institutions become upset because they feel as though they have been cheated of their money.

Debt Settlement: When a consumer legally declares that they can only pay half of their total debts. The consumer must pay a **lump sum amount**. This is half of the total amount of dischargable debts such as the credit cards and medical bills. Consumers need to be careful when listening to the advice of third party handling the debt settlement such as an attorney or company. This is because they may tell the consumer to stop paying their credit cards, student loans, and other bills claiming that they will eventually be forgiven. Such is very bad financial advice because the companies to whom the consumer owes money may take adverse actions such as garnishing the wages of the consumer or putting a claim on their property. The attorney or company will not be held responsible for these problems. In addition, some companies may tell the consumer to pay them money and on the behalf of the consumer, they will pay their monthly payments on the debts. There is no guarantee that the company will not simply pocket the money and not pay any of the debts. The damaged credit profile will be the problem the consumer.

Bankruptcy Codes
Chapters 7, 11, and 13 are all different types of bankruptcy. Each chapter is considered a bankruptcy code and has its own aspects such as the limitations to the debts that a consumer can discharge. Chapter 7 bankruptcy is meant more for consumers whereas Chapter 11 and Chapter 13 bankruptcy are meant more for businesses. Chapter 11 bankruptcy allows for the company to repay some of their debts and possibly transform themselves into a new business. Chapter 13 bankruptcy allows for the company or consumer to keep all their property such as a house but they still must repay some of their debts. Chapter 7 bankruptcy is similar to Chapter 13 bankruptcy but the consumer or company must give up more of their property and assets.

Two Types of Debts
Dischargeable debts can include collection accounts, mortgages, car loans, credit cards, and negative checking accounts. I am not a bankruptcy attorney and there may be more debts that can be discharged depending upon the financial conditions of the consumers. When consumers bankrupt on secured loan debts such as car loans and mortgages then they usually have to

surrender the collateral. This means they would have to surrender the car and house to the financial institutions. This is because the consumer is not repaying the debt and they cannot keep the house and car for free.

Debts that cannot be discharged with any type of bankruptcy or debt settlement are usually student loans, debt with the Internal Revenue Services, and child support or alimony payments. Such debts may be discharged in rare cases such as if the consumer has a major medical disability that prevents them from being able to do a job.

A bankruptcy or debt settlement ruins the credit scores of the consumer because it is considered the most negative information possible and usually stays on the credit reports for about 10 years. Unless a financial institution is "bankruptcy friendly" then it is unlikely consumers that have a bankruptcy or debt settlement reflecting on their credit reports will be approved for new credit accounts. Consumers may also struggle to open new checking or savings accounts that have no fees.

Due to the weak economy in the United States, very few financial institutions tolerate bankruptcy including subprime creditors. Subprime creditors are financial institutions that specialize in granting credit to consumers with bad or limited credit histories. Example of subprime creditors can include Capital One Bank, First Premier bank, and MetaBank.

Response of Financial Institutions to Bankruptcy

When consumers or businesses declare a bankruptcy or debt settlement then the companies to whom they owe money will usually try to claim their assets such as the money within their bank accounts. For this reason, some consumers after declaring bankruptcy will not deposit their money within a bank account and will use check cashing stores to cash their paychecks. Money within retirement account such as a 401k or IRA is protected from being seized by the companies. Consumers should _never_ claim the money within their retirement accounts and then declare a bankruptcy or debt settlement because it is likely that the money will be seized. Money taken out of retirement accounts has no protection.

Impact on Credit Reports

In most cases, when a consumer includes a debt in a debt settlement then the status of the debt on the credit reports will say "settled." This means the consumer paid some money to the financial institution. When a consumer includes a debt in a bankruptcy then the status of the debt on the credit reports will usually say "bankrupt" or "discharged." This means the consumer paid no money to the financial institution.

Bad Credit saved in Records

Many consumers think bankruptcy, debt settlement, or delinquent credit accounts will be erased from their credit reports after 7 to 10 years. This is not necessarily true information because some companies and financial institutions may save copies of past credit reports and credit accounts within their computer databases using the social security number of the consumer. When the consumer applies for credit then the financial institution may be alerted by the computer system that the consumer was not faithful in repaying their debts. This may cause the financial institution to approve the consumer with a higher than average interest rate or deny the consumer for credit. This is sometimes the reason why consumers choose not to do business with financial institutions at which they had delinquent credit accounts.

Bad Credit damages Economy

When too many consumers become unfaithful in repaying their debts then it causes the financial institutions and companies to have major losses. They start relying on the government for bailout money so the economic conditions remain stable and they can continue granting loans to entrepreneurs who want to expand upon their businesses and in doing so, create jobs. The bailout money that the government provides to the financial institutions comes out of taxpayer dollars and sometimes causes an increase with the national debt. Eventually, the financial institution has to make enough profit so they can repay the bailout money to the government. If the financial institution is unsuccessful in doing so and the government is still providing bailout money because too many consumers are defaulting on their loans then it raises the likelihood of a recession occurring within the country. In providing bailout money, the government is usually creating deficit, which is an excessive spent amount of money.

Bad Credit raises Needs to make Profit

To make more profit, financial institutions usually try and impose fees on consumers such as on their bank accounts and credit cards. They may start shutting down the credit accounts of current customers, decreasing their credit limits or loan amounts, and start increasing their interest rates. This can hurt entrepreneurs that want to start businesses. It will become more difficult for businesses to expand, diversify, and create new jobs. Financial institutions may also lay off their own employees and will be less likely to expand because such costs them money. A lack of profits may cause financial institutions to offer very little or no interest on the interest bearing deposit accounts of consumers such as interest checking, savings, money market, and certificate of deposit accounts. This is because financial institutions use part of the profits they make off of the interest charged on loans to hire employees and pay consumers interest on their deposit accounts. They use the funds of deposit accounts belonging consumers to grant loans to other consumers. There is a mutual relationship because consumers with loans and consumers with deposit accounts are both benefiting from each other but only when both groups are strong. A financial institution cannot grant many loans if they do not have enough consumers that open deposit accounts with sufficient funds. Some financial institutions may fail and close down. It is imperative for the financial institutions to pay back the bailout money and for this reason, it is equally important for consumers to pay all their loans and bills.

Bankruptcy and Debt Settlement Alternatives

Credit Counseling

When a consumer contacts a "credit counselor", it can be like a double edged sword. While the *credit counseling agency* is there to negotiate with the financial institution; they may also work for *collection agencies,* with which the consumer may have accounts. The credit counseling agency is able to get some or all of the late fees dismissed from the credit and collection accounts and do a "debt consolidation," in which all the collection account debts and credit card debts are combined. This is considered a payment plan for the consumer who is required to make a monthly payment, to the credit counseling agency and they have an agreement; with the credit counseling agency that in a certain number of months, all the debts part of the payment plan should be paid off. The credit counseling agency then uses the money and pays the credit card issuing companies and collection companies. However, the credit counseling agency does become a credit account itself that shows on the credit reports of the consumer.

Be Careful when Trusting Credit Counseling Agencies

The consumers should still check with their credit card issuers and other bills that have been part of the debt consolidation payment plan, to make sure they are being paid in a timely manner, by the credit counseling agency. This is because there is no guarantee that the credit counseling agency will be honest with the consumer, about paying their debts and may be using the money of the consumer for other purposes, which they did not ethically inform the consumer. Any late payments to credit cards may damage the credit profile of the consumer and late fees will be incurred. For the same reason, consumers cannot be late in making monthly payments, to the credit counseling agency, otherwise it is also possible that the credit counseling agency may cancel the payment plan but will still want the fees from the consumer for providing the service. If the consumer does not pay the fees then the credit counseling agency may sell their fees as a debt to a collection agency. The debt will become a collection account, which will immediately be reported as negative financial information to the credit profiles of the consumer. The collection agency will try collecting this new debt from the consumer.

Credit Counseling Fees: Pay HIGH Attention

The credit counseling agency may charge a fee to the consumer for their services. Consumers need to be on alert; if the fees are outrageously high then the consumer is better off not doing credit counseling and just paying the debts by themselves. Credit counseling agencies may have relationships with certain credit card issuers, which is why the credit card issuers may refer their customers that are financially struggling to specific agencies. The credit counseling agencies are paid commissions, by the credit card issuers and collection agencies. This is because usually consumers that are financially struggling are likely to default on their loans or declare a bankruptcy or debt settlement. If such happens then the financial institutions will have a loss. Credit counseling allows for the financial institution to get some of their loan money back, from the consumer and so it benefits them too. For this reason, the credit counseling agencies are able to get the financial institutions to extend their payment due dates, for consumers on their accounts.

Credit Counseling Limitations

Most credit counselors cannot help reduce interest rates on secured loans, such as automobile loans, mortgages (house loans), and any kind of loan in which the financial institution has a "collateral" worth of value, that they can repossess. Collateral can be thought of as a security deposit. For example, the collateral of an auto loan would be the car because the financial institution can repossess the car, in the event, that the consumer fails to pay on the auto loan. Although it is not as common now but many years back, consumers would purchase televisions, computers, furniture, and other major expenses by getting a secured loan. Very few financial institutions offer secured loans to purchase such minor items because it costs them too much money to repossess them, in the event that the consumer fails to make payments. These items lose value quickly. Secured loans tend to have low interest rates compared to unsecured debts such as credit cards. Financial institutions have the ability to repossess the collateral and so there is less need to charge the consumers so much interest or pay commission to credit counseling agencies for helping their customers. For this reason, credit counseling agencies cannot help consumers with secured loans. They specialize in helping with credit cards and collection accounts.

Credit Counseling is a Last Resort

Credit counseling should be a last resort for consumers, in great financial struggle. It is always better than a bankruptcy, debt settlement, or simply defaulting. Consumers should agree to credit counseling before letting the credit accounts become delinquent so the negative impact to the credit reports and scores can be avoided. Consumers that have already defaulted on a credit card or collection account should not waste too much time in contacting the credit counseling agency because there is no guarantee that the credit counseling agency will be able to get all the late fees and default interest dismissed from the accounts.

Consumers with zero percent offers on their credit cards should not bother getting credit counseling because it is unlikely the credit counselor will be able help them considering their interest rates are already so low. They should simply pay as much as they can on the credit cards with the intent of fully paying them off. In some financial situations, consumers are at best paying the minimum payments only on the zero percent credit cards that have balances and paying most of their money towards their loans that are accumulating large amounts of interest.

Seek Government Approved Credit Counseling Agencies

Consumers must look for non-profit credit counseling agencies that are approved by the government of their state and have positive consumer reviews. Most non-profit credit counseling agencies are part of the Consumer Credit Counseling Service, which is abbreviated as the CCCS. They are an organization that focuses on helping the financial situations of consumers, without aiming on making large levels of profit.

Please be aware that credit counseling agencies that claim they are legitimate because they have a good profile with the Better Business Bureau does not always have significance. This is because any business can pay money to be listed, with the Better Business Bureau. It is recommended that consumers conduct a complaints search by using the name of the business on a Google.com search. For the purpose of best avoiding illegitimate credit counseling agencies, consumers should attempt to get into business with credit counseling agencies that are affiliated with the National Foundation for Credit Counseling (NFCC) and this information can be found on www.nfcc.org.

Consumers can find an up-to-date list of government approved credit counseling agencies on http://www.justice.gov/ust/eo/bapcpa/ccde/cc_approved.html.

Risks of Credit Counseling and Its Impact on Credit

Consumers need to be aware that when they agree to do credit counseling, there are two cons that may happen, depending upon the policies of the particular agencies.

The credit counselors may not reveal this information, because they want to get the business of the consumers. When the credit counseling agencies negotiate with the creditors for lower interest rates; the creditors may close all the credit accounts of the consumer including accounts that have no balances. This is because the consumers that are doing credit counseling are considered financially weak and are likely to default; otherwise they would have had no need to do the program. For this reason, the financial institutions do not want them to build more debt by using the credit accounts. When the financial institutions close the credit accounts; they may say "closed by credit grantor", on the credit reports of the consumer. This can be considered negative information, because some financial institutions will wonder why the creditor closed the credit account, of the consumer. It may send them the message that the consumer was not responsible in handling their credit account; for this reason, the creditor may feel as though the consumer would not pay back the debt. As a result, the creditor would have a financial loss. They had to close the account down to avoid this. At all times, consumers need to make sure all closed credit accounts; showing on their credit reports say, "closed by consumer." Additionally, the closing of the credit cards will cause the FICO credit scores of the consumer to drop, because their debt-to-credit limit ratio will become higher. The FICO scoring model will then view the consumer, as having a higher utilization rate of their available credit. The credit account closure may shorten the average length of history established; on the open credit accounts. In seven to ten years, the credit account will drop off the credit reports and it will look like the consumer never had the credit account or its payment history. Furthermore, when credit accounts are closed too quickly especially if they have balances, then it sometimes suggests that the consumer experienced some kind of financial difficulties and could not afford to pay on the credit account.

Finally, some of the financial institutions may report to the credit bureaus that the consumers are doing credit counseling and it will show on the credit reports under each account included with the counseling that they are on a payment plan. This can be considered negative information if in the future, the consumer applies for credit. The financial institutions may feel as though the consumer is financially weak otherwise they would have had no need to do the credit counseling in the past. The financial institution will still value that the consumer paid their debts and did not do a bankruptcy, debt settlement, or just never paid on any of the accounts. For this reason, it is likely the financial institution will approve the consumer but with a low credit limit or loan amount and a slightly higher than average interest rate. Consumers can always build a positive payment history with the financial institution and later ask for a credit limit increase and a lower interest rate.

Get a New Loan with a Low and Fixed Interest Rate

Besides credit counseling, consumers can consider getting a new loan, preferably a secured loan. This is because secured loans tend to have lower interest rates than unsecured loans, which are credit cards and unsecured personal loan. Consumers can mention to the financial institutions putting their savings account, certificate of deposit, house, car, or some collateral worth of high value as a security deposit for the secured loan.

Using the new secured loan, consumers can pay off their debts including collection accounts and start making monthly payments towards the new secured loan. Getting a secured loan will mean a hard inquiry credit check will be done. Consumers want to make sure their credit check does not go to waste; and should research the different offers and interest rates being offered by the financial institutions. A recommended website for searching interest rates is www.bankrate.com. Consumers should check the interest rate of the secured loans with the financial institution, with whom that they have had the longest and positive relationship.

Credit Unions save Money

Consumers should also check the secured loan rates of "credit unions" which they are eligible to join. Credit unions are different than banks because most banks are supported by their stock shareholders. In contrast, credit unions are supported by their members. This explains why the members are usually required to pay a small fee; when opening up some type of account when joining a credit union.

Their deposits help support the credit union, which is why they are usually able to provide cheaper interest rates, on any type of loan. As evidence, credit unions that are part of the National Credit Union Association are not allowed to charge more than 18% in default interest rates to consumers that are late by sixty days, or more; on their credit card payments.

Another reason why credit unions are able to provide more consumer-friendly products than banks is because they are less focused; on making profits off of the consumers, due to the fact, they do not have highly paid executives and directors. For this reason, unlike banks, credit unions do not pay corporate taxes on their income. A corporate tax is tax paid, on the profits accumulated by a corporation. A corporation is recognized by law, as being a single body company, which has its own liabilities and authorities. Lastly, credit unions have more regulations and financial support from the government than banks.

Recommended websites consumers can use to determine which credit unions they are eligible to join are www.creditunion.coop, www.findacreditunion.com, and www.culookup.com.

In most cases, consumers are able to join credit unions based on the geographical location of their residence; and if their employers have business relationships with the particular credit union. A common reason why some consumers may not join a credit union is because credit unions have fewer branches, compared to banks. Credit unions usually have branches only within their designated city or state. This makes it difficult for consumers to take care of financial matters, including making cash deposits when they are traveling out of the state. To fix this problem, an increasing number of credit unions are forming business relations, with each other, called **co-op networks**. This will allow for members of one credit union to access their accounts at the branches of other credit unions, in state, as well as, out of the country; and perform transactions such as deposits, withdrawals, and making payments on loans without any fees. Credit unions that are part of the co-op networks are called **shared branch members**.

For example, Heather is a member of Orlando Federal Credit Union (OFCU), which is part of the co-op network. Heather travels to Texas and comes across the Texas Federal Credit Union (TFCU) branch; which is also part of the co-op network then it is possible Heather could go to the TFCU branch and have the branch representative access her accounts at OFCU. Heather could use the automated teller machine (ATM) that is attached to the outside wall of the TFCU branch; use her OFCU debit card, and access her accounts. She could even do a cash advance using the ATM system with her OFCU credit card. All consumers that are part of the co-network credit unions can access their accounts using their debit cards and do transactions at ATM systems located at Costco, seven-Eleven, Walgreens, and other stores nearby them, which they can locate using this website: www.co-opfs.org/btwoc-homepage.

National Credit Union Association

Consumers should only join credit unions that are part of the National Credit Union Association, which is abbreviated as NCUA. This is the government agency, of the United States, that monitors and financially supports the credit unions.

When a credit union is part of the NCUA, then it is considered NCUA insured; because the deposits of the consumers are protected up to $250,000, in the event that the credit unions fail. FDIC insurance is not for credit unions, but only for the deposits of consumers within financial institutions that are owned, by private businesses or families; because they are less regulated by the government. Credit unions are fully regulated by the government. FDIC and NCUA both serve the same purpose, of protecting the funds of the consumers.

Interest Rates are Never Guaranteed

Consumers should be aware that the financial institution offering a certain interest rate, does not guarantee the consumer will receive that rate. All loan products say, "subject to creditworthiness," which means that the consumer will only receive the advertised interest rate or possibly, a lower interest rate; if they have good credit.

When financial institutions advertise attractive interest rates on loan products then they are mostly targeting consumers, with good credit. Most financial institutions consider consumers, with no delinquencies or excessively high debts, to have good credit. Consumers should check their credit, with all four credit bureaus, before applying for the secured loan because there is no way to know which credit agency; the financial institution will use to pull the credit report. They may even pull credit from all the agencies. Consumers should dispute any inaccurate information, with the credit agencies, that may cause them to get denied or approved; with a higher than average interest rate, such as credit cards indicating they have balances but are paid off; multiple credit checks, from the same financial institution, for the same loan product; and accounts showing as closed but are actually open or vice versa. Only content on the credit reports can be disputed. Credit scores cannot be disputed. However, if the information on the credit reports can be corrected; then this can positively or negatively, affect the credit scores with an exception to Innovis because Innovis does not rank consumers using scores.

Credit Report Disputes can Improve Scores

Below are the websites, phone numbers, and addresses that can be used to submit the credit bureau disputes and resolve any credit report concerns. If there is a serious error on the credit reports, such as, if they are saying the consumer is deceased; then it is recommended that the dispute and a letter be submitted, using certified mail.

**Note: In order to submit a credit report dispute; a consumer first must order their credit report from the particular credit agency, because the online and written dispute forms ask for a credit report number. It is likely the credit bureaus do this so they can make money and in a sense, are not processing credit disputes for free.

Experian
P.O. Box 9556
Allen, TX 75013
(714) 830-7000
https://www.experian.com/consumer/cac/InvalidateSession.do?code=DISPUTE&channel=eight34two

Equifax
P.O. Box 740241
Atlanta, GA 30374-0241
(404) 885-8300
https://www.ai.equifax.com/CreditInvestigation/

TransUnion
P.O. Box 2000
Chester, PA 19022-2000
(312) 985-2000
http://www.TransUnion.com/personal-credit/credit-disputes/credit-disputes.page

Innovis
Attn: Consumer Assistance
P.O. Box 1640
Pittsburgh, PA 15230-1640
1-800-540-2505
https://www.innovis.com/InnovisWeb/pers_placeDispute.html

Balance Transfers Can Save Money

If credit counseling or getting a secured loan does not work; consumers have the option of paying off debt, by doing a "balance transfer" offer. A balance transfer is when consumers can bring the debts that they have, with multiple creditors, usually credit cards; and bring them over to another creditor, onto a single credit card. In this sense, the debts will be combined into one loan. It is possible for the consumer to bring only one debt over; from one creditor to another, when they do a balance transfer.

The purpose, of a balance transfer, is to save money; by getting a cheaper interest rate. Balance transfers usually have fees, depending upon the amount of the debts being transferred. The fee is usually three to four percent of the amount; with a minimum and maximum fee amount. The purpose of there being a minimum and maximum amount is so the credit card issuers make more profit. Depending upon the rules of the credit card issuer, consumers can do a balance transfer whenever they want or only when their credit card issuer sends them a promotional offer. The marketing departments of the credit card issuers usually send the balance transfer offers, because they are trying to get consumers to use their credit cards more or open new credit cards, so they can make more profits.

Example of a financial situation in which a consumer may consider doing a balance transfer to pay off their debts faster:

Mitchell receives a balance transfer offer from, Capital One Bank, indicating he will pay 0% interest for twelve months. He is already their customer and has a credit card with them; that has a credit limit of $10,000. The credit limit is the amount he has available to use, for doing the transfer. He cannot exceed the $10,000 amount otherwise he will be charged an "over the credit limit" fee. The offer indicates he will be charged a 3% fee based on the balance he is transferring. The minimum fee is $20.00 and there is no maximum fee amount.

Citibank Credit Card
Balance: $3,504.98
Interest rate: 14.24%

American Express Credit Card
Balance: $4,133.49
Interest rate: 18.24%

PNC Bank Credit Card
Balance: $1092.30
Interest rate: 13.49% and $25.00 annual fee

Discover Credit Card
Balance: $1000.20
Interest rate: 29.99% (This credit card was late by 60 days and the interest rate increased)

Total debts: $9,730.97 (Amount Mitchell will be transferring to Capital One Bank)

$9,730.97 x .03 balance transfer fee = $291.93 (Rounded)

The balance transfer fee is added to the balance. Mitchell is trying to transfer to Capital One.

9,730.97 + $291.93 = $10,022.90. This amount exceeds the $10,000 credit limit, which means he will be charged a fee.

Mitchell should pay $22.90 up front, so he can avoid the over the credit limit fee.

Successfully, Mitchell can combine and transfer; his debts from four credit cards, leaving only one with a balance. The four credit cards will be paid off. Mitchell now needs to focus on paying off his, Capital One credit card, which has the $10,000 balance, as much as possible, before the twelve months end. If he does not, then Mitchell will have to pay the standard purchase rate, of the Capital One credit card, on the $10,000 balance; which is 11.24%.

Methods to Request Balance Transfer

In order to do the balance transfer, Mitchell can fill out a balance transfer form; on the website of Capital One or mail in the form. However, there is no guarantee that the balance transfer will go through, because Capital One has the right to deny Mitchell doing the balance transfer.

Although financial institutions may send balance transfer offers to consumers, they may do a soft inquiry credit check on the consumer, if the consumer agrees to do a transfer. Soft inquiry credit checks do not affect the consumer, in anyway, because they do not mean that the consumer is applying for credit. They only mean that the financial institution is conducting an account review; or is trying to offer the consumer some kind of new promotional loan, credit card, or deposit account. Upon doing the soft inquiry credit check, if Capital One notices Mitchell has negative financial information; such as delinquent accounts, high number of hard inquiry credit checks, or excessively high debts; then Mitchell will likely be denied to do the balance transfer. This is, due to the fact, Mitchell has bad credit. It is likely Mitchell will default on the Capital One credit card. For this reason, Capital One cannot grant Mitchell a zero percent offer, because they need to make as much profit off of him, as possible, for the period he is making timely payments.

Financial institutions cannot approve risky consumers, with attractive offers, because then they will have weak business performance; and are more likely to fail. If Mitchell has good credit then it is unlikely Capital One will deny the balance transfer. His credit scores should increase, due to the fact; four credit cards have been paid. However, his scores will not be able to increase as high, as they can when credit accounts are paid, because of the fact he now has a $10,000 balance, on a credit card; that has a $10,000 credit limit. For this reason, it may be wise for Mitchell; to make a large payment, on the credit card, such as, $3,000 or more; so his credit utilization rate is not so high. He is less likely to go over the credit limit and be charged a fee. Mitchell is less likely to have the financial institution take a negative action towards him; such as closing his credit card account, because in some cases, financial institutions feel as though when a consumer is carrying an extremely high balance on a credit card; then they are not planning to pay it. Capital One may think Mitchell only did the balance transfer; so he can use all the available credit of his other four credit cards. Later, he will simply do a bankruptcy or debt settlement and all the financial institutions will have a loss.

Transferring Secured Loans to Unsecured Loans

Although it is uncommon, it is possible for consumers do to balance transfers with other loan types besides credit cards. Examples of such loans can include; car loans, mortgages (home loans), personal loans, student loans, and just any bill that is accumulating interest such as a collection account. Doing a balance transfer, with these loans to a credit card, does not always save money; but it can, in some financial situations.

From personal experience, my mother had a car loan with a bank that had a 7.5% interest rate; despite her having good credit. In order to get the interest rate down, I attempted to refinance the car, but I was only able to get the rate down to 6.8%. I did research over the internet and found a credit card; with Orlando Federal Credit Union, that was offering a 3.99% fixed balance transfer interest rate, on any new balances done with the credit card, upon opening the new account. There was no balance transfer fee for transferring the balance. Unless late payments were made, the 3.99% interest rate would stay fixed for the life of the balance. I asked my mother to open up the credit card, with Orlando Federal Credit Union. I then transferred the $16,849 car loan to the credit card; and my mother was able to pay off the balance much faster, because I was making payments above the minimum payment requirements. She saved hundreds of dollars on interest. The only con of doing the balance transfer from the car loan, to the credit card, was that in the beginning, my mother's credit scores dropped.

This was because when she opened the new credit card, it lowered her scores due to the facts a credit check was done; and the new credit account has no account history. However, the credit profile of my mother did not become bad, because credit scores can become low for minor reasons; which is what happened in her case.

Another reason why the credit scores dropped was because; when a consumer transfers a debt from an auto loan, which is a secured loan; to a credit card, which is an unsecured loan, the credit scoring models view the consumer as more likely to default on their unsecured loan debt. This is because unfortunately, some consumers do not take unsecured loan debt seriously, because if they do not pay it, then the financial institutions cannot repossess the items; that the consumer purchased whereas with secured loans, if they do not pay it then the financial institutions can repossess the items. The credit scoring models do not know that my mother transferred a car loan balance; and so they think my mother charged excessively, on her new credit card. For this reason, the credit scoring models and financial institutions may think she is financially weak; when they review her credit reports, in the event she applies for credit shortly after transferring the balance, from the car loan, to the credit card. It is not recommended that consumers apply for new credit shortly after doing a balance transfer; because it is likely they will get denied for credit. They should always pay off the balance; before seeking new credit. As the balance on the credit card; that was carrying the car loan balance was decreasing every month, positive payment history was being established on the new credit card. As a result, the credit scores of my mother were increasing. They eventually became higher than what they were before my mother opened the new credit card; because her report was now reflecting a paid in-full and on time auto loan; and paid open credit card. If we did not do anything with the auto loan and just kept everything the way that is was then it would have resulted in my mother paying hundreds in interest. It would have been more difficult for the credit scores to increase due to the fact the balance on the auto loan was decreasing very little every month, and it would taken more time to fully pay off the car. In the financial situation of my mother, transferring the car balance to the credit card was beneficial. However, it would not have been beneficial if my mother and I had a history of defaulting on loans; because had we transferred the car balance to the credit card and been late. Orlando Federal Credit Union may have increased the interest rate from 3.99% to anywhere from 29% and above. My mother would have ended up paying the price of three or more cars. For this reason, consumers should not transfer balances if they are likely to default on the loan. Consumers that have defaulted on their loans and have interest rates of 29% or higher should consider doing a balance transfer, to a credit card, which has a low purchase interest rate or a low promotional balance transfer interest rate.

Scenario in which Balance Transfer is Beneficial

For example, Maria defaulted on her World Financial Network National Bank credit card, which now has a penalty annual percentage rate (APR) of 29.95%. Her balance, on that credit card, is $3,113.27. Maria has three other credit cards; to which she could transfer the balance.

American Express credit card
Standard purchase annual percentage rate: 14.24%.
Balance transfer interest rate: No balance transfer option is currently being offered. Credit card issuers are likely to offer balance transfers to consumers, if as a business, they are growing strong.

Wilmington Trust credit card
Standard purchase annual percentage rate: 14.24%.
Balance transfer interest rate: 2.99% for six months and then the standard purchase interest rate will apply, to the transferred balance.

Pulaski Bank credit card
Standard purchase annual percentage rate: 16.24%.
Balance transfer interest rate: 0% for twelve months and then the standard purchase interest rate will apply to the transferred balance.

Depending upon how much Maria can pay towards the credit card every month; she should transfer the balance from the World Financial Network National Bank credit card to the Wilmington Trust credit card. She will save the most money, on interest, compared to how much interest she would pay; if she transferred the balance of the World Financial Network National Bank credit card, to the Pulaski Bank or Wilmington Trust credit cards. If Maria is confident she can pay off the credit card, in twelve months, and then she should transfer the balance of the World Financial Network National Bank credit card to the Pulaski Bank credit card.

She needs to be very careful when making this decision. It is possible Pulaski Bank or Wilmington Trust may deny her the balance transfers, if her credit history is poor. In this situation, she should try and transfer the balance of the World Financial Network National Bank credit card to any credit card she has; that will approve the balance transfer because usually, any standard percentage rate will be better than a 29% or higher default interest rate.

Limitations of Balance Transfers

Consumers cannot do balance transfers between credit cards issued by the same financial institution. Financial institutions make more profit when the consumer uses their credit card to bring over the debt from another company, rather than bring over the debt from another credit card issued by the same financial institution.

Example
Ebony has two credit cards with Amalgamated Bank of Chicago (ABOC). She has an ABOC MasterCard and ABOC Visa card.

ABOC MasterCard
Balance: $459.59
Interest rate: 15.24%

ABOC Visa card
Balance: $0
Interest rate: 10.24%

It makes sense for Ebony to transfer the balance, from her ABOC MasterCard to her ABOC Visa card; because the interest rate is cheaper, she will be able to pay off the balance faster. A cheaper interest rate means lower monthly minimum payment requirements; compared to the minimum payments she would pay on the ABOC MasterCard, and as a result, the credit scores of Ebony will increase faster because she will be debt free faster. Unfortunately, Ebony cannot transfer the balance from the MasterCard to the Visa card because the bank will not allow her to do so. They would rather Ebony use her ABOC MasterCard and Visa credit cards and bring over the balance to them that she has with another financial institution. Ebony has an American Express credit card with a balance of $2,493 and so ABOC would like it if Ebony transferred the balance from her American Express credit card to her ABOC MasterCard or Visa credit card. This is because as a business, ABOC will make more profit off of Ebony. They can charge her interest on the $2,493 balance and usually, when a balance transfer is done, the financial institution that is going to receive the debt; will send a check or electronic payment to the other financial institution with whom the debt is currently being held. In the situation of Ebony, ABOC will send a check to American Express, for the $2,493 debt, and when American Express cashes the check then ABOC makes additional profit. This is because American Express will have to pay a fee to cash the check; or process the electronic payment. ABOC collects this fee.

Denial of Credit Card and No Balance Transfer

For consumers that apply for a new credit card, because they want to do a balance transfer; they may get denied due to the fact, they have excessive debt. Usually, debt is considered excessive when more than 35% of the income of the consumer is going towards paying it off. This is making it difficult for them to save money; and be able to do anything more in life, than pay their debts. For this reason, the financial institutions may think the consumer is more likely to give up on paying their debts; and they are not going to want to grant the consumer a new credit card. Financial institutions do not know if the consumer will create new debt with the credit card or transfer a balance to it; and they cannot assume anything. For this reason, it is recommended when consumers apply for a credit card with the intention of doing a balance transfer, they should apply over the phone, so the representative of the financial institution can make a note on the application; stating the applicant that wishes to do a balance transfer, from one of their current credit cards; that has a balance. If they mail in a credit application, which is not recommended; due to the fact the mail can get lost, they should include a letter indicating they wish to do a balance transfer. Some online credit card applications may have an option to indicate the consumer wishes to do a balance transfer. In some way, consumers need to inform the financial institution that they wish to do a balance transfer, because they will lower the chances that the credit analyst of the financial institution will deny them for a new credit card. The financial institution will appreciate the fact that the consumer has integrity and is trying to pay off their debt.

If the consumer is still denied for the credit card after applying for it then they need to immediately send a letter similar or exactly like the one below to the financial institution asking for reconsideration.

Bank name:
Attention: Executive department
Corporate office address (consumers can find this information by doing a Google.com search) or the address from which the denial letter was received:
Date:

Application identification number or social security number:
Address of consumer that was on the credit application:

To Whom It May Concern:

I applied for a <u>Bank of America World Points credit card</u> (mention loan product name) on <u>October 14, 2010</u> (date on which the consumer had applied for the credit card) to take advantage of the <u>0% for twelve months balance transfer option</u> (indicate the reason why the consumer is applying for the credit card). I was denied for the credit card due to the reason of <u>"high revolving balances on accounts," which is the weakness in my credit profile</u> (indicate the reason for the credit card denial) that I am trying to fix. I have a Wells Fargo credit card on which <u>I am paying 18.24% and a $55 annual fee</u> (indicate the interest rate along with any annual fee on the credit card from which the consumer wishes to transfer the balance onto the new credit card) and I need to transfer its balance immediately so <u>I can save money, pay it off faster, and as a result, get my credit scores to increase due to the fact I will be in less debt</u> (consumers should indicate their financial goals because financial institutions are more likely to help consumers; that want to pay off their debts). For this reason, I was hoping my application could be reconsidered for an approval.

<u>I had accumulated the debt that I have from expenses; I had to pay for while I was in college</u> (consumers may want to explain how their debt was accumulated so the financial institution knows the consumer was not endlessly spending with the intention of never repaying the debt). If my application can be approved then I will submit payments aggressively until the balance is paid off and despite the debt, <u>I am considered creditworthy due to the fact, as reflected by my credit reports, I have never been late on my car loan, mortgage, or any of my 9 credit cards</u> (must establish financial strengths). I would never cheat Bank of America by stopping to pay and if Bank of America feels as though such will happen then <u>please feel free to garnish my wages, put a claim on my house, take me to court, or do anything possible to make up for the loan loss</u> (consumers need to make the financial institution feel confident that they will not have a loan loss). I say this confidently because I know I will never default.

Please approve my application immediately so that I may perform the balance transfer. <u>I am willing to accept a low credit limit</u> (consumers should mention this comment because then the financial institution will know they are not desperate for credit and thus, are less likely to default) and will transfer as much of the balance from the Wells Fargo credit card onto the new Bank of America credit card without going over the credit limit. If you need to contact me then <u>please call me at (407) 496-6005</u> (contact information is always needed).

Thank you for all your help in the matter,
Danny Singh

Pawnshop Loans

No Credit Checks
Consumers need to avoid getting loans from pawnshops offered by pawn brokers, who are considered the loan lenders. Pawnshop secured loans are similar to car title loans because pawn brokers do not check the credit profile of the consumer due to the fact they want the maximum amount of profit and do not want to pay fees to the credit agencies for obtaining credit reports.

Collateral
A consumer must sometimes offer an item worth of high value to the pawn broker. The item serves as the collateral, sometimes called a security deposit, of the loan. The consumer can borrow an amount up to the value of the item. The pawn broker will keep the item in the event that the consumer fails to pay back the loan and they are not at a complete loss. They will usually sell the item for the purpose of making profit.

Excessive Interest
Similar to car title loans, pawnbrokers charge outrageous interest on their loans. They do not report the payment history to the credit agencies, which does not help improve the credit scores of the consumer.

No Credit Data Reporting
Pawnbrokers may over exaggerate that they do report to the credit agencies simply to get the business of the consumer but they may not report any payment history. Consumers have the option of making monthly installment payments or can pay them the full amount at once with interest depending upon the policies of the individual pawn broker.

Cell Phones

Save Money on Cell Phones

Consumers need to be careful when choosing a cell phone provider, because contrary to what some consumers think; the cell phones are not free despite the fact that the phone providers are advertising them as free. They are a way for the cell phone companies to make high profit by charging consumers fees on text messages, going over the minutes, internet charges, playing games, or simply doing anything. Without granting the consumer a cell phone, the cell phone companies cannot charge consumers for anything. When consumers sign a contract then they are given a free cell phone or a very fancy cell phone at a discounted price and consumers are not allowed to cancel the cell phone service within the specified time of the contract, which usually last for two years, otherwise they will be charged a heavy penalty by the cell phone provider.

Consumers Should Not Pay for Phones

Consumers are best off to get the free cell phone, because if the fancy cell phone drops and breaks then the consumers will be out of their money that they paid for that phone. Before getting a cell phone, consumers must establish a strong and positive credit history by getting a credit card, using it lightly, and paying it off immediately, because the cell phone providers check the credit profile of the consumer using their social security number before granting the cell phone or even a regular home phone. They do so because they have no way of knowing whether or not the consumer will use the phone for a month and then when the bill comes, they simply will not pay it. This does happen and as a result, the cell phone companies have business losses. If the consumer has a limited or bad credit profile then the phone companies will ask for a security deposit. Giving a security deposit will make it more difficult for consumers to save money and be successful in paying their other bills in a timely manner. If the consumer does not pay their phone bill then the phone company gets to keep the security deposit money, which is their business purpose behind asking for it. In addition to keeping the security deposit money, the phone company will sell the unpaid debt to a collection agency that will then ruin the credit profile of the consumer. Having a bad or limited credit profile does not influence the monthly price that the consumer will pay towards their phone bill. There are small cell phone companies that cater to consumers with bad credit profiles because their services are limited, meaning consumers may not receive a phone signal in certain areas.

Qualities Sought in a Phone Plan

When consumers seek a cell phone provider, they should look for these features within a plan. The plan should have rollover minutes meaning if a consumer is given 200 minutes a month and they only use 100 minutes then the leftover 100 minutes, which are considered the rollover minutes, should be carried over to the next month; which will give the consumer a total of 300 minutes. A plan that does not have rollover minutes would simply cancel the leftover minutes and as a result, the money of the consumer is wasted. When consumers make monthly payments then they are paying for all the minutes even if they are not all used. Consumers will not get a refund for the unused minutes or a discount on their bill. For the purpose of being able to use the internet, consumers should not get a plan that requires for them to purchase a specific phone such as a smart phone. Some phone providers often charge an extra monthly fee just for carrying a smart phone even if the consumer is not using the internet. Consumers should get a cell phone plan that offers unlimited usage on weekends, and everyday usually after 9 or 10 PM, and unlimited usage when consumers are talking to other consumers that use the same cell phone company. Consumers should ask their employer if they have any business relationships with certain cell phone companies because those cell phone companies may give discounts to employees of businesses with whom they have relations.

SIM Cards save Money

If consumers break their cell phone, by dropping it or getting it wet, they should save the SIM (Subscriber Identity Module) card; which is located inside of the phone, purchase an unlocked pay-as-you-go cell phone at any retail store, and put the SIM card into that phone. The pay-as-you-go phone can be used as a regular phone, the consumer keeps the same phone number, and the consumer saves money because they do not have to purchase a fancy new phone. Consumers are discouraged from purchasing used phones from their friends or random online and physical stores; because there is no guarantee that the phones were kept in good conditions. If the phone breaks then the consumer has a major loss because now, they have to purchase another phone.

Another option for consumers who break their phone is to extend, also called renew, their phone contract with the cell phone company, because in most cases, the cell phone company will grant the consumer a new and free cell phone or a fancy new phone at a discounted price. The cell phone company does this so they can keep the business of the consumer and continue making large profits. Consumers should not extend their phone contract; if they are not pleased with the services of the cell phone company. If for whatever reason someday the consumer cannot afford to make their monthly cell phone payment, then they need to contact the company before becoming late on the account. They need to be honest with the company about not being able to afford their payments, and for this reason they need to cancel the cell phone contract early. Consumers should ask the company to waive or reduce the termination fee for canceling the cell phone contract early. Consumers are better off paying the termination fee rather than always receiving cell phone bills and not paying them because eventually; they will ruin the credit profile of the consumer. This will ruin the chances of the consumer at being able to earn a good job. The cell phone companies will work with the consumer and make arrangements with them to repay the debt, because the cell phone company makes more profit in doing so rather than selling the unpaid cell phone debt to a collection agency. The same rules apply to consumers in the event that they cannot afford to pay any type of utility, credit card, loan or service. Consumers can never simply let the bills come and not pay them. They must negotiate with their companies.

Cell Phone Insurance

Cell phone providers try to convince their customers into purchasing cell phone insurance, meaning if the cell phone gets stolen or broken, the cell phone provider will supply a replacement to the consumer. Agreeing to get cell phone insurance will cause the monthly bill of the consumer to increase by an average of 5 dollars, and as a result the cell phone provider will make more profit off of the consumer. Personally, it is not recommended that consumers purchase cell phone insurance, because at the time they need the replacement phone, they have to pay a deductible fee for using the insurance service to get another phone.

The amount of the deductible may range from $50 to $100 or more, depending upon the policies of the individual cell phone provider. Consumers paying 5 dollars a month is about 60 dollars within a year. For $60 plus the amount that would be paid as a deductible, consumers can purchase a brand new and unlocked phone themselves without needing any insurance. Consumers can find the best deals on phones on www.techbargains.com. Consumers do not need to get a fancy and expensive phone because they automatically get a new phone upon renewing their contract. Another fact about cell phone insurance is that the cell phone provider will usually not provide a brand new phone because it costs them too much money to do so. They will give the consumer a refurbished phone or a phone that is worth much less than the amount of money that the consumer has paid within the year plus the deducible. Therefore, cell phone insurance is a waste of money and this money should be going into a retirement account, paying off a mortgage, or helping children with their college education expenses.

Minors and Credit

Minors Should Not Ignore Bills

Although it is uncommon for minors to be receiving bills, considering most of them do not have a stable source of income, if they are receiving bills with their name; then they must pay for it or ask a parent to pay it, in a timely manner. If the minor did not sign up for the service or purchase the product for which they are being billed; then the minor or parent must contact the company immediately and let them know that fraud has happened.

They should contact the credit agencies as well as the police and freeze the credit profile of the minor. If minors do not have parents or guardians; then they must take up these responsibilities by themselves. They cannot ignore the bills because unpaid bills will <u>always</u> be reported as negative information to the credit agencies. It is possible for a minor to develop a credit report, with only negative information; because they have no positive credit accounts under their name. This can possibly ruin the future of the minor, because they may struggle to get student loans, a professional job, or any type of bank account.

Advice: Bad credit will always follow a consumer for up to ten years, and possibly longer if left unpaid, despite the consumer's age. Bad credit may cost the minor not being able to get a job in the future. For this reason, if the amount owed is small, it might be beneficial for the minor to pay the bill just to be safe while the police and the company are conducting a fraud investigation; unless the company or police request that the bill not be paid. Minors need to be aware that it is possible their parents or other family members may steal their identity and use the information to establish credit. For this reason, minors should be confidential of their information and be open to such possibilities because their family members may hide their shameful actions from the minors.

Be Honest about Financial Mistakes with Children

Some consumers indicate financial institutions took adverse actions against them for no reason at all, such as; increasing their interest rates, repossession, closing the accounts, or garnishing their wages or assets. Such consumers often leave out details regarding the mistakes that they made such as; paying late, not paying at all, building high debts, or doing other dishonorable actions that caused the financial institutions to look at them with increased risk. Financial institutions have to run a successful business. They have their own costs and expenses. They cannot afford to lend to consumers who are very likely to default. Consumers that do not pay their bills must be charged higher fees and interest because it is not fair to the consumers who always pay their bills at all times. If financial institutions do not take adverse actions against high risk consumers then consumers may lose respect for them and not take paying the bills seriously. Financial institutions cannot randomly take adverse actions against any consumer without having legitimate reasons otherwise they run the risk of being sued in court or being investigated and shut down by the Federal Trade Commission and the Office of Contempt Currency. The Federal Trade Commission is a government agency that ensures the consumer-protection laws are maintained by the financial institutions.

Unfortunately, there are consumers who purposely get loans, buy anything, and do everything possible to escape paying back the financial institutions. They often will falsely express that they are in financial struggles, after using all the credit. Such are the consumers that have taken advantage of financial institutions. Although part of the reason why the recession occurred was because financial institutions granted credit to consumers who did not qualify for them, consumers should have still done everything possible to pay back the loans. In most cases, consumers that claim to have financial struggles have ruined themselves by not being faithful in paying all the bills of their past lifetime. The bad credit histories are causing them to get expensive bills such as high interest rate loans and high insurance.

Consumers need to be honest, especially with their children, about any financial mistakes they made, which caused financial institutions to take adverse actions against them. In doing so, their children are less likely to make the same mistakes and ignorantly, ruin their financial futures. As evidence, I would not have learned all the financial concepts that I do had my mother not shared her financial information with me and I would not have had the financial successes that I did. Some children are misled by parents into thinking credit is bad and they should never use it. Credit is only bad when consumers do not pay it and a strong credit history must be established in order to get low interest rates, insurance, and be approved for a house, car, or any service. In some cases, parents who are very secretive about their finances with their children do so because they are hiding the financial mistakes they made—such as bankruptcy, a debt settlement, or late payments, which may cause the children to look at them dishonorably. Consumers with good credit are usually more open about discussing their financial information with others because they do not have dishonorable information to hide.

There are signs that sometimes suggest a consumer has a poor credit history:

Consumers are not depositing their money into deposit accounts and cash their checks, such as their paychecks, at "check cashing stores." Usually, consumers do this because they are worried that financial institutions will seize their funds in the deposit accounts due to the fact that the consumer did not pay their debts or declared a bankruptcy or debt settlement.

Consumers are changing companies that provide their services, such as their television provider. Sometimes, consumers change their companies because they are not planning on paying the company with whom they already have a service and so it makes sense for them to switch to another company. For example, Matthew has television service with Dish Network and he watches television for a month. Dish Network sends him the bill. Matthew does not want to pay the bill for his personal reasons. He immediately signs up for new television service with Bright House. Bright House cannot do anything Matthew for not paying his Dish Network bill. Bright House will not even know that Matthew did not pay his Dish Network bill unless Dish Networks converts his bill into a collection account and reports it to the credit agencies. By the time that the Dish Network bill is reported as negative information to the credit agencies, Matthew will have already signed up for the Bright House television service. It usually takes one to two months of being past due before a company converts a bill into a collection account.

Consumers are paying 29% or more on their credit cards. This means they have been late by sixty days or more on the credit account and now, they have to pay the penalty annual percentage rate.

The debit or credit cards of the consumer are declining at stores.

Financial institutions are always calling for the consumer and the consumer is purposely not answering the calls or changing their phone numbers, and as a result, financial institutions are calling family members, employers, or roommates seeking the consumer with the likely reason that the consumer has not paid on their loan or credit card. For this reason, consumers will change their phone number on purpose to avoid getting calls from the creditors because they have no intention of paying.

The bank repossesses an item such as a car.

The consumer often does **layaway**. Layaway is when the consumer has the merchant hold the item that they want and makes a down payment. The consumer is expected to make weekly or monthly payments on the item until it is paid in full, and then the consumer can officially take possession of the item. Some stores charge fees for their layaway programs and it makes no sense why a consumer would pay for layaway. Layaway can suggest that the consumer has no access to any credit and this raises the question why they do not. In most cases, not all, it is because they have not been faithful in paying their bills. Layaway does not benefit consumers because it does not report their payment history to the credit agencies.

The consumer is always purchasing used items such as televisions, cars, furniture, and houses because usually companies that specialize in granting products and service to consumers with bad or no credit, grant them products that are used or defective. This is because the company does not want to spend a great deal of money buying new products and lending them to consumers with bad credit who are unlikely to pay back the company. The company wants to make as much profit as possible for the purpose of offsetting the potential of risk.

The consumer often sells their items, such as; at pawn shops or garage sales. If consumers are in great need for money then it suggests they are incapable of paying their bills.

The services of the consumer are being canceled by the providers—such as if the phone, water, or electricity gets disconnected.

The consumer is always making excuses as to why they are paying late on their bills or not paying at all.

The consumer has little or no value for the items they purchase. For example, it would be considered unusual for a consumer to throw away a $3000 television they purchased or not bother getting it fixed when it became defective. This is likely because the consumer used a credit card to purchase it and is not planning on paying it. The consumer may include the credit card debt as part of a bankruptcy or debt settlement.

The consumer is struggling to get a professional job. The employer may be denying the consumer a job due to their bad credit profile.

The consumer is borrowing money from others. It is likely they have little or no access to credit otherwise they would not be borrowing money from other consumers.

Checks written by the consumer are bouncing, which means there was not enough money in the checking account to cover the expenses or the bill amounts.

The companies that the consumer is doing business with are known for catering to consumers with bad credit. The consumer has bad credit, which is why they are doing business with them and not a cheaper and more ethical company because such companies would require that a consumer has good credit.

Collection notices are being received in the mail.

The consumer cannot afford to purchase items that in financial relation to their income should be very inexpensive. It would be considered unusual for a consumer that makes a $100,000 annual income to not be able to afford a $15 DVD movie.

The consumer is stressed about their finances. A consumer usually stresses when they have defaulted on one or more of their bills and as a result, their other bills have become more expensive.

The consumer is saying they think it is meaningless to pay the bills and is not bothered by late payments.

The consumer is still struggling to pay the bills even after getting a new job or paying off a loan.

The consumer needs a cosigner in order to get approved for a credit card, apartment, or house.

The consumer is reluctant to apply for new credit or cosign for their children.

The credit applications of the consumer are being declined such as if the consumer applies for a store credit card at the store counter.

The consumer is purchasing items that are highly expensive using a credit card and they are not showing any concern about trying to find cheaper deals. It raises the question whether the consumer is planning on paying the credit card or not. For example, it would be considered unusual if a consumer wanted to stay at a hotel for a week that charged $400 a day. This raises the question why a consumer would not try and find a hotel that has a better daily rate.

Consumers are always being charged late fees.

Consumers that are always being charged returned check fees may be a sign that their credit profile is bad. This is because, unfortunately, some consumers with the intention to declare a bankruptcy, debt settlement, or ultimately, not pay at all, purposely pay the minimum payments on credit cards with checking accounts that do not have sufficient funds. This allows for the credit card to work for more purchasing power because the credit cards issuers do not immediately know that there are not enough funds in the checking account. When the consumer submits the payment, the credit card issuer processes the payment which takes three to five days, considers the credit account paid for the current month, and assumes there are enough funds. For this reason, they do not block the credit card. Later, the payment will come back returned to the credit card issuer after the issuer of the checking account rejects the payment. It is likely by the time that the payment is returned; the consumer has already used the credit card for more purchases. The financial institution will impose the returned payment fee along with the amount returned on the credit account, which will then both accumulate interest. Unfortunately, financial institutions do not always block the credit cards when returned payments happen. It is possible for a consumer to always have returned payments and when the credit card is completely maxed out then they will stop paying on it.

The consumer is never using a credit card. A credit card is a sign of financial success because it shows that a consumer handles their bills with honor and is responsible.

The consumer is living in an apartment. Some consumers are forced to live in apartments because they cannot get approved for a house loan or condominium loan. If a consumer cannot get approved for an apartment then it often suggests their credit is greatly poor. Consumers do not need loans for apartments. They submit a monthly payment to the apartment company. However, there is no guarantee that the consumer is going to send in the monthly payments and just not permanently leave the apartment without paying. For this reason, apartment companies must check credit.

Consumers that are stealing money or products sometimes sends the message that they have bad credit because if they are low enough to steal then it is likely they are low enough to not pay their bills.

Consumers are paying higher than average interest because insurance providers check credit, which helps determine the premium price.

Consumers that leave other consumers such as their spouses with all the bills can suggest that they have bad credit because it they are low enough to not share in the responsibilities then they are low enough to not pay their own bills.

Consumers cause other consumers to develop bad credit by not paying their bills such as on joint accounts.

Consumers are applying for credit under the names of other consumers. This means the consumer has bad credit otherwise it raises the question why they would be applying for credit using the credit profile of another consumer. If the intention is simply to make another consumer liable for all the charges then this bad intention may suggest that the consumer has bad credit because they have bad morals.

Consumers are always using prepaid debit cards, which have fees, may imply that they have bad credit because it raises the question why they could not get a free checking account with a free debit card at a credit union or bank. It is likely these consumers were denied a checking account because of negative information showing on their credit reports and/or ChexSystems reports.

Parents Abusing the Credit Profiles of their Children

There are an increasing number of cases in which parents are using the credit profiles, of their underage children to get services and products, by misrepresenting information on credit applications about the date of birth. Later, the consumers will leave the children, with all the bills. Finally, there are cases in which consumers that attend college will use the credit cards to pay for all the tuition, books, and other miscellaneous expenses. They will only make the minimum payments so the credit card continues working. When the student earns the college degree then they will declare a bankruptcy or debt settlement so they do not have to pay the credit card.

Employers often deny jobs to consumers with bad credit; because in their eyes, if a consumer is low enough to not pay their loans then they are low enough to do anything that could damage the reputation of a company. Consumers with bad credit may not have been motivated to pay the bills. This can sometimes make employers think that consumers will not be motivated to do their job with the best of their abilities and may become careless, which will result in a financial loss for the company. A company does not want to pay money for the training of candidates that are unlikely to bring success to the company.

Credit Card offers sent to Minors = Sign of Danger

Sometimes, when consumers are receiving credit card offers with decent interest rates and no annual fees unless there is an aggressive rewards program then this may be a sign that a consumer has good credit. In contrast, if consumers are not receiving credit cards offers then it may be a sign that they have bad credit. This can support why some credit card offers say "preapproved," which means the consumer passed the initial credit checks and is likely to be approved for the credit card if they accept the offer.

Consumers should try and avoid offers that say "prequalified" because this means the business needs to get more information before determining whether to approve or deny the consumer. Businesses are less likely to send decent credit card offers to consumers with poor or limited credit. Innovis, Equifax, Experian, and TransUnion share credit related information with financial institutions, and they use the information to send credit card offers to consumers often with good credit histories. Targeting consumers to send credit card, insurance, and other financial product offers is known as **prescreening**. The credit card offers consumers receive will usually say **"prescreened offers."** Underneath the "hard credit inquiries" section of all credit reports, consumers will see the "soft credit inquiries" section. The soft inquiries do not affect the credit score or credit report in any manner and can only be seen by the consumer. Soft inquiries are performed by financial institutions when credit bureaus share credit related information of consumers with them. It is likely when consumers sign up and are approved for credit card offers they receive in the mail, internet, or through telemarketing calls, that credit bureaus may be paid a commission by the financial institution. In fact, the credit bureaus will get paid even more money because the financial institutions will pay them fees when they perform hard inquiry credit checks on consumers who officially apply for the credit accounts. As the financial institution opens credit cards and other loans for consumers, the credit agencies hope to continue growing as a business along with the financial institutions.

Opt-out of Receiving Offers

Consumers have the right to "opt-out" of receiving credit card offers and block their credit profiles from being seen by outside parties other than employers and the financial institutions where they apply for credit. If minors, usually individuals under 18, are receiving credit card offers, then this is a dangerous sign that credit may have been established under their name and their information has been compromised by an identity thief. In this scenario, the parent or guardian must contact the credit agencies immediately, make sure no accounts were established, freeze the minor's credit reports, and place a fraud victim statement on each report. The credit agencies may request that a police report be submitted.

The only scenario in which it is possible for minors to receive credit card offers is when they are authorized or joint users on the accounts of family members, as permitted by the financial institutions. This is because when any individual is added as a joint or authorized user, some financial institutions will report this activity to the credit reports of the new individual. The financial institutions will also report the payment histories of the accounts, which may negatively or positively affect the credit reports of the new individual depending upon how much debt is being carried on the accounts and if their account holders have ever been late making payments on the accounts.

The credit agencies will share the credit related information of the authorized user with potential creditors that may want to get into business with the particular consumer. For this reason, they will send credit card offers. When my mother added me to all her credit card accounts as an authorized user, credit reports and scores were established under my name and I was benefiting from all the positive history on the credit accounts. Despite being a child, I received pre-approved credit card offers in the mail, and still do because of the excellent credit history. For consumers who are trying to build their credit, they should save the credit card offers, compare the interest rates, fees, rewards programs, and choose the offer that is the cheapest. Consumers are more likely to be approved by the financial institutions that are sending them credit card offers than they are to be approved by other financial institutions.

Consumers should not apply for multiple credit cards or loans at the same time because applying for credit aggressively hurts the credit profile. If consumers want to receive credit card and insurance offers then they should "opt-in." If consumers do not want to receive offers then they should "opt-out." Opting-in and opting-out can be done on this website: https://www.optoutprescreen.com. This does not influence the credit profiles in any way. Consumers who opt-in need to be careful that they shred the offers they reject because those offers may have some of the personal information regarding the consumer. Another option for consumers who want to opt-out is to call the opt-out phone number maintained by all the credit agencies. The number is 1-888-567-8688. According to the Federal Trade Commission, consumers can write letters to the addresses of the credit agencies below explaining that they want to opt-out.

Experian
Opt Out
P.O. Box 919
Allen, TX 75013

TransUnion
Name Removal Option
P.O. Box 505
Woodlyn, PA 19094

Equifax, Inc.
Options
P.O. Box 740123
Atlanta, GA 30374-0123

Innovis Consumer Assistance
P.O. Box 495
Pittsburgh, PA 15230-0495

High School and College Students Finances

Due to the rough economic times and the increasing number of students attending colleges, the costs of getting an education are increasing exponentially and globally. There is an increasing volume of students that are defaulting on their student loans, credit cards, and developing bad credit. Students are struggling to find jobs due to their damaged credit and the fees as well as interest on the loans are causing the balances to double and in some cases, triple. It is likely that student loans will become the next housing crisis in America.

For such reasons, students should try avoiding taking regular and prerequisite classes such Pre-AP or Pre-IB courses and take as many; Advanced Placement (AP), International Baccalaureate (IB), and other college credit courses as possible, while in high school. Although these courses will be challenging, the students will appreciate them more when they graduate, because if they pass the exams and score; a three or higher on the AP exams, a three or higher on the IB standard level exams, or a four or higher on the IB higher level exams, then it is unlikely they will have to take those courses in college. This means the students will be able to save thousands in paying tuition, student loan and credit card debt, and have more money for the classes that they do need in order to earn their college degree. Another choice a high school student has to get the maximum amount of college work done early and for a cheap price is to become a **dual-enrolled student**. Many high schools are now allowing for their students to attend an accredited community or state college to earn both high school and college credit for taking certain college courses such as Oral Communications. These courses will fulfill the general education requirements that are needed to earn a college degree and as a result, a student can earn their degree must faster and enter the workforce. High school students may have extra financial incentives for being dual-enrolled students such as getting a big discount on the tuition they would pay for taking the college courses. For this reason, high school students should check with their guidance counselor about becoming a dual-enrolled student and what financial incentives a student would receive, if any, for becoming one. High school students may need to have a certain grade point average in order for the high school to allow for them to become a dual-enrolled student. This is because low grades suggest the high school students are very likely to fail the college courses and the high school does not want such students becoming dual-enrolled students.

All consumers that graduate from high school should make the decision to earn a college degree despite their fears of getting into debt. It is the best financial investment a consumer can make and it is the only investment that has no risks but endless returns. In an economy, in which the majority of consumers have a well-rounded and advanced education then it is more likely that the highest levels of productivity will be achieved and sustained. In most cases, a college degree suggests the education level of a consumer. Without a college degree, it is not recommended that consumers start a business or become self-employed because it is common for consumers to use their credit cards and loans in order to expand upon their businesses. If the business fails then the consumers will have no source of income to pay their credit cards and loans and as a result, their credit profiles will become damaged and the financial institutions may take drastic actions against them. With a college degree, if the business fails, then the consumer will have better chances at being able to get a job and using the money that they earn to pay off their credit card and loan debts that were accumulated from the expanding of the business. Consumers are also discouraged to do "work-at-home" jobs until they earn their college degree because they usually require for the consumer to pay program fees and consumers will usually use their credit card to pay the fees. There is no guarantee how much, if any, income the consumer will be able to make from the job. If they make no or very little income then with the college degree, they have a higher chance at being able to get a job so they can pay off their credit cards and their credit profile is protected. The research of Careerbuilder.com and Monster.com shows in most cases that students who earn a four year degree or higher have better chances at earning higher than average paying jobs compared to students without any college work done. This is because employers will respect the fact that the students remained motivated to pursue higher education and they will think that the students are more likely to have a high level of motivation in successfully doing their job tasks. The employer may also think the education that the student absorbed while in college will help them better understand the concepts needed to do their job tasks and will be less likely to struggle and quit their job. This will result in a financial loss for the employer because employers spend money training their employees, which is why some employers require for a contract from their employees before hiring them. The contract will usually specify how long an employee must work for an employer.

They should attend a community or state college for their undergraduate years, which are primarily the freshmen and sophomore years. This is because almost all community and state colleges will accept the IB and AP credits whereas public and private universities may not accept them because they may not consider those credits to be college worthy. Even if a student did no college credit courses while in high school, a community or state college is still the best financial option for them.

There have been controversies that public and private universities do not accept the IB and AP credits because they want to make more profits off of the students. Public and private universities wanting to make profit is supported by controversies that they sometimes reject and accept students for reasons that are not related to their academic profiles but their residency, how many classes they would likely need to take at the university, and how much financial aid they have or how much they are likely to be granted. Public and private universities are going to make more profits off of out-of-state students that will pay out-of-state tuition than they are off of in-state students that will pay in-state tuition. Out-of-state tuition is always more expensive than in-state tuition. Students that have done very little or no college credit courses at their previous schools mean they will need to take many classes at the university, which means more money for them. Some university applications ask for how much financial aid a student has and how much income the student or their parents make, tax, or other financial-related information. None of such information has anything to do with the academic profile of the student and it raises the question why the university applications ask for such information. It makes sense for a financial aid office to ask for such information after a student has been admitted into the university. Finally, most university applications ask for an application fee just for reviewing the application. Reviewing an application does not require much labor or costs the university much money considering the students usually have to pay extra fees to their high school for sending their transcripts to the college. Considering a university makes so much profit off of the tuition costs of the student then it raises the question why they want extra fees from the student for doing trivial tasks. When candidates are seeking jobs and they submit their applications to employers, employers do not charge fees for job applications because the employees are going to contribute to the success of the company. Similarly, universities should not charge fees to students for submitting applications because the students are going to bring success to the university. Some universities claim the reason why they charge fees is because they get many applications and their time is valuable.

Employers also get many applications, their time is valuable, but they still do not charge fees. In fact, employers have to pay fees when reviewing applications to check the background and credit profile of the consumer and they do not compensate this from the candidate.

College Degree is never a Hole of Debt

It makes no sense for a student to attend a public or private university for their undergraduate years, build up large student loan and credit card debt, and then later be more likely in defaulting on that debt because large debts with high interest rates mean high minimum payments. If students do not make the full minimum payments then their loans will become delinquent. Bad credit will defeat the purpose of earning a college degree because the students will look bad in the eyes of the employer. The bad credit will cause the college degree of the student to lose credibility and the employer will not think of the student being as skilled as the degree may suggest to someone.

Along with the acceptance of the college credits, a community or state college will allow for a student to save more money for other expenses because they are less focused on making profits off of the students due to the fact they receive financial support from the government. This is supported by the evidence that not all state and community colleges charge college application fees and the ones that do, the average amounts are usually smaller than the application fees wanted by private and public universities. Students will have money to save in deposit and investment accounts, which will accumulate interest and can possibly be used for graduate school. Community and state colleges allow for better student and teacher interactions because their student-teacher ratios, which are the average number of students a teacher has per classroom, are usually smaller compared to the student-teacher ratios of most universities. Unlike university students; community and state college students are not placed into lecture halls with numerous other students and their professors, who do not know the names of all the students, academic strengths and weaknesses of the students, or notice that almost half of the students are sleeping in class, due to the fact they have lost interest in the subject or they do not understand any of the concepts.

Community and state college classes allow for better learning of the subject material and more academic success. Community and state college professors are not being paid for research and this makes them more likely to focus on teaching and helping the students. In contrast, there is controversy that some of the professors of public and private universities are more focused on conducting research regarding the subject that they teach and publishing their findings than they are in teaching and helping students. They get paid by colleges for doing research because it is hoped their research findings will bring a good reputation to the college so more students attend and they can make more money off of them. For this reason, some professors may have their research assistant students teach the course material in class. There is no guarantee that the research assistants are familiar with the concepts that they are teaching to the class and whether or not if the information being taught is correct. There is also no guarantee that the research findings of the professor has any significance or would contribute to society and that they are not doing it simply to get paid by the college. Such professors make it less likely that students will learn and fully understand all the course material. The quality of the education depends on the quality level of the professor. Many professors who teach at public or private universities also teach at a state or community college and so the education quality is not different. There is no guarantee if the public and private universities are as academically prestigious at they claim to be as justification for their tuition fees being so high. This is because there have been cases in which students graduated from college and did not learn all the course material. Potential employers will notice their ignorance when they try applying the skills that they were expected to learn to their job tasks. It is possible the employers may dismiss them from their jobs.

Another major difference between community and state colleges, with respect to traditional colleges, is in traditional colleges, part of the tuition paid by students support sports teams; such as the football teams. Community and state colleges do not have many sports teams and for this reason, they can offer cheaper tuition to students. Having little or no sports teams does not mean the education quality of a community or state college is weak. The likelihood of a student failing, at a community or state college, is less than at a traditional college, because unfortunately, some students focus solely on doing well in sports teams and become careless in regards to maintaining high academic marks.

Some students think attending a community or state college is disgraceful because such colleges do not have strict academic requirements, as traditional colleges do, about offering admission to students. There is a myth that students who could not get accepted into a traditional college must attend a community or state college. This is not true because some students attend a community or state college because they want to save money, they want to be in small classes, they do not want professors that are doing research, or they want to live near their families.

As proof, I was offered admission to Stetson University, Warner University, Florida Southern College, but I chose to attend Seminole State College because I wanted to stay close to my family and save money. It may be true that community and state colleges are not strict about offering admission, but it does not mean the students who attend them are uneducated or in general, have bad qualities about them. If anything, such students may be more motivated, than students who attend a traditional college, to get the best education possible and they want to defy all the odds to do so.

Motivation is what makes a student academically strong. A student can attend the most prestigious traditional college there is; but it does not mean they will be a success, because some students lose their motivation while in college and end up dropping out. My classmates, that attend Seminole State College of Florida with me, are some of the most brilliant students I have ever had the honor of meeting. Community and state college students will not have the burden of repaying, thousands of dollars in student loan debt, as will traditional college students.

I have been told, by some students that they choose to attend a traditional college, for the express purpose of connecting to the alumnae (female graduates) and alumnus (male graduates) for their all their undergraduate years, with the hopes of getting good jobs. There is no guarantee a student is going to be able to make such connections; or if the connections are even good. As evidence, some students, even after making social connections with previous graduates, still struggle to find a job after graduating. Connections do not guarantee they are going to be granted a job, because employers still look at the credit profile and background report of the candidate. The alumnus and alumni are not going to help the students repay their student loan debt. Paying thousands of dollars of tuition for connections with graduates is still meaningless, because students can make the same connections with the professors, alumnus, and alumni at the community or state college especially when they join clubs and organizations. If anything, students have a greater a chance of making connections to good employers, at a community or state college, than they do at a traditional college because due to the fact community and state college professors give individualized attention to students in the classroom. They can often see the interests and strengths of the individual students. Many professors have worked for advanced companies and facilities or may have family members that are currently working for well known companies. They may mention employment opportunities to students or students could ask their professors for opportunities whereas in a traditional college, it may be difficult to talk to professors and for professors to know each of their students due to the fact the professors are so busy with research and handling so many students at once.

To some extent, students that are attending a public or private university during their undergraduate years are wasting their money. When students pay tuition, they expect to get a high quality education that will potentially help them in the workforce. A high quality education does not involve; getting professors who are concerned about doing research, being taught by inexperienced research assistant students, being placed into lecture halls where students can barely listen to their professor, or going to a school that only wants to make profits off of the students or use their tuition money to support sports teams. For this reason, doing as many classes as possible from an accredited community or state college and then transferring to a public or private university is the best financial decision a student can make in their academic career. They will get the most value for their money.

Many community and state colleges are now offering junior and senior level courses, as well as bachelor's degree programs. If the program relates to what the student wants to do for a career; then it is the best financial decision for a student to do the bachelor's degree at the community or state college and save much money for graduate school. If desired the student can transfer their junior and senior level bachelor's degree courses to the public or private university that the student wishes to attend and earn the bachelor's degree from that university. The student can even become a **transient student**, and take whatever courses they need at the university and the community or state college. They will specify on the transient student application, from which educational facility they wish to earn the degree, and that educational facility will accept the credits as long as they are being done at an accredited school.

As an example, Seminole State College offers five bachelor's degree programs, which are business information management, interior design, architectural engineering technology, construction, and information systems technology. Although my major is finance, some of the courses required for the Finance major; are needed for the business information management major. At Seminole State, I am saving money to attend an Ivy League school, by taking the junior and senior level business information management courses. I will also become a transient student and take any junior and senior level courses that are not offered by Seminole State for a Finance major at the University of Central Florida. I will earn a bachelor's degree in business information management, from Seminole State, a bachelor's degree in financial management from UCF, and then I will transfer into an Ivy League school. The Ivy League school will honor the two bachelor's degrees and I will be able to earn a master's degree and doctoral degree in business administration. The bachelor's degree programs of community and state colleges are the solution to the looming student loan crisis, which has now hit 1 trillion dollars of debt and is still growing.

As support, ABC News reports the bachelor's degree programs at state and community colleges are about $400 less than annual in-state tuition at public universities. Taking into consideration student loan interest that ranges anywhere from about 5% to almost 7%, students possibly dropping out of classes or failing them, and all the other bills students have to pay such as rent, car insurance, gas for their car, car payments, credit cards, health insurance, utilities, books, and food. A savings of $400 a year is huge.

Some students worry that a community or state college degree may send the message to the employer that they could not get accepted into a regular public or private university. This is a common myth. If during an interview, employers were to question students about why they attended a community or state college; then students can respond by indicating they were always academically strong. They attended a community or state college because they were saving up money to attend a more advanced school and did not want to get into massive student loan debt and develop the chance of defaulting on it. Such a mature response will likely impress an employer, because they will respect the candidate more and it will add credibility to their college degrees. The employer will like the fact the student earned a graduate school degree because it suggests that the student has a great interest in the career subject, is motivated, and will be more likely to bring success to the company. However, it is unlikely an employer would question a student about going to a community or state college. After earning the bachelor's degree, students are encouraged to enter graduate school. According to www.Simplyhired.com, the average annual salary for college graduate students is $46,000.

Students are also encouraged to join the Honors programs at all the colleges and universities they attend; Honors programs often offer extra financial incentives to students, such as scholarships. As personal experience, I am part of the Art & Phyllis Grindle Honors Institute, at Seminole State College of Florida. Any Honors student who earns an A or B in an Honors class; gets a $150 scholarship return on each three credit class; for this reason, as of now, I have taken and passed five three credit Honors classes and earned back $750, which I have applied as payments towards my car insurance. I am planning on taking more Honors classes with the intention of saving more money.

Due to the fact the Honors programs offer more challenging curriculums; they offer students better chances at getting better paying jobs, because some employers ask for transcripts from candidates and the college degrees will usually indicate that the student successfully completed an Honors program. It sends a red flag to employers, if students have only taken regular courses. Honors programs offer smaller class sizes, which offers better communication between the professors and students. Such is especially useful for public universities; considering they have hundreds of students in some regular classes. Finally, they offer higher chances of transfer acceptance into higher ranking universities with potential scholarship opportunities.

The only financial scenario in which a student should consider attending a college or university, other than a community or state college, is if they are offered a scholarship that pays for most or all of the tuition. If the scholarship does not pay for all the tuition then students should compare how much they would have to pay for tuition, in attending that particular school, verses how much they would pay attending a community or state college possibility without any scholarship. They need to take into consideration; how long the scholarship lasts and depending upon the location of the college, the costs of moving out of state, because in some financial scenarios, the living costs will overpower the scholarship amounts. If the costs of attending a community or state college are the same for the student as going to a regular state or private university with some type of scholarship that lasts for all four undergraduate years, then the student should consider attending the regular college because it would not be wise for them to lose the scholarship. If the scholarship only lasts for two years then the student should consider attending the community or state college, because there will be better interactions between students and professors. The professors can write strong recommendations for the students; when they seek jobs and paid internships. Internships often turn into permanent jobs. Students will not have to worry about getting a job after graduating from college. They will be able to immediately start making large payments on their student loans and credit cards, which will lead to excellent credit and high chances of getting approved for a house and car. In fact, some intern employers may offer to pay for the college education expenses of their employees.

It is recommended any university or college a student attends; should be within their state of residency. This is because students can then pay in-state tuition, which in most cases, not all, are cheaper than the tuition they would pay to attend a private or out-of-state college or university. Colleges, at which the students can pay in-state tuition, give them special financial incentives because portions of the property taxes of their in-state properties help support the educational facilities, within the state of residency. They pass on these savings to the students. Private universities are usually more expensive than public universities and have the same tuition for both in-state and out-of-state students, because they receive little or no financial support from the government and little or no financial support from property taxes. In fact, for such reasons, they are stricter about accepting college credits, a student earned while in high school compared to community, state, or regular public universities.

Students that want to work immediately after getting some college credit are encouraged to earn at least a bachelor's degree and not get out of school until then. This is because considering the amount of tuition a student spends on their associate's degree alone, the average annual income they will be able to possibly make with that degree is $36,000 as reported by the National Center for Education Statistics. Taking into consideration that rough economic times are causing the overall expenses of consumers to increase such as with raising children, house loans, utilities, car maintenance expenses, insurance, credit cards, and any remaining student loan debt, $36,000 is not sufficient income to live a stress free life. Such income will make it less likely that the students will be proud of themselves for attending college and more likely that they will live a life of regret. Students should not wait until they are in their 30s or older to make the decision to go back to college to get their bachelor's degree. This is because in most cases, as consumers get older then their expenses increase especially when they have children and this makes it harder to pay college tuition and stay focused in the classrooms, which increases the likelihood of failing a class and the money for that class is therefore wasted. The bad grades may cause the student to lose any academic based financial aid. Some educational facilities may even require for students to pay out-of-state tuition to retake the failed classes. It may send a bad message to employers as to why it took a student so long to go back to college and if the student values education. They may think a student stopped with their associate's degree because they were not motivated to continue and could not handle the college work. In the eyes of the employer, this will raise the question that if a student could not handle the coursework while in college then what guarantee is there that they will be able to handle the tasks required by the job and be successful. This can support why it is more difficult for students who drop out of high school to get professional jobs. For this reasons, students should get their bachelors degree in their youngest years of life. As reported by the National Center for Education Statistics, the average annual income level of a consumer with a bachelor's degree is twice the amount that could be made by a consumer without a college degree. Consumers without college degrees are estimated to make an average $30,000 annual income and so it can be suggested that a consumer with a bachelor's degree could potential make a $60,000 or more annual income. Such an income will make it more likely a consumer will be able to live a stress free and healthy lifestyle. For this reason, it is <u>strongly</u> encouraged students accept the student loan to get a bachelor's degree or higher.

If students only want to do some college credit and get a certificate, specialized diploma, or associate's degree then they should always do research and contact all community and state colleges around their area to find out which one offers their desired program. They should attend the school that offers their program and is closest to their house location so their chances of being late to class are less and they are able to save money on gas.

If possible, they should always try to avoid technical, trade, vocational, for-profit, online, adult education, and career schools because in most cases, not all, these non-traditional schools over exaggerate about being accredited in anyway. These schools do not make the students take many prerequisite, general educations, or necessary core classes needed to fulfill the general education requirements of the state because these schools promise students that they can get their education quickly done with the business intention of attracting them and making profits. When the employer asks for a college transcript from the student then the employer will likely not respect that the student did not take a challenging curriculum and will think that the student will be unsuccessful in doing the job. Some employers also think that students who attended technical, trade, vocational, for-profit, online, adult education, and career schools did not earn their degree. Rather, the school granted them the degree because they were being paid so much money in tuition. In a sense, the school sold the degree to the student as a piece of merchandise. As a result of being denied jobs, the tuition that the student paid and any scholarships that may have been used will go to waste. Even if a student were to attend one of the schools and transfer into a top ranked college or university. The employer would still look and verify all the academic history of the student potentially using a website called <u>www.studentclearinghouse.org</u>. Getting a degree from a non-accredited educational institution or an educational institution with a bad reputation is a reason why many consumers are now struggling to get jobs.

Many of the non-traditional school types have numerous complaints against them if a consumer were to do an internet search using the school name. Due to fact most of these schools receive little or no financial support or regulations from the government, it is unsure if the schools are being ethical towards students when charging tuition. The tuition demanded is outrageously expensive compared to the tuition amounts of community, state, and in some cases, also private and public universities. Often admissions representatives call students and mail advertisements to get them to join the college because they get paid a commission for each student that joins. It makes <u>no sense</u> financially why a student would pay so much tuition considering they can get their education done at a fraction of the cost at a community or state college. Building up excessive debt with student loans or credit cards <u>always</u> has a negative impact on the credit scores and increased chances of denial for a house, apartment, credit card, or car. The average interest rates of student loans are expected to increase near the end of 2012 if not sooner. High debts send the message that the student is likely to default on the loans. An employer may think why a student went to a technical, trade, vocational, for-profit, some online, adult education, or career school because it may send the message they could not get accepted into a state, community, public, or private college. State, community, public, or private colleges can potentially deny admission to students due to their criminal records, past disciplinary problems, or convictions because they use the social security numbers that students provide to conduct background checks. Their systems will notify them of any negative information being found on the records. In contrast, it is likely due to the reason they are making so much profit, technical, trade, vocational, for-profit, online, adult education, or career schools may be more lenient about accepting students with negative background information. Some of these school types may not even conduct a background check because it costs them money to do so and they want to save and make as much money as possible. For this reason, they may not even be concerned about the previous academic records of a student such if they were or are currently on academic probation or if they successfully passed their middle or high school courses. To these schools, a student failing means they will be able to make more profits because the student will have to retake the course. There have been cases in which technical, trade, vocational, for-profit, online, adult education, and career schools shut themselves down, kept the tuition money, and did not compensate the students. As a result, the students had to file for lawsuits. The schools did not award the students any certificate, degree, or just any document that verified what education they completed and the students had nothing they could present to their employers or other colleges. In fact, if the school does present the student with a document that verifies their completion but they later shut down. The employer or college may think the school offered low quality education or was poor in some aspect because they would think why the school shut down. They will not be able to verify the challenge level of the curriculum that the student took because they will be unable to get a transcript from the school. Finally, these schools offer few or no extracurricular programs for students such as clubs because it costs them money. This may serve as a disadvantage for students because employers and other colleges may want to see outside involvement other than just academic work.

**Some of the school type names are used interchangeably and may be synonyms- words that have similar meanings. The definitions will be similar. The major difference is that not all school types offer the same programs.

For example, a technical school may teach office management whereas a trade school may not teach office management but welding.
Technical school: A school that teaches skills to students that they can use in the workforce immediately after graduating from the technical school.

Trade school: A school that specializes in teaching a particular skill that can usually be used in a limited number of workforce industries.

For example, a trade school may teach its students how to change the engine of an automobile. A student would only be able to use this skill in the automotive industry. This student would be unlikely to get a job within an industry that does not relate to the automotive industry because such an industry would have no need for their automotive skill.

Vocational or career school: A school that trains a student on how to do a job task such as the procedures involved. Unlike public and private universities, the vocational school would not teach a student general education or abstract concepts. For this reason, the student is not likely to have a well-rounded education.

For-profit school: Depending upon the policies of the individual schools, they may or may not offer general education courses and specialize in specific fields such as business, medicine, or psychology. They may offer career education to students who want to enter the workforce immediately and for this reason, they will not make them take general education courses. For-profit schools are run by private businesses or individuals who are the directors. There is controversy that the businesses or individuals get overly paid, which is why the tuition prices are so high. Some for-profit schools justify that the reason why their tuition is so high is because they are able to hire higher quality professors and in doing so, they can offer more advanced curriculums for students compared to the curriculums of other universities and colleges. For this reason, the for-profit schools think they can better academically nurture students to succeed. The controversy with this belief is that the success of a student can only come through their level of motivation. Examples of for-profit schools include DeVry University, University of Phoenix, Florida National College, and ITT Tech.

Online schools: Internet courses offered by accredited state, community, public and private universities or colleges are good for students that are parents or work long hour jobs or for students who want to save money on gas, tolls, or earn college credits more quickly. However, students should avoid some online schools because they offer online degrees, which is different than a degree from a traditional college. Some employers and colleges may think online degrees programs do not offer challenging curriculums because there are concepts and skills that students cannot always learn online.

Adult education school: These schools are beneficial for students who dropped out of middle or high school, or foreign students and want to complete their education. Some adult education schools charge outrageous fees for a General Education Diploma (GED) and are not accredited as they claim. For this reason, students may struggle getting a college or employer to accept the GED. Students should try to get their GED from an accredited community or state college. It will be easier for them to transfer into the degree-seeking program of the college.

Job Difficulties

There are an increasing number of cases in which consumers that never earned their college degree are now struggling to find a job. This is causing them to make the decision to go back to school and for this purpose; they choose to get a student loan and get into debt with the hopes they will be able to get a job more easily after earning their college degree. There is controversy whether or not going back to school is the best financial decision, if a consumer cannot find a job. Depending upon how much income a consumer makes and how much debt they owe, it may be beneficial to postpone going back to school and get any job as soon as possible even if it does not relate to their skills or qualifications or it is a short-term job. Earning some income is always better than earning no income.

If more than 35% of their income is going towards bills such as the housing payment, credit cards, utilities, and other miscellaneous expenses then a consumer should use some of the money they have in savings, checking, and any income they are making to pay down the bills for the purpose of protecting their credit, assets, house or apartment, and they are ensuring the bills will not double or triple due to compounded interest and fees. A consumer should cut their credit cards with scissors but not close them because credit account closures, with an exception to installment loans such as car and house loans, lower credit scores. When the consumer reaches the point to which only fifteen to twenty percent of their income is going towards the bills then it may be a wise decision to take classes at a community or state college.

Consumers need to be careful when choosing the class times and dates because they should not take classes at times that are in close time proximity to when they are expected to work. This is because they are at risk of running into stressful situations in which they may be late to work or school. In the case of being late to work then their employer could potentially dismiss them from the job and the consumer will have little or no funds to pay for the educational or living expenses. The employer will not serve as a good reference for the consumer when they try to get a new job. In the case of being late to school then the professor could potentially withdraw the student from class, the student will get an F in the course, they will get no credit for it, their grade point average will be ruined, and the money they paid for the class will go to waste because when a professor withdraws a student then in most cases, they cannot get their money for the class back. They just increased their student loan debt for no reason at all. If a consumer cannot find a class time that suits them then they should be safe and take online courses offered by the community or state college only. It is possible for a consumer to earn all the credits needed for the degree with the online courses. However, students should check with the college that if they were to earn all their credits with online classes then will they still be granted a traditional college degree or will it be an online college degree. Students want to try their best and avoid online degrees because some employers may consider online degrees to be unworthy since the students did not have a hands on experience or the experience of working with others. Online courses of the state or community college are usually the same prices as they are paying for the class to take at campus. If they are not the same price then they are usually in very close price range. Online courses also help save money on gas and in this regard, help reduce the amount of expenses for a consumer considering they have to pay for gas to drive to their job locations.

Consumers with degrees that are struggling to find jobs are due to some of the following reasons. Such are the reasons that the consumers would need to improve upon in order to increase their chances of getting a professional job. There is no guarantee that the employers will reveal the reasons as to why they denied a job to the consumer because they are not legally required to do so. For this reason, the consumer cannot assume that these reasons were not used in judging the credentials of the consumer.

Credit problems: Consumers that have delinquencies or excessive credit check inquiries need to write to the corporate offices of the financial institutions explaining why they were delinquent on the credit accounts and they need to question why the financial institutions performed so many credit checks. Consumers need to request that the delinquencies and credit check inquiries be removed. Consumers also need to dispute the negative information with the credit agencies. There is no guarantee that the negative information will be removed by trying is always better than simply giving up. Bankruptcy or debt settlements cannot be removed unless seven to ten years have passed and for this reason, they must be avoided at all costs. Consumers with derogatory public records need to negotiate with the courts to remove them from their credit profiles. Consumers need to mention that they are willing to do whatever it takes to get the public records removed. They may need to hire an attorney.

Negative background profile: Consumers need to avoid getting into trouble with the law officials because it is possible that the police records are reported by the courts to the background profiles of consumers. Consumers that are struggling to find jobs should check their background profiles to make sure there is no negative information showing. This is because employers may not disclose if the reason that the consumer was denied a job was due to negative information appearing in their background. To get the most accurate background profile report, consumers should order their background report from the Federal Bureau of Investigation (FBI) using their website, which is http://www.fbi.gov/about-us/cjis/background-checks. Consumers also have the option of ordering their background report from their residential state department of law enforcement. If negative information is found then the consumers need to contact the court or agency that reported the negative information and dispute it. If the agency or court does not cooperate then the consumer needs to find a credible attorney. Consumers should always ask attorneys for references because any attorney found in the phone book, internet, radio, or just any means has the potential of scamming the consumer. The consumers will not know this until the scam takes place and the attorney runs off with the money of the consumer. In addition, consumers develop a bad background profile when they post immature pictures of themselves, derogatory comments, or just any explicit information in general on social media websites like Twitter, Yahoo Personals, or especially Face book. Employers have access to this information and they may ask for the passwords to the social media accounts from their job candidates because there is nothing legally from preventing the employers from doing so. If the candidate refuses to furnish this information then it is very likely that the employer will think that the candidate is hiding a piece of information about themselves that could serve as a risk to the company such as for example, if the candidate has affiliations with gangs and is trying to get the position as a banker. There is no guarantee the candidate will not release confidential information about the company to the gang members which may allow from them to rob the company. For this reason, the employer is not going to take a risk and will deny the job to the candidate. It is also possible current employees could be dismissed from their jobs if their social media network accounts have inappropriate information. Other employees may talk about the inappropriate information and the rumors may reach the supervisor of the company.

Low demand for degree or training: Although choosing a career that a consumer would enjoy is important. Consumers also need to take into consideration if they will be able to get a job with the degree program they want to do. This is because it is unlikely a consumer will be proud of themselves for getting their degree or training if they are struggling to find a job and their credit profile is getting ruined because they have no means of paying their bills such as their student loans. Consumers will be upset with themselves and it is likely that they will struggle to survive. They will lose their home, automobile, and simply all their possessions if they cannot make the payments. In fact, consumers will not be able to express their talents that they developed from their career program if they cannot find a job and so getting the training that they did would have been a waste. When choosing a career path, it may be wise for consumers to contact other consumers who have completed the same career path and ask them about their struggles, if any, in finding a job. Consumers need to make sure that they choose to do a degree program that they will enjoy and will also have an economic demand in society. For example, due to an increasing number of consumers developing illnesses and needing treatments, nurses will always be needed in hospitals. For this reason, there is a high economic need for nurses. In contrast, although there is an economic need for artists because their paintings are sold and help merchants make money and create jobs. It is unlikely artists will be needed as greatly as nurses if the economic conditions start declining because it is likely a lower number of merchants will purchase the paintings and creations of artists. Consumers that have a degree of which there is a low economic demand may want to consider getting a job that does not relate to their career because making some money is better than making no money. Consumers can save up money and if they want then they can go back to school for retraining but they must be careful not to get into excessive student loan and credit card debt. For this reason, it may be wise for consumers to do some research if getting a higher level degree or getting a degree in another area different from the area in which the consumer already has a degree, will have a high economic demand in society.

Bad college or university: Before committing to attend an educational facility, consumers need to make sure that their degree programs as well as the facility itself are accredited. Any educational facility such as a college, career school, technical school, or university can over exaggerate about its accreditation and the consumers that do not verify the accreditation will not find out about the school over exaggerating until they start struggling trying to find a job. Employers may think that consumers who earn an unaccredited degree or earn it from an unaccredited educational facility completed an unchallenging curriculum or they could not attend an accredited university due to having a poor academic profile from the prior school that they attended. The United States Department of Education maintains an up-to-date database of accredited educational facilities and their programs at http://ope.ed.gov/accreditation/. The consumers should use this website to verify the accreditation. Additionally, consumers can check the reputation of the educational facility by doing a Google.com search with the name of educational facility and next to the name; they should type "complaints." For example, if consumers want to check the reputation of Seminole State College then they would type "Seminole State College complaints" on the Google search bar. Although it is unlikely an educational facility will have solid perfect reviews, consumers should read both the good and bad reviews and determine if the bad reviews overpower the good reviews. If this is the case then it is not recommended that they attend that particular educational facility. Consumers should pay special attention to student reviews of the educational facilities indicating the credits earned were not accepted by another educational facility when the student wanted to transfer. This should send a red flag to the consumer indicating that the educational facility has some major flaw otherwise there is no legitimate reason as to why another educational facility would not accept the credits. It is likely if the credits were not accepted then an employer will not honor the curriculum that the student completed at the educational facility. The most common reason why educational facilities do not accept the credits that the consumer completed at another educational facility is because that particular facility did not provide a challenging curriculum or its degree program was unaccredited.

Limited or bad references: Consumers should not become unmotivated in doing their jobs or become careless such as by arriving late to their job. This may result in the employers developing bad impressions about the consumers. Consumers that make mistakes should offer working extra hours or doing extra tasks to try and redeem themselves in the eyes of their employers. Making a good impression on an employer is vital for every consumer because it raises their chances of being granted a wage increase, a job promotion, and if they try and get a new job with another employer. The new employer may contact the old employers of the consumers that are listed on their resume, background profile, or credit reports. The credit reports reflect some or all of the most recent employers for whom the consumer has worked. If consumers do not list an employer on their resume that is showing on their credit reports or background profile then this may cause the employer to think that the consumer did not work diligently when they worked for the employer that they did not list. As a result, it is possible that the new employer may contact the employer that was not listed on the resume and ask about the performance level of the consumer. In general, employers have the ability to contact any employer and they are not required to disclose the comments that the previous employers made about the consumer, which may have caused them to be denied a job. For this reason, all employers for whom the consumer has worked to an extent are considered references. On the resume or cover letter, consumers can list two to three of their strongest references, who are usually previous employers that will likely talk about the contributions that a consumer can make to a company due to their particular skills, but there is no guarantee that the new employer will contact them. In some cases, if consumers do not have enough references then this could potentially cause an employer to deny them a job because the employer may not have sufficient information to determine if the consumer is a well-qualified candidate for the job or that the consumer has inadequate work experience. In order to have strong references, consumers simply need to work their hardest in doing their jobs throughout their lifetime with all employers. Employers will share information with each other.

Academic weaknesses: For consumers that do not have a great deal of work experience, it is likely any employer to whom they apply for a job may request an official transcript from the student or from all the colleges they have attended and focus on the academic marks that the student earned in each class. The employer may not even tell the consumer that they are going to look at their transcripts because they are not required by law to do so. For this reason, consumers need to focus on earning the highest academic marks in school. They are only harming themselves at their chances of being able to get a decent paying job by not academically performing their best. A tip that can be offered to help consumers perform academically well is to do all the assignments including extra credit if offered by the instructor. Consumers are taking a huge risk with their academic career by not doing extra credit because anything can happen which may cause them to do academically poorly such as a death in the family, they get ill and miss a test that cannot be made up, or they are suddenly loaded with tests and assignments from other classes. A second tip that can be offered is that consumers should always ask their instructor for help regarding concepts they do not understand. Asking an instructor for help or clarification is always better than doing poorly on the test. Instructors are more likely to do curves or special privileges for students who may not have the best grade in the class but have proven themselves to be academically strong on the tests or are making an attempt in trying to learn by asking for help.

After making the good decision to attend college, students can use this website to help them find all the colleges near their home area: http://www.50states.com/college/. It is encouraged that a student attend a community or state college that is closest to their house and if possible, has no college application fee, for the purpose of saving the most money on gas and getting into the least amount of student loan and credit card debt. If a college has an application fee, students should see their high school counselor for a college application fee waiver, which is usually offered to students who come from families with low incomes or have taken the **American College Test** (ACT) or **Scholastic Aptitude Test** (SAT). Students that are already enrolled in a college and want to transfer should check with their college guidance counselor to see if there are any waivers for paying the college application fee to the college to which they want to transfer. College application fees can get expensive and students should make every attempt to save as much money as possible because that is money they could potentially be using to pay towards their tuition. A student saving every penny is very important because it lowers their likelihood in defaulting on their student loan debt and as a result, developing bad credit.

FAFSA

Once students have applied to the college of their choice using the website of the college, they do not have to wait for the decision letter, the students then must then sit down in front of a computer with their legal parent or guardian and fill out what is called a *"Free Application for Federal Student Aid,"* which is abbreviated as a **FAFSA**. Consumers above age 24 do not need their parent or guardian because they are considered independent, which means they financially support themselves, but if they are underneath 24 then they are considered dependent, which means they are financial supported by their parents, and only the parents will know their own exact financial information. If the students indicate incorrect financial information regarding themselves of their parents on the FAFSA then they run the risk of the potential financial aid that is offered being revoked or the student will be required to do a verification in which they must bring in the financial documents of their parents, such as; tax returns or pay stubs to the college and this verification process can be considered annoying and time consuming. There are special circumstances in which consumers under the age of 24 can be considered an independent in the eyes of the government and colleges for the purpose of getting the most financial aid. Being an independent helps get more financial aid because it means the student is supporting themselves with their own income without any outside help such as from their parents. It is unlikely the student is going to make more income than their parents and so it makes sense for the government to give them more financial aid money.

It used to be that students could be considered an independent in the eyes of the government before age 24 but too much abuse was happening with FAFSA. In a sense, students were fraudulently obtaining excessive financial aid money. There were cases in which students were getting a job and filing themselves as an independent on their taxes but after getting and using the financial aid money, they would quit their jobs, and their parents would start claiming them again on their taxes as a dependent. The parents would get tax incentives from claiming their children. Additionally, there were cases in which parents would somehow clean out the funds from all their bank accounts, assets, and any college saving plans for their children for the purpose of getting the children more financial aid. The FAFSA asks how much money is in the deposit accounts of the parents so if there are low amounts then it is likely the student will receive more financial aid money. Finally, there were cases in which students were purposely spending all their income that they were making. They purposely saved little money in their accounts to get more financial aid. The government could not afford to provide so much financial aid, especially to some students who were not in great financial need. For such reasons, the age to be considered independent was increased. Currently, the abusive FAFSA practices that were mentioned are still happening but the increase in the age to be considered independent has helped lower the amount of abuse.

Consumers should <u>never</u> fill out a FAFSA on any other website besides www.fafsa.ed.gov because it is likely other websites are simply trying to steal personal financial information. Consumers need to be careful because there is an increasing number of cases in which criminals are creating bogus FAFSA websites, are mailing and emailing fake FAFSA assistance letters, and are asking for money from students and parents. FAFSA is controlled and regulated by the government and there are absolutely no fees. It records the tax and other financial-related information of consumers and their parents and electronically submits this information to the college that the consumer wishes to attend. The FAFSA will show the school all the financial aid for which the consumer qualifies such as grants, subsidized (interest free until graduation) as well as unsubsidized (interest bearing while in school) student loans, and need-based scholarships. The student loans granted through FAFSA are with the government and require no credit checks to be done but their payment histories are reported to the credit reports of the student that are maintained by the credit agencies. The school may use the financial information of the student and their parents as well as potential academic information reflecting on the transcript of the student to determine additional financial aid for which the student qualifies.

FAFSA Weaknesses and Criticisms

Students whose parents make high income usually $85,000 or more and their parents do not have many children, which are considered dependents, will receive very little or no financial aid in terms of grants and need-based scholarships. They will usually only receive loans. The FAFSA is assuming that parents who make high income can support the educational expenses, of their children. This is not true because some parents, despite their income, choose not to support their children or may have a great deal of liabilities, which are debts such as the mortgage (home loan), car loan, credit cards, insurance, medical and other expenses.

The FAFSA does not check the credit profile of the parents which would show their liabilities. In this sense, the FAFSA is assuming the parents have no liabilities. It is rare to find a parent that has zero debt. Additionally, due to the fact the credit profile is not checked, the FAFSA does not know if the parent has a bankruptcy or debt settlement and this information is not going to show on the tax documents. Parents that have a bankruptcy or debt settlement have less assets and funds that they can use to support their children. This is because when a bankruptcy or debt settlement happens, the financial institutions to whom the parents owe money seize as much of their assets and income as possible. Money that would seize can include the money within the bank accounts of the parents.

The FAFSA does not even take into consideration if one or more of the parents have had a foreclosure on their houses or car repossessions. It stands to reason that if a parent is not financially stable enough to pay for their house and/or car; then they cannot support their children despite making the high income. Some financial institutions attempt to garnish the wages of the consumers even after claiming the house or car. The FAFSA does not check if the wages of the consumers are being garnished and whether or not the students are financially supporting the parents. It is possible that the student and/or their parents may be able to negotiate with the financial aid office if their parents are in situations involving wage garnishment, parents are not supporting the students, house or car has been repossessed, or bankruptcy happened, but there is no guarantee the school will accept such situations as a reason for granting more financial aid. The government is catering financial aid money mostly to students whose parents make low income even for academic based scholarships. As evidence, according to collegeconfidential.com, "the *bad* news is that some colleges (admittedly not many) *do* require the FAFSA for *all* scholarships, whether need-based or not." Students that come from families with high income levels should not waste their time filling on applications for scholarships that require FAFSA. They should only apply for scholarships that do not need FAFSA and unfortunately, such scholarships are rare to find if any.

Some students that come from families with low incomes are misusing the grant money they are receiving such as the Pell grant. In fact, simply for the purpose of getting grant money, some students attend college and it is not because they want to earn their college degree. The grant money has very few, if any, academic requirements such as a grade point average that should be maintained. The grant money that the student receives is usually sent to the student in the form of a check or funded onto a debit card. The students can use the grant money to make any kind of purchase and the government nor does the school monitors what is being purchased. Some students purposely fail classes for the purpose of staying longer at the college so they can continue to receive grant money. For such reasons, an improvement needs to be made with the method that the government and the colleges use to determine which students deserve the grant money because they have legitimate needs to spend it on their educational expenses. A suggested improvement would be subtracting the grant money from the tuition, dorm, and book costs and then billing the student the remaining costs. Like academic scholarships, all grant money should have high academic expectations from students otherwise it is more likely they will fail their classes and the government will waste more money proving the financial aid. Excessive government spending raises the likelihood that the taxes will increase on everyone because the financial aid money is never free. The money that supports financial aid comes from taxes.

After processing the financial information of the student and the FAFSA, the college will then send a letter explaining all the financial aid for which the student qualifies and the student will then be required to accept or deny some or all of the financial aid. If the student applies to multiple colleges then it is likely that the student will receive a financial aid package letter from each college and each letter will have different financial aid. This is likely because the amount of financial aid a college can give a student depends on how many students have applied for admission into the college because it is likely, they are all seeking financial aid and the college has to balance how much financial aid is given to each student. It is recommended that the student attend the college that has the lowest tuition costs in relation to how much financial aid they are providing the student. Students should try presenting the financial aid letter from the college that is offering them the most financial aid to their top choice college and see if their top choice college can offer them the same or higher financial aid package compared to the package that is presented in the letter. Students would include the highest financial aid package letter with a financial aid appeal letter that they would send to their top choice college for the purpose of receiving more financial aid. In the financial aid appeal letter, students can mention their liabilities or the liabilities of their parents such as if their parents are jobless and the students are financially supporting them. It may be a good idea for the parents to also sign the financial aid appeal letter so it is more likely that the college believes what the student is saying on the letter. This is no guarantee that this strategy will result in the student being granted more financial aid but it never hurts to do so because the goal for all students should be to get the lowest amount of student loans. Student loans will become very expensive if their balances are high because high balances mean interest being compounded more aggressively. Finally, students can mention any significant academic achievements they have had since the time that the college application was submitted. The college is likely going to want academically prestigious students because they will likely give the college a better reputation and as a result, more students will choose to attend that particular college and the college will make more profit. Students need to be as convincing as possible in their letters as to why they should receive more financial aid. The letters need to be unique and stick out because there are thousands of other students also seeking more financial aid from the college.

Danny Singh

Here is an example of a college financial aid appeal letter
Source: http://money.howstuffworks.com/personal-finance/college-planning/financial-aid/financial-aid-appeal-letter1.htm

January 20, 2010
George Smith, Financial Aid Administrator
University of HSW
123 University Lane
Atlanta, GA 30326

Dear Mr. Smith:

Thank you for the offer of financial aid for attending the University of HSW. However, my family's financial status has changed since the application process.

The XYZ Company recently downsized several employees and my mother was one of those affected. As a result, my family is not going to be able to support my college education to the extent we expected during the application process.

I would be grateful if you could adjust my financial aid offer in light of this information. Please let me know what paperwork and information you need. Thank you for your attention.

Sincerely,
Student

222 Oak Lane
Gainesville, GA 30566
Home: (555) 555-5555

Part of the reason why a student may choose to go to a school that has expensive tuition is because the student has been rejected by the school that was offering the cheapest tuition. When colleges reject a student, the student cannot give up on trying to be granted admission. They need to do an appeal letter of the college decision explaining the reasons why the student should be offered admission. The student should indicate two to three of their strongest academic credentials and achievements. They should include certificates, DVDs, or documents that can verify the achievements. Students should get two to three of their teachers to write them a strong recommendation for admission into the college. The appeal letter along with the recommendations and documents verifying the achievements should be mailed to the college. An appeal letter may actually impress the college because it will suggest that the student is motivated on getting an education and performing academically well at the college otherwise they would not be trying so hard to get admission.

Here is a sample college decision appeal letter
Source: http://collegeapps.about.com/od/theartofgettingaccepted/a/sample-appeal-letter.htm

Ms. Jane Gatekeeper
Director of Admissions
Ivy Tower College
College town, USA

Dear Ms. Gatekeeper,

Although I was not surprised when I received a rejection letter from Ivy Tower College, I was extremely disappointed. I knew when I applied that my SAT scores from the November exam were below average for Ivy Tower. I also knew at the time of the SAT exam (because of illness) that my scores did not represent my true ability.

However, since I applied to Ivy Tower back in January, I have retaken the SAT and improved my scores measurably. My math score went from a 570 to a 660, and my reading score went up a full 120 points. I have instructed the College Board to send these new scores to you.

I know Ivy Tower discourages appeals, but I hope you will accept these new scores and reconsider my application. I have also had the best quarter yet at my high school (a 4.0 unweighted), and I have enclosed my most recent grade report for your consideration.

Again, I fully understand and respect your decision to deny me admission, but I do hope you will reopen my file to consider this new information. I was tremendously impressed by Ivy Tower when I visited last fall, and it remains the school I would most like to attend.

Sincerely,
Joe Student

Some personal recommendations that can be included within college decision appeal letters

1. Consumers can mention that if they are accepted into the college then they are willing to pay the tuition in advance for their entire degree program. It is unlikely the college will ask to get paid in advance for tuition in the event that they accept the student but they will value the fact that the student is committed in attending their college and academically succeeding. They may feel as though the student is confident. It stands to reason that students that mention to pay the entire tuition are less likely to drop out of the classes or fail them otherwise their own money goes to waste. The college wants to establish and maintain a high retention rate of students that successfully complete their degree programs because when students drop out then it hurts the reputation of the college and this is information that is available to the public. Students that do not complete the degree programs due to dropping out may suggest to future students that the college does not offer a curriculum in which their students feel motivated and engaged. Students are likely going to avoid attending such a college.
2. Consumers can mention any special circumstances that may have negatively influenced their grades such as for example, if they were working a job while attending school or if a family member passed away. Consumers should mention that grades do not necessarily reflect their motivation and the purpose behind doing the job was to save

up money for the college tuition for the purpose of plunging into the least amount of student loan debt. This may cause the college to think that the consumer is less likely to do academically poor in their classes and drop out because their motivation is strong. If the consumer did not have strong motivation then; it is less likely they would have saved up for their college tuition by getting a job. Consumers are more likely to work harder in classes that they paid for because they value their hard earned money. In addition, colleges will appreciate the fact that the consumer is trying to be financially smart and plunge into a low amount of student loan debt because in most cases, consumers that maturely handle their finances are more likely to perform stronger academically.

3. Consumers can mention any national or unique merits they have earned throughout their academic career that separate them from most other consumers. The college wants students that are unique and not just average consumers that want to get an admission into college. For this reason, consumers need to mention their distinctive qualities. High academic marks or test scores are not always distinctive qualities.

4. Consumers can indicate the programs, sports, and/or clubs that they want to join at the college such as the Honors program or science club. Consumers should mention what positions they would want to take within the programs and what they would hope to accomplish that other students have been unable to accomplish or did not even make the necessary attempts. Colleges are more likely to offer admission to students that want to get involved with the extracurricular opportunities offered by the college because these students usually tend to perform stronger academically. In fact, students will often use the incentive of getting to join special programs as motivation for trying to earn the best academic marks possible. This is because most college organizations require that a student have and maintain a certain grade point average.

5. Consumers can contact their senators, county commissioners, and governors explaining their distinctive qualities and asking for letters of recommendation to college. Consumers should include these letters with their financial aid and college decision appeal letters for the purpose of being granted admission and potentially being granted a larger academic scholarship amount. Another possibility is that the senators, county commissioners, and governors can mail the recommendation letters directly to the college. Additionally, it may be wise for consumers to contact their college admissions counselors and ask them if they would be interested in receiving recommendation letters from their employers that can possibly verify how hard the consumer worked in doing their job. If the college indicates that they do want to receive such letters then the consumers should immediately ask their employers for the recommendations.

6. Consumers can mention why they want admission into the college to whom they are writing the college decision appeal letter and why they think going to that particular college will benefit them in their lives. Colleges like admitting students that have a passion.

7. Consumers may want to mention previous family members, if any, that have attended the college because colleges sometimes will value family traditions of attending the same college.

8. Consumers can retake their ACT or SAT exams or both for the purpose of trying to earn higher exam scores. They need to mention in the appeal letter that have already retaken the exam and the college should receive the scores soon or that they will retake the exam. Among the ACT or SAT exam, whichever exam on which the consumer receives the best overall score is the one that should be forwarded to

the college. However, if growth occurred on both exams from the last time that the consumer took them; then they should forward all their scores to the college because the college wants to see academic growth. It lowers the likelihood that consumer made no academic progress in their life.

After getting acceptance into a college, students should make their commitment immediately, because they do not want to lose their spot. The next step would be to look for scholarships. Students need to be careful of scholarship scams. Students can often tell if a scholarship website, letter, phone call, or any correspondence is a scam because they usually only want to collect personal information of students such as addresses, phone numbers, and simply any information so that they may sell that information to companies with whom their have business relations. The companies will then use the information of the students to market them merchandise and services through junk email, letters, and phone calls. Scholarship scams of any type will often ask for fees from students and parents. Scholarships are always free and never require fees from students. Fees defeat the purpose of getting a scholarship and will give a bad reputation to the company that is offering the scholarship. Students should check reputable websites for scholarships such as www.findaid.org, www.fastweb.com, www.studentscholarships.org, and www.scholarships.com. Finally, consumers should check with the college that they are planning on entering for all their scholarship opportunities. Consumers should not spend too much applying for scholarships to the point that they are not having enough time to do their school work and as a result, their grades are becoming poor. Poor grades will ruin the chances of a student to earn a scholarship even if the student submitted a million scholarship applications. Grades are top priority. Top grades will usually surprise students with scholarships themselves because schools review grades for that purpose.

In most cases due to the weak economy, students do not receive all funding that they need for college through grants and scholarships especially if their parents make high income, the student is a dependent on their taxes, or if they are below age 24. Unfortunately, few parents are able to save for the college expenses for their children due to having to deal with their personal financial debts. For such reasons, students commonly take student loans, which can be the most dangerous debt that a consumer will have if they do not properly handle the loans. Most student loans are considered recourse loans meaning if the consumer does not pay on them then the student loan issuers can potentially sue the consumer, garnish their wages, or put a claim on their assets or property. Due to the fact that student loans must be repaid, this can support why they have a low average interest rate compared to most other loans in the United States.

On the financial aid package letter that the student receives from the financial aid department of the college, it will indicate what types of student loans for which the student qualifies.

There are two types of government student loans that students get through FAFSA
Subsidized student loan: The fixed interest rate loan will not accumulate any interest while the student is in school. The government is using taxpayer money and paying the student loan interest until the student graduates from college. After the student graduates then the subsidized student loan will start accumulating interest. Students should be careful not to get dismissed from their colleges for offenses or academic reasons because this may result in the subsidized student loan accumulating interest. The goal of students should be to get as much subsidized loan money as possible for the purpose of saving money on interest. Saving money on interest will lower the chances of students plunging into large amounts of student loan debt

and as a result, developing low credit scores. Students can contact their college financial aid office to request for more subsidized loan money.

Unsubsidized student loan: The fixed interest rate loan will start accumulating interest when the student gets the loan even if the student is in school. For this reason, if there are penalties for paying early, students should try to make payments on the unsubsidized student loans rather than the subsidized student loans because it is likely the unsubsidized loans will compound with the most interest. The subsidized student loan debt will mostly be the principle amount and little interest provided that the student is not often late on making payments after graduation because late fees cause the interest to compound more aggressively.

The government tries to balance how much subsidized and unsubsidized loan money that they give to each student. This is because they cannot afford to give too much subsidized loan money to students. If they do then they will have a difficult time trying to make more money for the purpose of lending that money made to other students that want to get an education. Regardless if they are subsidized or unsubsidized, government student loans are always cheaper than private student loans, which are provided by financial institutions.

College Cost Reduction Act of 2007

Congress passed the College Cost Reduction Act hoping to relieve students of their debt burdens. The act allows for $5,000 of student loan debt to be forgiven if the student chooses a career in pubic service such as a firefighter or teacher. The act raised the amount of Pell grant money given to students by up to $500. Finally, it lowered the interest rates on need-based student loans from 6.8% to 3.4%. To make these changes, the government reduced the amount of money they were paying student loan providers.

Specific Government Student Loans
The financial aid office of the college will determine if the student qualifies

Congress budgets the funds for each specific loan

1. **Perkins Loan:** The loan was named this in honor of a previous member of the United States House of Representatives who is Carl D. Perkins. The loan is for students with great financial need due to the fact their legal parents or guardians do not make a large amount of income. The government views that parents with low income levels are not able to contribute a great deal of money towards the education of their children. The Perkins loan has a fixed interest rate of 5% with a limit for undergraduate students up to $5,500 each year. For graduate students, the loan limit is up to $8,000 each year. Usually, after nine months from the date of graduation, students are expected to start paying on the Perkins loan otherwise they may face penalties such as negative marks to their credit profile or late fees unless they defer the payments or extend the life of the loan. If students choose to do so then they can payments on the loan after paying their unsubsidized (interest bearing) loans while in school and this will help raise the credit scores because upon graduation, the credit reports will reflect that the student has paid down their student loan debt to a certain amount. Upon reviewing credit reports, financial institutions will think the student is less likely to default on new loans and the financial institution can trust them with a lower than average interest rate and/or fees.

2. **Stafford Loan**: This is a fixed interest rate student loan and used to be called the Federal Guaranteed Student Loan Program. In 1988, it was renamed to the Stafford loan for the purpose of honoring a senator in the United States, Robert Stafford. The Stafford loan is available as subsidized and unsubsidized loans. The financial aid office of the college will determine, depending upon the income level of the student that is an independent or the income level of the parents of the student that is a dependent, how much Stafford subsidized and unsubsidized loan money will be available to the student. Students are encouraged to negotiate with the financial aid department for the purpose of getting the maximum amount of Stafford subsidized loan money as possible. They should mention such in their financial aid appeal letters. As of 2006, most unsubsidized (interest bearing) Stafford student loans have a fixed interest rate of 6.80%. Subsidized (bearing interest after graduation) Stafford student loans have a fixed interest rate of 3.40%. In the majority of cases, students are expected to start making payments on their Stafford loans after six months have passed from the date of graduation. As with all other student loans, if possible, students should make payments early on the Stafford loans especially on the unsubsidized Stafford loans for the purpose of preventing the interest from compounding too aggressively. Subsidized and unsubsidized Stafford loan amounts for undergraduate students go up to:

According to the Discover Student Loans, "Stafford subsidized and unsubsidized loans for graduate students can go up to $20,500 (certain programs for health professions may qualify for higher loan limits; see financial aid office for exact amounts)." Unfortunately, beginning July 1st, 2012, all students seeking graduate or higher level degrees will only be offered unsubsidized (interest bearing) Stafford loans and no subsidized Stafford loans. The subsidized Stafford loans offered to these students will have a fixed interest rate of 6.80%. The elimination of the unsubsidized Stafford student loans for graduate students was a con of the Budget Control Act that the United States President, Barack Obama, signed into law on August 2nd, 2011. Through this law, Obama was hoping to prevent the United States from failing due to the national debt because the economic conditions were so unstable.

Warning about ALL Stafford loans

Subsidized and unsubsidized Stafford loans currently have loan origination fees, which are fees just for getting the loan. The subsidized Stafford loan money has its own origination fee and the unsubsidized Stafford loan money has its own origination fee. They range from 1% - 4% of the loan amount. The higher that the loan amount will be then this will mean a higher loan origination fee. For this reason, students should not take out a huge student loan and live off of it because regardless of whether they use all the student loan money or not, they still have to pay the origination fee for getting the loan. Although it will not cause the loan origination fee to be cheaper, students should apply any leftover student loan money as payments towards the remaining student loan balance for the purpose of preventing the student loan from aggressively compounding with interest. For example, Marissa took out an $80,000 student loan from Suntrust Bank. She only used $10,000 of it to pay for her college expenses and so she should use the remaining $70,000 and pay back Suntrust Bank instead of spending it on games, jewelry, clothes, and her other wants in life. She is better off saving money for these items.

Parent PLUS Loan: A legal parent or legal guardian of a student can approach the financial aid office of the college to obtain this loan and a FAFSA will be required. Unlike with the Stafford and Perkins loan programs, a credit check is performed on the parent and student to see if they qualify for the loan and it may be easy for consumers with average to good credit to obtain this loan with an exception to if they have a bankruptcy or debt settlement showing on their credit reports. The parent uses the loan money to pay for the educational expenses of their children. The parent must make payments on the loan or defer the payment if they currently cannot afford to pay it. According to the Federal Student Aid, only the parent is responsible for repaying the student loan. However, as a personal piece of advice, if the payment history of the loan is appearing on the credit reports of both the parent and student then the student should also be focused on repaying the loan. Students should not take the huge financial risk of leaving it up to their parents to repay the loan because there is no telling whether or not that the parent will default on it and the student will have to pay the consequences with a damaged credit profile. This means high insurance premiums and many struggles to find a good job. The loan begins accumulating a 7.9% interest rate the minute that the loan money is released to the parent.

4. Graduate PLUS Loan: Students pursuing higher level degrees such as Masters and Ph.D. after earning their Bachelor's degree get this unsubsidized loan to pay for graduate school. It begins accumulating a 7.9% interest rate the minute that the loan money is released to the student and their parent but before even getting the loan, a 4% loan origination fee is charged on the loan. One of the legal parents of the student cosign for the student so they can obtain this loan. A credit check is performed on both the parent and student to evaluate their credit history. Like a Parent PLUS Loan, the parent uses the loan money to pay for the educational expenses of their children but this time for graduate school. The parent must make payments on the loan or defer the payment if they cannot afford to pay it. However, if the Graduate PLUS Loan is appearing on the credit reports of the parent and student then the student should be motivated like the parent to repay the loan because if either of them default on the loan then this will result in their credit profiles becoming damaged. Even if the student loan is only appearing on the credit report of the parent then to show appreciation, students should help their parents to repay the loan so their parents do not become homeless.

Access all government student loans, which are Stafford, Perkins, and Parent PLUS at http://www.nslds.ed.gov/nslds_SA/.

The Evil Private and Uncertified Student Loans

When students cannot get enough Perkins, Stafford, and Parent PLUS student loan money through the government to pay for their education then they get a **private student loan** that is granted by a financial institution. In most cases, if students still do not have enough funds to pay for college despite getting all the financial aid they were offered and are now considering getting a private student loan then it is likely that the college or university in which they are trying to get admission is very expensive and students are better off going to a community or state college. Students should never get into excessive amounts of student loan debt. It makes no sense to do so and does not raise their likelihood of being granted a more prestigious college degree or job. If anything, excessive loan debts lower the chances of a student being granted a professional job because it is likely the student loan debt will cause the credit scores of the student to become low and the employers may notice such when checking the credit reports and other financial related information of the student. For whatever reasons a student has for needing more loan money, they can consider getting a private student loan only from a credit union or community bank but students need to be aware that most private student loans have variable interest rates. Similar to variable interest rate credit cars and home equity lines of credit, if the prime rate that is published within the Wall Street journal is high due to the poor economic conditions then students can expect the interest rates on their private student loans to increase as high as 16%, 17%, and 18% or even higher.

According to www.dailyfinance.com, Zac Bissonnette indicates in, *Don't Ever Take out a Private Student Loan,* "Private student loans almost never have a cap" in regards to the interest rates. The interest rates increasing on the private student loans mean that the monthly minimum payment requirements will increase because a greater portion of the minimum payment requirement will be composed of interest and this raises the likelihood of the student defaulting on the loan depending upon the costs of their other monthly expenses. Students will not have as much flexibility defer payments on private student loans as they would government student loans, all private student loans are unsubsidized meaning they will start accumulating interest the day that the loan money is released, and students can only deduct up to $2,500.00 in student loan interest from their taxes. Like Stafford student loans, some private student loans have loan origination fees and the fees themselves compound with interest. For these reasons, if possible, students should always try to get private student loans with fixed interest rates because this means that the minimum payment requirements will be the same every month, the student is less likely to default, and they are more likely to deduct all or most of the interest that they pay on the student loans from their taxes. If students have a parent or close family member with a strong credit history only then they should ask them to cosign on the loan because it could mean a cheaper interest rate and lower monthly payment requirements.

Private student loans are available as a certified or uncertified loan, which is an option chosen by the student.

Students should avoid uncertified, sometimes called non-certified, student loans. A private student loan is considered uncertified because the financial institution does not contact the college to verify how much loan money is needed for tuition. Instead of the loan money being released to the college, it is released to the student meaning the student can do anything that they want with the money but it is expected that they use it for their college expenses. The financial institution will grant the student as much loan money as the student wants but they will take their credit profile information into consideration. The catch behind giving the student so much loan money is that the financial institution can make high profits by charging the student higher than average interest rates, loan origination fees, and possible prepayment penalties, which are fees accessed to the student when they pay off their uncertified student loans early. Most uncertified private student loans have variable interest rates.

Warning! The interest paid on the uncertified private student loans cannot be deducted from taxes. It makes no sense why a student would consider getting an uncertified private student loan. It is the most dangerous student loan available.

When the student requests for a certified private student loan then the financial institution will contact the school to verify how much loan money is needed to pay for the tuition. The school verifying the tuition amount means that they are **certifying** the loan. The financial institution will then release the specified amount of loan money to the school and not the student. A certified private student loan is less expensive than an uncertified student loan because it will tend to have cheaper interest rates, little or no loan origination fees, and little or no prepayment penalties. Unlike an uncertified private student loan, the interest paid on a certified student loan can be deducted from taxes. The financial institution is taking on less loan risk by granting the student a certified student loan than an uncertified student loan because it is more likely that the student will get an education and be able to get a job. For this reason, the financial institution feels more comfortable granting a cheaper interest rate because there are an increasing number of cases in which students are using the uncertified student loans to make purchases that have nothing to do with their education. They struggle to get a job and default on their student loan payments. More certified private student loans have fixed interest rates than uncertified student loans.

Here is the sequence that students should follow when obtaining student loans with the highest number being the most student loan money type that should be acquired because it has the cheapest interest rate. As the list goes down then it means the interest rate of the loan is more expensive than the one prior to it.

1. Perkins loan.
2. Subsidized Stafford loan.
3. Unsubsidized Stafford loan.
4. Unsubsidized parent plus loan. Unfortunately, there are no subsidized parent plus loans.
5. Certified private student loan with fixed interest rate only.
5. Uncertified private student loan with fixed interest rate only.
6. For whatever reason more loan money is needed then students should get a job or the cheapest secured loan with a fixed interest rate from a credit union or community bank. It should cause major concern if a student needs so much loan money because there should be no need to get into so much debt. The credit scores will become very low due to the excessive debt. Do not obtain variable interest rate loans.

Students can track the balances on all their government student loans on http://www.nslds.ed.gov/nslds_SA/.

Crucial Tips for ALL Private Student Loans (and other Loans too)
Before Submitting the Applications

1. Some financial intuitions give the option to the consumer to select a variable interest rate or fixed interest rate on their loan. Consumers should not get fooled by the fact that the variable interest rate is cheaper than a fixed interest rate because in the beginning, the variable interest rate can be cheap but it can go up at any time along with the minimum payment requirements. The variable interest rate could potentially double in amount compared to the fixed interest rate. Consumers are more financially prepared for loans with fixed interest rates because the minimum payment requirements are the same every month. Consumers are less likely to default on fixed interest rate loans and be accessed late fees. Some financial institutions offer variable

interest rate loans that have a zero percent interest rate promotion for up to a certain time period such as twelve months. Financial institutions do so for the purpose of getting more consumers to sign up for the variable interest rate loans rather than the fixed interest rate loans. Consumers should not get fooled by the zero percent offers because it is likely the financial institution plans on making up for the time in which the consumer was paying zero percent by charging them a really high interest rate after the promotional interest rate period has ended. For example, if the consumer signs up for a variable interest rate loan that will charge zero percent for 6 months verses signing up for a loan with no promotional interest rate but a fixed rate of 7 percent then it is likely after 6 months, the interest rate on the variable interest rate loan will go up to 8%, 9%, 10%, or even higher. As a result, the zero percent interest rate loan promotion did not ultimately help the consumer save money. In anything, such a loan cost them more money. Consumers should always choose to get fixed interest rate loans even if they have no promotions. In most cases, promotions have catches; the financial institutions are not going to give loans out for free. They want money for granting money.

2. Before applying for any loan such as a private student loan, students and their cosigners, if any, should use as much money as they have saved up, to pay off their current debts as much as possible if not in full such as their credit cards, auto loans, other student loans, or other liabilities, which mean debts, that are showing on their credit reports. This is because often the financial institutions use the current debts that the student and their cosigners have against them by approving them with a higher than average interest rate. This is because financial institutions think that a consumer with many debts in relation to their income, even if all the debts are being paid in a timely manner, suggests that the consumer is likely to default because they will not be able to make all the payments. Consumers with low debts are very likely to be granted a low interest rate because their debt-to-income ratio is low. They are more likely to pay off the student loan successfully and in a timely manner.

Example
Consumers will see this on the student loan application on the section where it talks about the interest rate calculation
"Index plus margin of 7.75% to 14.25%, depending on the applicant's creditworthiness"—This was taken from Credit.com.
The "index" is referring to the interest rate that is published in the Wall Street Journal. If the loan has a fixed interest rate then the consumer will not see that there is an index rate on the loan. Only variable interest rate loans have index rates. Index rates are sometimes called prime rates.
The "margin" is referring to the marginal interest rate that the financial institutions will combine with the index interest rate. The marginal interest rate is determined by the financial institution based on the "creditworthiness" level of the consumer. Creditworthiness is the likelihood of the consumer in repaying the loan. A high level of creditworthiness means the consumer has little or no debts in relation to their income on which they have not defaulted and for this reason, they are very likely to successfully repay any new loans that they obtain. The goal of consumers is to have the least amount of debts so they can be approved for the cheapest marginal interest rate.
If the consumer were to get approved for a marginal interest rate of 7.5% then the total interest rate would be calculated as 3.25% (Wall Street Journal prime rate which is considered the index

rate) + 7.5% (marginal interest rate) = 10.75%, this is the interest rate that a consumer would pay on a variable interest rate loan such as a private student loan.

3. If given the option on the loan application or by the loan representative, consumers should always agree to set up an automatic payment plan because this often means a discount with the interest rate. When a financial institution sees that the consumer has set up an automatic payment plan then they feel that the consumer is less likely to default on their loan and for this reason, the consumer deserves a cheaper interest rate.

4. Before applying for the private student loan, the students and their cosigners should check their credit reports with Equifax, Experian, and TransUnion and dispute any incorrect information. Information that should be disputed includes excessive credit check inquiries, incorrect loan balances, delinquent credit accounts, and late payments. There is no guarantee that the information will be removed or corrected immediately but trying is always better than not trying to improve the credit profile information. Credit check inquiries often show the date on which they will drop off the credit report with the specific credit agency. If possible, the consumers should wait for most or all of the credit check inquiries to drop off and not apply for new credit before they apply for the private student loan. Excessive credit check inquiries can make a difference when getting approved for an interest rate. It is very likely consumers with many credit checks, which are usually 4 or more, will get approved for a higher than average interest rate on their student loan. This is because credit checks mean the consumer is seeking loan money and wants to get into debt, which raises their likelihood of defaulting on the student loan. Consumers should send letters to the companies that performed the credit inquiries and ask them to remove the inquiries. If credit was granted by the company then the consumer should not request for them to remove the credit check inquiry.

Consumers should only send this letter to companies that denied them for credit and request for the credit check inquiries to be removed because it is lowering their scores. Consumers also need to provide their credit reports that show the credit checks along with the letter. Companies need to be able to provide proof to the consumer that an application for credit was submitted by the authentic consumer and not a theft criminal otherwise the company should remove the credit check inquiry. Consumers should use certified mail when sending letters that have personal information, which in this case, is the social security number and credit report. Certified mail lowers the likelihood of the letter getting lost by the post office.

Attention: Name of company
Corporate mailing address of company
Date letter was written

Name of consumer
Social security number of consumers (Financial institutions need this number in order to pull up the records on the consumer)
Address of consumer
Phone number of consumer

Details of credit check inquiry
Date credit check was done
Which credit agencies (Equifax, Experian, TransUnion, and/or Innovis) are showing the credit check inquiry

To Whom It May Concern:

On my <u>Equifax credit report</u> (mention which credit report is showing the credit check inquiry), I noticed a <u>hard inquiry credit check</u> (consumers need to indicate the credit check was a "hard" inquiry otherwise some financial institutions may assume they are talking about a "soft" inquiry, which does not influence the credit scores, and the financial institutions will take the letter less seriously) inquiry was done by <u>Citibank</u> (indicate the name of the company that performed the credit check) on <u>June 19, 2005</u> (indicate the date that is reflecting on the credit report as to when the credit check was done). <u>I called Equifax and they said only the company that performed the credit check can send a request to them to have the inquiry removed</u> (this statement is vital to include with the letter otherwise the company will not be motivated to help the consumer and will simply tell them to contact the credit agency for the purpose of getting the credit check removed). I do not remember applying for credit with Citibank. For this reason, I ask that <u>Citibank furnish a copy of the credit application</u> (consumers need to request for the company to provide a copy of the application that was submitted to them for credit which is why they did a credit check on the consumer) that was submitted to them under my social security number. If the <u>application cannot be found then it means a credit check inquiry was done on me without my authorization</u> (if the company has no loan application on the consumer then a credit check should never have been done, it is unfair to the consumer, and must be removed from their credit report) and should be immediately removed from my credit report <u>because it is lowering my credit scores</u> (financial institutions like helping consumers that are concerned about maintaining good credit because it is less likely such consumers would abuse their loans by not repaying them). <u>I need to refinance my house so I can get cheaper monthly payments</u> (consumers should mention the reason why they would like the credit check removed, what is their purpose behind trying to improve their credit profile).

<u>Please contact me as soon as possible at (407) 496-6005</u> (a contact phone number should always be mentioned) confirming the retrieval of this letter and <u>do everything possible to get the inquiry removed</u> (state the purpose for writing the letter). If I am unavailable then please leave me a voice message and I will promptly return your call. I greatly appreciate your assistance in the matter.

Thank you,
Danny Singh

5. Consumers should not get so much loan money because they want to use it for their everyday expenses such as food, clothing, and housing. In this sense, the consumer is planning on living off of the loan money. Unfortunately, many students are currently getting so much student loan money with the intention of living off of it but they are also blowing it on unnecessary purchases such as fancy computers, iPads, drugs, televisions, and cell phones. Student loan money should only be used for the necessities for getting an education such as food, books, and supplies. It is recommended students get a part-time job without failing classes and take the least amount of student loan money for the purpose of preventing the loan from

compounding with interest so aggressively. When consumers obtain higher than average loan amounts then they welcome the aggressive compounding of interest without even realizing it and as a result, it takes them 30, 40, 50 years, or more just to make student loan payments and not be able to do anything in life. A $20,000 student loan will become a $40,000 student loan. A $40,000 student loan will become a $60,000 student loan. Taking into consideration that the student may be late, may often defer their payments, or the government decides to interest the interest rates on all student loans then a $60,000 student loan may become $100,000 student loan or more. These consumers, especially students, raise their chances of defaulting because higher than average loan amounts mean high monthly minimum payment requirements. This is because more of the minimum payment will be requiring interest to be paid by the consumer and the consumer cannot deduct all the interest from their taxes because there is a limit to how much can be deducted. Defaulting on a loan means little or no chances at being able to get a job and no income gives the freedom to the student loans to continue compounding with interest and late fees. For whatever reasons, if a consumer needs more loan money, then they can request it but it makes no sense to get a huge amount of loan money that is not needed in the majority of cases. Consumers do not want to pay their whole life paying interest.

6. Consumers should make a habit of making payments on their student loans and ultimately, all loans, early before the arrival of the due date. Students with government student loans (Perkins, Stafford, Plus) all have the same interest rates that the government can change at any time depending upon the conditions of the economy so the credit history does not influence their rates. However, the interest rates and loan origination fees, if any, of certified and non-certified private student loans are influenced by the credit histories reflecting on the credit reports of the consumer. The financial institutions periodically check the credit profile of the student by doing a soft inquiry credit check on the credit reports, with all the agencies to ensure that all the bills are being paid. If they notice that a powerful credit history is being maintained along with payments being made early on the student loans then the student will be more likely to convince the financial institution to grant a cheaper fixed interest rate on the loan or convert the variable interest rate into a fixed interest rate. Financial institutions consider consumers that are always paying early as low risk to their business because it is unlikely they will default. The business risk management software financial institutions use records the dates as to when the payments are being received and will give the consumer a positive status if payments are being received early. Consumers have to call the student loan issuers and request for them to review the student loan for a cheaper interest rate. If possible, variable interest rates should always be converted into fixed interest rates.

7. Consumers should sell investments such as stocks for the purpose of getting into the least amount of student loan debt because it is unlikely the earnings made by the investments will overpower the interest charged to the consumer by the student loans. Consumers that already have student loans may want to consider using the money made from selling their investments to pay off the debt because student loans cannot ever be eliminated. When selling investments, consumers need to be careful that most of the money that was made does not get consumed by heavy fees and/or penalties for selling the investments.

World renowned financial expert, Suze Orman, expresses that in the current economy, students are stopping to pay on their loans thinking they will go away but in the majority of cases, student loan debt cannot be discharged in any bankruptcy or debt settlement. Paying late or not paying at all on any loan will damage credit and considering the severe credit crisis that is happening, this will make it almost impossible for students to get approved for a decent apartment, car, insurance premium, or simply anything because a credit history is the only way companies know that the consumers will pay them back. If too many consumers default on their student loans then eventually, interest rates will skyrocket and there will be a severe economic downturn. The national debt may increase because the government will have to spend more money to support the student loan programs and this will likely mean higher taxes that the consumers will eventually have to pay. For such reasons, here are some personal tricks to pay off the student loan debt in the most efficient and effective manner.

1. If there are no prepayment penalties (fees for paying early), without letting other bills become late, consumers should make payments now on the unsubsidized private and government loans because they begin compounding with interest the day that the consumer gets them. If consumers have already paid off their unsubsidized loans then they should immediately start paying their subsidized loans because even though they do not start accumulating interest until after graduation, Time magazine reports that Congress may increase their interest rates from 3.4% to 6.8% on July 1. It normally takes students about 20 to 30 years to pay off their student loan debts. If the interest rates increase then it will probably take students about 40 to 50 years to pay off their student loans, which is why it is encouraged that students make payments while in school. Students can ask their financial aid office for the website where they can make the student loan payments online. Students are discouraged

2. If there is no additional fee then consumers should use a debit or credit card to make payments on the student loans because they have rewards, which save money. Do not use debit or credit cards that have monthly or annual fees. This defeats the purpose of the savings. Without going over the credit limit, using a credit card and paying it off immediately will mean higher credit scores because the credit reports will reflect a paid on time student loan and credit card. This will mean cheaper insurance premiums for houses and cars and the savings can be applied as payments towards student loans.

3. Do NOT carry balances on credit cards even if they have a 0% no interest charged on the balance offer. Consumers should never carry a balance on the credit card that they are using to pay off the student loan otherwise they are creating more debt instead of paying it off. When consumers carry balances on credit cards, their health insurance, life insurance, car insurance, and home owner's insurance become more expensive because in the eyes of the insurance providers, balances on credit cards or just loans in general raises the chances that the consumer will one day stop paying on their insurance premiums. Consumers should use credit cards that have the lowest purchase interest rates and highest rewards. Always call provider every 2-3 months for a lower interest rate even if the balance is being paid at the end of month because there have been cases in which consumers lost their jobs and could not pay off the credit cards immediately. It is better to have a cheap interest rate and be safe than sorry. 11% and below on a credit card with no annual fee is excellent!

4. If possible, do not use debit cards or paper check account numbers on the internet on unknown websites. The bank account can potentially get cleaned out of all its funds and consumers will have no money on which they can live and pay other bills. Consumers are better off using a credit card because they are always safe.

5. Before buying books at the bookstore, consumers should always check the internet to see if the books can be purchased for cheaper prices. Consumers should always buy used books using a credit card because they are cheaper than new books and when they are done with them then they should sell them and use the money to make payment towards their student loans and other debts. The credit card rewards help save money. Books that relate to the major of the consumer should not be sold. For example, if the major of the consumer is Biology then they should not sell Biology textbooks because it is likely they will need them again for assignments and projects. Students sometimes purchase books from the college bookstore due to the fact they can use financial aid such as loan and grant money. Students are better off depositing the loan and grant money into their bank accounts and then using a debit or credit card to make the book purchases online. Despite the fact students can use financial aid at the college book stores, they do not save money because they end up three times as much, if not more, because the bookstores are trying to make profits for the colleges. Students also have to pay interest on the student loans that they use to purchase the books and the fact that that they are in so much student loan debt means they will have to pay expensive car insurance premiums. High student loan debts suggest that the student will one day stop paying on their car insurance or will be late in making the payments. The cheapest websites from which consumers can purchase books are Amazon.com, Half.com, Ebay.com, and Betterworldbooks.com. Better World Books always offer free shipping to consumers.

6. Before becoming late on a student loan or credit card, students should always contact the provider, and defer the payment or work out a payment plan. Paying extra interest and protecting their credit profile is always better than paying late fees and the credit profile of the consumer gets damaged due to the late payments, which means low chances at being able to get a good job. Extended repayment and income-based repayment offer the lowest monthly payments but they offer the greatest amount of interest which may cause the loan amount to double or even triple if they defer many payments. Paying late can eliminate student loan payment relief options because the loan issuers do not want to help consumers who did them wrong by not paying.

7. Always pay above the minimum payment on ALL loans especially the unsubsidized student loans because they begin accumulating interest the day that the student receives the student loan money even if the student is in school. Paying off debt faster means higher credit scores and higher chances of getting approved for a lower interest rate and a good job. Any left over grant money should be used to make student loan payments.

8. If consumers transfer to another school then they should become a transient student and take as many courses as possible at a community or state college. This reduces the amount of potential student loan and credit card debt. Many state and community colleges offer junior and senior level courses due to the fact they offer Bachelors

degree programs. At all colleges, students are encourages to join the Honors programs because they often offer extra financial incentives such as scholarships.

9. Students should not drop classes if they will not get a refund for them. Instead, students should take them, pass them, and raise their grade point average. This raises the chances of being awarded a scholarship and a job. It makes no sense for students to waste their own money by dropping classes. When a student drops a class, their transcript shows the class was dropped. Employers and future colleges may think the student is academically weak, which is why they dropped the class. Getting a C in a class is better than dropping it. Some students drop classes because they are using a student loan and think they will simply not repay it. Student loan debt can never go away for it must be repaid with interest. They cannot escape it.

10. Consumers should not make a habit of doing this but if they cannot pay off their credit card and other bills at the end of the month then they should use their student loan and/or grant money to pay it off because they do not want their credit card to accumulate interest and fees.

    For whatever reasons, if consumers cannot make payments on their student loans after graduation and cannot defer the payments then they should take a loan against their 401(k), which must be repaid within five years so the 10% tax penalty can be avoided. Two other options to make payments on the student loan and protect the credit profile is to rollover (transfer) most of the funds within assets such as a CD, money market, savings, traditional IRA, and 401(k) into a Roth IRA, pay any necessary income taxes, and take the money without paying the 10% tax penalty. A Roth IRA has no 10% tax penalty as long as the consumer does not take the earnings (interest) but only the contributions (deposits) that they made towards the account. The final option consumers have is getting a secured loan such as a home equity loan from a credit union or community bank and using that loan money to make payments. The loan should have a fixed interest rate. Ideally, if consumers are using loan money to pay other loans then this is major financial weakness and consumers should immediately seek to get a second job even if it does not relate to their major. Consumers should never get payday loans, car title loans, pawn shop loans, cash advance loans, tax refund loans, or any loan with exorbitant interest to make payments towards their student loans. The interest paid on loans with exorbitant interest rates cannot be deducted from taxes and if the companies say otherwise then the consumer should check with a tax advisor because it is likely the company is over exaggerating so they can win the business of the consumer.

11. Students with multiple student loans have the option of consolidating, which means combining, them into one big student loan. Students do loan consolidations for the purpose of avoiding having to make payments to multiple student loans, which makes it harder for them to handle their other expenses and raises their likelihood of defaulting on one or more of the student loans. Currently, the government student loans (Perkins, Stafford, Plus) that are granted through FAFSA can be consolidated together and often, students may receive an interest rate discount. Private student loans, which are the loans, granted by financial institutions to students, cannot be consolidated with the government student loans. Private student loans can only be combined with each other and there be an interest rate discount. In regards to the

government student loans, students should not consolidate those if some of the loans are subsidized meaning they are not accumulating any interest until after graduation. If students consolidate the subsidized loans then they will start accumulating interest with the unsubsidized loans. If possible, students should only consolidate the unsubsidized loans, which begin accumulating interest the day that the student acquires the student loan money. Students should not consolidate private student loans with each other unless they have fixed interest rates. If students have private student loans with variable interest rates then the students should request for the financial institutions to convert them into fixed interest rate private student loans before consolidating them. If students consolidate private student loans with variable interest rates then they are taking a huge risk. It is cheaper to have multiple private student loans with small balances and variable interest rates than have a big private student loan with a huge balance and variable interest rate. If the financial institution will grant a fixed interest rate if the consumer consolidates all their private student loans then the consumer should immediately do the private student loan consolidation because it will save a large amount of money.

Example
Erica has 3 private student loans with variable interest rates and she is considering consolidating them all to Suntrust Bank.

Private student loan with Suntrust Bank
Balance: $3,778.21
Variable interest rate is set for 6% in April

Private student loan with Bank of America
Balance: $945.45
Variable interest rate is set for 7% in April

Private student loan with Chase Bank
Balance: $2,495.51
Variable interest rate is set for 10% in April

Here is the situation Erica will have if she consolidates all the private student loans to Suntrust Bank
Private student loan debts: $2,495.51 + $945.45 + $3,778.21 = $7,219.17, which is the total amount of the consolidated (combined) student loan with Suntrust Bank

Consolidated student loan with Suntrust Bank
Balance: $7,219.17
Variable interest rate is set for 6% in April.
Danger: The variable interest rate may be 6% in April but it is possible that in May, the prime rate that will be published in the Wall Street Journal will be much higher than what it was in April or the financial institutions may increase their marginal interest rate. Financial institutions add the prime rate that is published in the Wall Street Journal with their marginal interest rate to determine the total interest rate that the consumer will have to pay. This means the interest rate on the consolidated private student loan could become 18% or more because there is no cap on the increase of the interest rate. 18% or a higher interest rate on a $7,219.17 balance could be over a thousand dollars or more worth of interest especially if the student defers their payments or is late in making them. If the interest rate increases greatly then the monthly

minimum payment requirements increase too to the point that a consumer may not be able to afford to pay them and will result in the student loan becoming delinquent. Unless Suntrust Bank could make the 6% interest rate permanent on the consolidated student loan then Erica is better off having multiple private student loans with small balances. 18% or more on private student loans with small balances is cheaper than a consolidated private student loan with a huge balance. Financial institutions that are offering incentives of some type for consolidating the student loans should be avoided unless they can guarantee a permanent, which means fixed, interest rate.

12. Students should not drop classes unless they are guaranteed a 100% refund for the class. It makes no sense to drop a class if there is no refund given because then a student just wasted their own money. Some students that are using scholarships and/or student loans think it does not hurt them to drop a class because they will choose not to repay their student loans. They think the scholarships are free money. These students are unaware that student loans never disappear, they keep growing with compounded interest and late fees if left unpaid, and cannot be wiped out in any bankruptcy or debt settlement unless the student has a major disability that is preventing them being able to do labor and can be somehow verified by the government. If students fail or drop their class then the scholarship money must be repaid based on the price of the class. The providers of the scholarships are not going to let their money get wasted. They have academic expectations for the students to whom they grant the scholarships. Additionally, when the time period passes in which a student can drop a class and get a full refund, if a student drops a class after this period then their transcript will show a "W" letter next to the title of the course. The W means withdrawal and when employers see the transcript of the student and notices that the student withdrew from a class then they may think the student is academically weak because they would not understand why a student would withdraw from a class. Such a decision made by the student takes credibility away from their college degree. For this reason, students are better off earning a C in a class rather than withdrawing from it. If students currently have a D or F in their class then they should talk to their professor about doing extra credit or redoing a major assignment or project for a higher grade. Although it is unlikely a professor would allow for a student to do something extra for the purpose of trying to improve their grade, this does not mean that a professor would not give the chance to the student if they feel as though the student has been putting forth a great deal of effort in the class. Most professors value dedication and effort. Students should be honest with their professor that they do not want to fail and have to retake the course because they do not want to get into excessive student loan debt. Professors will value the fact that students are trying to be financially smart.

13. At times, credit card companies may send balance transfer offers to new and current customers. A balance transfer is when a debt is brought over from one financial institution to another for the purpose of receiving a cheaper interest rate on the debt. New customers will be required to apply for a new credit card if they want to accept the balance transfer offer. Consumers should consider doing a balance transfer with their student loan if the interest rate they will receive through the balance transfer is cheaper than the current interest rate they are paying and the interest rate will be fixed for life. If the balance transfer interest rate is fixed for life then it may be worth it to pay the 3-5% balance transfer fee. However, consumer should not transfer their

student loan to a credit card if they think they will default on it someday because then the interest rate will be increased to about 30% or more and will cause the debt to significantly increase instead of decrease. Consumers should not accept balance transfer offers that last for a certain number of months because in most cases, it is unlikely that the student will be able to repay all the debt with the specified time period of the balance transfer offer. If they are unable to repay it within that time then the interest rate will increase to the regular purchase rate of the credit card, which is usually anywhere from 10% - 18% variable or fixed. If students do not have a high enough credit limit on their credit card or loan to conduct the balance transfer then they should call the financial institution and explain that they want to transfer student loan debt for the purpose of trying to save money. It is likely the financial institution will conduct a hard inquiry credit check for increasing the credit limit or amount of the loan but in this situation, the credit check is worthwhile because the student should want to save money on interest. The business purpose behind performing a credit check is that when a financial institution grants more loan money such as through a credit limit increase or approves a new credit account, they do not want other financial institutions to immediately grant more loan money to the consumer. This is because it raises the chances that the consumer will use all the loan money and put themselves into a bad position in which they cannot repay any company. The credit check lowers the likelihood that the consumer will get approved for new credit accounts or more loan money because new financial institutions are not going to want to grant more loan money to a consumer that was recently granted new loan money. For example, if Carmen was granted a Nordstrom Bank credit card and two weeks later, she applies for a Citibank credit card. Citibank is likely going to deny Carmen for a new credit card because Citibank and Nordstrom Bank does not want that Carmen use the entire credit limits of her Nordstrom Bank and Citibank credit cards and as a result, she cannot repay either of them. Citibank will notice the credit check that Nordstrom Bank did on her and so they know Carmen had recently obtained new credit. If Citibank had granted credit to Carmen then the business risk management software of Nordstrom Bank would detect a change in her credit profile and they would potentially consider closing the Nordstrom Bank credit card or reducing its credit limit. The credit check helps the financial institutions, which in this case are Citibank and Nordstrom Bank, protect themselves from business losses.

14. Even when consumers receive no bill from the student loan issuer then they should still continue making payments on the student loan with any extra money in their possession. Every dollar helps save money significantly on interest. Consumers should make all payments for all bills online so the payments are not lost and money is not being wasted.

15. If possible, students should use a credit card to pay as much as possible for their tuition. They should use the credit card that has the most rewards and no annual fee. This is because the rewards program helps save money as long as the student does not carry a balance on their credit card because then they will get charged interest. Students should use their student loan money to pay off the credit card immediately. Many credit cards offer cash back or points that can be redeemed for airline tickets, gift cards, or simply cash that the student gets to keep provided that they are faithful in paying their credit cards.

16. If consumers are working to the point that they are earning low academic grades in courses then they need to immediately quit their job or reduce the amount of hours they are working because they are not making any money by doing poorly in classes. Consumers are losing money because they will not earn credits for the courses in which they do poorly and as a result, they will have to retake the courses. Retaking courses will likely cause them to spend beyond the amount of money that they are earning within their job especially if they are using student loan money to pay for the classes because the student loans will compound with interest. Students are better off using more student loan money to pay for their expenses and spend less time working at their job and more time focusing on their courses. Bad grades will jeopardize any scholarships the students may already be receiving and it will also jeopardize any future scholarships for which they apply and chances at earning a good job. Little or no scholarship money along with a bad or no job means more expenses and debt.

Student Loan Relief Fraud

Students should <u>never</u> respond to the advertisements they see on television, the internet, or hear on the radio about phony companies claiming they can eliminate student loan debt. The truth is student loan debt can never be eliminated unless the student fully repays it in an efficient manner. The phony companies tell the students to stop paying on their student loans. They then have the student send them the money that they would normally use to make the student loan payments claiming the student is no longer liable for the debt and the company will handle it for them. They may over exaggerate to the student that they will get the student loan debt cut in half, its interest rate reduced, or have it permanently discharged in someway. They charge the student exorbitant fees for their scam services. After a certain number of months or years have passed, the phony companies may contact the student loan providers and make a deal with them to buy the student loan debt claiming that the student cannot pay it, which is why they have not been making any payments. The student loan provider will refuse to sell the debt, they will take adverse actions against the student, and it is likely the phony company will take off with the money by erasing their business website, address, and phone number. The phony "student loan relief" companies have no liability if the wages of the student are garnished, the student receives no tax refunds, the student is sued by their student loan providers, or if the student loan providers levy the bank accounts, which means they withdraw all the money belonging to the student.

Some phony student loan relief companies do nothing but collect money from the students with the intention of running off with it and erasing their business information so the police neither the students can find them. They may collect personal information from the student such as their student loan account number, social security number, and date of birth so they can somehow open up credit accounts and make the student liable for all the charges. Finally, the phony student loan companies may somehow take the student loan money, keep it as profit, and the student now must repay the huge balance on the student loan. If consumers are currently dealing with a phony student loan relief company, they should report them immediately to law officials and stop paying them any money. The only companies that should be receiving money are the authentic student loan providers.

Student Loan Relief Options

For whatever reasons if a student is delinquent on their student loan and the delinquency is reported to the credit agencies so they can put a negative mark on the credit reports of the student. The student should not stop making payments. Instead, they should call the provider immediately and ask them to waive the late fee as a one time courtesy. Students should never be careless about getting late fees refunded because in time, they can add up to a great deal of money considering they are compounded with interest and this will cause the credit scores of the consumer to plummet. The late fees cause the debts to grow increasingly and debt always lowers the credit scores. Even if the student one day manages to repay the entire student loan debt, it still may raise questions to employers as to why they had so much student loan debt. Students should request for the customer service representative of the student loan company to make a note on their student loan account indicating why they were late in making their payment. The purpose for doing this is so the student loan provider does not think that the student has the intention of defaulting because as a business, the productivity function level of the student loan provider becomes weak. A student loan provider is more likely to be willing to remove the negative marks off of the credit reports of the student on that one month they were delinquent if the student manages to redeem themselves by never being late on any payment due since the time that the delinquency had occurred. When a student requests for their student loan provider to remove the negative marks off of their credit reports then they are requesting for a process called **loan rehabilitation**. Students that have negative marks on their credit reports under the student loans should always ask for loan rehabilitation from each student loan provider. It will cause the student loan providers to review the payment histories of the student loans and then they will decide whether or not the student deserves to have the negative marks removed. They will see the notes made on the student loan accounts explaining why the students were late in making their payments on the months that the negative marks were reported to the credit reports of the consumer. The student loan providers may deny the request to the students to remove the negative marks but the students should continue maintaining a strong payment history and should later again ask for loan rehabilitation. Students do not want their employers and insurance providers to see the negative marks on their credit reports.

When students are successful in making payments all the time or they manage to redeem themselves in the eyes of the student loan issuer by always making payments in a timely manner since the last time they were late then the students have payment relief options. Keep in mind, these options do not eliminate student loan debt or make it cheaper, they actually make the student loan debt more expensive because it is likely the issuer will charge extra interest on the balance, but they are awesome alternatives if a student were to lose their job or source of income. This is because the credit profile of the student is protected from a delinquency (late payment) being reported by the loan issuer and the student is protected against late fees, which compound with interest themselves. Students will not qualify for all the options because it depends on their payment history, information on their FAFSA, what type of government and private student loans they have, and the issuer may ask for a copy of their tax documents such as the tax returns to verify how much money, if any, to which they have access. Students have to ask the issuer which student loan relief options for which they qualify and some of them are similar. Due to the rough economic conditions, some of the student loan relief options may have been eliminated or will be eliminated and for this reason, students should get the least amount of student loan money as possible. Students need to be aware that there are less payment relief options for private student loans, which are bank issued loans, than government student loans. For this reason, students should not get themselves into a position in which they need private student loan money.

1. Economic hardship payment deferment: Students that have most or all of their income going towards student loan payments to the point that they cannot afford to provide for themselves or their family can defer their payments.

2. Unemployment payment deferment: Students that currently have no job or source of income can defer their monthly minimum payment for the time that they are unemployed.

3. Military payment deferment: Students are serving in the military, armed forces, or the navy can defer their payments.

All the payment relief options, regardless of their name, are considered a deferment, because a student is postponing on making the payment or is stretching the payments to make the minimum payment requirements smaller. There may be a limit to how many times a student can defer their minimum payment depending upon what the polices are of the student loan provider. Students should ask such information when calling the provider. Payment deferments can get expensive because it is possible the student may end up paying extra interest on interest, it will take them longer to pay off the student loan, and the excessive debt can cause their credit scores to remain low. Paying extra interest is the cost of deferring the payment.

Example
Krista has a student loan of which the minimum monthly payment requirement is $55.39.

When the minimum payment of a student loan, credit card, or mortgage is calculated, it includes two portions. One portion is interest whereas the other and very little portion is principal. It is likely most of the minimum payment is interest because the goal of the loan issuer is to make the maximum profit off of the consumers.

Krista cannot afford to make the payment in December and so she calls the loan issuer and defers the payment. The $55.39 goes into the principal student loan balance of $2,859.11, which is considered the student loan being capitalized because it is growing instead of decreasing. Capitalization is when the interest becomes part of the principal balance. Whatever portion of the $55.39 is interest is now becoming part of the student loan principal balance when a student defers the payment.

The student loan has an interest rate of 6.8% fixed. When the $55.39 goes back into $2,859.11 primary student loan balance, the portion of the minimum payment that is interest will be charged the 6.8%. Thus, interest is being charged on interest. For this reason, students should defer their payment only if it is their last resort to protecting their credit profile from a delinquency.

Repayment plans in which the students can make payments but their monthly minimum payment requirements will be very small. Some of these payment plans may be similar but are not available on all the government issued loans as well as loans on which the student has defaulted.

Danny Singh

Warning: Lowering the minimum payment requirements can cause the loan amount to double or even triple. For this reason, even if students are in a special repayment plan, at any time if they get extra money, they should pay above the minimum payment requirements. Doing so also has a positive impact on their credit scores because their overall level of debt is less.

Forbearance

According to Sallie Mae, students can defer their payments for up to 1 year and pay nothing. However, other loan providers may allow the students to defer their payments for a longer or shorter time frame depending upon their policies.

Standard Repayment

The loan is structured so it can be fully paid off within 10 years or less. Standard repayment allows for the student to save the most amount of money in interest compared to the other repayment options but for this reason, it has the highest monthly minimum payments. If students cannot afford to make the monthly minimum payment then they should not do a standard repayment student loan plan otherwise they will be hit with late fees and eventually, the student loan provider will report the student loan as delinquent to the credit agencies and this will kill the chances of the student being able to earn a good job and getting a cheap insurance premium. The standard repayment plan makes it unlikely that the student loan amount will double or triple provided the student is not always late in making payments because the late fees with interest are very expensive. Students should not do standard repayment if they feel as though their job is not secure meaning they are at high risk of losing it, if they are expecting children, or another major expense.

Extended Repayment

The student loan can be stretched out to be repaid at any time frame within 12 to 30 years but the longer that the student makes the time frame then the more interest that they agree to be charged. Such is the price for making the monthly minimum payments so small.
-Students should make the extended repayment plan as long as possible for the purpose of being safe against the student loan damaging the credit profile due to a delinquency. Although the monthly minimum payments will be small, students should pay as much as they can above the minimum payment and in doing so, they can pay off the student loan much faster than the loan term they have set with the issuer. Paying above the minimum payment will allow for the student to save a **huge** amount of money paid on interest with any loan. The extended repayment plan makes it easier to pay the other expenses but students should always aim at fully repaying the student loan faster than the time frame term they have set with the issuer. Paying extra will mean higher credit scores.

Graduated Repayment

Similar to an extended repayment plan, the time frame to repay the student loan can be anywhere from 12 to 30 years and if students stretch out the loan term too long and only make the minimum monthly payments then they run the risk of the student loan doubling or tripling due to aggressively compounded interest. The major difference between a graduated repayment plan and an extended repayment plan is that with a graduated repayment plan, every two years, the monthly minimum payment will increase but the interest rate will remain the same. The purpose of the minimum payment increasing is so the student can repay the student loan immediately and not pay so much interest.

Income-Contingent Repayment (ICR)

The maximum term to repay the student loan is 25 years. The monthly minimum payment amount is based on the income level and amount of debt belonging to the student. For this reason, it is likely the loan issuer will ask the student for a pay stub or W-2 for the purpose of verifying their income. After 25 years, any remaining student loan debt is forgiven but students may have to pay taxes on that forgiven debt depending upon the current laws of the government and the policies of the student loan issuer. For this reason, students should try their best to pay off the student loan before the 25 years comes to an end.

Income-Sensitive Repayment (ISR)

Similar to the income-contingent repayment (ICR) plan, ISR bases the monthly minimum payment off of the loan amount and income level of the student but the loan must be repaid within 10 years. Due to the fact that the consumer is repaying the student loan faster with an ISR plan than they are with an ICR plan, the monthly minimum payments are going to be higher with an ISR plan than with an ICR plan. A certain percentage of the income of the student is used to determine the payment amounts so the loan can be repaid within 10 years or less.

Income-Based Repayment (IBR)

An income-based repayment plan makes the monthly minimum payments no more than 10% of the income belonging to the consumer. The loan provider will ask for a W-2 or pay stub of the consumer to verify their income every year. The loan term can be stretched out to 25 years and if students are never late in making the payments then the debt will be forgiven. For students that work in the military or public service industries then their debt will be forgiven in 10 years.

Note: Compared to all the student loan repayment options, the income-based repayment and extended repayment plans offer the lowest monthly minimum payment and they are ideal for students that have many expenses. However, students should <u>always</u> pay above the minimum payment for the purpose of preventing the student loan amount from doubling or tripling due to excessive interest. It is recommended students do an income-based or extended repayment plan because if a financial emergency happens then they can afford to take care of it along with making the student loan payments. When the emergency is over then they can make payments above the minimum payment requirements. Consumers can always switch their repayment plan. For example, Austin can switch from a standard repayment plan to an extended repayment plan. Consumers should always call their loan issuer and switch their repayment plan immediately before becoming delinquent for the purpose of protecting their credit profile.

Word of caution: Before doing a payment deferment or repayment program, students should always ask their student loan provider how they will report the payment history of the student loan to the credit agencies in the months of which the payments are being deferred or the minimum payment requirements are very low. Students do not want the student loan providers to report to their credit reports that they are doing a special payment program because although this is better than delinquencies from being reported, payment programs may send the message to future financial institutions that the consumer is financially weak otherwise it raises the question to them why the consumer would have had the need to do any payment plan program. However, they will appreciate the fact that the student did a payment plan program verses simply letting the student loans become delinquent.

For the purpose of minimizing student loan debt, students should ask their college for **work study** opportunities. Work study is when the student is given a job at the school such as a library assistant and they get paid for doing the job and this income goes towards tuition. Unfortunately, work study opportunities are based on the information that is found on the FAFSA profile of the student. The reason for this is because the government is trying to give work study to students whose parents make very little or no income because it stands to reason they would need work study more than other students. Students that come from low income families need more money to pay for their tuition. Students, regardless of the income level, should ask the financial aid office of their college for work study opportunities. However, students should never do so much work study to the point that they have little or no time to focus on their academics.

Obama Student Loan Reform

On March 30, 2010, President Barrack Obama signed into law the student loan reform act, which was hoped to cause more students to make the decision to enter college due to the fact they would have less financial struggles to pay for the tuition. The student loan reform act would supposedly cause students to have access to more financial aid money and with a college degree; they could enter the workforce more easily. As a result, this would keep the economy strong and stable within the United States. All the changes of the student loan reform act would go into effect in 2012.

1. The government will no longer pay money as fees to the financial institutions to issue government supported student loans to students. They will only be issued through the college and Department of Education using FAFSA. As reported by the New York Times, this is expected to cause about $68 billion dollars in savings over 11 years and should cause the Pell grants to increase from $5,550 to a maximum of $5,975 by the year 2017. It will also provide 820,000 more grants to students by the year 2020. However, currently, private student loans, which are the variable interest rate loans supported mainly by the financial institutions, will still exist.
Personal advice: It is recommended students do not waste the extra Pell grant money on unnecessary items such as drugs and instead, use it to make payments on their student loans so they can be out of debt much faster and will not struggle to get a job, cheap insurance, apartment, house, or car.

2. For the next four years beginning in 2012, about two billion dollars will be invested into community and state colleges for the purpose of creating career training programs such as the bachelor's degree programs. The colleges can expand and it is hoped students will have access to a more advanced education.
Personal advice: Students should take advantage of the bachelor's degree programs and other courses offered by the community and state colleges. The investment of the government should not go to waste and it will allow for a student to save a substantial amount of money on student loan debt. After earning the bachelor's degree, the student should continue their education at a graduate school and pursue the highest level degree possible.

3. Students who take out government supported student loans such as Perkins, Stafford, Plus, will not have to make monthly payment amounts more than 10% of their income. Currently, students do not have to make payments more than 15% of their income on their student loans. Personal advice: If possible, students should try their best to save money and make payments more than 10% of their income for the purpose of preventing their student loans from rapidly growing with compounded interest and fees. Payments less than 10% of the income may cause the student loan amounts to double and in some cases, triple, because the primary balance is still considered high. The interest rate attacks the primary balance. High student loan balances also mean low credit scores and expensive car, life, health, and house insurance premiums.

4. Students can consolidate meaning they can combine guaranteed and direct student loans and as a result, earn a discount on their interest rate.
Personal advice: Students should not consolidate the student loans if the monthly minimum payment will become too expensive for them to afford. This will raise their chances of defaulting on the consolidated student loan and being hit with late fees that will compound with interest themselves. If the monthly payments for the guaranteed and direct student loans are cheaper separately then the students should not do anything with them. If the monthly minimum payment will be affordable then the students should consolidate their student loans. Students can and should ask for an estimation of how much the monthly minimum payment will be if they consolidate the student loans.

5. Instead of 25 years, after 20 years of successfully making payments on the government supported student loans, any remaining debt is forgiven and the student is done in making payments. For students that pursue a career in nursing, the armed forces, or teaching, their student loan debt is forgiven in 10 years. However, private student loans, which are the loans issued by financial institutions, last forever and they are never forgiven.
Personal advice: Students should not be late on making the student loan payments otherwise they may struggle in getting the debts forgiven after 10 or 20 years depending upon their career path.

The student loan reform act may have benefits but along with the weak economic conditions due to the credit crisis, it may be partially responsible for the government eliminating subsidized Stafford loans for students wishing to enter graduate school and the current danger of student loan interest rates increasing on Stafford subsidized student loans from 3.4% to 6.8% for all students effective July 2012. The interest rates increasing may cause a recession within the United States because it will cause the monthly minimum payments on the Stafford student loans to increase and this will raise the chances of the student defaulting on the loans. It will be especially difficult for students to make payments considering taxes may be increasing, gas prices, insurance premiums, and the overall costs of living. The student loan debts dropping in 20 years and 10 years for nurses, members of the armed forces, and teachers may be dangerous for the economy of the United States because debt never disappears and it is likely the national debt may increase from the many student loans being forgiven.

Quest Bridge

Students who come from low income families but they want to attend college should visit www.questbridge.org. This website uses their academic credentials to match them up to top ranking colleges and universities who will offer them a significant scholarship. The scholarship can pay to 100% of the tuition costs provided the student has strong academics and assessment scores. Students have nothing to lose and should visit the website immediately.

"School-as-Lender" Program

Students need to be very careful of colleges and universities that are part of the "school-as-lender" program. This program is when the school has business relationships with multiple private lenders such as Sallie Mae or Citibank and uses their money to grant student loans to students. After the student agrees to get the student loan, the school forwards the student to the private student loan lending company. The student has to repay the loan lending company. The student loan lending company pays the school a commission or fee for getting them the student. This is similar to how car dealership forward consumers to financial institutions who grant them an auto loan with a higher than average interest and the money made from the interest is used to pay a commission to the car dealership for getting them new business.

Both the school and lending company make money through the "school-as-lender" program. According to a 60 Minutes segment on CBS News aired on May 7, 2006, they discussed the school-as-lender program when they were discussing the business practices of Sallie Mae and they had indicated that schools try to get students to get private student loans, which can go up at any time to 18 percent similar to a credit card and usually has fees just for getting the loan. According to the Huffington Post, the average student loan debt amount in America is greater than $25,250 and being accessed an 18 percent interest rate on a $25,000 loan is a nightmare especially if the student attended a private or for-profit school and has almost $100,000 worth of debt. $100,000 is the price for some houses in America and consumers usually have a mortgage interest rate anywhere from 4 to 6 percent. As seen in the 2000s housing crisis, millions of consumers failed to make their mortgage payments and as a result, the financial institutions foreclosed on their houses. This raises the question if so many consumers could not handle paying their mortgages, which are dischargeable in bankruptcy, then how can the majority of students be successful in repaying their student loans. The answer is many students will default and the student loans crisis will emerge in America causing a recession similar to the housing crisis.

Some schools justify the school-as-lender program as being beneficial to students because some of the profit they make is used to create grants and scholarships for other students. This is true but the issue arises why some students have to pay high interest on student loans, which raises their likelihood of defaulting and struggling to earn a job, for the purpose of funding grants for other students. As a personal analysis, this program does not seem fair because all students have expenses and must save money for the purpose of living. For this reason, please always avoid getting private student loans and do not get fooled by the encouragement of the school to get one. Only get Perkins, Stafford, and other federal government loans because the overall costs of getting them are much cheaper than private student loans. If consumers are in a position in which they have no choice but to get a private student loan in order to pay for college then they should **really** consider going to a cheaper school. There is nothing wrong with doing so because consumers will eventually have other expenses in their lives and they cannot afford to have excessive student loan debt. This could lead to their houses and cars becoming repossessed and not being able to save money for their children. Consumers should not worry about what people will think about them if they choose to attend a cheaper school because a life filled of debt is **never** a good life.

Weddings and Finance

Weddings do not mean Debt

According to Reuters, the average cost of a wedding, within the United States is $27,021. Part of what makes weddings so expensive is that many consumers use loan money to pay for them. Consumers should never do cash out refinance or obtain a home equity line of credit, to pay for a wedding; because cash out refinances have high closing costs and fees up to $5,000 that compound with interest themselves.

The interest rate of a home equity line of credit can increase at any time up to 18% along with the monthly payment making it likely that a consumer will default and be hit with late fees. The late fees will compound with interest themselves. Unless the consumer has saved up enough money in savings to pay off the balance immediately, using a credit card even if it has a 0% promotional interest rate, to pay for a wedding is very dangerous because if the consumer is late in making the payment then they will be charged an expensive late fee usually of $35 or more that will compound with interest itself and after 60 days, the credit card provider will increase the interest rate to 30%. The safest and cheapest loan to use for a wedding is a secured loan from a credit union or a home equity loan if the house has available equity meaning value that can be converted into loan money. Although a wedding is a time of joy and excitement, consumers need to make sure the expenses do not cause them to live married lives of being bankrupt, and eventually, divorced because debt usually causes major stress between couples.

Home Equity Loan is Sometimes a Safe Method to Finance Wedding

Home equity loans have a fixed interest rate, which does not change, even if the consumer defaults. Unless the consumer has a past due balance, then the monthly payment amount is the same every month. Consumers should not get home equity loans, if they have expensive closing costs or fees in general or if their employment is not secured; because if they do not pay the home equity loan then the financial institution will foreclose on the house and if it is a recourse home equity loan, then the financial institution will demand money from the consumer even after taking the house.

In addition, I do not suggest taking a loan against a 401(k) or 403(b) plan, to pay for a wedding, because taking a loan against a retirement plan should only be meant for saving the house from foreclosure or saving a loan from becoming delinquent; so the consumer does not become homeless or struggle to find a job.

Roth IRA can be Safe Financing Method for Wedding

The best way to save for a wedding, is if a consumer works for an employer that does company matching; meaning the company will contribute an additional amount to the 401(k) or 403(b) plan, equal to the exact amount that the consumer contributed; then consumers should contribute as much money as possible, without exceeding the contribution limit to their 401(k) or 403(b) plan for the purpose of maximizing the company matching benefit.

Afterwards, consumers should rollover (transfer) the money from their retirement plan into a Roth IRA, pay the necessary taxes, and then take the money and not the earnings (interest). They will not have to pay the 10% tax penalty or wait until they reach the age of retirement to take the money.

Saving money within a regular savings or money market will likely not make as much earnings as the money would make within a Roth IRA but it is ideal for consumers that for some reason, cannot get a Roth IRA. Whatever deposit account consumers open for the purpose of saving for their wedding should have an account bonus such for example, $100 for opening a new account. Consumers find the best bank bonus offers on www.ibankdesign.com and www.ibankbonus.com

Consumers need to pay attention to the fees and should never get an account that has a monthly fee, because this will offset the money made through the account bonus. Finally, consumers should never open an account, despite the bonus, with a financial institution that is not FDIC or NCUA insured. Consumers should use a credit card to pay for all the wedding expenses for protection against scams and then use the money from the Roth IRA or deposit account to pay off the credit card, without closing it. Consumers will save money through the rewards program and may be able to save even more by calling their insurance providers for cheaper premiums now that their credit scores have likely increased. After getting married, the two partners should immediately take a term life insurance plan for each other.

Ways to Keep Low Expenses for Wedding

1. Consumers should ask their friends for connections to florists, designers, DJs, or better yet, if the friends can do the tasks themselves. For example, instead of paying $1,000 or more to a DJ, consumers can get speakers and hook up an iPod or computer to automatically play the music. A friend or family member can monitor everything for technical difficulties.
2. Instead of expensive halls, consumers can get married in a public park, or the church they attend.
3. Consumers should go to outlet stores or stores going out of business to purchase wedding jewelry, dress, suits, and other items.

Pregnancy and Finance

A growing number of teenagers and young adults are having sex before getting married and this results in many unplanned pregnancies occurring. As a result; the consumers are dropping out of school, are struggling to do well in school, or are using their grant and student loan money to support their children. As support, www.teenhealth.com reports 80% of teenage pregnancies are unintended and 79% of these teenagers are unmarried, within the United States.

Only one-third of teenage mothers completes high school and receives their diplomas. By age 30, only 1.5% of women who had pregnancies, as a teenager, have a college degree. It is likely because their motherly responsibilities distract them from their academic responsibilities; which raise their chances of failing classes and getting into student loan debt. This causes them to struggle in earning a decent job and they begin relying on the government, for financial support. In personal experience, I have met several brilliant women, at my college and high school; who became pregnant and dropped out of school and the women were even younger than me.

Dropping out of school ruins the future of a consumer and this can support why one half of the unmarried teenage mothers; go on social welfare. The United States spends an estimated seven billion dollars each year on supporting teenage mothers. The seven billion dollars comes from taxpayer money. Social welfare and not having a college degree, considering the many expenses consumers have within a lifetime, causes teenage mothers to struggle in making a living for themselves and their children.

Time Magazine reports it costs more than $220,000 to raise a child and this does not even include the costs of sending them to college. It is especially hard for teenage mothers to work if they are carrying a child within themselves. Part of the reason why this is happening is because the male partners are leaving the female partners; due to not having any integrity or good morals to take care of their children. The children cannot likely grow up in a financially healthy household, with only one parent in charge of all the expenses.

In fact, the Brooklyn Young Mothers' Collective (BYMC) indicates it is believed more than 75% of children born to single teenage parents in the United States grow up in poverty. For this reason, young adults and teenagers should only have sex after getting married; because if the partner does leave then they can be sued for alimony and child support as part of the divorce or separation decree.

Without marriage, it is true teenage mothers can get only child support; but it may be difficult to do so without getting an attorney, unless the partner is very willing to pay the child support. According to www.lawfirms.com, attorney and court fees range from $4,000 to $25,000. It is unlikely a teenage mother will be able to come up with so much money with ease; and it is always possible that a parent may stop paying child support, which may require for the teenage mother to take them to court and pay the fees again. When a parent stops paying child support; then it is reported as negative information to their credit reports and they may struggle to get a job, because employers may think they are low in character for not supporting their children.

Additionally, from personal experience, child support alone is very little or no money. When my mother and father divorced, my mother was only paid $300 a month and that only paid the monthly payment of our car. She had to pay for the mortgage, credit cards, car insurance, health insurance, life insurance, utilities, home owner's insurance, food, taxes, maintenance of the car and house, and the home owner's association bill; by herself and had to work long hours so she could make enough money. Child support only lasts until the child reaches age 18. For this reason, women should never think that if they get pregnant and are paid child support then they will be able to live an average to good lifestyle. Marriage will help teenage mothers get child support and alimony and they need that money to help support their children; otherwise they could end up becoming homeless and the partner will not care about them. It is also possible that the wife could leave the husband with the child. In this situation, it is possible for the husband to get child support and alimony from their wife. Alimony and child support will be even more beneficial if the parent later finds out he or she may be living with a disease; because it will cost them more money to pay for the medical treatments.

Some women and men think it is okay to have sex before marriage; if they use contraception methods such as birth control pills or if they abort the child. Contraception does not always prevent pregnancy and some of the methods are dangerous; especially for the women. For example, according to MSN Health, birth control pills increase the risk of the woman developing cervical and breast cancers, migraines, liver tumors, blood clots and infertility which means they can never have children in their lifetime. This is because birth control pills along with other chemical contraception methods; use artificial hormones that damage the bodily functions of the woman in order to prevent them from becoming pregnant. Abortion is not considered a contraception method. It is not healthy for women because the chemicals that the medical physicians use to end the life of the child are dangerous. They may be a reason why women that have done at least one abortion in their lifetime face a 2.3 times higher risk of having cervical cancer compared to women that have never had an abortion, as reported by the Elliot Institute.

Unless they already have strong assets, when consumers have a child, they should always get term life insurance, preferably from a credit union or community bank, so if they die then their child will be protected. Women should get the life insurance policy the day that they find out they are pregnant; because if they pass away while giving birth then their baby is protected. Consumers have to inform the insurance company that they are pregnant because there is special type of term life insurance for pregnant women; due to the fact the baby is not yet born.

When the money within an IRA account and/or 401(k) or 403(b) account is plentiful then the consumers can cancel the term life insurance and name their children as the beneficiaries on the accounts meaning the children will get all the money within those accounts when their parents die. However, before naming the children as beneficiaries, the consumers need to ask if they name a minor, which is an individual under age 18, will the money within the retirement accounts become blocked. Consumers never want to put their children into a position in which they cannot claim the money within their retirement accounts if they become deceased.

Finance 101: The Whiz Kid's Perfect Credit Guide

Financial Protection and Safety Strategies

Safety Precautions

Consumers should shred all their open plastic credit cards, to lower the risks of them being stolen or the consumers unknowingly using all of them. Consumers should only carry one to two bank credit cards and their store branded credit cards with them. When a consumer closes their credit card; they need to shred the plastic card immediately. Even though it is closed, a criminal could potentially use the account number, reopen the account, and go on a shopping spree. Some criminals can even use the account number to somehow steal the identity of the consumer. Consumers should not carry their social security card or large cash bills with them. Consumers should not take such risks because a robbery can happen at any time.

Scam College Aid

Consumers need to avoid websites that ask for money, so they can apply for scholarships or the website representatives will apply for scholarships on the behalf of the consumer. These websites do no guarantee that the consumer will get any financial aid for college. They are gimmicks and consumers do not get refunds. Consumers could get into legal trouble if the companies misrepresent information; about the consumer on scholarship applications such as their ethnicity because some scholarships are only for certain ethnicities. Consumers may receive postal mail too from companies claiming they can get the consumer a scholarship or grant if the consumer first pays them money and provides their personal information. These companies may also fraudulently use the information of the consumers to do financial damage to them and ruin their credit profiles.

Credit Card Abuse

Consumers should never apply for credit cards and loans; for the purpose of depositing the money into an interest bearing account; with the intention of not repaying the loan. The damaged credit profile will offset any interest they make because they will struggle to find a job and all their insurance companies will increase the premiums. For consumers that do have the intention of repaying their loans and want to deposit the loan money into bank accounts, this is a very dangerous investment that is personally not recommended. Consumers have to make a monthly payment on the loans and credit cards and if they are late in doing so; then they will be charged late fees and on credit cards, the interest rates will be increased to 30% or more. Using all the loan money to deposit into interest bearing accounts will cause their credit scores to significantly drop because it looks like the consumer is getting into a high level of debt. Low credit scores are going to cause the insurance premiums to increase and cause employers to look at the consumer as being irresponsible. The interest made within deposit accounts are taxable so the consumer is getting little or no return especially considering they likely paid fees to use the loan money of the credit card, which are balance transfer fees, or the loans, which are closing costs, for the purpose of depositing it all into their bank accounts.

Personal Line of Credit

A personal line of credit is similar to a credit card, because the consumer accesses loan money whenever they need it. The consumer is not given all the loan money at once, unless they want to access all of it. Consumers can use the personal line of credit and attach it to their checking account for the purpose of avoiding overdraft fees. The line of credit will pay for the transactions for which the consumer does not have enough money. Consumers can get a secured personal line of credit; meaning they provide a security deposit to the financial institution or they can get an unsecured personal line of credit meaning they provide no security deposit to the financial institution.

A **secured** personal line of credit will always have a cheaper interest rate and overall costs than an unsecured personal line of credit; because the financial institution will keep the security deposit money if the consumer chooses not to repay the loan. Consumers access the loan money of a personal line of credit, by writing a check to a merchant or by transferring the loan money into their checking account. They can then withdraw the money from the bank account as cash. However, a personal line of credit does not help save money because it does not have a rewards program like most credit cards and almost all personal line of credit products have annual fees. This is a flat fee that the consumer pays every year to the financial institution; regardless if they use the line of credit or not.

Not all credit cards have annual fees; which is why they are better than a line of credit product. A personal line of credit is dangerous because most of them have variable interest rates that can go up at any time to 17%, 18%, or 19% depending upon the conditions of the economy and the prime rate that is published, within the Wall Street Journal. This will cause the monthly payments due every month to be different every month and if the interest rate becomes too high; then the minimum payment will likely become very high because consumers will have to pay more interest with the payment. Some financial institutions may charge application fees, sometimes called closing costs, for the consumer to get the line of credit product. Consumers should request for these fees to be waived or reduced. Credit cards do not charge application fees or closing costs. Additionally, a personal line of credit product does not have the advanced consumer protection, like all credit cards do, against fraud or scam merchants. If a consumer used loan money from a credit product to send a check; or get cash and the merchant took off with the money, then the consumer has a financial loss. Unlike a credit card, consumers cannot use a plastic card to access the loan money, of their line of credit. Plastic cards such as credit and debit cards; make transactions safe because they give the right to the consumer to do a chargeback against the merchant; meaning the consumer can work with their financial institution and the money that the consumer paid the merchant will be taken back. For the purpose of being best protected, if a consumer gets a personal line of credit then they should transfer the money into their checking account and then use a high level rewards debit card to pay merchants.

Thanks to the Electronic Fund Transfer Act, all debit card users within the United States are given the right to do a chargeback, similar to how all credit card users are given the right to do a chargeback thanks to the **Truth in Lending Act**. A reason why some consumers may get a personal line of credit, instead of a credit card is due to the fact; if they default on the personal line of credit then their interest rate will not be increased to 30% or more, but they will still be charged a late fee and negative information will be reported to the credit agencies regarding the late payment.

If a consumer defaulted, on a credit card; then their interest rate would be increased to 30% or more, a late fee would be charged, and their credit profile would get damaged. Like all loan products, consumers should always get a line of credit product from a credit union or community bank and if possible; they should ask if there is any line of credit product with a fixed interest rate and obtain this product. Consumers are required to pay interest only, minimum monthly payments, on a line of credit product; but the interest cannot be deducted from their taxes and as personal advice, consumers should pay more than just the interest; otherwise the personal line of credit balance will continue compounding with more interest.

The minimum payment only pays 1% to 2% of the balance. The consumer will put themselves into a situation where they will owe a huge balance, to the financial institution and this will cause their credit scores to drop. Due to the fact the minimum payment due every month is low; a personal line of credit will be beneficial for consumers that have limited funds or have defaulted on credit cards. They should transfer the balances from the delinquent credit cards, onto the line of credit, because even if the variable interest rate goes up to 19%, this is still better than paying 30% on a credit card. When consumers pay off a personal line of credit; then they should not close it because similar to closing a credit, the closure of the line of credit will result in the credit scores going down. This is because the closure, of a line of credit product, sends the message that the consumer cannot handle the financial responsibility. It is worth it to pay the annual fee to maintain the line of credit account and just not use it. Consumers should lightly use the line of credit, spending no more than 30% of the loan money amount, and pay it off immediately; so it is not closed for inactivity and as a result, lowers the credit scores of the consumer. Consumers should periodically ask the financial institution to remove or reduce the annual fee without closing the line of credit product.

Timeshare

A timeshare is property owned or leased by multiple consumers who use it as a vacation home at different times. Usually, consumers are only allowed to use a timeshare for no more than one week every year; or they can rent their time to use the timeshare, to another consumer; for the purpose of trying to make money. Timeshares are usually apartments or condominiums located within resort areas. When a consumer gets a timeshare, then they send in money every year; to pay for it, its property taxes, and its maintenance. The timeshare company may collect additional fees from the consumer to make more profit. Timeshares can get expensive, because the amount of money that the consumer sends every month; could be used to make payments towards a student loan, mortgage, or save up for a house purchase. Despite being within resort areas, the timeshares are not worth the amount of money that the consumer pays and there is no telling how the other consumers will take care of the timeshare. For this reason, ABC News indicates; timeshares are one of the biggest scams in the country. Unless consumers work very little and have little or no debt; then a timeshare is not the best investment and consumers need to understand that it will be difficult for them to sell the timeshare. Consumers should do an internet complaints search on any company before getting a timeshare from them; or selling a timeshare to them. Companies want fees for selling timeshares, which are usually above $1000, because they claim they can guarantee to get the timeshare sold and they will take care of its maintenance until it is sold.

Auto lease

When consumers lease a car in simplest terms; they are renting the car and after the car reaches a certain number of miles; then the consumer will return the car, to the car dealer, or they can buy it. There is no obligation to purchase a car after the lease term is over. Consumers choose to lease a car because usually, the monthly payments for leasing a car are cheaper than buying a car and consumers do not have to make a down payment unless their credit profile is very poor. Consumers may lease a car, because they want to get familiar with it. For example, if a consumer is leasing a car that burns a great deal of gas; or they have a hard time driving it; then it is likely the consumer will return the car immediately and will not consider buying it. Some consumers lease a car, because they always want to have a new car every couple of years and so it makes no sense for them to purchase a car, pay for its maintenance, and then purchase a new car because now they have to pay for the maintenance, auto loan payments, and insurance policies of two cars. Some consumers may choose to sell the second car, but doing so can be a pain and for this reason, they choose to lease a car so they do not have to put up with the troubles of owning multiple cars. Consumers cannot exceed a certain number of miles when they are leasing a car, because if they do then they will be required to pay more money to the car dealer. If consumers are planning on driving to many destinations using a leased car; they are far better off buying a car, otherwise the lease will be more expensive. Consumers should not damage the leased automobile, because the car dealer may ask for money to repair the damages. Leasing or buying a car, does not affect its insurance premium, in any aspect. However, consumers should always ask the car dealer, if they are going to check the credit profile of the consumer every time they lease an automobile. If this is the case then consumers should wait at least two years every time they lease a car because the credit check drops off in two years. Consumers do not want to lease a new car every couple of months because then their credit profile will begin to get damaged from the excessive credit checks and this may cause their insurance premiums to increase.

Saving for Children's Education

A 529 college savings account and an education IRA are not the same; and they are two different financial products, that parents should consider getting for the purpose of paying the future college expenses for their children. Consumers should consider these products the moment that their children are born. These products will lower the chances of their children becoming too reliant on student loan money and as a result; the chances of a student loan crisis emerging and a recession happening will be low. All parents should motivate their children to pursue a degree.

529 College Savings

These plans are sponsored by the state agencies. The plan is available to families of all income levels.

The state tells the consumer how much money they can put into a 529 account every year. Before money goes into a 529 plan, taxes must be paid on it and for this reason, the amount of money that is deposited cannot be deducted from the taxes of the consumer. Parents never pay taxes, on the interest (earnings), that the money makes within the account. When the student begins taking the money, which is when they go to college, they do not pay any taxes on that money. Students cannot use the money to pay for something other than the expenses of college otherwise they will have to pay a 10% tax penalty and ordinary income taxes on that money. There is no age requirement when the student must use the money within the 529 account. They will face no penalties.

Any consumer, such as; an uncle, aunt, grandparent, grandmother, cousin, or just any family member can make a contribution (deposit) towards the 529 plan of a student. However, there is a limit to how much money they can contribute every year, otherwise they may face gift tax penalties, which is when consumers pay taxes on the money they donate or give to others. Consumers can find out the limit by calling the 529 account issuer.

When a 529 account is opened for a student then the parent must name the student as the "designated beneficiary"; so if the parent passes away then the student still gets all the money within the account and can pay for college. If the student makes the decision that they do not want to attend college or earn a scholarship; then they can withdraw the money from the 529 account without paying any penalty but they will have to pay taxes on the money. The money within a 529 account can be used to pay for any in-state or out of state college or university. However, the goal of all consumers should be to save as much money as possible within the 529 account, because after graduation, they can use the leftover money to make a down payment on a house or make another investment. For this reason, consumers should be smart and attend a community or state college because they have cheap tuition costs.

529 accounts have some risk because the money within them is growing due to the performance of stocks. If the stock market does poorly, then the money loses value. For this reason, when consumers are structuring the 529 account for their children, they should not invest too much money into stocks. Instead, they can purchase bonds, CDs, or leave some of the money within a money market account as part of the 529 account. The money that is kept within bonds, CDs, and the money market account does not make a great deal of earnings but it has no risk in money being lost. Consumers can find the 529 account issuer of their state by going to http://www.savingforcollege.com/.

Education IRA (Coverdell Education Savings Account)

Parents can make contributions (deposits) up to $2,000 per year, to an education IRA, to pay for the college expenses of their child. The contributions cannot be deducted from their taxes. Different from a 529 account, the money within an **Education IRA** must be used by the child when they turn age 30 or transferred to another family member if the child chooses not to attend college so tax penalties can be avoided. The money within an **Education IRA** cannot be used for expenses, other than college; otherwise the money will be taxed with a 10% tax penalty and ordinary income taxes.

Another difference between an Education IRA and a 529 account is that consumers can use the money, within an Education IRA, to pay for the educational expenses of their children that attend costly, usually private, elementary, middle, and high schools. The consumers will not have to pay taxes on the money; when they withdraw it to pay for such expenses including college expenses. An Education IRA has risk because the growth of its money depends on the conditions of the stock market. For this reason, consumers should not invest too much money into stocks. They should structure the Education IRA so most of the money is held within a money market account, CDs, and bonds. Consumers should get an Education IRA for their child at a credit union or community bank.

Third Party Manages Store Branded Credit Cards

When consumers apply for any store branded credit card, a third party, which is the financial institution, is handling all the management for the store credit card and will determine whether the consumer is denied or approved. The store is not handling the management of the store credit cards, because they pay a fee to the financial institution to handle all the management for them. The financial institution pays the store some type of commission from the profits generated, from the store credit cards to the store. For example, the Dillard's store credit card is not managed by Dillard's; but by their third party financial institution, GE Money Bank. GE Money Bank decides if the consumer who applies for the Dillard's credit card should be approved or denied, if they should be approved for a Dillard's store card or a Dillard's American Express bank credit card, and pays Dillard's a percentage of the profit that is accumulated from the credit card business. GE Money Bank collects the payments, reports the payment history of the consumer on the credit card as data to the credit agencies, and the payment history appears on the credit reports belonging to the consumer. Dillard's does not do the management for the credit card; even through the credit card has the Dillard's store brand. This is because it would cost Dillard's more money to purchase credit risk management software and hire credit risk analysts, financial analysts, and other positions needed to successfully run a credit card business than it would for them to hire a third party financial institution to do their credit card management for them because the financial institution already has the people and software needed to successfully run a credit card business.

When consumers have issues with the regular store branded credit card or the store branded bank credit card such as; billing issues, then they must call the number on the back of their credit card that will connect them to the third party financial institution. In relation to the example of the Dillard's credit card, if consumers called the number on the back of their Dillard's card then a representative would answer the call and indicate they are with the Dillard's credit card customer service department. The Dillard's credit card customer service department is a division within the GE Money Bank Corporation. Each store card has its own customer service division, within the bank, meaning the GAP credit card would have its own department within GE Money Bank, the Old Navy credit card would have its own department within GE Money Bank, and JC Penney credit card would have its own department within GE Money Bank. At any time, the store can break its business relationship with the third party bank and manage its own credit cards or hire another third party bank that may charge fewer fees to the store, which enables the store to make more profit. As an example, currently, the TJ Max credit card is managed by Chase Bank. If TJ Max thinks Chase is charging them too many fees; then TJ Max will break the credit card business relation contract that was established with Chase Bank. Chase Bank will no longer be responsible for handling the TJ Max credit cards. TJ Max would look for another third party financial institution to handle their credit cards but one that charges them fewer fees than Chase, so they can make more profit. TJ Max could approach HSBC Bank and HSBC may offer them a better contract compared to the conditions they had on the contract, with Chase. TJ Max would agree to the contract with HSBC Bank and as a result, HSBC would manage all the current and new TJ Max credit cards issued to consumers. TJ Max will make more profit, with their credit card business relationship with HSBC Bank; than they would with Chase Bank. Consumers that have a TJ Max credit card would contact HSBC Bank, instead of Chase Bank to resolve any issues.

Similar to stores hiring a third party; to manage their credit cards for their customers, some financial institutions hire another financial institution to manage their credit cards for them. This is usually because the financial institution is not large enough to have their own credit card management department; and it would cost them too much money to manage it. They make more profit, when they hire a larger financial institution to manage the credit cards. The third party is usually paid a commission or both parties somehow share in the profits generated from the credit card business. For example, a credit card with Regions Bank is not managed by Regions Bank but FIA Card Services. For this reason, on the back of the Regions Bank credit card, it would say "this card is issued by FIA Card Services."

FIA Card Services is a division of Bank of America. Bank of America manages the credit cards of Regions Bank, because Bank of America is much larger. Bank of America and Regions Bank have a business relationship agreement, in which; they share the profits generated from the credit card business.

Similarly, if a consumer were to apply for a Charles Schwab credit card; the credit card would be managed by FIA Card Services who is a division of Bank of America. This is because Charles Schwab is not as big as Bank of America and they are mostly an investment firm company. Due to the fact the Charles Schwab and Regions Bank credit cards are being managed, by FIA Card Services, then on the credit reports of the consumers, it would not say Regions Bank and Charles Schwab, but FIA Card Services for the title of each credit card account. At any time, Regions Bank or Charles Schwab could break their business relationship with FIA Card Services and manage their own credit cards. Some financial institutions manage their own credit cards; such as Fifth Third Bank, Wells Fargo, Bank of America, HSBC, Barclays Bank, and Capital One.

Most credit unions, not all, manage their own credit cards. The credit unions usually do not hire a third party to manage their credit cards otherwise it would cost them more money and they would likely not be able to offer consumers cheap interest rates.

Some financial institutions offer store branded bank credit cards; such as, the Macys American Express card, Saks Fifth Avenue MasterCard, and Best Buy MasterCard. A store branded bank credit card is any credit card that has the Discover Card, American Express, Visa, or MasterCard credit card program logo and can be used anywhere besides the store. When consumers apply for store credit, they are first considered for the bank store branded credit card, but if their credit is not strong then they are only granted a store card, such as; a regular Macys card, Best Buy card, or Saks Fifth Avenue card. A store branded credit card can only be used, in the store, because financial institutions cannot greatly trust consumers with limited or average credit profiles to use the credit card outside the store and fully repay the credit card. Store branded credit cards tend to have lower credit limits (spending limits); than the limits of store branded bank credit cards. Financial institutions grant store branded bank credit cards to consumers, with excellent credit histories; because they think such consumers will use their cards greatly, they will likely repay the credit card, and as a result, the financial institution will be able to make more profit. Store branded bank credit cards have more rewards programs, than store branded credit cards, and this can explain why it costs more money for the financial institutions to operate them and so they cannot afford to grant store branded bank credit cards to consumers that are unlikely to repay it. Consumers with store branded credit cards, after building an excellent credit history; may request for their credit card to be upgraded to a store branded bank credit card, by calling the customer service department. This may cause a positive impact, on the credit profile, because future financial institutions will know other financial institutions trusted the consumer with a store branded bank credit card rather than simply a store branded credit card. On credit reports, store branded credit card are known as, **charge accounts,** but do not get this mixed up with a **charged-off account**, which means the credit card was never repaid and the financial institution gave up trying to collect the debt. In contrast, on credit reports, store branded bank credit cards are known as, **bank credit cards** or **bank revolving accounts.**

Store branded bank credit cards that can be used everywhere may have another feature, depending upon polices of the financial institution. They can be considered a dual-credit limit, sometimes called a dual-credit line, credit card. The financial institution will consider granting dual-limit credit cards to consumers, with excellent credit profiles when they apply for the regular store branded credit cards. A dual credit-limit credit card means the individual store branded bank credit card has two separate spending limits attached to it. Each spending limit is considered an individual credit account. Therefore, the single credit card will be reported, as two credit accounts to the credit reports, of the consumers. One spending limit is used for purchases; within the store, whereas the second spending limit is used for purchases outside of the store. When companies review the credit reports; it will look like the consumer has two of the same credit card and this can cause the credit scores to be higher. This is because it looks like the consumer is maintaining an excellent payment on two accounts instead of one.

Example
Ratna applies for a Saks Fifth Avenue credit card. The current issuer of that credit card is HSBC Bank. HSBC reviews the Equifax credit report of Ratna, notices she has a powerful credit history, and as a result, HSBC approves Ratna for a Saks Fifth Avenue MasterCard credit card, which is considered a store branded bank credit card. Her total credit limit on the credit card is $2,000. They know Ratna is very likely to repay the credit card; they can make profit, and for this reason, they want Ratna to be able to use the credit card at stores outside of Saks Fifth Avenue. The Saks Fifth Avenue MasterCard is considered a dual credit-limit credit card; because it has two separate spending limits of $1000. One limit, of $1000, can be used for purchases only within Saks Fifth Avenue where as; the other limit of $1000 can be used for purchases outside of Saks Fifth Avenue any store where MasterCard credit cards are accepted such as Wal-Mart, Kmart, Sears, and JC Penney. The credit reports, of Ratna, will reflect the two $1000 limits; as two Saks Fifth Avenue credit card accounts with different account numbers. One account will reflect it is a store only credit card account meaning; the card can be used to make purchases only within the certain store whereas the other account will reflect it is a bank credit card meaning; the card can be used to make purchases anywhere. The Saks Fifth Avenue MasterCard will know which credit limit to pull money from; because when the cashier swipes the card then electronically the credit card will know if the consumer is making a purchase at Saks Fifth Avenue or a store outside of it.

Some credit card providers, of dual credit limit credit cards, may give the consumer two physical cards. One card can be used, in the store program, of the credit card, such as; Saks Fifth Avenue, whereas the other physical card can be used in stores outside of the store. The providers, of dual credit limit credit cards, assign two credit limits because they do not want that the consumers use the entire spending limit to do shopping only at the certain store. In the case of Ratna, HSBC does not want that she use the full $2000 spending limit at Saks Fifth Avenue, because when consumers use the credit card outside of its store program; then the financial institutions can make more profit, due to the fact, the stores pay credit card payment processing fees and a portion of the fees money is collected by the issuer of the credit card belonging to the consumer. HSBC makes more profit when Ratna uses the Saks Fifth Avenue MasterCard credit card at; for example, Wal-Mart, Best Buy, and Red Lobster; than they would if she only used the credit card, at Saks Fifth Avenue. This is because HSBC and Saks Fifth Avenue have a business relationship; due to the fact HSBC manages their credit cards. Saks Fifth Avenue has to pay, little or no, credit card payment processing fees; when consumers use their Saks Fifth Avenue credit card. The financial institution makes less profit and Saks Fifth Avenue is able to save money. Saving money is why stores often send coupons to their credit card customers, so the customers are more likely to use their store cards for the purpose of getting the savings on the merchandise.

Not just store branded bank credit card, but any bank credit card may have special rewards programs names, such as; "World Platinum," "World MasterCard, "Gold Platinum," "Elite," "Visa Signature," "Premier" and other similar rewards names. The name of the rewards program will show on the front of the bank credit card, with an exception to credit cards issued by American Express or Discover Card because these programs are offered by the MasterCard or Visa Card network and not the financial institutions. The MasterCard and Visa Card networks are paid, by the financial institutions, to offer their rewards program products to consumers; that have excellent credit profiles. To make up for the money, the financial institutions pay the MasterCard and Visa Card networks, they usually charge consumers an annual program fee, on their rewards credit card accounts. The reward programs help consumers get special benefits, such as; discounts on merchandise, access to special event tickets, and accelerated rewards on purchases made using the credit card.

Consumers should be careful not to get too many credit cards with annual fees, because despite the rewards, they can get expensive to use. Consumers have to do a high level of spending, in order to get any "worthy" savings, from the credit cards and this means the consumers will plunge themselves into excessive debt. Additionally, consumers with bad or limited credit profiles need to be careful not to get tricked, by some credit card providers, specifically the subprime providers that cater to consumers with bad credit profiles, who attempt to get consumers to sign up for credit cards that are supposedly rewards credit cards due to their fancy names but in reality, these credit cards have no rewards programs.

For example, I have a "Platinum Student MasterCard" with Capital One Bank and the name of the credit card makes it seem like it is a rewards credit card, but truthfully, the card has no rewards program. Before signing up for any credit card, consumers should ask about the rewards program, on the credit card. Without a rewards program, consumers will not be able to save money on purchases. Store cards usually do not have rewards programs, due to the fact, store card holders receive coupons and with the coupons, they are saving money. Consumers with limited or bad credit profiles may not be able to get rewards program credit cards, because the financial institutions are taking on a high level of risk lending to such consumers that are very likely to one day stop paying on their credit cards. It costs money for the financial institutions to operate the rewards programs; and they cannot afford to grant them to consumers with bad or limited credit histories. If the consumer stops paying, then the financial institution has a major loss.

Some bank credit cards; especially rewards credit cards, American Express credit cards, and a few store cards, do not report the credit limits (spending limits) to the credit agencies, but only the payment history of the credit accounts. Consumers with excellent credit profiles have been granted a **flexible spending credit card;** meaning they can spend a certain amount over their credit limit and as a result, the financial institution will be able to make more profit. On the credit reports of the consumer, the credit cards that are flexible spending credit cards will indicate so next to the "account type". The consumer will not be charged an over-the-credit limit fee, on a flexible spending credit card, as they would on a traditional credit card; if they went over the credit limit. The business intention, behind flexible spending credit cards, is to make consumers ambitious towards earning credit card rewards and spend; to the highest extent without worrying about their credit profile because on traditional credit cards, if consumers spent over the credit limit or close to it then their credit scores would drop.

For example, on a credit report, if Vanessa has a HSBC regular MasterCard credit card with a limit of $4,000 and she spends $3,800. Her credit reports will record her "high balance," which is considered the highest amount spent on a loan, as $3,800. Her utilization level, of the credit card, would be considered $3,800/$4,000, which equals a ratio of 95%. Such is considered high utilization, on a credit card, even if Vanessa pays it off immediately. This is because financial institutions have to take into consideration that if Vanessa is excessively utilizing credit cards; then she is likely to get into so much debt that she will put herself into a bad position in which she cannot repay any company. If Vanessa was using a flexible spending credit card; her credit reports would not reflect the $4,000 limit she has on the credit card and the financial institutions. The credit agencies would not know whether or not Vanessa is spending close to; or beyond her credit limit. This protects her credit scores, because there is no evidence she is excessively utilizing a credit card. There is no way for a consumer to go to a bank; or the internet to apply for a flexible spending credit card. Upon reviewing the application, for the credit card, the financial institution will decide whether or not to grant the consumer a flexible spending credit card. It will reflect, on the credit reports, if the credit card is a flexible spending credit card and it will not show the credit limit of the credit card. Some credit cards, especially Visa Signature Rewards credit cards and a few store cards; such as Macys, do not have to be classified as a flexible spending credit card on the credit reports in order for the financial institutions not to report the credit limits.

For example, my mother has a Macy's store credit card with a limit of $2,000, but her credit reports do not reflect the limit and Macys confirmed the reason for this is because she could potentially spend over the credit limit. The Macys store card is not considered a flexible spending credit card on the credit report. It depends on the policies of the financial institution; if they want to report the credit card account as a flexible spending credit card.

However, regardless if a credit card is a flexible spending credit card or not, consumers should never spend close or beyond the credit limit unless they can pay off the balance immediately; otherwise they are creating excessive debt on which they may default and it will ruin their credit profile anyway. When consumers have flexible spending credit cards or credit cards that do not report the credit limits, to the credit agencies then the credit scores cannot increase as easily as they could if the credit limits of the credit cards were being reported and the consumer was utilizing less than 30% of the credit limits on the credit cards. This is because without knowing the credit limits of some of the credit cards, because they are not showing on the credit reports, the credit agencies cannot calculate the most accurate debt-to-credit ratio, which influences 30% of the credit scores. They cannot figure out how much of the total available credit (total amount of loan money) is being used by the consumer. The credit agencies want to see that consumers are using a small portion of all the loan money (credit) to which they have access through all their credit cards and loans with a credit limit.

Example
Chase Bank MasterCard credit card
Balance: $1,294.04
Credit limit: $2,000.00

Bank of America Accelerated Rewards American Express credit card
Balance: $2,053.49
Loan type: Flexible spending credit card
Credit limit: N/A

Kohl's store credit card
Balance: $34.11
Credit limit: $200.00

Credit card balances: $1,294.04 (Chase Bank credit card) + $2,053.49 (Bank of America credit card) + $34.11 (Kohl's credit card) = $3381.64, which is the total amount of revolving debt. Revolving debt is balances that are being carried every month on loans such as credit cards with spending limits.
Credit limits (total amount of loan money that is available to the consumer): $2,000 (Chase Bank credit card) + $200.00 (Kohl's credit card) = $2,200.00.
Note: The Bank of America credit card is a flexible spending credit card so its credit limit is unknown by the credit agencies.
Debt-to-credit ratio: $3,381.64 (total debt)/$2,200 (total amount of loan money) = 154% (rounded).

In the eyes of the financial institutions, a 154% debt-to-credit ratio suggests the consumer is excessively using credit; and is very likely to default on some kind of bill otherwise they would not be using so much loan money. This will result in the financial institution having a loan loss. The Bank of America credit card has a credit limit of $6,000; but due to the fact it is a flexible spending credit card, only the consumer and Bank of America knows that, but not the credit agencies because the consumer can spend over the credit limit if they decided to do so. Unfortunately, consumers cannot request for the financial institutions to report the credit limits. For the purpose of maintaining the credit scores to be as high as possible, consumers should not carry balances on credit cards or any loan with a credit limit such as a home equity line of credit because then their debt-to-credit ratio will always be 0%, which is perfect. This means the consumer is not spending beyond their means, is unlikely to default, and will receive the cheapest interest rates and insurance premiums. The debt-to-credit ratio is not influenced by mortgages, car loans, home equity loans, and loans that do not have a spending limit, also called a credit limit.

Revocable Living Trust

When consumers have children or get married then they need to establish a revocable living trust, with an attorney. It is a document that indicates how the assets and property of the consumer will be distributed to their family members; or whom ever they choose after they die. Consumers can make changes to their revocable living trust such as removing or adding beneficiaries or designating how much money is inherited by each beneficiary.

Statue of Limitations

In the event that a consumer is sued by a financial institution; or company to repay a debt then consumers will have to talk to an attorney if the statue of limitations of their state considers that debt to be expired meaning the company cannot sue the consumer to repay the debt. The statue of limitations prevents the company from suing the consumer in court if the debt has been living for a certain number of years but consumers are still obligated to repay the debt otherwise their credit scores will continue going down. Consumers just cannot get sued anymore. When a company cannot sue a consumer to repay a debt then the debt is considered a time-barred debt. However, to avoid the problems of going to court and paying an attorney, consumers should simply make arrangements with the company to repay the debt.

Finance 101: The Whiz Kid's Perfect Credit Guide

Building and Rebuilding Good Credit

To get anything in the world, consumers must have an established and positive credit report otherwise they will always be denied for places to live, services, utilities, and loan or they will receive them at higher-than-average interest rates and/or fees because there is no way for the business to know if the consumer is going to pay them or not. Businesses have their own expenses and they have to make money off of consumers. Employers that check the credit profile of the candidate will honor the fact that the candidate is financially responsible if they have good credit. Such will add credibility to their degree and integrity. There is no way to escape building credit and the easiest and cheapest way to build credit is to sign up for a credit card. When consumers turn the legal age in their state that allows for them to get a credit card and they have a job then they should get a credit card immediately because they want to establish the longest history possible. Consumers do not immediately establish good credit; they have to establish year's worth of good payment history. For consumers that have no credit profile or a damaged credit profile, getting their first credit card may not be easy and the process of getting one should be handled responsibly. Consumers have a bad habit of applying for credit several times when they are denied for credit. In doing so, they are damaging their credit profile rather than strengthening it. This is because every time they apply for credit, a credit check is done on them by the financial institution, and the record that the credit check was done shows as an inquiry on the credit report. When financial institutions see the credit check inquiries, regardless whether or not the consumer has any credit history, then they think the consumer is financially weak otherwise it makes no sense to them why a consumer would keep applying for credit despite the fact they keep getting denied. They sometimes assume that the consumer was approved for every credit account for which they applied that the credit checks are showing and the accounts have not yet appeared on their credit reports because there is no way for the financial institutions to know if the consumer was denied for credit. When they see many credit checks, they have to take into consideration the possibilities that a criminal may be applying for credit under the social security number of the consumer or the consumer desires to get into a large amount of debt using loan money. Even if the consumer has no credit scores, the fact that so many credit checks took place on them is negative information and it will stay on their credit reports for two years. When a consumer is approved for credit then the negative impact of the credit check is not as severe but a consumer, after getting approved for their first credit card, should stop applying for credit until at least two to three years have passed.

Consumers should be careful when asking for a credit limit increase because some financial institutions, not all, perform hard inquiry credit checks to grant the extra loan money. Consumers should only ask for a credit limit increase if the financial institution can confirm the credit check will be a soft inquiry because such does not affect their credit scores. It may be a wise idea for consumers to temporarily freeze their credit reports and then ask for a credit limit increase because there have been cases in which financial institutions said they would perform a soft inquiry credit check actually performed a hard inquiry credit check, which negatively affected the credit scores of the consumer. This happened because the customer service representatives gave inaccurate information to the consumers. If the financial institutions are being authentic when they say they will perform a soft inquiry credit check for the purpose of granting a credit limit increase then the security freeze will not prevent the soft inquiry credit check from being done. The freeze will only prevent hard inquiry credit checks, which will protect the credit profile of the consumer. Credit limit increases do help increase the credit scores because they send the message that the consumer is creditworthy otherwise the financial institution would not grant them more loan money. However, consumers should not be aggressively asking for credit limit increases because it may raise the question why they want so much loan money. A credit limit increase request every two to three years is healthy. Hard inquiry credit checks should only be done when a consumer applies for a new credit card or loan and there is no way to escape them.

Consumers that already have good credit history due to a student loan or other type of loan still need a credit card because their credit profile is considered underdeveloped. Consumers must have a variety of loans showing on their credit reports for the purpose of achieving and maintaining the highest credit scores possible. Consumers with a variety of non-delinquent loans are less likely to default in the eyes of the financial institutions because it stands to reason they are financially strong.

Here are the steps consumers should follow for the purpose of minimizing their chances in getting denied for credit.

1. Before applying for credit, consumers need to check their personal information with the credit agencies, Equifax, Experian, TransUnion, and Innovis to make sure their social security number, date of birth, address, name, and other information is correct. Even if the consumers have no credit history, the credit bureaus still have personal information stored on them using public records. Consumers need to dispute any inaccurate information online on the websites of the credit agencies or if for whatever reasons, they cannot view their credit reports or personal information online then they need to call the credit agencies. Consumers should not apply for credit before checking their credit reports because if the information that the consumer puts on their credit application does not match the stored information that the credit agencies have on the consumer then it is possible the financial institution may deny the consumer for credit thinking a criminal is applying for credit using the personal information of the consumer. Consumers that have negative financial information such as collection accounts need to contact the companies that have reported the negative information and ask them to remove it. Consumers will need to pay them any debt that is still owed and it is worth it to pay the debt.

2. After making any corrections to the credit reports, consumers should accept one of the credit card offers that they receive in the mail with their name that has no annual fee or fees just for having the credit card. The offers that consumers receive in the mail mean they passed the initial soft inquiry credit check that the financial institution had done on them for the purpose of being able to mail the credit card offer. Financial institutions are not going to want to send credit card offers to consumers with bad credit profiles because they are wasting their money in doing so since they will likely not approve such consumers for credit. They are trying to expand their business by sending credit card offers to consumers that are likely to get approved.

3. If consumers receive no credit card offers or are denied for the credit card offer they received in the mail then they should apply for store branded credit cards because they tend to be easier to get than bank credit cards. This is because it costs less money for the financial institutions to operate the store branded credit card programs and they make more profit off of them due to the fact most store branded credit cards have

purchase interest rates above 20%. Items sold by the stores or their catalogs that offer the store branded credit cards usually have higher than average prices. They can make enough profit off of the consumer that overpowers the risk they are taking by lending to consumers with limited or bad credit profiles. Consumers can avoid paying any interest by immediately paying off the balance, which is how they should handle every credit card and loan. However, consumers that have a bankruptcy or debt settlement showing on their credit reports should call the credit card issuer before applying for the card and ask if they grant credit to consumers that have filed for a bankruptcy. In personal experience, the easiest store branded credit card to obtain is the Firestone/Bridgestone card. Consumers can apply for this credit card on their website, which is www.firestonecompleteautocare.com/credit_card/. The second easiest store branded credit card is Fingerhut, which can be found on www.fingerhut.com. The third easiest store branded credit card is Valero Gas and can be found on https://ccc.valero.com/Applications/apply_now.aspx.

Other store cards for consumers with limited or slightly damaged credit profiles
Macys: https://www.macys.com/service/credit/applynow/creditapp.ognc
Bloomingdales: https://www.bloomingdales.com/service/credit/applynow/creditapp.ognc
Talbots: https://www.talbots.com/online/myaccount/talbots_charge_application.jsp
Gettington: http://www.gettington.com/home.jsp
Dillard's: https://www.onlinecreditcenter2.com/eapplygen2/load.do?cHash=7332168838&subActionId=1000 or www.dillards.com
Victoria's Secret: https://c1.comenity.net/victoriassecret?Action=ApplyOnline.jsp or www.victoriassecret.com Wal-Mart: http://www.walmart.com/cp/Credit-Cards/632402

Besides the websites, consumers can apply for some of the credit cards in the physical stores or by calling the application phone number on the website.

**Note: In most cases, catalog store credit cards are easier to get than retail store credit cards. This is because due to the fact catalog store companies have less business expenses than retail stores considering they do not have to hire many employees, they are able to make more profit off of consumers and for this reason, they can grant credit more easily. Consumers can sometimes determine whether or not they will be approved for a specific credit card using the credit information of previous consumers that has applied for that same card and were approved or denied. This information can be found on www.financeglobe.com.

4. The best way to save money while building credit is to save up the coupons that the store branded credit card issuers will send to their consumers and use them to make purchases. However, consumers should never spend beyond their means otherwise they will end up building large amounts of debt and this defeats the purpose of saving money in using the coupons. At times, the store branded credit card issuers may have promotional events for their consumers such as for example, consumers can save 3% off on all children's clothes purchased on Monday using their store branded credit card.

5. If consumers are denied for a credit card then they should stop applying for credit. They should wait for the letter that indicates the reason why they were denied. Consumers should challenge the reason and send a reconsideration letter to the address indicated on the denial letter. The reconsideration letter should have all the reasons why the financial institution should approve the consumer and these reasons should overpower the reason that the financial institution used to deny the consumer for credit.

6. Consumers that are denied credit and do not hear back from the financial institution after sending the reconsideration letter or hear back from them and they say that the application is still denied, should not lose their motivation to obtain credit. The only way to build or rebuild credit is to use credit again and using debit cards or cash all the time does not resolve the issue. Consumers should go to a credit union or community bank and get a secured credit card. Consumers with bankruptcy or a debt settlement may be denied for a secured credit card and for this reason, before applying, they should ask if the financial institution will approve consumers that have such information showing on their credit reports. If the financial institution says they do not cater to consumers that have filed for a bankruptcy or debt settlement then consumers simply have to wait for the negative information to fall off or become very old. There are subprime lending companies that extend credit consumers with a bankruptcy or debt settlement but they are <u>many</u> fees for getting the credit and the interest rates are exorbitant. In doing research, the subprime lending companies offer credit cards with interest rates of up to 79% or higher and these cards have application fees, fees for using the website, annual fees, and monthly maintenance fees. Overall, the fees are almost over $150 a year in addition to interest if the consumer chooses to carry a balance on the credit card. For this reason, consumers should not go to such companies.

Most secured credit cards have annual fees, which is a flat fee a consumer would pay every year for having the car, because they are specialized products for consumers with little, no, or bad credit profiles. For this reason, the financial institution needs to make as much profit as possible off of the consumer because they are likely to one day stop paying the bill. Financial institutions cannot assume consumers with no credit histories will pay the bills. They have to treat them as they would consumers with bad credit histories.

In personal research, the financial institution that is offering the cheapest secured credit card is Fifth Third Bank. Their secured MasterCard product has an annual fee of $24: https://www.wellsfargo.com/credit_cards/secured/. The second cheapest secured credit card is offered by Wells Fargo Bank. Their secured Visa card product has an annual fee of $25: https://www.wellsfargo.com/credit_cards/secured/. The third cheapest secured credit card is offered by Capital One Bank. Their secured MasterCard product has an annual fee of $29: http://www.capitalone.com/creditcards/mastercard-secured-credit-card/. Before applying for any of these cards, consumers should contact credit unions and community banks around their area to see if they can offer a cheaper secured card product. The amount of money that a consumer offers as a security deposit for the secured credit card is the spending limit, also called a credit limit. The security deposit money goes into an FDIC or NCUA insured savings account. The security deposit money is not used to make payments on the secured card and when consumers spend using the secured credit card, money is not pulled from the security deposit. The security deposit is insurance for the financial institution that the consumer will pay their credit card bill. If the consumer does not pay their credit card then the financial institution keeps the security deposit money. However, the credit profile of the consumer is ruined because the financial institution reports that the consumer did not make their payments. The financial institution should have had no need to keep the security deposit money. The consumer should have made payments on the secured credit card. The consumer eventually gets back the security deposit money after they have proven themselves to be trustworthy in the eyes of the financial institution in repaying their loans and the financial institution can trust them with loans without needing the security deposit money.

Example
Ian applies and is approved for a Chase Bank secured credit card.
Chase requires that he provide a security deposit of $300 because he has no credit history. Ian provides Chase with the $300 security deposit and now Chase can trust Ian with $300 of their loan money. The $300 security deposit money sits in a Chase savings account for safe keeping.
If Ian charges $25 for gas on his secured credit card, he must pay Chase $25 on or before the due date or Chase charge him a late fee and after a certain number of days (usually 60), they will report that his credit card is late to the credit agencies. Chase will not extract the $25 from the $300 security deposit money. Ian will ruin his credit by not repaying Chase. After so many months pass and Chase still does not receive any payments from Ian then they will report the secured credit card as a charged-off account to the credit agencies and the credit profile of Ian will be ruined. He can expect to struggle finding a job and he will have to pay expensive insurance on everything. It will be difficult for Ian to save money.

7. When consumers spend money using their secured credit card, they cannot spend beyond the credit limit or their card may decline, they may be charged an over-the-limit fee, and the fact that the consumer spent beyond the limit of the secured card may be reported to their credit reports. When future financial institutions notice that the consumer went over the credit limit then they may think the consumer is more likely to spend beyond their means and build up excessive debt that they will not be able to repay the financial institution. As a result, the financial institution may have a loan loss and they are going to try and avoid having such a loss by denying the consumer for credit or approving them with a low credit limit and a higher than average interest rate and/or annual fee. Consumers should not spend more than 30% of the credit limit on any credit card, regardless if they are secured or unsecured. When consumers spend on their secured credit card, they have to pay it and preferably, to achieve the best credit profile possible and avoid paying interest, they should pay off the balance immediately on the day that they make the charges.

8. As time passes, consumers should deposit more money towards the security deposit of the secured credit card so on the credit reports, the credit limit becomes higher. The credit limit is the total amount of money that the consumer has given to the bank as a security deposit. Growing credit limits causes the credit scores to increase because the utilization level of the consumer is becoming less and it looks like they can handle more loan money. Consumers should never carry a balance on a secured or unsecured credit card otherwise their credit scores will drop due to excessive debt. Consumers should be persistent with the financial institution, after building years of positive payment history, to remove or reduce the annual fee and upgrade the credit card from a secured loan type to an unsecured loan type meaning the financial institution can return to the consumer their security deposit money and can trust them with the credit card blindly. An unsecured credit card will help the credit scores increase more because it sends the message that the consumer is trustworthy in repaying their loans.

9. At some point in time, without closing their current secured or unsecured credit card, the consumer should think about getting 1 to 2 more bank type unsecured credit cards without annual fees such as a Visa, MasterCard, American Express, or Discover Card through a credit union by using a non-profit website called www.creditcardconnection.org. The website will ask the consumer for their zip code and will show them the credit union credit cards available to them based on the credit unions that are located nearest to their location. In personal experience, very few, if any, credit unions offer American Express and Discover credit cards

for the likely reason it costs them too much money to operate these credit card branded programs. Discover and American Express credit cards tend to give their users rewards more aggressively than Visa and MasterCard credit cards but the con is that consumers have to spend a great deal of money. In terms of achieving the highest credit scores, it does not matter if a consumer has a Visa, American Express, Discover, or MasterCard credit card. They are all considered bank type credit cards but they are competitors because each credit card brand offers its own benefits. Credit union credit cards are especially ideal for consumers that are currently carrying balances on bank issued credit cards because consumers can save a significant amount of money on interest and as a result, pay off their debt much faster.

10. Consumers with good and bad credit profiles should never keep applying for credit if they are getting denied because the credit checks will cause their credit scores to become too low. This may cause the insurance providers to increase the insurance premiums on them. Employers may also find it bizarre that a candidate has so many credit checks showing on their credit reports. If consumers are denied for credit then they always need to ask for a reconsideration convincing the financial institution that they will never default on the credit card.

11. Consumers should never carry a balance on any of their loans or credit cards and they should pay off the balance the day that the credit card is used or at the end of the month to avoid paying interest. They should never spend over or more than 30% of their credit limit otherwise the financial institutions may think they are spending to the point that they will default on some type of bill and are living off their credit cards. Consumers should always ask for a cheaper interest rate and/or annual fee for the purpose of preparing themselves for using their credit card in an emergency. Usually, it is difficult to get an interest rate on a credit card cheaper than 11%. To maintain excellent credit, consumers should always monitor the loans on which they cosign including joint credit cards and never trust anyone to pay their bills for them including family members.

Finance 101: The Whiz Kid's Perfect Credit Guide

Incarceration

Notice of Deficiency

If a consumer receives a Notice of Deficiency, also called a 90-day letter, from the IRS (Internal Revenue Service) then they need to get a tax attorney immediately and show it to them. A Notice of Deficiency is sent to a consumer when they owe money to the IRS; because they did not pay all their taxes on their income and sources of money, which must be reported to the IRS, and the debt is now past due. If the amount owed is very little then consumers should simply pay it; because the fees to get a tax attorney can get more expensive, than the IRS debt.

When consumers do not pay all their taxes then the money they still owe to the IRS grows with high interest and penalty fees. Consumers have 90 days to repay the debt. In some cases, the IRS makes a mistake in sending the consumer a Notice of Deficiency; because the tax information was not reported or recorded correctly and so consumers can dispute the amount that they owe to the IRS, as indicated on the Notice of Deficiency, with the IRS and the United States Tax Court. A local tax court office can be found on http://www.ustaxcourt.gov/. Consumers must resolve this issue immediately; because the IRS has the power to levy the bank accounts of the consumer, stop their tax refunds, put a claim on their assets or property, and ruin their credit profile if they have not done so already. If negative information is showing on the credit reports of the consumer due to the unpaid tax debt then consumers should notify the United States Tax Court; when they are submitting the dispute. Consumers should submit a dispute to the credit agencies to remove the negative information. Consumers must pay the debt if it was not a mistake and like student loan debt, IRS debt is not dischargeable in bankruptcy or a debt settlement unless the consumer has a major health disability that is preventing them from working. Consumers should use a high rewards level credit card or debit card to pay the IRS debt because the rewards programs help save money. If years pass and consumers are not paying their income taxes then they are very likely to receive a notice of deficiency.

Tax Audits are Serious

Consumers need to make sure they file their taxes properly or hire someone credible to do so, while paying attention to the fees they will be charged. Avoid hiring tax preparation firms or individuals that claim they can "guarantee" consumers to receive tax refunds, because this is impossible. If the taxes are not submitted properly, the Internal Revenue Service (IRS) can select a consumer for a tax audit. The consumer will receive a notice that they have been selected and will need to provide certain documentations verifying the income they have reported is correct, as well as, expenses they indicated on the tax documents.

If the IRS determines the consumer did not report all their income properly, then the consumer will be subject to penalties and fees. The IRS may get the impression that the consumer was trying to escape paying their taxes or they were trying to collect big tax returns. If consumers receive a notice that they have been selected for an audit then it is recommended they get a tax attorney immediately; because it is possible the IRS may garnish their wages if they do not take any action to resolve the audit in a timely manner. If consumers do not have a job then they must still file taxes and use a fixed interest rate loan, a loan against a 401k plan or 403b plan, or the money within a Roth IRA to pay the taxes otherwise the penalties will be very expensive. Consumers also have the option of negotiating payment plans with the Internal Revenue Service, and can possibly defer the payments until they find a job or source of income.

Tax Evasion

When the IRS selects a consumer for a tax audit, they may think the consumer is responsible for tax evasion; meaning that they are illegally trying to hide some of their income to avoid paying taxes on it or make illegitimate tax deductions for expenses they never had in their life. An example of a tax evasion can be if a consumer deducts student loan interest off of their taxes, but in reality never had a student loan.

Incarceration Damages Credit

Although records of being incarcerated may not appear on credit reports, they will appear on background checks. Some financial institutions check the background reports of consumers when they apply for credit or their credit account is reviewed. Depending upon the circumstances as to why the consumer was incarcerated, the financial institutions may take adverse actions against the consumer. The most common action they would take is to close down the credit account or deny the consumer for new credit.

As support, Jeremy M. Simon is a staff reporter for www.CreditCards.com and in his article, "How going to jail impacts your credit," he indicates that Citibank "says [a] [credit card issuer] will close a credit card account once [the] issuer learns the cardholder is incarcerated." This is because in the eyes of the financial institutions, incarcerated consumers are very likely to default on their credit accounts. This is because in most cases, incarcerated consumers have financial struggles due to the fact that they have to pay for court, attorney, and probation fees. In fact, to pay for such expenses, incarcerated consumers often take high interest and fee-based loans and thus, they will have less money to pay their other bills such as the credit cards.

Incarceration suggests No Integrity to Repay Bills

In some cases, if consumers are low enough to do the actions that they did; which caused them to get incarcerated then it may cause financial institutions to think that the consumers are low enough to not pay their bills. When credit accounts are closed by financial institutions; then it may negatively impact the consumer, because the credit accounts will indicate "closed by credit grantor" on the credit reports. The credit scores will decrease because the closure of credit accounts reduces the amount of total available credit to which the consumer has access and as a result, the credit utilization ratio will become higher. It will look like the consumer is using a high amount of their total available credit, and thus they are considered financially weak.

After 7-10 years, the closed credit account will drop off the credit reports along with its payment history, and this will lower the average length of history established on the credit accounts, which influences fifteen percent of a FICO credit score. In order to avoid facing credit problems, consumers need to avoid getting into trouble with the law. For consumers that are incarcerated, after getting released from prison, consumers need to have the negative public records removed from their background reports and in some cases, also their credit reports.

They can dispute the negative public records from their credit reports with the credit agencies. Consumers would need to ask the courts as to how they can dispute the negative public records from their background reports. They may need to find a very credible attorney to do so. By removing the negative public records, consumers will increase their chances of being able to find a professional job more easily.

Certified Checks and Starter Checks

Certified Check
A check that is written by the consumer and the money will be taken from their bank account to pay the bill issuer. Before the money can be taken, the financial institution managing the checking account of the consumer can use the certified check to verify with the bill issuer that there is enough money within the account. When the financial institution is verifying the amount of money within the account then in a sense, they are "certifying" the check. If there is enough money then the bill issuer can be successfully paid. The consumer will not have to pay any returned payment or check fees.

Starter Check
When a consumer first opens a deposit account, usually a checking account, then the financial institution gives them about 5 starter checks until the consumer receives the regular checkbooks in the mail. Starter checks are similar to regular checks because they have the bank routing number and checking account number of the consumer but they are different because they usually do not have the name of the consumer or their address. Consumers must fill out their name and address on the starter check before paying a merchant and they need to verify if the merchant accepts starter checks. Some merchants do not accept starter checks and if a consumer pays them with one then the consumer could potentially face returned check fees. The reason for this is because criminals can potentially perform many fraudulent activities with starter checks by filling out the information of any consumer. Merchants are taking on risk by cashing starter checks because it costs the merchant money to cash checks and if the check turns out to be fraudulent then the merchant has a business loss. Businesses do not want to deal with the hassles of starter checks. Regular checks are more secure.

Retirement

Seek Cheap Utilities

Consumers can find their local home phone, cell phone, and other utility providers such as television, internet, and security systems, by using these websites: www.allconnect.com, www.connectmyphone.com, or www.phonesystempricequotes.com. Consumers without internet access can call All Connect at 1-866-684-7629 or they can call Connect My Phone at 1-877-213-1057. These companies, that match consumers with their local providers, do not collect any fees from the consumer; but from the company whom they forward the consumers. The websites or customer service representatives will tell the consumers the monthly payment of each company that could potentially provide the service to the consumer. Consumers should be financially conservative and get the cheapest services available so they have more money to pay the big bills such as their mortgage, student loans, car loan, credit cards, and insurances.

For example, it makes no sense for a consumer to purchase a television plan that offers over 100 channels, if consumers do not often watch television or do not watch that many channels. They are unnecessarily wasting money and this raises their chances of becoming delinquent on another bill and ruining their credit profile.

Another example of being financially conservative is; if consumers are always out, do not often talk on the phone, or do not have a large family then it makes no sense for them to have both a cell phone and regular home phone. Consumers are better off just keeping a cell phone and putting the money that they would pay towards a regular home phone into a retirement account or 529 plan for the college education expenses of their children. If consumers have high credit card or student loan debts and insurance premiums, then they should remove text messaging, internet, and the other fancy features off of their cell phone plans and use the saved money to pay more towards credit cards and then student loans. Credit cards tend to have high interest rates and fees compared to student loans. Even the smallest amount of savings, such as; $10 will make a huge difference in saving money on credit card interest, late fees, and protecting their credit profile because for some consumers, $10 or less is just the minimum payment due on a credit card. If consumers do not save money by being financially conservation then they will struggle to pay off their debts, the debts will compound with interest, the credit scores will remain low, and the insurance premiums will increase instead of decrease because the debts are suggesting the consumer is very likely not to repay some kind of bill.

Self-employed Consumers have Unique Retirement Accounts

SEP-IRA: Simplified Employee Pension Individual Retirement Account is for the owners of small businesses or self-employed consumers. Consumers deduct the amount of money that the put into the SEP-IRA from their taxable income and do not pay any taxes on the growth on the money until they withdraw it at the age of retirement. Consumers can contribute up to $40,000 a year towards a SEP-IRA. If consumers have any type of IRA, 401(k), or 403(b) account and they become self-employed then they convert their retirement accounts into a SEP-IRA. Consumers can get an SEP-IRA with any company where they have an IRA.

Keogh: A retirement program for self-employed consumers or owners of small businesses that allows for them to save up to 25% of their income within an account. Consumers pay taxes on all the money that they contribute and its earnings when they begin withdrawing the money at the age of retirement. It is a tax-deferred account. For this reason, consumers cannot deduct the amount of money they put towards their Keogh plan from their taxes.

Retirement Accounts of Government Employees

Thrift account: This retirement account is offered to the employees of the federal government and members of the armed forces such as the military. It is managed by the Federal Retirement Thrift Investment Board. The agency that the employee works for makes the contributions (deposits) into the thrift account by deducting a certain amount of money, specified by the employee, from their paycheck. The amount of contribution that can be made towards a thrift account every year is $16,500. Consumers can deduct the amount of money they contribute to the thrift account from their taxes but when they withdraw the money at the age of retirement then they must pay taxes on it. The age of retirement for a thrift account is 59 ½. If consumers develop a permanent medical disability; then they can withdraw the money early without paying the 10% tax penalty. Like on any type of retirement account, consumers need to name their spouse or children as the beneficiary on the account meaning if the consumer passes away then the beneficiary gets all the money. Consumers should not name children that are under the age of 18 on any type of retirement account because it may be difficult for minors to obtain the money within a retirement account.

Saving Money

Save Money on Gift Cards

Many consumers buy gift cards for their family members and friends. What I absolutely hate about the bank gift cards, such; as the MasterCard, Visa, and American Express gift cards is that they usually charge a consumer a $3-$6 fee, just to buy the physical gift card. For this reason, consumers should only buy a gift card from a credit union or community bank, where ever the gift card will be sold for the cheapest price; because the goal is to pay the cheapest fee possible. If possible, consumers should buy only store branded gift cards, such as; Macys, Kohl's, and TJ Maxx. Store gift cards, do not charge the consumer extra fees just to buy the physical gift cards.

Two legitimate websites I use, myself, to purchase family members and friend's gift cards are www.plasticjungle.com and www.monstergiftcard.com. These websites charge no money for shipping and consumers can buy gift cards, at discounted prices. The gift cards will usually have a higher value than what the consumer pays for them.

For example, if a Macys gift card is worth $25.00 then a consumer will likely only have to pay, anywhere in the range of $20 - $23, and there are several gift cards that have higher discounts, up to 30%. Consumers should take advantage of the discounts.

Self-Publishing is a Great Source of Extra Money

Consumers who have a passion and want an extra source of income should consider writing and publishing a book. They can self-publish the book on www.CreateSpace.com and pay only $25.00 for the distribution; so the book is listed on book stores all over the internet. There is no annual fee that the consumer will have to pay or other fees; unless they want a professional book cover to be produced.

For the book cover, consumers can ask their friends or family for help. From the sales of the book, consumers can get anywhere from 20% to 40% in royalties deposited directly into their bank account. Literacy helps the economy grow. Self-published books can eventually be picked up by major traditional book companies, and this means even more money for the consumer.

Name Brands can be Wallet Killers

Some consumers get fooled by the marketing and promotion of fancy named branded products, such as with; batteries, medicines, or clothes; thinking they are better than generic brands. For this reason, they spend more money on products, with the fancy names, such as; batteries, Duracell or the cough medicine, Robitussin. There is no research indicating fancy brands are better than generic brands.

In my opinion, named branded products and generic branded products are usually the same in quality with an exception to foods. For this reason, whenever I walk into CVS or Walgreens, I always buy their generic branded products and over time, save a great deal of money that I apply towards making my auto loan payments and save money on interest. If possible, consumers should purchase generic branded items.

Premium Gas

Gas prices are expensive and saving the maximum amount of money is important. For this reason, unless the automobile requires special gas, consumers should always get regular gas and not the premium gas or gas with fancy names. There is no research indicating premium gas is better than regular gas in terms of quality, get better mileage, or helps the vehicle better function. As support, the Federal Trade Commission indicates "using a higher octane gasoline than [the] owner's manual recommends offers absolutely no benefit" and this means the consumer is wasting their money on premium gas.

Fees for Checking in Bags at Airports

Most airline providers, such as; Delta, Southwest, and US Airways, charge a fee for checking bags. In most cases, when consumers want to check in a bag that weighs more than 50 pounds, they must pay an expensive fee, usually $50 or more. The amount of money they pay in the fees can be used to buy new clothes when they arrive at their destination. For this reason, consumers should not check bags if they can avoid paying the fee, which is a waste of money. Consumers should not take so many items with them when traveling, because it raises the likelihood that they will lose or damage them as they change flights. Consumers should try to restrict themselves to carry-on luggage.

Newspapers

Consumers can avoid paying hundreds of dollars per year to a newspaper provider, by reading the news for free, on the internet. They will not have to deal with the hassle of disposing the newspapers.

Surge Protector Power Strips = Inexpensive Electricity Bill

Televisions can consume up to 40% of its operating power, even if they are turned off in standby mode, and this causes the electricity bill to be more expensive. Consumers should use surge protector power strips, and turn them off at night before they go to sleep.

Avoid Expensive Gyms and Health Care Clubs

Consumers should go to parks for exercise, instead of paying for expensive gym memberships. They are better off buying weights, verses paying monthly membership fees to a gym. The amount of money consumers spend on a gym or health club membership can be used to purchase a lot of equipment.

Avoid "Gas Saving" Devices

Consumers must avoid buying expensive devices, for their automobiles, that claim they can save money on gas, such as; devices that will cause the car to operate on water or another source. These devices may damage the car and the companies offering them will not reimburse the consumer.

Dollar Store Deals

Dollar stores can be an ideal way to save money on everyday expenses, but consumers need to be aware that not all items within dollar stores are a good deal.

Categories of items that are usually good deals include:
1. Cleaning supplies such as laundry detergent or dish soap.
2. Party supplies such as gift wrap paper and ribbons.
3. Shampoo.
4. Kitchen accessories.
5. Car maintenance accessories.
6. Greeting cards such as for birthdays or anniversaries.

Saving Money on Sending Mail

Consumers should use United States Postal Services (USPS) to send mail, because they are always cheaper than privately owned companies, such as; FedEx, DHL, and United Postal Service (UPS). In personal experience, paying more money for supposedly faster shipping options is a waste because there is no guarantee the item will arrive within the specified amount of time that the mail delivery provider is claiming, and if the item does not arrive on time then it is unlikely the mail provider will refund the consumer their hard-earned money. For this reason, consumers are better off paying for regular mail delivery.

Avoid Hotel Fees

Going on vacation can be expensive, and part of what makes it expensive is hotel fees. Consumers need to be on the lookout for these fees and if they get charged them then they should ask for a refund.

- Internet
- Parking
- Receiving or sending packages
- Phone calls
- Towel
- Replacement room key

Safe Deposit Boxes are Not Insured

Consumers should keep their valuables within a safe deposit box, at a credit union or community bank. The safe deposit box will cost them money, but it is worth paying because their valuables are protected. However, consumers should get some kind of insurance plan for the items that they put within the safe deposit box, because the FDIC or NCUA insurance does not protect them if they were to get damaged or robbed. This is confirmed by CBS News who in *12 things to keep in a safe at home, not at a bank*, indicates the contents of a safe deposit box are rarely insured. For this reason, consumers should not put money within a safe deposit. Consumers should check with their homeowner's insurance company if they can include the possessions that they place within the safe deposit box such as jewelry, to be protected with their policy.

Extended Warranties on Items

Be careful of purchasing extended warranties on items, because they are a strategy a business strategy to make more money off of consumers. Warranties have exclusions, meaning they will not pay for certain damages. Consumers should always ask about the exclusions.

Fake Charities

Consumers should avoid giving money to random people who call them or walk to their door requesting for donations for a cause. Anyone can claim to be a charity when in reality they are criminals performing a scam.

Vacation Finance

When seeking the cheapest airline tickets, hotel rooms, car rentals, and other travel deals, please check www.statravel.com, www.mobissimo.com, and www.hotwire.com. Students may be able to get special discounts on travel packages especially on STA Travel. I recommend going on www.retailmenot.com, which offers several coupons not just for travel agency, websites but also many websites and businesses. In my experience, these coupons save money.

Rent-to-Own is Expensive

Consumers with any type of credit profile need to avoid "rent-to-own" and "lease-to-own" online and physical stores. They sell merchandise, usually of poor or unknown conditions because they do not want to spend too much money, to consumers such as; televisions, furniture, weights, computers, and simply anything to earn a sale out of consumers. The consumer is expected to make monthly payments on the merchandise. Rent-to-own stores do not check the credit profiles of consumers, because it costs them money to do so; but they will report negative information to the credit agencies if the consumer fails to make payments as a way of trying to get the consumers to make payments again. Although the rent-to-own stores may not admit to it and it may not show an interest rate on the paperwork; they make consumers pay interest ranging from 48% to over 100% on the merchandise.

The market value of the merchandise is very low compared to the amount of money that is desired, by the rent-to-own stores. Most of the monthly payments go towards paying interest. This can support why the Consumers League of New Jersey express that the rent-to-own stores charge "loan shark rates" and their business is "immoral", even though it is legal. Matt Breed from Money Crashers indicates rent-to-own stores could be one of the biggest scams around. In addition, some of the rent-to-own stores may want money upfront before selling the furniture to the consumer because they are trying to compensate for the potential that the consumer may choose not to repay them. They have to do so because the bad or limited credit profile of the consumer makes them not trustworthy.

Example: Ross gets a Dynex 19 inches television, at a rent-to-own store. He agrees to send $15.00 as payments over the next sixty weeks. This means he will end up paying $900 for the television. This same television Ross could have purchased, at Best Buy, for $180.00. Assuming $180.00 is the market value of the television, this means the rent-to-own store made 50% interest because $900.00 (amount that Ross paid)/$180.00 (market value of television).

The rent-to-own store may have charged Ross additional fees before they sold him the television and this can mean they made more than 50% interest in profit.

Consumers such as Ross are better off saving the money to buy furniture, they can go to garage sales that sell used furniture at very cheap prices, or they can ask for furniture items from their family members. Ideally, consumers should avoid developing bad credit or they should fix their credit profile by building an excellent payment history on a credit card, so they can use credit to buy furniture from regular stores such as Wal-Mart.

Companies that Buy Gold

Consumers, despite their financial conditions, are encouraged not to sell their jewelry; especially if the jewelry cost the consumer a large amount of money to buy it. Many consumers use a credit card to buy jewelry, pay for its maintenance such as keeping it clean, and pay interest on it; which raises the total cost of buying the jewelry. There are "we-buy-gold" companies that make advertisements on the internet, the radio, and television for consumers to sell them their unused jewelry and they will get paid money for it. This may sound like an attractive offer, but these companies are scams because they pay consumers a significant amount below the market value of the jewelry. It costs them money just to mail the gold to the company, because some companies, if any, do not pay for the mailing costs of sending the jewelry. The consumer makes little or no money compared to what they had paid for the jewelry. Consumers need to be on alert that some of the "we-buy-gold" companies claim they offer a "100% Satisfaction Guarantee or your jewelry returned." This is not true because most of them require that consumers contact them within a certain number of days such as 10 days from when the check they pay the consumer with is dated. It takes time for the consumer to receive their payment from the company and if 10 days pass, then the consumer cannot return the payment and receive their jewelry back.

According to Consumerism Commentary in their article, *Cash 4 Gold: Scam! Real Tips for Selling Your Gold Jewelry*, they indicate if the consumers agree to receive a direct deposit payment from the company then they "automatically WAIVE [their] rights to have the items returned." On Fox News, Chris Fichera, a Consumer Reports Money agent, expressed that the "we-buy-gold" companies did not pay well for the jewelry compared to coin stores, pawn shops, and local jewelry stores. Fichera had mailed multiple "we-buy-gold" companies the same 18K gold chain that was purchased for $175. He received these offers from the companies for that gold chain.

    Cash4Gold $7.60
    $7.60/$175 = 4% return (rounded)

    GoldKit $7.81
    $7.81/$175 = 4.5% return (rounded)

    GoldPaq: $8.22
    $8.22/$175 = 5% return (rounded)

Safe Online Shopping

Consumers should try not to do business with any online store if they do not accept Paypal, Google checkout, or some type of online credit or debit card payment processing service. This is because if the consumer sends the business a money order or check as a form of payment then there is nothing stopping the business from cashing the check and running with the money. There will be nothing that the consumer can do to reclaim their lost money and some criminals can even use the checking account number located on the check to withdraw money from the checking account belonging to the consumer. A money order is a little safer than a check because it does not show the account number. Consumers can buy a money order at some retail stores such as Publix. It is when a consumer hands the store a specific amount of money such as $100 and the stores give the consumer a check in that amount. The consumer must pay the store a small fee for the money order service because it costs money for the store to buy the checks. If consumers are paying a delinquent debt such as a collection account, seriously late credit card, or loan then they should always use a money order to pay the debt.

Emergency Fund

Consumers should always put their extra money left over from paying the bills and other expenses into a high interest-bearing savings or money market account. If possible, consumers should put their children on the account as beneficiaries or joint account users. The money within the account will be considered an emergency fund that consumers can access to pay all their bills and everyday living expenses in the event that they become unemployed. If the parents pass away then their children can possibly access the money and it is never lost. However, consumers need to check with the financial institution if they will allow for a minor to access the money in the event that the parents die.

Consumers should save up enough money so they can pay ten months worth of expenses and should never touch that money for any other purpose. Consumers can determine how much money they need within an emergency funds account by multiplying the amount of money they spend within one month times 10. The amount of money within the emergency funds account should match or exceed this amount but if it is below the amount then they need to continue saving money aggressively. This is because a consumer could lose their job at any time.

Most consumers should be able to get a job within 10 months or less. Some financial experts say an emergency fund should be able to support consumers for eight months or less. 10 months is a personal recommendation due to the fact there is a possibility of a recession occurring within the United States due to the student loans crisis. During the recession, it is likely many consumers may lose their jobs and the prices of services and merchandises will increase. Gas prices are still increasing and for some consumers, this makes it difficult to save money for food alone. A 10 months emergency fund will best protect consumers from becoming homeless.

Danny Singh

****

I want to end this book by thanking you, the reader, so much for your purchase and support. Again, all profits from each book sale are donated to The Children's National Medical Center in Washington, DC because my goal is to spread financial literacy as well as change for the benefit of society. For this reason, I am asking you to write to your senators, governors, state representatives, and anyone you can about some of the changes below that I feel as though will greatly benefit our generation so another housing crisis will not arise.

The government is considering increasing the interest rate on Stafford student loans to 6.8%, which will cause the monthly minimum payments to be much higher to the point some students will default and will be charged late fees that will compound with interest themselves. They will struggle to find a job due to their damaged credit profile. If too many students default then taxes will likely be increased on all consumers because the government will need more money to make up for the student loan losses. Please advocate that the interest rate not be increased at all costs! Putting students into debt is not a good solution for the economy.

Currently, private student loans issued by financial institutions have variable interest rates with no cap and this is scary because they can become as high as 18%. This will cause the monthly student loan payment to skyrocket. Most students make the minimum wage salary, if not less and considering that most of them pay for housing, car insurance, utilities, and other bills, there is no way a student will be able to afford to make the monthly payment unless they do not pay another bill, which is not a good solution. Please advocate that private student loans have a cap to their interest rate or that private student loans should only be granted with fixed interest rates, which are much safer.

Payday loan companies, pawnshop loan companies, cash advance stores, and car title loan companies need to have more financial restrictions placed on them by the government as to how much they can charge to consumers in interest and fees. Payday loans specifically should not have interest rates ranging from 100% up to 800% in addition to charging the consumer fees that will compound with interest themselves. It is unethical even for consumers with bad credit profiles because some of them have children for which they must provide food and shelter. They still have to save for their retirement.

The variable interest rate on a home equity line of credit can go up to 18% and the variable interest rate on a personal line of credit can go up to 19%. When the interest rates increase then their monthly payments do as well and this makes it more likely that the consumer will default and will be hit with late fees. Almost all personal line of credit and home equity line of credit products charge an annual fee to the consumer which compounds with interest itself. The government needs to place a lower interest rate cap on home equity line of credit and personal line of credit products and put a restriction on the annual fee amount. If possible, the government should not allow for the financial institutions to charge an annual fee considering the consumer is already paying so much interest.

Rent-to-own and lease-to-own stores that grant merchandise to consumers with exorbitant interest rates and/or fees need to have restrictions placed on them. It would be better if they could ask the consumer for a security deposit so they can trust the consumer with a cheaper interest rate and still grow as a business.

There needs to be a cap on the amount of cash advance loan money consumers are allowed to take from their credit cards because cash advances are usually charged more than 20% in interest in addition to being charged a $10 or higher amount fee that will compound with interest itself. Some consumers use cash advances to pay their other bills including their mortgage, other credit cards, or they put the cash advance money into their bank accounts and eventually bankrupt their credit card debts. It would benefit financial institutions and consumers if cash advances from credit cards were limited or eliminated. Some credit card companies allow consumers to take cash advances up to 40% of their credit limit meaning if a consumer has a credit limit of $8,000 then they can take up to $3,200 as a cash advance. Consumers should never be allowed to take more than 5% - 10% of their credit limit as a cash advance.

Financial institutions should be required to report the interest rate that the consumer is paying on their loan as information to appear on the credit reports because future financial institutions will be less likely to have a loan loss. It is likely if consumers are paying high interest rates on their loans then this means their monthly payments are high and it is more likely they will default on a new loan or credit card. Seeing the interest rates consumers are paying will allow for the financial institution to better market their credit card and other loan products to consumers for the purpose of trying to get them a cheaper interest rate and this will allow for the consumer to save money. Financial institutions should not grant credit to consumers that are paying an average 17% or more on all their loans and credit cards that have balances.

All need-based scholarships and grants such as the Pell grant must have academic requirements that the student must maintain while they are in school. Some students get scholarship and grant money despite doing poorly in school and this is not fair to students that are working extremely hard to maintain good grades. Additionally, the government needs to have a way of monitoring how the students are spending their financial aid money. Some students use the financial aid money to purchase drugs, use it to gamble, or on items that have no connection to their education. Money is being wasted and this money should be going towards students that authentically need financial aid to pay for their school expenses. Instead of sending the student a check or depositing the financial aid money into their bank account, the colleges should deduct the financial aid from their tuition bill in the form of discounts. This will prevent the money from being misused.

Credit Report Dispute Forms

Source: Equifax.com

Research Request Form

You may initiate an investigation request via the internet at www.investigate.equifax.com.

Or, mail this document to the following address:

Equifax Information Services LLC
P.O. Box 740256
Atlanta, GA 30348

Email Address (please print clearly): _____

Please provide your email address if you would like to be informed once your reinvestigation is completed and if you would like to view the results of your reinvestigation online.

Would you like Equifax to hide the first 5 digits of your social security number on our response to you? Circle: Yes   No

Confirmation Number (please provide if you have a confirmation number): _____

Intentionally making any false statements to a consumer reporting agency for the purpose of having it placed on a consumer report is punishable by law in some states. To ensure that your request is processed accurately, please enlarge photocopies of any items that contain small print (i.e. driver's license, W2 forms, etc.). Photocopies that are not legible or contain highlighting may cause us to request that you resubmit your request for clarity.

If your identity information differs from the information listed on this form, please fill in the correct information in the space provided for each item. Please provide a photocopy of your driver's license, social security card, or recent utility bill that reflects the correct information.

Identification Information

Name _____   Social Security Number _____   Date of Birth _____

Current Address _____

Previous Address(es) _____

Daytime Phone Number _____   Evening Phone Number _____

List other names which you have used in the past _____

Account Information

Company Name _____   Account Number _____

Reason for Investigation: ☐ Not Mine ☐ Paid in Full ☐ Current/Previous Status Incorrect ☐ Account Closed

☐ Other (Please explain) _____

Company Name _____   Account Number _____

Reason for Investigation: ☐ Not Mine ☐ Paid in Full ☐ Current/Previous Status Incorrect ☐ Account Closed

☐ Other (Please explain) _____

Company Name _____   Account Number _____

Reason for Investigation: ☐ Not Mine ☐ Paid in Full ☐ Current/Previous Status Incorrect ☐ Account Closed

☐ Other (Please explain) _____

Source: Innovis

Danny Singh

Source: Transunion.com

Experience with Financial Institutions
Thank you for the Honor of doing Business for the Past 8 Years

Amalgamated Bank of Chicago
American Express
Amtrust Bank
BB&T—Better Banking and Trust
BBVA Compass Bank
Bank of the Ozarks
Barclays Bank Delaware
Capital One Bank
Citibank
Commerce Bank
Countrywide Home Loans
Credit First National Association
Crown Jewelers
DSRM National Bank
Department Stores National Bank (Macys and Bloomingdales)
Discover Card
FIA Card Services
Fifth Third Bank
First Bank and Trust (Revolution Card)
First Convenience Bank
First National Bank of Texas
First Premier Bank
Ford Motor Credit
GE Money Bank
HSBC Bank
Metabank
National City (PNC Bank)
Nordstrom National Bank
Orlando Federal Credit Union
Regions Bank
Scottrade
Sterling Jewelers
TD Ameritrade
Talbots National Bank
Target National Bank
Town North Bank
Trustco Bank
Wachovia Bank (Wells Fargo)
Washington Mutual (Chase Bank)
Wilmington Trust
World Financial National Network Bank/World Financial Capital Bank

Credit Department Contact Numbers

*Note: This information has been taken from the contact information source found at http://ficoforums.myfico.com/t5/Credit-Cards/Backdoor-Numbers/td-p/408066

Company	Phone Number
American Express Credit Bureau Unit	1-800-874-2717
American Express	1-800-567-1083
American Express Oasis Program	1-888-232-3261
Barclay's Customer Care	1-888-232-0780
Barclay's Credit Analyst	1-866-408-4064
Best Buy CSR	1-800-365-0292
Best Buy Application Status	1-800-811-7276
Best Buy Store Card	1-800-305-0533
Bank of America Application Status	1-866-421-8153
Bank of America	1-888-503-6090
Bank of America Secured Accounts	1-888-260-4696
Bank of America Secured And Partially Secured Accounts	1-800-824-5895
Bank of America Credit Analyst for Existing Cardholders	1-800-718-6072
Bank of America Loan Department	1-800-881-4730
Bank of America Credit Department Fax	1-888-500-6270
Bank of America/FIA	1-888-831-4181
FIA Credit Analyst	1-866-421-8153
BP/Amoco Application Status	1-800-365-6204
Capital One Account Specialist	1-800-625-7866
Capital One Customer Relations	1-800-951-6951
Capital One Application Status - Automated Only	1-800-548-4593
Capital One Account Retention	1-877-513-9959
Capital One Debt Recovery	1-800-258-9319
Capital One Secured Platinum Card	1-800-219-7931
Capital One Senior Escalation Account Managers	1-800-707-0489
Chase Application Status	1-800-436-7927
Chase Application Reconsideration	1-888-270-2127
Chase Credit Analyst	1-888-245-0625
Chase Executive Office in Illinois	1-888-622-75-47
Chase Product Change Status Questions	1-800-955-9900
Chevron/Texaco Biz Card Application Status	1-888-243-8358
Chevron Underwriting	1-800-243-8766
Citi New Application Approval Status	1-888-201-4523
Citi AA	1-888-662-7759
Citi Application Status	1-800-645-7240
Citi Retention Department	1-800-444-2568
Citi Credit Bureau Dispute Fax	1-866-713-5028
Discover	1-888-676-3695

Discover Retention Department	1-866-219-0214
Élan Financial Services	1-800-685-7680
Exxon/Mobil Biz Card	1-800-903-9966
FIA Credit Analyst	1-866-421-8153
GE Money bank	1-866-419-4096
Home Depot Store Card Credit Analyst	1-800-677-0232
Home Depot Store Card Application Status	1-423-467-6957
Home Depot MasterCard (Commercial)	1-800-720-0649
HSBC Application Status	1-866-574-4421
HSBC Credit Analyst	1-866-551-0258
HSBC Executive Resolution Unit	1-866-280-0118
JCPenney	1-800-542-0800
Juniper Credit Analyst	1-866-408-4064
Juniper/Barclays Corporate Offices	1-866-750-6031
Key Bank Application Status	1-888-201-4523
Key Bank MC	1-800-288-4653
Key Bank Credit Research Fax	1-216-357-6404
Lowes Application Status	1-800-445-6937
Lowes Biz Account Underwriting	1-866-232-7443
Lowes Fraud/Underwriting/Credit Department	1-800-444-1408
Macy's Credit Department	1-800-627-2909
Macy's Recovery Services	1-800-543-9617
Meijer's MC	1-801-517-5560
National City Credit Department	1-800-762-0974
Nationwide Visa	1-866-757-2720
Sam's Club Underwriting	1-800-301-5546
Sam's Club/Wal-Mart Escalated Help Desk	1-877-294-7541
Sears	1-800-599-9710
Shell Fleet Card Commercial Accounts	1-800-223-3296
Shell Application Status	1-800-223-3296
Shell	1-800-377-5150
Staples	1-800-767-1291
Sunoco Corporation Card	1-800-935-3387
Sunoco	1-800-310-4773
Target Biz Card	1-800-440-5317
Tiffany's	1-800-770-0800
US Bank Underwriting	1-800-947-1444
US Bank Corp. And Commercial Cards	1-800-344-5696
Wal-Mart	1-877-294-7548
Wal-Mart Underwriting	1-877-294-7541
WaMu CSR	1-800-356-0011
WaMu Application and New Accounts	1-888-687-2273
Wright Express	1-888-743-3893

Acknowledgements

I never thought in my life I would write a book but I was given the encouragement to do so by several people who mean the world to me. Although there are many names, it does not mean I typed up a random list. Any success with this book would not have been possible without the support of these people who are the most brilliant and amazing individuals anyone can meet. I mean this from my heart.

University High School International Baccalaureate Class of 2011

Kathleen Acevedo
Joshua Aguilar
Marissa Alonso
Chynna Bambico
Christine Barbosa
Iman Boudlal
Maria Carrasco
Matthew Castner
Ian Chin-See
Caisey Cole
Sean Conte
Alan Dang
Kim Dang
Ashley de Haas
Glisairis Depena
Melissa Dinh
Elizabeth Eby
Melissa Eby
Manu Elias
Elizabeth Escobedo
Rosana Eustache
Cristina Flores
Victoria Flores
Reimar Francisco
Natalia Frias
Carla Gabaldon-Torrents
Ashley Garrett
Lemuel Gorion
Matthew Gorion
Lizbeth Guzman
Richard Haddock
Alinnette Hernandez
Brittany Jean-Pierre
Paul Jenny
Peter Jiang
Parth Kataria
Elizabeth Kilian
Elizabeth Knorr
Brandon Laines

Vladimir Llarch
Daniel Lockaby
Timothy McCarthy
Rachel McLeod
Tanisa McLeod
Tanisa McMillian
Christopher McNamara
Jillian Mendoza
Rebecca Miller
Deandra Modeste
Cameron Neilson
Nicole Neilson
Jennifer Newton
Paul Nguyen
Pete Oshkolup
Samuel Pan
Mitchell Quach
Erika Ramirez
Suraj Ramnarain
Kirstin Raymond
Paola Rodriguez
Jared Ruddell
Angel Santiago
Friedrich Schulte
Stephanie Silvius
Charlotte Smith
Kenlyn Soucy
Matthew Stover
Roberto Telleria
Daniel Toro
Francine Vassell
Jabril Vilmenay
Nadia Williams
Michelle Windish
Alexis Wood
Sheran Xavier
Ashish Yamdagni

Other friends and supporters of www.facebook.com/studentsfinance

Addie Nicole Waver
Adrian Del Toro
Adrian Lopez
Agunk Riot
Aldrin D. Hicks
Alen Dumonjic
Alex Weston
Alexandra Olivia Ahab
Amanda Berins

Danny Singh

Amanda Leigh
Ana Salmoran
Anais Sanchez
Andrea Salcedo
Andrew Colarte
Andrew Figueroa
Andrew Hall
Angelica Garcia
Ant Nee
Anthony Fernandez
Anthony Joseph Battad
Aracelis Bellorin
Arisa Ramirez
Artemis Tursi Otaiza
Austin Delic Barnard
Bailee Leidich
Baka Serkoukou
Brandon Grega
Breana Marchwinski
Brendon Knapp
Brett Sandh
Bria Blossom
Brittany McChesney
Brittany Sapp
Brittany Shamp
Britton Sheely
Brooke Jacques
Bryan Perez
Cady Coe
Caleb Astacio
Camille Vasquez
Carline Marie Barnes
Carlos Perez
Carlos Romero
Carmen Ramirez
Cedez Swan
Celine Parietti
Chantel Chiu
Charlie Faircloth
Chelsea Quindardo
Chelsea Quindardo
Chris Wilson
Christian Carter
Christina Leung
Christinah Cross
Cindy Moore Diaz
Clara Leung
Cory Campbell
Cyrus Smith

DaLisa M Jackson
Dameon Brown
Damian Durana
Daniel Alejandro Leon
Daniel Dickie
Daniel Dupuy
Daniela Suarez Cardenas
Danielle Montanez
Destiny Nazario
Devoree Davis-Halter
Douglas Rintoul
Dylan Elliot
Ebony Charity
Eddie Duarte
Edmarie Collazo
Eduardo Quintero
Edwin Perez
Elif Ipek Kuguoglu
Elisha Guilfoyle Borak
Elizabeth Ferguson
Elyessa Rivera
Emily Grace Moon
Emily Lilia Block
Emily Sue McCarta
Erica Lisa Lazzano
Erica Lisa Lazzano
Erica Reidy
Evelyn C-Sampolski
Gabe Brohammed Ali
Gabriella Lubinsky
Geoffrey Mompoint
Gic Fiestan
Gisela Fernandez
Gloria Alicia
Grant Hitchins
Hailee Rae
Hailey Sayers-O'Neill
Haley Shea
Haley Ulrich
Hanna Read
Heidi O'Donnell
Holly Mass
Ingrid Schulte
Isa Adney
Ivan Espinoza
Ivonne Valentin
Jacob Reagan
James Seymour
Jasmine Yampierre

Danny Singh

Javier Acevedo
Jawn J. Arevalo
Jay-Shing Wang
Jay Shah
Jay Swift
Jazib Malik
Jennifer Gomez
Jennifer Stone
Jessica Anderson
Jessica Phamnguyen
Jimmy Sebastien Demosthenes
Jocelyn Abate
Jocelyn Penagos
Jodie Zapatier
Joey D. Charles
Johan Sebasian Rueda
Johanna Bellorin
John Soderberg
Jonathan Spillman
Jorge Daikigen Lanza
Jorge Mode
Jose Miguel Rosales
Joseph Munio
Joy Emery
Julissa Henry
Justin Solomon
Jyoti Ramdat
Kaitlyn Pennington
Karissa Berkey
Katie Drake
Katie Panetti
Katie White
Katrina Rew
Katy Rivera
Katyria Medina-Utreras
Kelly Flanagan
Kelly Reidy
Kelly Thompson
Kelsey Cotter
Kelsey Wyatt
Kim Brown
Kim Stansfield
Kimberly Davis McDonald
Kirollos Masood
Krista Bartlett
Kristen Ashley Basco
Kristi Ann Malanga
Kristina Mercado
Kyle Brown

Lacey Friedman
Lacey Kresen
Lauren Forster
Lauren Mouser
Lauren Vinson
Lawrence Leung
Leshi Wang
Lexci Pelletier
Libna Campos
Lina Camboulin
Lindsey Coffey
Lizbeth Lorena Perez
Lopez Juan
Lorna Lew
Lucdwin Luck
Luisairis Soto
Luke Browning
Mai Bui
Margot Prince
Maria Moya
Mariah Pelton
Marwin Briesen
Mary Angelica
Matt Forrest
Matthew Sullivan
Maya Elias
Megan Alders
Megan Ann Siedzik
Megan Emily Pye
Meghan Mangrum
Meissa Lopez
Melanie Cello
Melissa Cordero
Michael Li
Michael Martinez
Michael Papania
Michelle Gabrielle Madrigal
Michelle McDaniel
Mido Ahmed
Monica Kiefer
Morgan Holman
Muna Arabraham
NSette Simpson
Nancy Masood
Nargis Azim
Natalie Marie Cortes
Nayara Alves
Nick Bartlett
Nick Portillo

Nicole Cardinale
Nicole Cyntra Dudenhoefer
Nikki Kushel
Nikolay Oshkolup
Paul Antonio
Polly Harding
Quincy Bundrage
Rachael Mack
Rebecca DeJesus
Rebekah Haddock
Rebekah Verdejo
Richard Byron Twaits
Robert Jarden
Rochelle Denard
Roger Orta
Roy Scott Rhodes
Rupa Nayee
Ryan Browne
Ryan Ochse
Sabryna McIntosh
Sabryna McIntosh
Sallekh Shakya
Sam Del Carpio
Samady Vazquez
Samantha Hart
Samantha Jo Johnson
Sara Gudino
Sarah Ferguson
Sarah Sperling
Shaleine Mahadeo
Shannon Gallegos
Shelby Block
Shelby Hunter
Shyla Christyne
Sidney Richardson Jr.
Stannon McCreary
Stephanie Marie Vargas
Stephanie Ortiz
Steven Johnson
Steven Silvernail
Sun Dae
Tanethia Wade
Taylor Curtis
Taylor Gibson
Thuy Tran
Tiffany Soriano
Timothy Duke
Timothy L. Johnson
Tony Lucena

Tyi Gardener
Tyler Waide
Valerie Seranno
Vanessa Alonso
Victoria Massiel
Vikram Dhillon
Vivian Hernandez
Vu Chau
William Perez
Wiselet Rouzard
Yazzy Spookster
Yogi Nayyar
Zach Smith
Zach Thorne

2011-2012 The Art and Phyllis Grindle Honors Institute at Seminole State College of Florida

Adriana Tartaglia
Alexandra Worthen
Ali Hussein Yusufali
Alyxis White
Amanda Leigh Mullens
Ana Zuccarini
Anayjay Sparrow
Andre Vega
Andrew Wexler
Angela Dowe-Warren
Ashley Thompson
Austin Gilbert
Austin Kent
Austin Mittan
Austin Wheeler
Brandon Hart
Brian Qualls
Bridget Henry
Bryan Malave
Callme Sally
Cameron Krane
Charles Bilyue
Chelsea Ann Carrera
Chelsea Honeycutt
Christen Fraas
Christopher Posey
Colin Jaye
Crystal Lamson
Daniel Fitzsimons
Devin Walker

Diane Castillo
Elisa Carvalho
Elise Pearson
Estefania Trujillo
Fatema Hassanali
Fiorella Gallo
Grace Love
Heather Fox
Jacqueline Stough
James Herzig
Jessica Flachner
Jessica Viera
Joshua Debaere
Joshua Nawrocki
Katie Odell
Ken DeMoya
Kevin Anderson
Khadija Tufail
Kiersten Connor
Kristina Dingeman
Luis Martinez
Maggie Wolff
Matthew Quinones
Medge Parcily
Mell Leonard
Michael McCloskey
Miguel Carvajal
Nicole Brown-Goldman
Nikolas Schulz
Ourmela Persaud
Phillip Martin
Pooja Salooja
Ratna Okhai
Richard Christel
Ricky Ashby
Sarina Lambert
Sean Moskal
Sergio Almarez
Shacquilla Thompson
Simone Bodecker
Tarik Hamiliton
Tucker Crawford
Vanessa Karpf

I want to acknowledge two special people. During their lives, they made positive impacts to the lives of many including myself and they are Kelly McConnell, who was an inspiring student, at University High School, part of the International Baccalaureate class of 2009, and Rebecca DeJeasus, who was an administrator and loved teacher at University High School.

Finance 101: The Whiz Kid's Perfect Credit Guide

My Recognition of Excellence

Throughout my academic career, I have had the honor of being educated by some of the best teachers in the world. They have helped nurture my advanced academic skills and thinking, which I have reflected throughout my book.

Riverdale Elementary School in Orlando, Florida
(Class of 2004 Graduate)

Principal
Ms. Sylvia Lorraine Boyd

Teachers
Albert Cervellera
Amy Keenan Pruett
Cheryl Smith
Connie Robbins
Debbie Arthur
Donna Cosio
Jack T. Warren
Keaton Schreiner
Lea Anne Moore
Margaret Ragley
Naomi Montilla
Patty McKenna
Sharon Komperda
Susan Curtis
Terri Davidson
Timothy Brewer
Vonda Daniels
Wendy Clyde

Danny Singh

Odyssey Middle School in Orlando, Florida
(Class of 2007 Graduate)

Principals
Dr. Christopher Bernier

Mrs. Patricia Bowen-Painter

Teachers
Another Dunem
Becky Jones
Dana Hopper
David Santiago
Dominic Eckhoff
Holly Hodges
Jennifer McConkey
Jiae Dy
Josh Counce
Karen D'Angelo
Kimberly Jenkins
Kimela Graves
Laura Richardson
Linda Torres
Lisa McChesney
Michael Cush
Michael Rochkind
Maxima Harmon
Richard Gotham
Sandra Fleming
Scott Evans
Steve Wise
Suzanne Hakimipour
Timothy Douglas
Windy Lopez

A very special thanks to my science teacher, Dana Hopper, I met Mrs. Hopper the day I first began my journey at Odyssey. She is one of the most motivating teachers a student could ever meet. Through her humor, it is so easy for her to make any student love class. I joined her Science Olympiad club and then followed her when she started a new club with Mr. Dunem called "Science Technology Club."

University High School in Orlando, Florida
(International Baccalaureate class of 2011 Graduate)

Principal
Dr. Michael Armbruster

Teachers
Chris Burley
Dora Paz
Doug Klinkerman
Earl Rowland
Eric Saxon
Frank Valenza
John Bruehl
Kathleen Richardville
Lee Ann Spillane
Lisa Tempest
Martha Heine
Melissa Juergens
Mimi Mendez
Oswald Thomas
Philip Rohleder
Ross Klongerbo
Sejal Jagirdar
Sherry Viersen
Stephen Richardville
Teresa Middleton
Timothy Arnold

A very special thanks to my Latin teacher, Philip Rohleder, I met Mr. Rohleder the day I began at University High. I had his Latin course for all four wonderful years and although I struggled, Mr. Rohleder continued pushing me academically and I was able to learn many new skills perfecting my language skills. He is the only teacher I have had for four wonderful years of my life and I cannot thank him enough for being there for his students.

Danny Singh

Seminole State College of Florida in Oviedo, Florida
(The Art & Phyllis Grindle Honors Institute class of 2012 Graduate)

President
Dr. E. Ann McGee

Vice President
Dr. Marcia Roman

Guidance Counselor
Rebecca Lorenzana

Professors
Alan Kraft
Baboucar Jobe
Chris Wright
Collin Morgan
Debra Socci
Diane Wenzel
George Bernard
Howard Sonn
Jeffrey Smith
Jeri Rogers
Kevin Konecny
Laura Dickinson
Mary Dettman
Melissa Bork
Monique Byrnes
Rachel Braaten
Sarah Hernandez
Susan Bell
Teresa Walsh

I want to express a heart-warmed thank you to my favorite professor, Honors director, and role model, Dr. Debra Socci, for encouraging me to write this book and make the best decision in my life by joining the Art & Phyllis Grindle Honors Institute. I still remember the first day I called her asking about joining the Honors program and she asked me to come into her office, take a writing test about sayings from motivational speakers, and I was so nervous. When I graduated University High School, I was unsure of my career path but thanks to Dr. Socci, I was able to fully unlock my passion for Finance and Business. She helped organize my financial seminars, informed the Seminole State media department who then did a story on me that got picked up by the Fox 35 news station, and granted me the opportunity to do one of the seminars at the Florida Collegiate Honors Conference.

I was able to win several Honors scholarships thanks to her recommendations. I have made connections with several amazing professors that along with her have helped me grow as both a student and person. For this reason, my negative perception of community colleges had changed and now I am an advocate that attending a community college is the best financial decision that can be made by a student.

Dr. Socci taught Biology at the University of South Florida, conducted award-winning brain pathology research, and earned a Ph.D. She has been at Seminole State College since 2001 and with so much professional experience, there is no professor more qualified to teach Biology than her.

There are so many positive words that can be used to describe Dr. Debra Socci. Whenever a student or professor needs her or has a problem then she is there for them. It is so admirable how dedicated she is in helping students achieve their dreams. She has prepared me so well to take on bigger challenges in life. Even after graduating Seminole State, I hope to keep in contact with Dr. Socci so I can continue following her guidance and mature into a leader only the Art & Phyllis Grindle Honors Institute can bring to the world.

Family Acknowledgements

Thank you to my loving Singh family for their encouragement including my uncles, Ajit and Nirmal, and aunts, Indira and Priya. A special thanks to my mother, Rita, for her financial support in getting this book published and for the trust she bestowed upon me for the past eight years, which allowed for me to develop my financial skills.

Thank you to my grandfather, Andy, and my grandmother, Sudha, for their motivation to pursue a Ph.D. and embrace my financial talents. Although my father, Sandip, passed away in November of 2009, I thank him for watching over me till this day. Any writer needs happiness in order to write successfully and my happiness comes from my little brothers, Tusya, Gerik, and Gullu, and my little sister, Natasha.

I want to thank news anchors Shelly Slater (WFAA news), Amanda Evans (Channel 13 news), and Tracy Jacim (Fox 35 news). I want to thank reporter Brittni Johnson (East Orlando Sun) and producer Lisa McDonald (Local 6 news). Thank you to Jay Davis and Loraine O'Connell, both part of the Seminole State College media and marketing department. Thank you to Joe Rubble of the WBDO FM 96.5 radio station.

News interviews can be viewed with these links:
http://www.youtube.com/watch?v=nineNfipdX_xOg
http://www.youtube.com/watch?v=tBIGMAvryIo&feature=related
http://www.youtube.com/watch?v=xtwoGFNNtwofuones&feature=related
http://www.youtube.com/watch?v=oneDUaIsFzMeightc
http://www.eosun.com/news/2011/jul/21/finance-whiz-kid/
http://www.seminolechronicle.com/vnews/display.v/ART/2011/11/0two/foureb14sevennine20sixeetwo?in_archive=one
http://www.seminolestate.edu/newsroom/articles/fiveoseven/Whiz-kid-coaches-fellow-students-on-finances
http://www.myfoxorlando.com/dpp/good_day/110two11-financial-whiz-kid-danny-singh-talks-money
http://yourlisten.com/channel/content/11025five/Danny_Singhs_Financial_Seminar
http://yourlisten.com/channel/content/11025six/Financial_Seminar_Part_two

To make it simpler, I have listed all the interview links on

http://www.facebook.com/Studentsfinance under the "info" section or
http://www.youtube.com/user/Dannyasingh/videos.

ydg | studios

I had the most amazing book cover produced by Andrew Dang and Ashish Yamdagni of YDG Studios and want to greatly thank them.

As a financial tip, I encourage you to contact them for all your media needs. Andrew and Ashish will work with you to produce the highest quality products ever at the most competitive prices.

andrew@YDGStudios.com

ashish@YDGStudios.com

"To my friend Danny: Congrats on finishing the book, I hope to see more from you in the near future. Good luck, and all the best!"—Ashish Yamdagni

My Rays of Light Publishing assisted with the formatting and editing of this book. They can be contacted at:
www.myraysoflight.com
myraysoflight@hotmail.com

"Danny, it has been an extreme pleasure working in this project with you. Your financial knowledge will, no doubt, help many people. Above all else, your humanitarian efforts are commendable, may you be blessed in all endeavors."
-Jen, My Rays of Light Publishing

Index

Finance 101: The Whiz Kid's Perfect Credit Guide
The Teen who Refinanced his Mother's House and Car at 14

A

ABA number   51-2
Account bonus   66, 284
Account number   40, 51-2, 54, 110, 134, 155, 209, 275, 287, 308, 316
Account review   3-4, 19-20, 39, 80, 97, 210, 222
Active duty alert   115
Adjustable-rate mortgage   177, 185-6
Advanced Placement   239
After-tax dollars   58
Aggregate demand   16, 169, 173
Alimony   103-4, 109, 120, 201, 213, 285-6
Allpoint Network   31-2
American Bankers Association   51-2
American College Test   252
American Express   21, 24, 29, 36, 75, 85, 93, 99-100, 106, 221, 224-5, 292-3, 295, 303-4, 323-4
Amortization   179-80, 182
Annual fee   15, 18, 25-8, 37, 42, 74-5, 84-5, 96, 98, 105, 120-1, 226, 289, 302-4, 318
Annual percentage rate   21, 23-4, 42, 98, 107, 172, 203, 224, 233
Apartment   10, 48, 58, 107, 118, 120, 127, 131, 140, 163, 167-8, 188, 192, 205, 235-6
Appeal letter   255-8
Application   15, 28, 79, 91, 109-12, 115, 122, 132-6, 225-7, 240-1, 252, 255-7, 265-7, 300-2, 324-5
Appraiser   73, 174-6, 189-90, 197, 203
Appreciate   87, 99, 101-2, 111-12, 135-6, 154-5, 181, 190, 226, 239, 258, 267, 280
Approval   109, 131, 133, 174, 226, 324
Arbitration   40
Assets   45, 49-50, 52-3, 55-6, 80, 97, 111-12, 116, 128, 135-6, 140, 142-3, 146-7, 169-70, 253-4
Associated Credit Bureau Services   117
Assumable mortgage   177
ATM   29-32, 42, 55-6, 63, 105-6, 219
Attorney   70, 76, 85, 97, 104, 108, 137, 143, 156, 176-8, 212, 249-50, 285, 297-8, 305-7
Auto-enhanced   8, 11
Auto lease   289

Auto loan   1-2, 8, 45, 81-2, 88, 96, 127, 145-6, 150-2, 154-9, 162, 203, 216, 223, 282
Available credit   4, 9-10, 26, 39, 45, 83-4, 86-8, 90, 94, 132, 143, 172-3, 194-5, 217, 306
Average daily balance   17, 24, 53, 55

B

Background profile   211, 249-51
Bad credit car dealerships   147-8
Bailout money   55, 68, 170, 214
Balance transfer   23, 37, 43, 97, 159, 183, 221-7, 273-4, 287
Balance type   21-3
Balloon mortgage   177
Bank of America World Points   111, 136, 226
Bank revolving   92-3, 97, 99-100, 293
Bank-to-bank transfer   65
Bankrupt   22, 45, 139, 155, 170, 182, 212-13, 283, 319
Bankruptcy   56-8, 61-2, 70, 80-1, 97, 100, 108-9, 116, 142-3, 204-5, 212-13, 215-17, 233-6, 254, 301-2
Bankruptcy codes   212
Bankruptcy friendly   213
Barack Obama   16, 261
Beacon   14
Behavior score   123
Beneficiary   59, 140-1, 147, 149, 291, 297, 310
Better Business Bureau   v, 108, 142, 176, 216
Bill pay   53-5, 67
Billing cycle   23-4, 176
Blacklist   129
Bonds   57, 204, 291
Boom-and-bust cycle   169
Bounced checks   33, 64, 128
Brooklyn Young Mothers' Collective   285
Building credit   ix, 44, 96, 299, 301
Business   7-8, 10-14, 30-3, 40, 44-7, 75-6, 108, 114-15, 120-5, 140-2, 160-1, 216-18, 237-9, 274-6, 292-5
Business credit cards   40

C

Car dealer 146, 151-2, 154, 289-90
Car insurance 37, 146, 153-4, 160-2, 165, 244, 269-70, 286, 318
Car title loans 50, 203-4, 228, 271
CARD act 16-23, 27-8, 39-40
Card member agreement 19
Career school 246-7, 251
CarMax 149
Cash advance 23, 38, 43, 100, 200, 219, 271, 318-19
Cash equivalence 128
Cash flow 53, 121, 168, 173
Cash-out refinance 183
Cash value 78
CE Score 14
Cell phone insurance 230-1
Center for Responsible Lending 72
Certificate of Deposit 20, 33, 50, 56-7, 66, 76, 104, 131, 204, 214, 218
Certified check 308
Certifying 264, 308
Chapter 7 bankruptcy 212
Chapter 11 bankruptcy 212
Chapter 13 bankruptcy 212
Charge account 99
Charged-off account 93, 99, 101-2, 124, 293, 303
Chase Sapphire 74
Check cashing stores 213, 233
Check Free Corporation 53, 55
Check identification number 52
Check kitting 64
Checkbooks 51, 54, 67, 308
Checking account v, ix, 21, 24, 29, 33-4, 36, 43-4, 51-5, 63-6, 201, 234-6, 288, 308, 316
ChexSystems 29, 32-4, 55, 63-4, 68-9, 76, 201, 210-11, 236
Child support 37, 88, 103-4, 109, 120, 201, 205, 213, 285-6
CIGNA 164
Claim 56-9, 61, 70-1, 110-12, 128, 134-6, 142-3, 147, 162-3, 167-8, 189-90, 212-13, 240-1, 305, 314-15
Closed by consumer 19, 87, 126, 217
Closed by credit grantor 30, 87, 117, 126, 217, 306
Closed for inactivity 39, 126, 289

Closing costs 38, 73-4, 78, 150, 158-9, 174, 176-9, 181-4, 186, 193, 197, 283, 287-8
Co-op network 219
Collateral 61, 70-1, 73, 82, 88, 94, 96, 104, 145, 162-3, 190-1, 201, 203, 216, 228
Collateralized debts 88
Collateralized loans 88
Collection account 102-3, 108-9, 124, 201, 204, 215-16, 223, 233, 316
College Cost Reduction Act 260
College degree 127, 236, 239-41, 244, 246, 248-9, 254, 262, 273, 280, 285
Commission 62, 118, 125, 150, 160, 172, 207, 216, 232, 237-8, 246, 282, 292, 312
Community bank 31, 49-51, 57, 72, 97, 116, 140-1, 145-6, 148-50, 156, 166-7, 176, 182, 186, 263-4
Community college vii, 241, 249, 338
Community home buyer's program 179
Company matching 60-1, 167, 283
Compound 21, 24, 26, 42-3, 78, 151-2, 158, 178, 180, 183, 185, 260, 275-6, 283, 318-19
Condo 163, 167
Consequences 20, 109, 111, 126, 135, 185, 262
Consolidations 271
Contributions 56, 58-60, 62, 192, 204, 252, 271, 291, 310
CoreScore 200, 204, 206
Corporate office 85, 110-11, 134-5, 137, 140, 155, 176, 226
Corporate tax 218
Cosigner 10, 17, 75, 140-1, 146-7, 149, 235
Countrywide Home Loans 113, 323
Coupons 36, 132, 294-5, 301, 314
Coverage v, 48, 68, 104, 140, 146, 157, 160-3, 184
Credibility 127, 131, 161, 189, 241, 244, 273, 299
Credit agency 6, 14-15, 32, 79, 91, 102, 117-18, 133, 174, 219-20, 266-7
Credit analyst 3, 20, 91, 122, 132, 226, 324-5
Credit card 1-4, 13-21, 23-32, 34-47, 65-7, 77-90, 93-103, 105-12, 132-6, 221-7, 234-41, 269-71, 273-4, 291-7, 299-306
Credit check 2-6, 13, 25-6, 67, 85, 98-9, 101-2, 111, 130, 134-5, 174-5, 222-3, 266-8, 274, 299-300
Credit counseling 17-18, 37, 97, 104, 108, 116, 142-3, 148, 215-18, 221
Credit counselor 215-16

Credit crisis   17, 40, 145, 170-3, 269, 281
Credit disclosure notice   174
Credit-healthy group   121
Credit life insurance   165
Credit limit   9-10, 26-8, 38-41, 43-4, 83-90, 95-8, 117-18, 125-7, 131-3, 193-5, 221-2, 274, 294-7, 299-300, 302-4
Credit limit increase   90, 111, 135, 217, 274, 299-300
Credit limit reduction   26-7, 118, 195
Credit lines   30
Credit needy   5
Credit protection   27, 171
Credit report   2, 8-9, 11-15, 45, 76-7, 93-4, 102-3, 110, 117-18, 134-5, 171, 200, 206, 219-20, 266-7
Credit score   7-9, 11-14, 45, 85, 111, 117, 125, 135, 171-4, 196, 237, 306
Credit union   37-8, 48-51, 67, 81-2, 140-3, 145-6, 148-50, 156, 158, 166-7, 182-3, 186, 218-19, 223-4, 302-4
Creditor   1, 7, 11, 74-5, 78, 84, 87, 90, 117, 121, 129, 217, 221
Creditworthiness   11, 99, 120, 122, 171, 173, 191, 219, 265
Criminal   3, 5, 13, 30, 34, 44, 50-1, 54, 56, 63, 68, 102, 111, 207-10, 299-300
Customer service   v, 15, 30-1, 53-4, 84-5, 87, 109, 133-4, 155, 161, 176, 276, 292-3, 299, 309

D

Debit   21, 29-34, 44, 51-2, 54, 63-6, 105-6, 146, 152, 184, 195-6, 219, 236, 269-70, 288
Debt   9-13, 36-8, 81-6, 88-90, 115-16, 145-9, 154-8, 168-73, 176-83, 192-7, 212-17, 225-6, 258-66, 273-83, 295-305
Debt settlement   3, 7, 56-7, 61-2, 70, 97, 109, 116, 143, 204-5, 212-13, 215-17, 233-6, 254, 301-2
Debt-to-credit ratio   26, 83, 296-7
Debt-to-income ratio   88-90, 125, 151, 173, 265
Decline   6, 22, 26, 40-1, 62, 64, 91, 126, 132, 140, 169-70, 173, 196, 204, 303
Deductible   37, 161, 179, 192, 230-1
Default   3-5, 16, 18-20, 22-3, 35, 75-7, 80, 112-14, 136, 171, 215-18, 222-4, 262-6, 296-7, 318-19
Defer   37, 104, 106, 108, 141, 260, 262-3, 268, 270-1, 277-8, 306
Deficiency judgment   70
Deficit   214
Delinquency   v, 20, 46, 81-3, 92-3, 98, 101, 103-4, 107-8, 129, 276-8
Delinquency ratio   81-3
Demand account   51
Denial   68, 91, 93, 97-9, 101-2, 105-7, 109-11, 118, 132-5, 171, 205, 225-6, 246, 301
Deposit   20-2, 32-5, 48-51, 53, 55-8, 65-72, 76-7, 123-4, 166-7, 169-70, 213-14, 228-9, 287-8, 302-3, 313
Depreciation   128, 152-3, 190, 197
Derogatory   92, 102-4, 108-9, 128-9, 249-50
Dischargable debts   212
Discharged   168, 205, 212-13, 269, 275
Discover Card   29, 75, 93, 99, 293, 295, 303, 323
Discover Student Loans   261
Disease insurance   165
Dish Network   233
Dispute   28-30, 52, 96, 100, 102, 108-9, 117-18, 129, 146, 148, 206, 219-20, 249-50, 305, 307
Distribution age   57-8
District attorney   143
Dividends   57
Double-cycle billing   20
Double taxation   141
Down payment   58, 73, 147, 149, 152, 157-9, 173, 175, 178-9, 181, 186, 191, 234, 290-1
Drive Time   147
Dual credit-limit credit card   294
Dual-enrolled student   239

E

Earnings   56, 58-61, 140, 167, 184, 187, 204, 268, 271, 284, 290-1, 310
Economic hardship payment deferment   277
Economy   16, 22, 25, 46-7, 50, 70, 74-5, 168-9, 173-4, 187-8, 196-7, 199, 213-14, 268-9, 280-1
Education IRA   290-1
Electronic Fund Transfer Act   288
Emergency fund   37, 182, 186, 317
Empirica Score   14
Employment   3, 88, 107, 116, 118, 123, 164, 168, 186, 200, 243, 283

Entrepreneurs 16, 72, 214
Equal Credit Opportunity Act 125
Equifax 2, 6-8, 11, 14-15, 69, 92, 117-19, 148, 171, 200, 210-11, 220, 237-8, 266-7, 294
Equity 10, 81-2, 95-7, 141-2, 149-50, 156-8, 169-70, 175, 178, 181, 186, 188-99, 283, 297, 318
Escrow 159
Eviction 205
Executive 85, 109-11, 133-5, 226, 324-5
Experian 6-9, 11, 14-15, 69, 79, 92, 118-19, 148, 171, 200, 210-11, 220, 237-8, 266-7, 300
Extended repayment 270, 278-9

F

FAFSA 252-5, 259, 262, 271, 276, 280
Fair and Accurate Credit Transaction Act (FACTA) 211
Fair Credit Billing Act 29-30
Fair Credit Reporting Act 115, 170
Fair Isaac Corporation 5, 7-8, 14, 117, 200
Fannie Mae 169-70, 179
Fannie Neighbors mortgages 179
FDIC 48-50, 55, 57, 60, 67-8, 166, 219, 284, 302, 313
Federal funds rate 74
Federal Housing Administration 178
Federal Reserve 16, 22, 28, 50-2, 74, 100, 168-70, 184
Federal Trade Commission 118, 125, 172, 207, 232, 238, 312
FIA Card Services 293, 323
FICO 4, 7-8, 12, 14, 45, 88, 95, 125, 172, 174, 200, 217, 306
Financial advisor 62
Fiserv 53-5
Fixed-rate mortgage 183-6
Flood insurance 163
For-profit school 248, 282
Forbearance 137, 139, 278
Foreclosure 56, 58, 61, 70, 139-43, 170, 172, 181, 187, 199, 254, 283
Fraud ix, 5-6, 11, 30, 34, 42, 44-5, 49, 52, 54, 69, 115, 172-3, 206-11, 232
Freddie Mac 169-70
Freezing credit 130

G

Gap insurance 154
Garnish 71, 110-12, 134-6, 163, 198, 226, 254, 259, 305
Gas v, 29, 132, 182, 208, 244, 246, 248-9, 252, 281, 290, 301, 303, 312, 317
Gift card 28, 66, 85, 311
Gold 295, 315
Gold Platinum 295
Grace period 43-4, 176
Graduate PLUS 262
Gym 312

H

Hard inquiry 2-4, 6, 13, 25-6, 44, 91, 94, 96, 99, 101, 109, 130, 133, 184, 299-300
Health savings account 166
High balance 9, 36, 38-9, 93, 106, 117-18, 141, 173, 222, 296
Home equity line of credit 13, 175, 178, 181, 186, 189, 192-7, 283, 297, 318
Home equity loan 81-2, 97, 105, 107, 141, 150, 156, 158, 175, 178, 181, 186, 189-97, 271, 283
Homeowner's insurance 48, 163, 184, 313
Honors vi, 244, 258, 271, 333, 338-9
Household review 79-80
Housing crisis 48, 142, 168-71, 173, 178, 181, 197, 199, 239, 282, 318
Hurricane insurance 163
Hybrid mortgage 177

I

Identity theft 11, 170, 172
Incarceration 305-6
Income 17, 61-2, 77-9, 84, 87-90, 113, 119, 121-3, 125, 245-6, 248, 253-4, 259-61, 279-81, 305-6
Income-based repayment 270, 279
Income-contingent repayment 279
Income-sensitive repayment 279
Individual retirement account 48, 56, 108, 123, 204, 309
Inflation 47, 168
Innovis 6, 8, 14-15, 69, 91, 117-19, 133, 148, 171, 200, 210-11, 219-20, 237-8, 267, 300

Installment credit   8, 11-12, 92, 94-6, 107, 145, 158, 190
Insurance agent   160
Insurance broker   160
Insurance risk   8, 11
Interest   15-28, 34-47, 49-53, 71-8, 93-8, 131-43, 145-53, 166-87, 192-7, 203-5, 216-19, 223-6, 259-66, 268-84, 317-19
Interest-only mortgages   170
International Baccalaureate   vi, 239, 326, 334, 337
Internet crime center   211
Investment firm company   293
Investments   24, 50, 57, 62, 119, 141, 197, 268
IRS   62, 78, 108, 128, 141, 182, 192, 200, 204, 305-6

J

Joint account   75, 109, 134, 317
Jumbo mortgage   177

K

Keogh   309-10

L

Late fee   18, 25, 27, 43, 46, 124, 193, 276, 283, 288, 303
Late payment warning   17
Lawyer   139, 157, 205
Layaway   234
Length of history   4, 8, 10, 44-5, 86, 98, 106, 110, 134, 143, 193, 195, 217, 306
Levy   29, 71, 82, 142, 275, 305
Liability   30, 63, 73, 122, 124, 129, 139, 157, 205, 275
License tag   153
Lien   70-1, 82, 104, 109, 128-9, 162, 205
Life insurance   78, 104, 140, 146-7, 149, 160, 165, 186, 269, 284, 286
Loan against their 401(k)   141, 149, 156, 168, 181, 204, 271
Loan modification   137-9, 141, 144
Loan rehabilitation   276
Loan sharks   75, 114
Loan term   95, 145, 158, 179-80, 185, 278-9
Loan-to-value ratio   73, 173, 175-6, 190-1

Logbook loans   203
Lump sum amount   212

M

Maintenance   31, 35, 68, 73, 127, 148, 150, 152-5, 157, 181, 188, 199, 245, 286, 289-90
Making Home Affordable   144
Margin interest   23
Market value   70, 128, 145, 148, 151-3, 169-70, 178, 189, 203, 314-15
Marketing   3, 75, 221, 311, 340
Marquette Bank decision   47
Maturity   56, 177, 192, 194
Maximum fee amount   221
Medicaid   164
Medicare   164, 166
Merchants   29, 40, 42, 46, 51-2, 55-6, 100, 192, 250, 288, 308
Microloans   72
Miles   85, 98, 110, 134, 148, 165, 289-90
Military payment deferment   277
Minimum payment   17-18, 21-2, 24-5, 35-6, 40-1, 43, 79, 107-8, 168, 179, 196, 263-4, 277-9, 281, 288-9
Minimum payment warning   17
Minors   94, 232, 237, 310
Money laundering   49, 123
Money market   20, 22, 29, 33, 52-3, 55-8, 63, 65-6, 68, 72, 74, 76, 100, 140, 291
Money order   191, 316
Mortgage broker   176
Mortgage score   200, 206
MSN Health   286
Municipal bond funds   57
Mutual funds   57

N

National Consumer Law Center   72, 203
National debt   55, 178, 214, 261, 269, 281
National Foundation for Credit Counseling   142, 217
NCUA   48-50, 55, 57, 60, 67-8, 166, 219, 284, 302, 313
Negative checking account   201
Newspaper   312
No-income verification   113
Non-consensual lien   70-1, 82, 109, 128, 162

Non-recourse loan   70-1
Nontaxable income   147
Notice of deficiency   305
NSF fees   33, 123, 211
Numerical coding   91, 133

O

Obama student loan reform   280
Office of Contempt Currency   232
Officers   91, 122, 132
Open ended credit   145
Opt-in   238
Opt-out   19, 25, 41-2, 64, 237-8
Origination fees   73, 78, 96, 150, 193, 261, 263-4, 268
Out-of-state   240, 245
Over-the-credit limit fees   26-7, 40
Overdraft fees   ix, 21, 31, 33-4, 38, 44, 65-6, 123, 211, 288
Overdraft protection   21, 23, 63-6

P

Paid as agreed   92, 102
Parent PLUS   262, 264
Parents   46, 80, 119, 149, 168, 205, 232-3, 236, 240, 248, 253-5, 259-62, 285-6, 290-1, 317
Patriot Act   123
Pawn broker   228
Pawnshop loan   318
Pay stub   17, 79, 115, 200, 279
Payday loan   200-3, 318
Payment history   4, 8-12, 15, 30, 36, 71, 96-9, 106, 137-8, 148-9, 204-5, 217, 228, 276, 292
Pell grant   254, 260, 280, 319
Penalty APR   23, 42
Perkins   260, 262, 264, 268, 271, 281-2
Permanent loan modification   137, 139, 144
Personal line of credit   287-9, 318
Pink slip loans   203
Plus score   14
Points   13, 34, 44, 74, 98-9, 111, 136, 146, 171, 184-5, 226, 257, 274
Portfolio risk department   4
Pre-approved   25-6, 238
Pre-tax dollars   58
Pregnancy   285-6
Premium   46, 118, 161-2, 184, 192, 236, 269, 278, 290, 312
Prepaid   29-32, 34, 44, 105-6, 236
Prepayment   96, 107, 146-7, 168, 192-3, 197, 263-4, 269
Prepayment fees   193
Prescreened offers   237
Prescreening   237
Prime lending   74, 81
Prime rate   22-3, 50, 74, 192, 196, 263, 265, 272, 288
Private college   247
Private mortgage insurance   149, 174-6, 178-9, 186
Private student loan   96, 262-6, 272-3, 277, 282
Productivity function level   22, 121, 276
Professor   vi, 169, 193, 241, 243, 249, 273, 338-9
Property taxes   70, 174, 179, 182, 188, 245, 289
Public record   92, 102-4, 108-9
Purchases   5, 10, 13, 21-3, 34-6, 39-40, 52-3, 57, 63, 105-6, 150-1, 153, 169, 204, 294-5

Q

Quest bridge   281

R

Real estate agent   167-8
Receipts   40
Recent credit   9
Recession   ix, 17, 46-7, 49, 84, 170, 173, 188, 214, 233, 281-2, 290, 317
Reconsideration   45, 91, 109-11, 132-5, 226, 301-2, 304, 324
Recourse loan   70-1, 178, 181, 191
Refinance   74, 101-2, 110, 128, 134, 137, 140-1, 158, 175, 180, 183-4, 186-7, 192, 194, 197
Rent-to-own   314-15, 318
Rental insurance   163
Repossession   58, 61, 70, 104, 138, 146, 148, 154-6, 158, 232
Returned check   33, 52, 64-6, 201, 235, 308
Reverse mortgage   178
Revocable living trust   297
Revolving   10, 13, 86, 92-100, 105, 109-10, 133-5, 145, 194-5, 226, 293, 297
Rewards   29, 63, 74-5, 85, 98-9, 131-2, 146, 152, 161, 184, 191, 195, 269-70, 295-7, 304-5

Rollover   61-2, 140, 156, 167, 186, 229, 271, 284
Roth 401(k)   61
Roth IRA   58-9, 61, 116, 140, 156, 167, 181, 187, 204, 271, 283-4, 305
Routing number   51-2, 308

S

Safe deposit box   313
Saks Fifth Avenue credit card   294
Sallie Mae   278, 282
Savings account   29, 33, 43, 55, 65-6, 97, 100, 110, 128, 134, 140, 166, 200, 290-1, 302-3
Scam   42, 108, 139, 143, 147, 176, 250, 259, 275, 287-8, 314-15
Scholarship   168, 244-5, 258-9, 271, 273, 275, 281, 287, 291, 319
Scholastic Aptitude Test   252
School-as-lender program   282
ScoreX   14
Secured credit card   26, 70, 88, 98, 129, 148, 302-3
Secured loan   71-2, 212, 216, 218-19, 221, 223, 264, 271, 283, 303
Security deposit   1, 4, 61, 70-1, 82, 94, 118, 167, 201, 216, 218, 228-9, 288, 302-3, 318
Self-employed   239, 309
Self-publishing   311
SEP-IRA   309
Settle   143, 154
Shared branch members   219
Shares   viii, 57, 75
Short-term loans   72
Signature-based transaction   63
Signature loans   71
SIM card   230
Sioux Falls   46
Small businesses   60, 100, 164, 309
Snapshot   165
Social security   5, 13, 15, 30, 68-9, 97, 110-11, 116, 118, 123-4, 134-5, 160-1, 207-10, 266-7, 299-300
Social welfare   57, 285
Society of Human Resources Management   129
Soft inquiry   2-4, 26, 94, 99, 130, 184, 222, 268, 299-300
Spending limits   26, 194-5, 293-5, 297
Spouse   76, 80, 85, 104, 120, 140, 149, 153, 178, 192, 211, 310
Stafford   261-4, 268, 271, 281-2, 318
Standard repayment   278-9
Starter check   308
Statement   17, 21, 23-5, 31, 55, 108, 111-12, 115, 135-6, 193, 210, 237, 267
Statue of limitations   298
Stimulus packages   57
Stock brokerage   57, 62
Stocks   57, 62, 197, 268, 291
Store branded credit card   291-3, 300-1
Student loan relief   275-6
Student loans crisis   282, 317
Subprime lending   75, 81, 114, 120, 302
Subsidized   94, 253, 259-61, 264, 269, 272, 281
Suze Orman   31, 269

T

Tax audit   305-6
Tax benefits   48, 60-1, 192
Tax deduction   192-3
Tax evasion   306
Tax exemption   192
Tax-free   59, 61
Tax penalties   57-8, 61, 108, 123, 166, 291
Tax refunds   37, 107, 141, 275, 305
Taxes   55-9, 61-2, 68, 78, 140-1, 166-7, 174-6, 178-9, 186-8, 192-3, 204, 263-4, 289-91, 305-6, 309-10
Term life insurance   140, 146-7, 149, 186, 284, 286
Terms and conditions   v, 19, 22-3, 26, 28, 41-2, 70
Thrift account   310
Timeshare   289
Trade lines   118
Trade school   247
Traditional banks   49, 140, 142, 197
Traditional IRA   58, 61-2, 140, 186, 204, 271
Transient student   243, 270
TransRisk score   14
TransUnion   6-8, 11, 14-15, 69, 92, 110, 118-19, 134, 171, 200, 210-11, 220, 237-8, 266-7, 300
Trial loan modification   137-9
Truth in Lending Act   19, 288
Tuition   39, 236, 239-48, 252, 255-8, 263-4, 274, 280-1, 291, 319

U

Umbrella insurance 157
Uncertified student loan 264
Undergraduate 240-3, 245, 260-1
Unemployment 107, 156, 159, 171-2, 277
Universal default 3, 19-20
Universal life insurance 147
Unsecured loan 97, 223, 303
Unsubsidized 94, 253, 260-4, 269-70, 272
Usury 46-7, 200
Utilities 1, 33, 37, 73, 124, 131, 244-5, 248, 286, 299, 309, 318
Utilization 4, 10, 39, 83-4, 87-8, 90, 93, 132, 194, 217, 222, 296, 303, 306

V

VA mortgage 179
Vantage Score 7-9, 12, 174
Variable interest 18, 22, 50, 74, 96, 150, 177-80, 185, 196, 263-6, 268, 272, 280, 288-9, 318
Variable life insurance 78

W

Wages 60, 70-1, 76, 79, 110-12, 134-6, 162-3, 194, 198, 212, 226, 232, 254, 259, 275
Wall Street 22, 50-1, 170, 192, 196, 263, 265, 272, 288
Warranty 153
Wedding 191, 283-4
Whole life insurance 140
Wire transfer 65
Withdrawal 25, 53, 204, 273
Work study 280
World MasterCard 295
World Platinum 295

Z

Zero percent interest 265

Whiz Kid's Book Raises Awareness of Student Loans Crisis and Donates to Charity

Economists and business commentators are increasingly concerned about the high levels of debts carried by Americans.

Danny Singh "financial whiz kid" is not taking this issue lightly.

"The amount of Americans in debt seems to be increasing every year and that to me is a huge issue. We need to focus on spreading financial literacy," says 19-year-old Danny Singh. But this self-taught financial guru is making it his goal to prevent an emerging student loans crisis in America by educating students on how to best manage their finances.

And he should know. Singh has refinanced a house and a car at age 14, paid the family bills on time each month for eight years and achieved a pristine credit score for his mother – all before he turned 19.

He also raises concerns that the student loans crisis will cause a recession in America which could possibly be worse than the housing crisis, because unlike home loans, student loans are not dischargeable in bankruptcy and have exceeded 1 trillion dollars.

Singh is now providing expert advice in his finance book, *Finance 101: The Whiz Kid's Perfect Credit Guide*. He is also running his own independent and non-profit credit advisory agency called "Students' Finance Success" from his home in East Orlando, helping families save homes from foreclosure, save cars from repossession, and helping them fix their credit reports.

Singh's own story started when he took over his mother's finances, at just 11 years old.

"My mother began working more than 60 hours a week, and she was working long hours too. She was overwhelmed by our financial situation and turned to me for help," said Singh.

Rita Singh added her 11-year-old son as an authorized user on all of her accounts so the companies would release her information to him. A finance whiz kid, Singh was dedicated to the cause, learning everything he could by talking to the customer service representatives on the phone, diligently researching information on the internet, scrutinizing the fine print on account statements and quizzing his mother.

As a result, for the past eight years he has been successfully managing his mother's IRA, paying all her bills and making sure the deposit accounts do not pass into the red. Singh established perfect credit record for his mother – all the while maintaining his own strong academic record.

"I worked with more than 30 different banks, who have each contributed to my skills. One major accomplishment was getting the interest rates reduced and the annual fees removed on several of my mother's credit cards," Singh said.

He didn't stop there. Singh increased the credit limits on his mother's credit cards, linking them to checking accounts to prevent overdraft fees, which achieved increased credit scores. The 14-year-old 'finance whiz kid' was then able to refinance the mortgage.

"The mortgage interest rate was reduced to 4.86 percent fixed with a 30-year loan term. Then I set to work refinancing the car. I asked my mother to open a new credit card, which meant I could transfer her 7 percent interest rate car loan onto it and obtain a fixed interest rate of 3.99 percent for life," he said.

To reduce the expenses of the car and house further, Singh negotiated cheaper premiums with the insurance companies, using his mother's new high credit scores.

While proactively reducing his mother's debt, Singh's financial diligence has also prevented some anomalies that might otherwise have gone unnoticed.

"When I was 18, I discovered my mother was being charged the wrong interest rate by a credit card company, so I simply contacted the corporate office. The bank confirmed it was their mistake and we were refunded over $1,300 in interest and fees," Singh said.

When a fraudulent company was found stealing money from his mother's bank accounts, Singh reported the issue to the Better Business Bureau and the Internet Complaints Board, and then worked with the bank to return all her money.

Friends and family have also benefited from Singh's help with their mortgage problems. He solved a credit issue for his grandmother, ensuring she was approved for credit after first being denied.

When Danny was 13, he made a financial mistake that later turned out to be a blessing in disguise. Danny had purchased his mother a $1,000 ring from a jewelry store as a gift for her on mother's day using the credit card his mother had given him. She was not upset and thought it was sweet but it was his responsibility to make the monthly payments. Danny successfully paid off the credit card and was never late but regretted paying interest. The experience thought him the importance of not overspending and using credit wisely.

Now aged 19, Danny Singh is working to raise awareness of credit issues amongst his fellow students at Seminole State College of Florida and further afield. His financial seminars at the college educate the students on the most effective plans to pay off their loans and other debts.

"I recommend students do the maximum number of classes at a community or state college to get into the least amount of student loan debt, and reduce financial stress," he said.

Singh is donating all the royalties he receives from his book, *Finance 101: The Whiz Kid's Perfect Credit Guide*, to the Children's National Medical Center in Washington DC to support HIV research.

And while he is helping others with their financial dreams, Danny Singh has his own goal to achieve.

"I'm planning on having a role at Chase Bank as a financial adviser when I finish my MBA and PHD in two years. But above all, I want to ensure my mother is mortgage-free," he said.

About Danny Singh
Singh is the grandson of late Narendra Singh, more popularly known as Bachcha Babu, famous for plying steamers between Palheja Ghat in Patna and Hajipur prior to the construction of Gandhi Setu. He has been taking care of his mother's finances since he was 11 years old, is a first generation college student, and 2011 graduate of University High School's International Baccalaureate program and is part of the Art and Phyllis Grindle Honors Institute at Seminole State College of Florida. His financial genius has attracted several news stations, Governor Rick Perry, First Lady Anita Perry, Seminole County Commissioner Bob Dallari, Florida State Representative Jason Brodeur, and Senator Marco Rubio – who have all recognized him as the 'financial whiz kid'. It took 7 months to finish his book, *Finance 101: The Whiz Kid's Perfect Credit Guide,* which is available to buy on Amazon.com and other online booksellers.

Media Contact
Rita Singh
(407) 496-6005

www.ingramcontent.com/pod-product-compliance
Lightning Source LLC
Chambersburg PA
CBHW081233180526
45171CB00005B/416